Selected Literary Criticism

Volume I: 1859–1885

W. D. HOWELLS

Selected Literary Criticism

Volume I: 1859–1885

Text Selection and Introduction
by Ulrich Halfmann

Notes to the Texts by
Ulrich Halfmann and Christoph K. Lohmann

Texts Established by
Don L. Cook, Christoph K. Lohmann,
and David J. Nordloh

INDIANA UNIVERSITY PRESS

Bloomington and Indianapolis

1993

CENTER FOR EDITIONS OF
AMERICAN AUTHORS
AN APPROVED TEXT
MODERN LANGUAGE
ASSOCIATION OF AMERICA

The paper used in this publication meets the minimum requirements of American
National Standard for Information Sciences—Permanence of Paper for Printed
Library Materials, ANSI Z39.48-1984.

 ™

Manufactured in the United States of America

Library of Congress Cataloging-in-Publication Data
Howells, William Dean, 1837–1920.
    Selected literary criticism / W.D. Howells.
        p.   cm. — (A Selected edition of W.D. Howells : v. 13, 21,
30)
    Text selection and introductions by Ulrich Halfmann, Donald
Pizer, and Ronald Gottesman.
        Contents: v. 1. 1859–1885 — v. 2. 1886–1897 — v. 3. 1898–1920.
        ISBN 0-253-32857-8 (v. 1). — ISBN 0-253-32858-6 (v. 2). — ISBN
0-253-32859-4 (v. 3)
    I. Halfmann, Ulrich.   II. Pizer, Donald.   III. Gottesman, Ronald.
IV. Title.   V. Series: Howells, William Dean, 1837–1920.
Selections.   1968 : v. 13, etc.
PS2020.F68 vol. 13, etc. <Rare Bk Coll>
818'.409 s—dc20
[809]   91-7615

0-253-32860-8 (3 vol. set)

1 2 3 4 5   97 96 95 94 93

Acknowledgments

THE editors of this volume and the Howells Edition Center are grateful for the gracious assistance and cooperation of Professor William White Howells and the heirs of W. D. Howells. We also thank the Collection of American Literature, Beinecke Rare Book and Manuscript Library, Yale University; the Princeton University Library; and the American Literature Collection, University of Southern California Library for the use of W. D. Howells' manuscripts, which are specifically identified in the Textual Apparatus of this volume. In making the selections for this volume, we have had the thoughtful advice of Professors Donald Pizer and Ronald Gottesman, the editors of the other two volumes in this series; their informed judgments have contributed much to our own efforts. The late Frederick Anderson inspected this volume at the request of the Center for Editions of American Authors, and we are grateful for the thoroughness and expertise which he brought to this task. We also gratefully acknowledge funding received from the Ball Brothers Foundation of Muncie, Indiana, to defray part of the cost of publication.

Finally, we express our gratitude to George Warren Arms, whose dedication to the study of American literature in general and W. D. Howells in particular has so influenced our own thinking. Here is the model of scholar and friend—generous in sharing his knowledge, thoughtful and kind in guiding colleagues and students, delightful in exchanging wit and the pleasures of reading.

Contents

Introduction

THE coming of age of W. D. Howells as a serious *littérateur* is concentrated in the years 1859–1861. Though he had been publishing a wide variety of things—from poems to legislative reports—in Ohio newspapers since 1852, and though he became a staff writer for the *Ohio State Journal* in November 1858, it was the acceptance by James Russell Lowell in July 1859 of a poem for the esteemed *Atlantic Monthly* ("Andenken," published in January 1860) that constituted the first step away from the protective and nurturing encouragement of provincial audiences and toward genuine recognition as a writer by journals and critics of established reputations in the East and West. That first step was followed by a rush of acceptance and a testing of literary skills over the next two-and-a-half years. In December 1859 Howells appeared as co-author (with J. J. Piatt) of *Poems of Two Friends* and in September 1860 as contributor to *Poets and Poetry of the West* (edited by James T. Coggeshall). Also in 1860 he found occasion to express his abolitionist ideals in a campaign biography of Abraham Lincoln. He wrote as a critic not only for his father's *Ashtabula Sentinel* and the *Ohio State Journal* but also for Henry Clapp's bohemian New York *Saturday Press*, which published Howells' review of Aldrich's *The Ballad of Babie Bell* in July 1859 and reprinted an essay on *Leaves of Grass*, as "A Hoosier's Opinion of Walt Whitman," in August 1860. That same month Howells spent traveling—or pilgrimaging, as ironical minds have it—to New York and the literary centers of New England. He came away disappointed by the Manhattan metropolis and disenchanted by much of its literary life, but he was deeply impressed by Boston, Cambridge, and Concord, whose literary giants welcomed the young Westerner generously.

Howells returned to Columbus knowing—or at least sensing—that his future lay in Boston. "I look forward to living there some day—being possibly the linchpin in the hub," he wrote to James T. Fields, whose assistant and successor as editor of the *Atlantic* he was later to become.[1] The remarkable success of Howells' trip was no doubt due in part to his charm, social adaptability, critical intelligence, knowledge, and serious honesty, as well as his

---

[1] WDH to Fields, 22 August 1860, *W. D. Howells: Selected Letters*, volume 1, ed. George Arms, Richard H. Ballinger, Christoph K. Lohmann, and John K. Reeves (Boston, 1979), p. 58.

veneration of the Brahmins and eagerness to follow in their footsteps. But there was more. It was highly significant that Hawthorne, in their brief and monosyllabic meeting at Concord, had asked Howells "about the West, and [had] wisht he could find some part of America 'where the cursed shadow of Europe hadn't fallen' ";[2] and that Holmes had talked ominously of the "apostolic succession."[3] This "young man" had something acceptably new and desirably different to offer: a genuine Western Americanism which, along with his personal integrity and stamina, carried the promise of a vigorous progressive alternative to imminent epigonic stagnation.

This rush of recognition had deep effects on Howells, effects that changed the direction of his intellectual life. Less than half a year after his return from the East, he applied for a consulship to Europe. Back in Ohio he had been seized by a deep *ennui* which filled him with dissatisfaction at his position on the *Ohio State Journal* and doubts about the advancement of his literary career. "Is this indolence a pause in the scheme of my developement [sic]?" he brooded in a letter to the younger Holmes in 1861; "Have I come to the end?"[4] Howells was actually experiencing something more complex— and less threatening. He and "the scheme of [his] developement" had undergone changes resulting from what could be called the trauma of his New England success. Having suddenly widened and stimulated his ambition, he suffered all the more from the obvious impossibility of fulfilling it in the local journalistic position he was holding. Besides, Howells was self-critical enough to have come away from his conversations with Lowell, Fields, Hawthorne, Holmes, and others with a sharp sense not of his inferiority but of his present inadequacy, his lack of experience and urbanity. To leave Columbus was thus both logically and psychologically a plausible course. When his application for a place on the New York *Post* failed, Howells applied to Lincoln's new administration for the consulship in Munich, in order to pursue the study of German literature. After some months of uncertainty and considerable bureaucratic confusion about possible vacancies in Munich, Leipzig, Cardiff, Vienna, and Rome, he was given the post at Venice. Howells sailed on 9 November 1861—but not before he had paid another visit to Lowell, Fields, and Holmes.

If the choice of Venice was largely accidental, Howells left little else to chance during the ensuing "voluntary exile"[5] which lasted until 1865. Having won new self-confidence, he set out to live and work according to a program of even more intensive self-education than that which had filled his adolescent solitude. It included the study of Italian and French, the reading of the Latin and Greek classics and of Italian literature, the writing (and

---

[2] WDH to Moncure D. Conway, 5 March 1890, *W. D. Howells: Selected Letters*, volume 3, ed. Robert C. Leitz, Richard H. Ballinger, and Christoph K. Lohmann (Boston, 1980), p. 276.

[3] "My First Visit to New England," *Literary Friends and Acquaintance* (Bloomington, Indiana, 1968), p. 36.

[4] WDH to Oliver Wendell Holmes, Jr., 24 February 1861, *Selected Letters*, 1:72.

[5] WDH to James Russell Lowell, 21 August 1864, *Selected Letters*, 1:195.

publishing) of poetry, and the keeping of "a journal from which I hope to make a book about Venice."[6] Some of these plans faltered or failed. Many of his poems, for instance, were rejected by the magazines, causing moods of dejection in the humiliated author and—as it seems in retrospect—a fortunate shift of creative effort from poetry to prose. Other plans succeeded perfectly. In March 1863, essays expanded from his journal began to appear in the Boston *Daily Advertiser* as "Letters from Venice," which afterwards grew into *Venetian Life* (1866), a book that marked Howells' first great literary success. The following year, a letter from Lowell sent Howells "up to heaven at once,"[7] marking what he himself later designated "the turning point of my life."[8] Lowell informed Howells of acceptance for the *North American Review* of a long critical article on "Recent Italian Comedy," the fruit of Howells' systematic study of Italian literature. Beyond the notification that the article was already in print and the invitation to "write us another on 'Modern Italian Literature,' or anything you like," Lowell dealt out praise and advice: "You have enough in you to do honor to our literature. Keep on cultivating yourself."[9]

In terms of its emotional force, the impact of this letter on Howells equalled that of his New England trip five years earlier. Yet this time he was not thrown off-balance. He knew that another phase of his development had come to an end, and in his reply to Lowell he announced that he was going to resign his office and continue his studies at home. In a sense, Venice had from the beginning been a preparation for his literary career, and now he was anxious to return, afraid that he might already have "fallen out of the American procession of progress."[10] He left Venice on 1 July 1865.

During his four European years he had become more mature, more urbane, and more scholarly. He had virtually given up poetry; his prose, he himself felt, had "grown earnester in style, and solider in matter."[11] His criticism, largely a combination of "sensitive" reactions and "smart" rhetoric during the Ohio years, had gained a new tone based on learning and insight into aesthetics and history as well as human nature. All in all, Venice had been a catalytic force in the process of his self-realization. To what Hawthorne had called the "cursed shadow of Europe" this Western American had remained singularly immune.

In September 1865 Howells settled in New York. Immediately and ener-

---

[6] WDH to Victoria M. Howells, 26 April 1862, *Selected Letters*, 1:113.

[7] Lowell's letter that gave Howells so much pleasure was dated 28 July 1864; see WDH to James Russell Lowell, 21 August 1864, *Selected Letters*, I: 193–196. However, the quoted phrase was used by Howells ten years later in a letter to Lowell of 25 May 1874; see WDH to James Russell Lowell, 25 May 1874, *Selected Letters*, volume 2, ed. George Arms and Christoph K. Lohmann (Boston, 1979), p. 60.

[8] "The Turning Point of My Life," *Harper's Bazar*, XLIV (1910), 165.

[9] Lowell to WDH, 28 July 1864, *Letters of James Russell Lowell*, ed. Charles Eliot Norton (New York, 1894), volume 1, p. 338.

[10] *Interviews with William Dean Howells*, ed. Ulrich Halfmann (Arlington, Texas, 1973), p. 307.

[11] WDH to Charles Hale, 25 October 1863, *Selected Letters*, 1:163.

getically he started elbowing his way through the crowd of free-lance writers: selling his stock of old poems, reading manuscripts for Hurd (the publisher of *Venetian Life*), and writing "Letters from New York" for the Cincinnati *Gazette*, as well as editorials for the New York *Times*, book reviews for the *Round Table*, and miscellaneous literary criticism for the *Nation*. Of all these activities and connections the last two soon proved most important. The editors of the *Round Table* and the *Nation*—Edwin L. Godkin, Thomas Bailey Aldrich, Edmund Clarence Stedman, Richard Henry Stoddard, and William Winter, some of whom he had met in 1860 and 1861—became Howells' influential friends. Their two young periodicals, centers of the principal literary activity in New York, provided him with excellent platforms for the criticism which was now becoming his most immediate and serious occupation. By the end of October Howells' reputation was solid enough to draw an offer from Godkin to write exclusively for the *Nation* on a monthly salary. Less than three months later, from Cambridge, where his New York activities had been watched attentively, came Fields's offer to become assistant editor of the *Atlantic*, "that great periodical" which Howells had always admired.[12] He talked the matter over with Godkin, consulted Lowell, accepted in early February, and assumed the duties of his new position on 1 March 1866, his twenty-ninth birthday. "These duties I understand to be," he carefully recorded in his letter of acceptance,

> examination of mss. offered to the "Atlantic," correspondence with contributors, reading proof of the magazine after its revisal by the printers, and writing the critical notices of books; for which I am to receive fifty dollars a week, while anything I may contribute to the body of the magazine shall be paid for on such terms as we may agree upon.[13]

Howells was modest enough to attribute his appointment mainly to his experience as a practical printer and proofreader. The contract with the *Atlantic*—notably the fact that Howells was put in charge of the magazine's distinguished "Reviews and Literary Notices" department—suggests, however, that the competence and discernment he had shown as a literary critic must have been a strong motive in Fields's offer. Five years later, on 1 July 1871, Howells became editor-in-chief. He held the position for ten years— truly "the linchpin in the hub" he had dreamed of becoming in 1860.

It would be difficult to sum up the fifteen years of Howells' editorial affiliation with the *Atlantic* (1866–1881) and the following four years as a free-lance novelist and critic.[14] Yet the mere enumeration of a few significant facts suggests what these years meant for Howells' personal development and

---

[12] WDH to John J. Piatt, 10 September 1859, *Selected Letters*, 1:41.

[13] WDH to James T. Fields, 6 February 1866, *Selected Letters*, 1:249.

[14] For a full background, see the following dissertations: Elizabeth B. Stanton, "William Dean Howells: A Study of His Literary Theories and Practices During His *Atlantic Monthly* Years, 1866–1881" (Ohio State University, 1943); Robert E. Butler, "William Dean Howells as Editor of the *Atlantic Monthly*" (Rutgers University, 1950); and Walter Gauss, "Die Entwicklung von

literary achievement. In terms of social status, they meant rapidly growing recognition that finally secured for the one-time "raw youngster"[15] from Ohio a respected place among the established *literati*: Howells was invited to the exclusive Century Club in 1865 and to Longfellow's even more exclusive Dante Club in 1866–1867; he dined, talked, and corresponded regularly with Lowell (who often addressed his letters "my dear boy" and sometimes signed them "el viejo"); he was lionized on visits to New York in 1872 and 1878 by Aldrich, De Forest, Hay, Harte, Stedman, Warner, and others; he "settled the true principles of literary art" in many "famous evenings and walks" with Henry James,[16] who remained a life-long brother-in-arms and intimate critic; he became one of the closest friends of Mark Twain; and he prospered financially, settling in August 1884 among the social elite of Boston on the water side of Beacon Street. Professionally, the same period launched Howells on three distinguished simultaneous and interrelated careers: by 1885 he was almost universally recognized as one of the foremost novelists, critics, and literary editors in the country.

II

Several writers have noticed with considerable puzzlement that Howells, himself a prolific critic for nearly sixty years, repeatedly scoffed at the office and object of literary criticism with harsh words. "Criticism," reads a notorious sentence from *My Literary Passions*, "ever since I filled myself so full of it in my boyhood, I have not cared for, and often I have found it repulsive."[17] An earlier letter to a Mr. Ernst insists that "criticism, as it exists, is absolutely useless to art of any sort" and that it is consequently "the idlest think [sic] in the world."[18] And in a letter to Aldrich in 1901 he declared: "I hate criticism. . . . I never did a piece of it that satisfied me."[19]

These claims are not, however, as unequivocal as they may seem. In their respective contexts they do not add up to a universal condemnation of literary criticism, but rather reflect Howells' distaste for certain forms of criticism "as it exists" and his uneasiness with the pressures under which he, as a critic, was forced to work. He suffered especially from the permanent pressure of editorial obligations and deadlines, from a painful awareness of the

William Dean Howells von 1866 bis 1881: Howells Tätigkeit als Hilfs und Chefredakteur am *Atlantic Monthly*" (Freie Universität Berlin, 1957).

[15] WDH to James Russell Lowell, 21 August 1864, *Selected Letters*, 1:194.

[16] WDH to Edmund Clarence Stedman, 5 December 1866, *Life in Letters of William Dean Howells*, ed. Mildred Howells (Garden City, N.Y., 1928), volume 1, p. 116; WDH to Charles Eliot Norton, 12 November 1868, *Life in Letters*, 1:137.

[17] *My Literary Passions* (New York, 1895), p. 235.

[18] WDH to Ernst (possibly C. W. Ernst, editor of the Boston *Beacon*), 4 June 1887 (MS at John Hay Library, Brown University). Quoted by permission of Brown University Library.

[19] WDH to Thomas Bailey Aldrich, 21 May 1901, *W. D. Howells: Selected Letters*, volume 4, ed. Thomas Wortham, Christoph K. Lohmann, and David J. Nordloh (Boston, 1981), p. 265.

"limitations of the mere book-noticing critic's work"[20] and increasingly from the feeling that the perpetual writing of reviews and literary notices was not only marring his reading with a bitter alloy but imposing too heavy a burden on his work as a novelist—all reasons which motivated his resignation from the *Atlantic* in 1881. At the same time, Howells objected emphatically to much of the published criticism: both the "attributive" impressionism (à la Ruskin)[21] and the prejudiced normative dogmatism (à la Brunetière), as well as the various pseudo-critical manifestations of "partisan feeling, envy of a rival, personal dislike, ecclesiastical terror, or mean malevolence of any sort."[22]

This negative catalogue reveals to some extent what Howells demanded of a good critic and thus of himself: a "constructive criticism"[23] which conceives of itself as an honest and modest service to the reader, which strives to objectify its methods and premises, and which derives its standards of value not only from an educated and refined taste and a thorough competence but above all from a faithful interpretation of experienced reality. In his essay "Literary Criticism" (1866), which along with his review of Thomas Purnell's *Literature and Its Professors* (1867) is the best statement of his early critical theory, Howells wrote that "True criticism is the function and the natural habit of every intelligent and candid mind";[24] that is, it is essentially an act of common sense which is concerned with diagnosis and discrimination (rather than with emotional impressions or aesthetic precepts) and which ultimately transcends its literary object, tending towards a larger criticism of life. Done conscientiously, it becomes a "stern and responsible duty: the exercise of discernment between the good and the bad, the false and the true, the sincere and the sham." And when "such . . . exercise is honestly and loyally put into print for the general perusal," Howells asked, "pray is not the public the gainer?"[25]

Though Howells did not always live up to his own standards, though he produced book notices "the poorness, the wretched meagreness" of which later made him blush,[26] the critical *Nation* felt that the public was indeed the gainer when Howells took charge of the *Atlantic*'s "Reviews and Literary Notices" in 1866.[27] Howells, reticent in public yet humorously self-assured in private, apparently agreed. "The Nation often has good notices," he re-

---

[20] Howells' review of Oliver Wendell Holmes, *The Poet at the Breakfast Table*, *Atlantic*, XXX (1872), 746.

[21] Howells' review of W. H. Pater, *Studies in the History of the Renaissance*, *Atlantic*, XXXII (1873), 497–498.

[22] Howells, "Literary Criticism," item 11, below.

[23] Howells' review of James Russell Lowell, *Among My Books: Second Series*, *Atlantic*, XXXVII (1876), 493.

[24] See item 11, below.

[25] *Ibid.*

[26] WDH to Charles Dudley Warner, 18 December 1876, *Selected Letters*, 2:144.

[27] Comments about Howells' "department" appeared in the *Nation* on 2 August and 29 November 1866, 29 October 1868, and 3 February 1870.

marked to his sister Annie, "but on the whole I think The Atlantic's the best in the country—even though I don't always write them."[28] Howells was in illustrious company when praising his own achievement. As early as 1868 Lowell had saluted Howells' critical *"savoir dire"* in the *Atlantic*, predicting that he was going "to beat us all in prose."[29] Holmes, another of the magazine's founders, congratulated Howells on the "brilliant and commanding position" he had "fairly won" for himself.[30] Of the younger American writers, Mark Twain testified to his respect for Howells' competence and authority in his own characteristic way: "Yours is the recognized critical Court of Last Resort in this country; from its decision there is no appeal."[31]

There were others, to be sure, who judged differently. Charles Eliot Norton, for one, lamented Howells' lack of formal education and "culture"—the absence of "some acquaintance in childhood with Homer and Vergil and the historical stream of imagination in literature."[32] Henry James agreed at least occasionally: "The principles on which [Howells] edits the *Atlantic*," he commented to Thomas Sergeant Perry, "indicate a low standard, certainly, & the vulgarity of that magazine often calls a patriotic blush to my cheek."[33] (More frequently, James praised Howells highly as both editor and critic—and may have blushed at the contradiction.)[34] Lafcadio Hearn bluntly classified Howells' literary philosophy as "that of a school-boy" and his power of criticism as "limited to Sunday-school standards."[35] Bernard Smith, in his *Forces in American Criticism*, dismissed Howells' critical career up to 1886 as a time during which "he reveled (worshipfully, of course) in the prejudices and attitudes of the aristocratic natives" of New England. Howells as a literary critic, Smith suggested, was a distinctly undistinguished *quantité négligeable*

---

[28] WDH to Anne T. Howells, 3 February 1873, *Selected Letters*, 2:12. Although he claimed in 1866 that he wrote "nearly all the literary notices" (WDH to Mary D. Howells, 19 June 1866, *Selected Letters*, 1:261) and no doubt "almost wholly" controlled the *Atlantic* reviews during his editorial tenure (WDH to Thomas Wentworth Higginson, 24 December 1869, *Selected Letters*, 1:348), Howells apparently soon called in other reviewers. Since all reviews and notices appeared anonymously and since the *Atlantic Index* (Boston and New York, 1889; Supplement, 1903) is incomplete, a positive identification of all of Howells' contributions to the "Reviews and Literary Notices" may ultimately turn out to be impossible. See Textual Commentary, below, for a comment on the attribution of essays included in the present volume.

[29] Lowell to WDH, 31 October 1868, *New Letters of James Russell Lowell*, ed. Mark A. DeWolfe Howe (New York, 1932), p. 130.

[30] Oliver Wendell Holmes to WDH, 14 December 1879 (MS at Houghton Library, Harvard). Quoted by permission of the Harvard College Library.

[31] Mark Twain to WDH, 19 October 1875, *Mark Twain-Howells Letters*, ed. Henry Nash Smith and William M. Gibson (Cambridge, Mass., 1960), volume 1, p. 107.

[32] Norton to S. Weir Mitchell, 22 December 1905; quoted in Kermit Vanderbilt, *Charles Eliot Norton: Apostle of Culture in a Democracy* (Cambridge, Mass., 1959), p. 180.

[33] James to Perry, 31 August 1880, in Virginia Harlow, *Thomas Sergeant Perry: A Biography* (Durham, N.C., 1950), p. 308.

[34] Henry James, "William Dean Howells," *Harper's Weekly*, 19 June 1886, p. 394, and "Letter to Mr. Howells," *North American Review*, CVC (1912), 558–559.

[35] "Sins of Genius" (1886), reprinted in *Essays on American Literature*, ed. Albert Mordell and Sanki Ichikawa (Tokyo, 1929), p. 192.

until, setting out on a "new tack" in 1886, he "first put forth his major critical ideas" in the "Editor's Study" of *Harper's Monthly*.[36]

III

The present collection of more than seventy reviews and critical essays from the twenty-seven years before 1886 enables the reader to form his or her own independent opinion of the historical status and the stature of Howells' early criticism. For far too long the need to attack or defend has determined the discussion of Howells' work. Insufficient knowledge of the texts, as well as dubious motives, were nothing short of a tradition among at least four decades of commentators: both Van Wyck Brooks and Sinclair Lewis ridiculed Howells' novels without having read them,[37] and Bernard Smith commented without knowing even a few of Howells' more important early critical pieces. Now that a representative cross-section of these texts is available, a disinterested reappraisal is not only possible but may be encouraged by a few observations on characteristic elements of Howells' early criticism.

1. Although personal in tone, often *en passant* and *à propos* in attitude, and not advancing an explicit aesthetic system, Howells' reviews and essays before 1886 nevertheless display a fundamental unity of outlook and continuity of development. They represent the evolution of a concept of the nature and function of literature which, at some time in the early 1880s, began to be called "realism" in America. This concept was not one of literature alone, and it was not invented by Howells. "No one invented realism," Howells wrote in 1886; "it came."[38] It came *to* Howells, whose background and temperament predisposed him for its acceptance to such a degree that it almost appeared as his "native growth."[39] It then came *through* Howells who, in the criticism here collected, first evolved realistic critical standards in a country where shoddy romanticism and arrogant culturism were flourishing. He advocated modest honesty and clear and truthful adherence to reality, fidelity to the authentic, the experienced, the observed instead of romanticistic abstraction, sentimentality, and pretense. His criticism was built on respect for the common as the naturally human *par excellence*. In adhering to principles and techniques of narration which serve these ends, it valued the prevalence of character revelation over plot invention, "dramatic" presentation over authorial intrusion and didacticism, and organic over superimposed structure. These standards, to be sure, did not emerge simultaneously and ready-made. They were the product of a long search for aesthetic—and not only aesthetic—criteria for a new art based on a new fidelity to reality.

---

[36] Bernard Smith, *Forces in American Criticism* (New York, 1939), p. 161.

[37] On Brooks, see *Interviews with William Dean Howells*, pp. 368–371 and 406, n. 98; on Lewis, *Howells Sentinel*, VI (1 November 1962), 5.

[38] WDH to Thomas Sergeant Perry, 28 January 1886, *Selected Letters*, 3:153.

[39] Vernon L. Parrington, *Main Currents in American Thought* (New York, 1930), volume 3, p. 248.

They crystallized from careful analyses of fiction that testified to their validity either by demonstrated superiority (as in the works of Turgenev, Björnson, De Forest, Mark Twain, and James) or by blatant disregard for them (as, above all, in innumerable historical romances and adventure stories but also in some of the novels of Dickens, Thackeray, and Trollope). At what time exactly these critical standards first became clearly discernible in Howells' criticism—in 1866, as George Bennett suggests, or not until 1872, as Everett Carter maintains[40]—is one of the issues the reader may want to examine. By the end of 1885, at any rate, they were fully operative.

2. Howells' "passion for the common"[41]—the commonplace, the common man, the common human experience, the common idiom of speech, and the utility of common sense—makes it clear that his realism has underlying idealistic-melioristic premises. "I should be ashamed and sorry," Howells wrote to Thomas Wentworth Higginson, "if my novels did not unmistakably teach a lenient, generous, and liberal life: that is, I should feel degraded merely to amuse people."[42] This view had been even more pointedly expressed several years earlier in a review of Ralph Keeler's *Vagabond Adventures*: "A book has no business to be merely literature; and such a book as this especially ought to teach something,—ought to disenchant youth with adventure, and show Poverty in her true colors."[43] For Howells such sentences do not signify a relapse into authorial didacticism. He believed that the realistic work is objective rather than subjective—its "didacticism" is inherent in the salutary contact with (that is, the faithful representation of) reality which the work affords. In realistic art, Howells stated later, "truth to life is suffered to do its unsermonized office for conduct."[44]

Just as literature and life were inseparable in Howells' mind, so were his aesthetic and his humanitarian interest, his commitment to realism in literature, and his call for tolerant and responsible conduct manifestations of one and the same conviction: his belief in "the brotherhood of men," the "true spirit of Democracy."[45] In this sense, Howells' novels, his critical comments on social conditions, and even many of his editorial decisions on the *Atlantic*, were acts of literary criticism. The Howells who wrote about Landor "that a man achieves little who refuses to be his own contemporary,"[46] is the same Howells who ridiculed anachronistic Bostonian snobbery in *A Chance Acquaintance* and attacked both sentimentalism and social Darwinism in *The Rise*

---

[40] George N. Bennett, *William Dean Howells: The Development of a Novelist* (Norman, Oklahoma, 1959), p. 30; Everett Carter, *Howells and the Age of Realism* (Philadelphia and New York, 1954), p. 47.

[41] Howells, "Recollections of an Atlantic Editorship," *Atlantic*, C (1907), 600.

[42] WDH to Higginson, 17 September 1879, *Selected Letters*, 2:238.

[43] See item 31, below.

[44] *Literary Friends and Acquaintance*, p. 102.

[45] Howells' review of Goldwin Smith, *Cowper*, item 68, below; WDH to William Cooper Howells, 20 April 1873, *Selected Letters*, 2:24.

[46] See Howells' review of *Cameos: Selected from the Works of Walter Savage Landor*, item 46, below.

of Silas Lapham, who pilloried slavery as early as 1860 ("All men shall rise where slaves have trod"),[47] and who accepted Henry Demarest Lloyd's "Story of a Great Monopoly" for the *Atlantic* "with pleasure."[48] Perhaps no other motive was more essential for Howells' entire literary productivity than that which his fictional *persona*, Basil March, later called "the interest of human enlightenment."[49]

3. On the occasion of Whittier's seventieth birthday and the twentieth anniversary celebration of the *Atlantic* in 1877, Charles Dudley Warner praised the "fair share" the magazine had had "in the total revolution of the character of American literature—I mean the revolution out of the sentimental period" and the emancipation "from fear of or dependence on English criticisms."[50] Of that fair share a fair share belongs to Howells. As editor, he never tired of rejecting and ridiculing what Lowell called belated British attempts at "provincializing us again";[51] in 1882 he serenely reaped the British whirlwind he had sown by suggesting that "the art of fiction has, in fact, become a finer art in our day than it was with Dickens and Thackeray."[52] More important still than this private feud with British criticism is his belief in the "fundamental identity of American experience" and the essential goodness of the "right American manner." It was the basis on which Howells encouraged, both as critic and editor, all serious literary attempts to depict American life faithfully.[53]

When he left the *Atlantic* in 1881 Howells had established himself as probably the most distinguished discoverer and promoter of talent in American literature: a "literary Columbus,"[54] godfather—as *Cosmopolitan* editor Perriton Maxwell later called him—"to a flock of brilliant essayists, poets, and storytellers whose voices would have died in the echoless wilderness of un-appreciation had he not been the conscientious listener for the newer notes borne Bostonward from everywhere in these broad States of ours."[55] The barest list of American authors whom Howells helped to break through to general recognition before 1886 is impressive indeed. It includes Henry James and Mark Twain as well as Edward Bellamy, George Cary Eggleston, J. W. De Forest, E. W. Howe, and Sarah Orne Jewett. Better than anything else, these names testify to the competence, discernment, and vision of Howells' early criticism.

---

[47] Howells, "Old Brown," *Ashtabula Sentinel*, 25 January 1860, p. 1.
[48] WDH to Lloyd, 6 December 1880, *Selected Letters*, 2:270.
[49] *The Shadow of a Dream* (Bloomington and London, 1970), p. 111.
[50] "The Atlantic Dinner," Boston *Evening Transcript*, 18 December 1877, p. 3.
[51] Lowell to Grace Norton, 12 June 1879, *Letters of James Russell Lowell*, 2:244.
[52] "Henry James, Jr.," item 71, below.
[53] Bennett, *William Dean Howells*, p. 50; Howells, "Editor's Study," *Harper's Monthly*, LXXII (1886), 323–324.
[54] Theodore Dreiser, review of Abraham Cahan, *Yekl*, *Ev'ry Month*, II (1896), 22.
[55] "Howells *the* Editor," *Book News Monthly*, XXVI (1908), 737.

IV

Some words need to be added in explanation of the principles by which the present volume was compiled. Between the later 1850s and the end of 1885, Howells published more than four hundred items of literary criticism (mainly book reviews, some critical essays, a few miscellaneous articles) which statistically constitute more than forty percent of his total literary output from that time; more than ninety percent of it was written in the two most productive periods, 1859–1861 and 1866–1880.[56]

This selection, which offers about one–fifth of Howells' work during these years, attempts both to represent Howells and to present the best of Howells. Only such reviews and essays were chosen as, in the complete unabridged form of their first publication, stand out as well-reasoned, coherent, illuminating samples of literary criticism. (Editorial cutting of individual essays or of independent sections of multi-part reviews was ruled out on principle.) These samples were then reconsidered and resifted in the light of their contextual relevance for the development and articulation of Howells' realistic concept of the form and function of the literary work of art. The deliberate, persistent working out of that concept to the point of explicitness is the main achievement of Howells' criticism before 1886. It is also the implicit *leitmotif* of the criticism here collected.

A special editorial problem was posed by Howells' "Italian essays"— eleven lengthy articles on Italian literature, nine of which were later reprinted with omissions and revisions in *Modern Italian Poets* (1887). The product of systematic study begun at Venice in 1863–1864 and continued in Cambridge and Boston where Howells lectured on "New Italian Literature," "Modern Italian Poetry and Comedy," and "Italian Poets of Our Century" at both Harvard and the Lowell Institute (1870–1871), these essays differ from Howells' other critical writings in at least two respects. First, their main objective is precritical rather than critical, namely to *inform* a largely ignorant American audience of the existence of certain authors, works, and tendencies of "modern" Italian literature; the emphasis is on description rather

---

[56] Prior to 1861 Howells published a relatively large number of anonymous and as yet unidentified contributions (including literary criticism) in the *Ashtabula Sentinel*, the *Ohio State Journal*, and other newspapers and magazines. Similarly, Howells' reviews and literary notices in the *Atlantic* (see n. 28, above) were also anonymous, and some of them may not yet have been identified. The magazine's index is incomplete in this respect; contributions to its "Contributor's Club," which Howells started in 1877, are, for instance, not listed in the index. Recent efforts at identification—Philip B. Eppard and George Monteiro, *A Guide to the "Atlantic Monthly" Contributor's Club* (Boston, 1983)—have identified only one item (on dreams) by Howells. William M. Gibson's and George Arms's *Bibliography of William Dean Howells* (New York, 1948) has so far been supplemented only to a relatively modest extent. For addenda in the realm of literary criticism before 1886, see George Monteiro, "Howells on Lowell: An Unascribed Review," *New England Quarterly*, XXXVIII (1965), 508–509, and Ulrich Halfmann, "Addenda to Gibson and Arms: Twenty-three New Howells Items," *PBSA*, LXVI (1972), 174–177. See Textual Commentary, below, for a comment on the attribution of essays included in the present volume.

than analysis and on biography rather than the literary works themselves. Secondly, in striking contrast to Howells' other criticism, they are written from the point of view of an outsider who felt himself being pushed into the role of expert in a field "where my solitude, if not my magnitude, would give me monumental distinction."[57] Hence, in nearly all of his Italian essays we find a strong indebtedness to secondary sources, an often fragmentary knowledge of an author's work, and a resulting vagueness and indecision in critical judgments. Hence, the present volume omits all of these essays with the exception of a single one, which stands as a document worthy of our attention: "Recent Italian Comedy." Published in 1864, it is not only Howells' first but also his most successful article on an Italian literary subject— "an effective blend of history, cultural analysis, human interest, and literary criticism."[58] Both Norton and Longfellow, surely two of the most competent American judges, praised it; even Italian critics and authors (among them Dall'Ongaro) expressed their appreciation.[59] Biographically, its acceptance by Lowell and its publication in the *North American Review* in 1864 marked another memorable stage in Howells' career, the "turning point" at which the now mature professional writer directed himself away from poetry toward criticism and fiction.

U. H.

---

[57] "The Turning Point of My Life," p. 165.

[58] Edwin H. Cady, *The Road to Realism* (Syracuse, N.Y., 1956), p. 108.

[59] See James L. Woodress, *Howells & Italy* (Durham, N.C., 1952), pp. 92 and 95; also WDH to William Cooper Howells, 21 June 1865, *Selected Letters*, 1:220: "My article on 'Comedy,' has made me quite a reputation in Italy, amongst the Italian literati, and the English living in Italy."

REVIEWS AND ESSAYS

1

A Book Read Yesterday.

[Thomas Bailey Aldrich, *The Ballad of Babie Bell*]

WHEN a book comes to you well dressed, in a surcoat of pleasantly brown cloth, and arrayed in fine linen paper (tinted a thought saffron), and printed with those uncouth, old-fashioned type, which are just now so much the mode in the book-world; when a book comes to you in such a guise, it is very likely you fall in love with it at first sight. It is possible that a better acquaintance with this volume will cure your passion; and, indeed, I have survived, during the present year, two very violent prepossessions of the kind. One was that exuberant "Life and Times of Sir Philip Sidney," in which the poor gentleman was quite lost sight of amid a gorgeous pageantry of contemporary events (continually marched before the reader), and a halo of the most dazzling panegyric. The other was "A Bachelor's Story," which had a queer, faint smack of "The Reveries" and "Dream Life," as warmish water might have of wine when rinsed from a bottle in which there had been champagne.

I am a reader of books, but I do not believe the critics so much as I once did, and commonly read with an unmade-up mind. It is really a great luxury to form your own opinions, and it is astonishing how few people indulge in it. The gratification is within the reach of the slenderest purse, and yet we go using over again the notions of others, until we cheat ourselves out of what little is original and real in our thoughts. There is no slavery so abject as that of the unemancipated mind to the critic; and freedom is all the sweeter for the recollection of the old bondage. I like to retaliate with sleeve-laughter upon my old tyrants—take two of equal authority, and read them on the same subject. It is pleasant to see how easily, by a certain line of reasoning, and a certain art of Italicized quotations, each makes out his case for or against the book. If you read two criticisms, and think about them afterwards, your reading will have been of profit, as well as pleasure. It is a sad thing to be a man of one book, but it is a sadder thing to be a man of one critic.

Fine precepts! Can I practice them? Dear knows.

It was of Aldrich's poems I wanted to speak. We have vast numbers of verse-writers (that sounds like the preliminary hemming and hawing of a puff in the Boston *Palimpsest* or the New York *Patchquilt*), but true poets we have not in such abundance that we can suffer anything of that nature to go down to oblivion without calling upon him to stand, in the prince's name. If he do not stand, he is of course not the man we took him for, and we shall at once permit him to steal out of immortal company.

It is a few years only since T. B. Aldrich's poems first began to "attract attention," and they have run the gauntlet of the press from one end of the land to the other, until he has now, perhaps, a wider newspaper reputation than any other of our young poets. His poems have that obvious beauty which catches the thought at once, and there is a richness and passionateness about them that pleases us, though we call ourselves not sentimental as a people. I like a little affectation in a poet, as I like it in a woman, and there are certain little airs in Mr. Aldrich's style that do not offend me. I think I know where they come from, and I love them all the better for what they remind me of. Mr. Aldrich has been among our dear old ballad-makers— those bluebirds of English song, whose quaint, broken notes preluded the full chorus that has since shaken the sky of our poetic June—he has been among the sadder and sweeter German poets, say Heine and Uhland,—he has been among those

———"rogues of cazonite and serenades,"

the Spanish lyrists, who made Spain great before her kings did. And Mr. Aldrich is come back from all these people, with a touch of mannerism from each, but also with much of their excellence assimilated to his native genius—like a gentleman polite with travel.

Somebody said, the other day (before I had the chance to do so, for the same idea ran in thought in my mind, and I was just about to bottle it up in words, and serve it to the public, with the inventor's seal on the cork, and a fac-simile of his signature on the wrapper), that it was too much the custom of critics to find fault with the lily because it was not an oak, the lark because it was not an eagle, and so forth. This sort of criticism is so cheap, one can afford it at half the price of a genuine article. It is easy to say of a poet that he is not strong like another poet, nor terrible like another, nor profound like another. It is much easier than to prove that he has not an hundred graces, for which one would cheerfully give strength, terror, and profundity, with boot. But I recommend this method of criticism to all dull people.

His daintiness of style and delicacy of thought is something that may be objected to Mr. Aldrich by such people; and I am afraid that he may be tempted to write some day a poem in the wish to show that he can be what they object he is not. I sincerely trust he will fail.

In the volume before me (I got that out of my inkhorn-full of newspaper expressions), I like best of all the little poem "Nameless Pain." It is the worthiest proof that Mr. Aldrich is a poet, and better than an epic for him. All hearts, however dulled by care, and doubt, and wrong, feel sometimes the Nameless Pain, only different in degree. How it thrills and trembles in the heart of the poet he has—described? No. Expressed? No. We do not, even the greatest-tongued of us, describe or express intense sensation. The best that any can do is to let the soul be seen for an instant with the secret lightning of feeling playing through it, and illuming it—"*flammae inter nubes.*"

And this is not to be done by any elaboration of words, but suddenly and briefly, as Heine does it in his line-long revelations of Passion and Sorrow, in that rhyme commencing—

> "Mein Herz, mein Herz ist traurig,
> Doch lustig leuchtet der Mai,
> Ich stehe gelehnt an der Linden,
> Hoch auf der alten Bastei."

The picture of the boy fishing in the lazy moat, the far-seen fields and meadows, the pleasure-houses, the maidens bleaching the linen, the mill-wheel scattering its diamonds with its "fernes Gesunen," and the sentry on the old gray tower, marching up and down before his box, with his musket twinkling in the sun, and at last the imagination brought back to the said *haupt-figur* of the scene, with this passionate cry—

> "Ich wollte er schösset mir todt!"

This is the art which makes me doubt art; and this is the art which I love in Mr. Aldrich's poem of "Nameless Pain."

> "In my nostrils the Summer wind
> Blows the exquisite scent of the rose!
> O, for the golden, golden wind,
> Breaking the buds as it goes—
> Breaking the buds, and bending the grass
> And spilling the scent of the rose!
>
> "O, wind of the Summer morn,
> Tearing the petals in twain,
> Wafting the fragrant soul
> Of the rose through valley and plain,
> I would you could tear my heart to-day,
> And scatter its nameless pain."

Of a different beauty are the poems: "Cloth of Gold," "The Faded Violet," "We knew it would Rain," and "Tiger Lilies,"—all so honey-worded, and so delicate-thoughted, so exquisite and true, that I am tempted to take back my avowal of preference for the poem I have just quoted. I take it for granted that every reader of the *Saturday Press* is acquainted with Mr. Aldrich's poems, and I need not quote them. "Babie Bell" is a lament not to be touched with the commonplace of praise. The mother-heart will love that and honor it best in silence.

"Palabras Cariñaeas" is worthy to wear so melting a Spanish name. There is nothing more luscious and tender in all Tennyson. The song "Sing it, Ring it, Silver Throat," pleasures me also, and the same rich and luscious fancy is at play in all the amorous trifles of the book.

I do not like that dramatic sketch, "The Set of Turquoise," though I like many of its lines. Mr. Aldrich's sonnets are as far from being unreadable as any sonnets I have yet conquered. His "Invocation to Sleep" brings back the old dream in which I read the "Lotus Eater" first. Hark!

> "The bell sleeps in the belfry—from its tongue
> A drowsy murmur floats into the air,
> Like thistle down."

Do you hear it?

"A Ballad of Nantucket" is as pretty and unaffected and touching as may be; while "The Ghost's Lady" is poor in fancy and quite barren of thought. How is this, Poet? I have borrowed your book of a friend who bought it, and do you talk to me of "quaint little snakes in the grass, lifting their heads to the moon?" Do your quaint little snakes ever do anything of that nature? Go to!

Ah! Mr. Aldrich, if I could but talk down upon you as a critic should do, I would close these notices (which a long habit of pen has, I fear, very nearly converted into a puff,) by telling you how to become a greater and better poet than you are. I would assume that superiority which interprets emotions without pretending to have felt them, and which explains what poetry should be, without having written it. But the office is something difficult, to me; and, indeed, your little book gave me so much pleasure, that I wish you would write another just like it. I do not deny that you can become better, and it is possible for you to be worse. But, shall we scourge a poet and then dip him in brine, that he may

> ————"suffer a seachange
> Into something rich and strange?"

[New York *Saturday Press*, 30 July 1859]

2

Hawthorne's "Marble Faun."

THE people who have read this beautiful book will hardly wish to have the story feebly rehearsed. Those who have yet the pleasure of reading it before them, could only be vexed by glimpses of its incidents.

For the reader's sake, therefore, we repress whatever desire we have to tell Mr. Hawthorne's tale again, and permit ourselves only allusion to the idea of the book.

Of all this author's romances, "The Marble Faun" is the most darkly sad, the most subtly mysterious. In it you glide forever through a dream of exquisite sorrow, with the dim life of antiquity vaguely haunting the shadowy groves, and mixing with lives of the present, so far exalted out of the common-place and vulgar. Hawthorne, indeed, seems to have wreaked his soul upon the expression of the emotion which rises from the thought of Death, and the story, fine and precious as it is, is but the clay in which he shapes and moulds the idea to make it palpable to coarser vision.

In no other atmosphere than that of Rome is such a work possible, and there the scene is laid—in that city, where life, constantly confronted with eternal Art, seems so cruelly brief and little, and where old Nature is ineffably sad with the secrets and sorrows of her dead children, the Generations.

Yes, the Idea of the book is Death. Not that ghastly thing which triumphs over our joy, and shows itself grinning and hideous at our feasts—but Death, the old attendant of our race, inevitable, and universal, standing in wait for us at the end of the journey, and embracing the beggar and the prince with wide arms that know no difference. Death the moss-bearded,—death the vague but not the terribly mysterious,—death the rest but not the punishment,—death the inexorable but not unkind—venerable, serene.

The little stream of life and love that goes glimmering through this Valley of the Shadow is sweet enough; the flowers of our common delighte spring upon its banks, and kiss its waters; and the woods that group themselves along its course, are full of sylvan creatures, and gleam with exquisite works of art.

Kenyon the sculptor is a real and noble man; Hilda is marbly pure and tranquil as a saint, preciously carved out of stone; Miriam is—Miriam—and Donatello, the poor Faun, who found a soul in sin—there is only one other man like him that ever lived, and he lived in "The House of Seven Gables"—

Clifton Pyncheon, in whom destiny annulled all the rich and beautiful purpose of nature, and mocked with the terrible earnestness of grief, the soul that was born for enjoyment and happiness.

[*Ohio State Journal*, 24 March 1860]

3

Bardic Symbols.

WALT. Whitman has a poem of this title in the April *Atlantic*.

Swift denunciation comes always from either ignorance or prejudice, or passion—no less in literature than in any other living affair; and it carries no force with it except to the ignorant, the passionate, and the prejudiced.

It is a pity that criticism should ever forget this; but criticism does; and the newspaper critic particularly seems to think that so he makes a great wind in his angry scoop, he carries conviction with him, and strikes dead the poet whose heart he cannot understand, and cannot find.

Walt Whitman has higher claims upon our consideration than mere magazine contributorship. He is the author of a book of poetry called "Leaves of Grass," which, whatever else you may think, is wonderful. Ralph Waldo Emerson pronounced it the representative book of the poetry of our age. It drew the attention of critics, but found no favor with the public, for the people suspect and dislike those who nullify venerable laws, and trample upon old forms and usages. Since the publication of his book, Walt Whitman has driven hack in New York, and employed the hours of his literary retiracy in hard work. Some months ago he suddenly flashed upon us in the New York *Saturday Press*, and created eager dissension among the "crickets." Now he is in the *Atlantic*, with a poem more lawless, measureless, rhymeless and inscrutable than ever.

No one, even after the fourth or fifth reading, can pretend to say what the "Bardic Symbols" symbolize. The poet walks by the sea, and addressing the drift, the foam, the billows and the wind, attempts to force from them, by his frantic outcry, the true solution of the mystery of Existence, always most heavily and darkly felt in the august ocean presence. All is confusion, waste and sound. It is in vain that you attempt to gather the poet's full meaning from what he says or what he hints. You can only take refuge in occasional passages like this, in which he wildly laments the feebleness and inefficiency of that art which above all others seeks to make the soul visible and audible:

"O, baffled, lost,
Bent to the very earth, here preceding what follows,
Terrified with myself that I have dared to open my mouth,
Aware now, that amid all the blab, whose echoes recoil upon me, I

have not once had the least idea who or what I am,
But that before all my insolent poems the real one still stands
  untouched, untold, altogether unreached,
Withdrawn far, mocking me with mock-congratulatory signs and bows,
With peals of distant ironical laughter at every word I have written
  or shall write,
Striking me with insults till I fall helpless upon the sand."

If indeed, we were compelled to guess the meaning of the poem, we should say it all lay in the compass of these lines of Tennyson—the saddest and profoundest that ever were written:

"Break, break, break,
  On thy cold gray stones, O sea!
And I would that my tongue could utter
  The thoughts that arise in me!"

An aspiration of mute words without relevancy, without absolute signification, and full of "divine despair."

We think it has been an error in Whitman to discard forms and laws, for without them the poet diffuses. He may hurry forward with impulses, but he is spent before he reaches the reader's heart through his bewildered understanding. Steam subject, is a mighty force; steam free, is an impalpable vapor, only capable of delicate hues and beauty with the sun upon it.

But O, poet! there is not a sun in every sky.

[*Ohio State Journal*, 28 March 1860]

4

[Whitman's Leaves of Grass]

Leaves of Grass.—By Walt. Whitman.—Thayer and Eldrige. Year 85 of the States. (1860–61.)

WHO is Walt. Whitman?

The person himself states his character, and replies to this question in the following general terms.

"Walt. Whitman, an American, one of the roughs, a kosmos.
Disorderly, fleshy, sensual, eating, drinking, breeding.
No sentimentalist—no stander above men and women, or apart from them.
No more modest than immodest."

This is frank, but not altogether satisfactory. From the journals therefore, and from talk of those who know him, we gather that Walt. Whitman lives in Brooklyn, that he has been a printer, and an omnibus driver, that he wears a red flannel shirt, and habitually stands with his hands in pockets; that he is not chaste nor clean, despising with equal scorn the conventional purity of linen, and the conventional rules of verse; that he is sublime and at the same time beastly; that he has a wonderful brain and an unwashed body. Five years ago, he gave to light the first edition of the "Leaves of Grass," which excited by its utter lawlessness, the admiration of those who believe liberty to mean the destruction of government, and disgusted many persons of fine feelings. We remember to have seen a brief criticism of the book in dear, dead *Putnam*, by a critic, who seemed to have argued himself into a complete state of uncertainty, and who oracularly delivered an opinion formed upon the model of the judge's charge in Bardell and Pickwick. Ralph Waldo Emmerson, however, took by the horns, this bull, that had plunged into the china-shop of poetical literature, threatening all the pretty Dresden ornaments, and nice little cups with gold bands on them; and pronounced him a splendid animal—and left people to infer that he was some such inspired brute as that Jove infurried, when he played Europa that sad trick.

But presently the bull—being a mere brute—was forgotten, and the china-shop was furnished forth anew with delicate wares—new-fashioned dolls, bubble-thin goblets, and dainty match-safes.

Nearly a year ago, the bull put his head through the New York Saturday Press' enclosure, and bellowed loud, long and unintelligibly.

The mystery of the thing made it all the more appalling.

The Misses Nancy of criticism hastened to scramble over the fence, and on the other side, stood shaking their fans and parasols at the wretch, and shrieking, "Beast! beast!"

Some courageous wits attempted to frighten the animal away by mimicry, and made a noise as from infant bulls.

The people in the china-shop shut and bolted their doors.

Several critics petted and patted the bull; but it was agreed that while his eyes had a beautiful expression, and his breath was fragrant with all the meadow-sweetness of the world, he was not at all clean, and in general, smelt of the stables, and like a bull.

But after all, the question remained,—"What does he mean by it?"

It remains yet—now when he stands again in front of the china-shop, with his mouth full of fresh leaves of grass, lilies, clover-heads, buttercups, daisies, cockles, thistles, burrs, and hay, all mingled in a wisp together.

He says:

> "I celebrate myself,
> And what I assume you shall assume,
> For every atom belonging to me, as good belongs to you."

And so proceeds, metreless, rhymeless, shaggy, coarse, sublime, disgusting, beautiful, tender, harsh, vile, elevated, foolish, wise, pure and nasty to the four hundred and fifty-sixth page, in a book most sumptuously printed and bound.

If you attempt to gather the meaning of the whole book, you fail utterly.

We never saw a man yet, who understood it all. We who have read it all, certainly do not.

Yet there are passages in the book of profound and subtle significance, and of rare beauty; with passages so gross and revolting, that you might say of them, as the Germans say of bad books—*Sie lassen sich nicht lesen.*

Walt Whitman is both overrated and underrated. It will not do to condemn him altogether, nor to commend him altogether.—You cannot apply to him the tests by which you are accustomed to discriminate in poetry.

He disregards and defies precedent, in the poetic art. It remains for Time, the all-discerning, to announce his wisdom, or his folly to the future.

Only this: If he is indeed "the distinctive poet of America," then the office of poet is one which must be left hereafter to the shameless and the friendless. For Walt. Whitman is not a man whom you would like to know. You might care to see him, to hear him speak, but you must shrink from his contact. He has told too much. The secrets of the soul may be whispered to the world, but the secrets of the body should be decently hid. Walt. Whitman exults to blab them.

Heine in speaking of the confidences of Sterne, and of Jean Paul, says that the former showed himself to the world naked, while the latter merely had holes in his trousers. Walt. Whitman goes through his book, like one in an ill-conditioned dream, perfectly nude, with his clothes over his arm.

[*Ashtabula Sentinel*, 18 July 1860]

5

[Poets and Poetry of the West]

The Poets and Poetry of the West: with Biographical
and Critical Notices. By W. T. Caggeshall, Columbus.
Follett, Foster & Co.

IN this superb volume of nearly seven hundred pages, we have evidence that
Western Poets and Poetry certainly exist as to quantity, whatever else may be
said of them. The contents of the book, indeed, are like the quality of mercy,
in one respect, and its magnitude is partially attributable to the motive which
we had better let the editor explain himself.

"It has been the intention of the editor," he says, "to include in this
collection, every person legitimately belonging to the West, who has gained
recognition as a writer of reputable verse."

He has therefore, with this catholic intention given us poems and biographical notices of one hundred and forty-two writers of the West, of which
number sixty-nine were born in the West, and thirty-nine in Ohio alone. In
poet-bearing, Kentucky comes next, Indiana next, Michigan and Illinois
next, after Ohio.

When this book was forthcoming, we said (glancing at the advance
sheets,) that the rhymings of the West had nearly all been desultory; that few
western men had made literature a profession,—that

"In almost every locality of the vast region from which the materials of
this book have been drawn—Kentucky, Ohio, Indiana, Illinois, Wisconsin,
Michigan, Iowa, Kansas—some bird has piped his songs in the spring of
youth, and as the summer of life advanced, has taken to the more practical
business of building nests, and substantialy beautifying and peopling the
primeval solitudes that echoed to his earlier strains. Whatever is good in the
"airy nothing" of such singers, Mr. Coggeshall has caught and given in his
work "a local habitation." Then, again, those people who have "never got
over it,"—through whose lips the divine afflatus has never ceased to
breathe—who despite the jostling, and punching, and pushing, which must
disturb the reveries of star-gazers in the streets of our go-ahead towns and
cities—these are represented here in full, and the best that they have written
is offered to us, who "have not time" to read *all* they have written. The
younger poets—the bardlings of both sexes, who make our present poetical
literature, are gathered from the four winds of the newspapers and magazines, and put in this book, to which no doubt, if

"They love to read their own dear songs,"

they will turn hereafter with more tenderness than pride."

Looking over the complete work, we do not find cause to vary the estimate formed of it above; but have rather to express our satisfaction with the thorough manner in which the editor has discharged his task. It is one, indeed, for which he has been peculiarly fitted by his earnest belief in the excellence and the wrongs of Western literature, as well as his peculiar talent and industry. Few men in the country could have brought so much patience and ardor to the work—no other man in the West could have done so. Eager to render justice—perhaps too eager to encourage—yet keeping the endurance of his reader in view, he has made a book entirely creditable to himself.—And we think it creditable to the West, too.—One constantly encounters pleasant surprises in turning over its handsome pages. Here is John Findley's "Bachelor's Hall," which has crossed and recrossed the Atlantic, as the humorous extravaganza of Thomas Moore; here is that wild and powerful poem of John L. Harney's, "The Fever Dream," which was one of the horrible delights of our boyhood; here is Perkins' "Young Soldier,"——

> "O were ye ne'er a school-boy,
>   And did you never train,
> And feel that swelling at the heart,
>   You ne'er can feel again."

God bless us! Were we not, indeed? What else should give that rare and subtle music to the refrain,

> "March, march away"

but the fact that we used to do it?

Then we have all that is best in Gallagher's verse; all that is best in the poetry of the Cary sisters, Mrs. Nichols, Amelia Welby, Fosdick, William Ross Wallace, Coates Kinney, and then later, Wm. W. Harney, (whom we account among the best,) Piatt, "Ruth Crayne," "Mary Robbins," and a score of others to whom we must deny mention.

The critic writes to little purpose, if he fails to show wherein he is wiser than his author, and we are tempted to tell Mr. Coggeshall and the public how much better we could now make this book. But it is a good book as it is—a very good book, and we refrain from a display of superiority at once proper and inexpensive.

Nay let us be lavishly generous, and give the publisher his due, for issuing one of the handsomest volumes which has appeared from the American press. We greet it with pride—and we trust that it will meet that abundant success, which it deserves. There is an historical value in the work, which through a secondary merit, should not be overlooked. The biographical notices, following each other in chronological order, form a complete history of poetical literature in the West, and present many facts of interest, as well as a large amount of information, in regard to personal history nowhere else to be found.

We believe the book is sold entirely by subscription.

[*Ohio State Journal*, 1 September 1860]

6

Some Western Poets of To-Day.

Wm. Wallace Harney.

Mr. Coggeshall's book of "Poets and Poetry of the West," is such a remarkably suggestive book in so many ways, that it is hard to keep the animadversive pencil out of it. Indeed, the present impulse is to write a series of brief papers upon the later poets of the West, who are also the best with one or two exceptions, but who are crowded into such a narrow space at the close of the volume, that the general effect is that of a bird-fancier's shop, rather than the well-known wild wood grove, in which songbirds of all kinds are supposed to disport themselves in the most expansive and advantageous manner. It is the generous impulse to give these thronged, half-throttled singers an airing, one after the other; but the impulse hardly amounts to an intention, and this series of brief papers may open and shut in the first essay. The business is not without dangers and risks. There are plumes that may be ruffled; there are performances that must be criticised, and out of the same beaks often come piping and pecking—with here and there a dash back at the benevolent critic. Nevertheless!

And the first poet in our mind, and one of the first in the book, is Mr. William Wallace Harney. We account him among the first, because he has shown in one or two poems that he possesses that poetic art, equally divine with the poetic impulse, which many of the earlier, and many of the later western poets have lacked. They have forever enacted the fable of Icarus, mounting on pinions of wax, that melted from them whenever they rose to the fervor of the upper skies, and let them down with ungainly falls, alike uncomfortable to themselves and their readers. Or if a western simile is insisted upon, (we are good at any kind,) theirs are the wings of the flying squirrel, useless except to alight with from some height already scrambled up to. It could not perhaps, be altogether otherwise, for western poets are workers as well as singers, and their performances are all more or less furtive and hurried. Yet, because we hope there shall some day be a different order of things—because we trust that after while the poet shall cease to hunger amid the abundance of our sea-wide cornfields—because we believe he shall not always be regarded as an alien in his own land,—we speak these words of kindly criticism that he may be worthy of the future that awaits him. Yes, in that Some-day, where we have all "located" our happiness, we like to think that the Western poet shall be the first of American poets. But they found

that the sweetest grape of Italy soured upon the hill-slopes at Cincinnati; and
they had no good wine till they took the harsh vine of their own woods, and
mellowed its blood with generous culture. And the wine of western poetry
must have the life and strength of a native past in it, mellowed by that light
and warmth which must always come from the orient.

There has been much vain talk about Western poetry. Some who have
contrasted its rude graces, its aboriginal audacities, with the exquisite fault-
lessness of its elder sister of the east, have been ready to deny its claim to
kinship. Its native beauties are forgotten in the grotesqueness of some of its
rhetorical finery, which hangs upon it like the cheap splendor borrowed from
a dubious civilization, on an Indian girl. On the other hand, (unluckily for
western poetry,) there has been a number of ill-advised friends, who have
insisted that it was already a literature, and have made themselves uncomfortable about the fancied slights and wrongs it has suffered at the hands of
eastern criticism. It has been shut out, they say, from eastern collections of
poetry; and eastern magazines have smothered all the babes of western song,
in the secrecy of those dungeons appointed for the reception of rejected
contributions. These enthusiastic, but mistaken persons, have insisted in
many cases upon cultivating wild gooseberries instead of wild grapes; and
when the eastern, or other critics, have made wry faces over the dreadful
juice of that abominable fruit, the indiscriminate friends of western succu-
lence have cried out: "Good Heaven! here is a nice-stomached man for you!
His prejudices, sir, his *jealousy* wont let him acknowledge that this well-
flavored drink is sparkling Catawba."

But this is an article on Mr. Harney, of Kentucky, we believe. Persons
who wish to know him biographically will go to Mr. Coggeshall's book. He is
now the editor of the Louisville *Daily Democrat*, and is a native of Indiana.—
He is represented in the book of "Poets and Poetry," by five poems: "The
Stab," "The Buried Hope," "The Suicide," "The Old Mill," and "Jimmy's
Wooing." The first of these poems is the briefest and the best. It is so good,
indeed, that we quote it—though many of our readers are doubtless already
familiar with it:

> THE STAB.
> On the road, the lonely road,
>   Under the cold white moon,
> Under the ragged trees he strode;
> He whistled and shifted his weary load—
>   Whistled a foolish tune.
>
> There was a step timed with his own,
>   A figure that stooped and bowed—
> A cold, white blade that gleamed and shone,
> Like a splinter of daylight downward thrown—
>   And the moon went behind a cloud.

But the moon came out so broad and good,
 The barn fowl woke and crowed;
Then roughed his feathers in drowsy mood,
And the brown owl called to his mate in the wood
 That a dead man lay on the road.

There is one figure in this poem, which may have pleased some persons by its audacity, but which is entirely false and bad, and mars terribly a poem in which there is no other defect. We mean the comparison of the knife to

—"A splinter of daylight downward thrown."

The poem is eminently suggestive, but it suggests no possibility by which daylight can be splintered. The raggedness and *tearing* emotion suggested is well, and has its proper effect upon the nerves; but why daylight, *how* splinter of daylight? We doubt if Mr. Harney approves this image himself, but he was probably loth to touch in correction, a poem that must have had a movement all its own and seemed to end without his volition, and had in it at after-glance an inscrutable perfection and symmetry, unfelt while it flowed from his imagination. It belongs to that class of poems which impress the reader like the glimpsed career of a cataract which is seen and is not heard to fall, but which thunders ever after in the heart. It is of the "wayward, modern" school; it is German. It does not belong to the arithmetical three-into-nine-go-three-times, or the Jones-is-dead-but-he-is-in-heaven-and-therefore-we-wont-cry, lyrical school. It doesn't pin a poetic moral to a cork; but the shadow it casts upon you is winged.

"The Suicide," is an attempt in the same spirit with the poem we have quoted, and we think a failure. There is a lamentable inadequency of expression here and there; the imagery is occasionally revolting, and it is rather the Corpse than the Horror of a suicide that the poet presents.

"The Buried Hope," is tender and touching, and though treating of a dead child, has none of that loud varnish-smell, with which coffin-poetesses perfume their mortuary verses.

"The Old Mill"—ah! we have been there! If we shut our eyes, we see it where it stands,

"The lichen hangs from the walls aloof,
And the rusty nails from the ragged roof,
 Drop daily, one by one.

"The long grass grows in the shady pool,
Where the cattle used to come to cool,
 And the rotting wheel stands still;
The gray owl winks in the granary loft,
And the sly rats slinks, with a pit-pat soft,
 From the hopper of the quaint Old Mill."

Now and then the elevator in Mr. Harney's mill breaks, and the ground wheat does not reach the cooling-floor, and is not bolted; but for the most part it remains all right in the Old Mill.

We account "Jemmy's Wooing" one of the sweetest little idylls that has ever been written. It is full of country summer scents, and rainy sights, and breezy sounds, and there is an old ballad simplicity in it, most dear to us. Not even Drayton's "Dawsabel," who—

"Who went forth to gather Maye,"

pleases us more. It is one of the few popular poems which has deserved the newspaper celebrity it has attained; and it suffers re-perusal marvelous well.

It is customary, we believe, to wind up a criticism with a few general observation—a sort of "May-Heaven-have-mercy-upon-your-soul" address to the poet, and some remarks by way of warning to the reader. But as nothing particularly novel in this way occurs to us, we will offer in reference to Mr. Harney, the comprehensive sentiment, "Many returns of the same."

We like Mr. Harney's poems, because he shows an individual power, even when his themes are not original. The poetic impulses of the time are palpable in what he does—in his felicity of expression, his aversion of a really prosaic word, and his daring recognition of poetry in the commonest ideas; and in his suggestive style. He has not yet published a book; and is now so "absorbed in his duties as a journalist (his biographer tells us,) that he has not that leisure for the cultivation of his reputation as a poet that his friends could wish, and the pure spring of Helican has been neglected for the dirty pool of politics."

Looking to Mr. Harney's future, are we not sure that he is not wiser than his friends, in giving himself for a while to politics and journalism. The pool of politics is dirty or not, according as it is a cleanly or uncleanly person immersed in it. We cannot forget that Dante (not to mention lesser names) was a fervid politician. The profession of journalism, too, with its wide opportunities of knowing men and things, may teach the poetic nature, prone to look back and sigh,

"Ah! well-a-day for the dear old days!"

that no age has been so grand as our own, and that none has been so falsely and stupidly called prosaic. The poet dreams of yesterday and to-morrow; journalism can teach him to value to-day. His art is the sublimest when it is true to his own time. There has been no time so great and earnest as this. If he remembers the world's grandeur now, it shall remember his hereafter.

[*Ohio State Journal*, 25 September 1860]

7

[Recent Italian Comedy]

1. *Opere Drammatiche di Paolo Ferrari*. Milano.
2. *Teatro Scelto di Paolo Giacometti*. Milano.
3. *Le Commedie del Dottore Teobaldo Ciconi*. Milano.
4. *Florilegio Drammatico*. Milano. (Containing various comedies by Francesco dall' Ongaro, Luigi Gualtieri, August Bon, Leone Fortis, Riccardo Castelvecchio, Prof. Botto, etc., etc.)
5. *Intorno alla Natura e all' Ufficio dell' Arte Drammatica; Studj di Prof. F. dall' Ongaro*. (Two articles in the *Politecnico* of Milan, October and December, 1863.)

THE writer of this paper has sometimes found a certain pensive amusement in comparing experiences with other foreigners in Italy, and in noting how they had one and all been confined, as by some fatality, to the same range of authors in their efforts to become acquainted with recent Italian literature. Manzoni, Pellico, Guerrazzi, D'Azelio, and perhaps Grossi:—one counts on the fingers of one hand the inevitable names which embody this literature to such readers, and they must needs have patience and courage if they can persist in the faith that there are modern Italian writers who represent in the literature of their nation something besides its scholarly culture, its religious sentimentality, its revolutionary speculation, and its tendency to seek the romantic and picturesque only in the past. Even when these readers have cleared the bounds set them by the great names mentioned, they must be gifted with rare cheerfulness and enthusiasm, if they can suppress a sigh of disappointment at the barrenness of fields which in English literature teem with continual blossom and harvest.

The student of a language usually turns first to its fiction, and the English student naturally seeks in Italian fiction a class of society-romances corresponding to the novels of Thackeray, Bulwer, Dickens, Brontë, and Stowe, as a means of acquainting himself at once with the best living authors of the language, and the social life of the people. But in fact there are no such romances in modern Italian literature, and the few which do exist may be safely said to reflect the manners, thoughts, feelings, and lives of no class of the modern Italian population. There are, it is true, some brief tales, and even some more ambitious works, which profess to deal with themes and people of the present civilization; but their worth and success may be fairly judged by the fact that the Italians themselves never speak of them, and scarcely know them by name when they are mentioned. A sufficiently just notion of English society, and in lesser degree of our own, may be formed by reading our contemporary fiction; but the only Italian writer who deals attractively with Italian life of the present century—life so various, so interesting, and seemingly so favorable to the purposes of romance—is Ruffini, who writes in English for the English. The Italians who write novels to amuse their own countrymen give them historical romances, of which tedious species of composition they are fond.

The temptation is great to pronounce this absence of the romance of society an absolute want in Italian literature, but one learns to resist the temptation on further acquaintance with the literature and character of the Italians. The want is really supplied from a source which has wellnigh run dry in English letters; and perhaps recognition of this fact, which involves toleration of a defect in ourselves, will help us to bear with a difference in the Italians. Nay, it may be that the wonder after all shall seem, not that they have done so little where we have done so much, but that, with their recent emancipation as a people, and their yet incomplete destiny, they should have surpassed us in another direction.

The Italians care more to have their social life reproduced in the scenes of the theatre than in the pages of narrative fiction. They seem, as a people, to have an utter indifference, if not a positive distaste, for the class of novels which we find so delightful. They neither encourage their own authors to write them, nor do they borrow them from other languages. It is a rare thing to see translations from any of the authors of social romances whom we have named, with the exception of Mrs. Stowe, whose great work unites the most pleasing features of the historical novel and the drama. We have never seen a line from Thackeray translated into Italian; there are versions of Dickens, but he is not liked, and is little read; only the historical romances of Bulwer are translated; while the novels of Scott and of Cooper are endlessly reproduced in every variety of edition.

This peculiarity of taste is partly to be accounted for by the conditions which have formed modern Italian civilization, and which deserve consideration, in whatever light we view the Italians. We have no novels of society, they say, because till now we have had no Italian society. Codini,[1] office-holders, and spies have heretofore formed the recognized and approved society of Italy. And these characters, however favorable for the purposes of satire, were not just the characters with whom a spirited author could amuse his readers, inasmuch as literature existed only by their consent, and was sufficiently obnoxious to them in its very essence, without taking a personally disagreeable form. All the elements which the author would have used in a novel of contemporary life were forbidden him. The virtues which genius must applaud were only to be found in characters dangerous to good government; bad faith, intolerance, pedantry, ignorance, and servility were specially protected and favored by authority against the humorist and the wit. It is true that people in Florence, in Milan, in Naples, lived, loved, married, succeeded, and failed, and experienced all life's good and ill, before the year 1859; and no doubt there were effects enough to be studied in the social situation of the miserable poor, the sordid money-getting middle classes, and

---

[1] *fogies*, or, in American, *hunkers*. Literally, pig-tails.

the idle, corrupt, and unmanly nobles. But it is only perfect freedom which can produce and enjoy the novel of society as we have it. Under the former governments of Italy, it would have been wholly impossible for an Italian to give in narrative fiction a faithful picture of Italian society. If it was bad, it had been robbed of the power of self-regeneration by a church and a state to which its weakness and wickedness were necessary, and to which the very hope of better things was irreligion and treason. Genius, contemplating these conditions, which it was forbidden to criticise and powerless to affect, had the choice either to take refuge from present sorrow and degradation in dreamful study of the glorious and heroic past, or to utter its cry against the wrong, and pass into prison or exile. That is, if it were genius which could not find expression in drama. The wholly different way in which the comedy, which occupies the same place in dramatic composition that the society-romance holds in narrative fiction, deals with the features of a contemporary civilization, so as to present a picture of the social life belonging to it, has always made it possible even under the most despotic government; and this difference preserves our facts from the fatality of proving too much, and rendering the existence of Italian comedy illogical in the state of things alluded to. From a time long before Goldoni, and ever since the time of that painter of national manners and character, the comedy in Italy has constantly employed itself with the portraiture of the contemporary social phases unseen in Italian romance; and has even, now and then, trusting to what Giacometti calls the providential ignorance of censors, ventured to agitate a question not merely individual, but civil and Italian, and to speak, in the theatre, of the Italians as a people, of their sorrows and of their follies. There is a certain fugitive essence in the drama, taking life from the utterance, the manner of the actor, which might well escape a censor the most vigilant of public tranquillity. But the novel must contemplate and comment; it can leave nothing unexpressed and trust no secret effect to elocution or action. Moreover, while comedy deals with character as it exists and manifests itself in action, narrative fiction must bare the causes which produce character, and reveal all the feelings and explain the circumstances which influence men to action. The novel of society must needs censure conditions in which odious human traits and characters flourish when it depicts them; the play can laugh them to scorn without a syllable of criticism on the state of things to which they owe their existence. Molière was possible under the *ancien régime* in France, but Victor Hugo could not have been.

No doubt, then, comedy owes something of the ascendency which it holds over the social romance with the Italians to these extrinsic causes; but it owes infinitely more to the dramatic temperament of the race. It is a trite thing to say that the temperament of the Italians is dramatic; but the fact acquires wonderful freshness and interest from experimental knowledge of their civilization. It is the first thing in the character of the people which strikes the passing stranger; it is the trait of all others, which develops and grows upon the observation of the sojourner and student of human nature in Italy. The babe seems to suck in the spirit of drama with the milk; the little children are born actors. This spirit modifies and influences the whole life of the people; it shapes the manners of all classes; it inspires every movement and gesture of the least conscious individual of a race without bashfulness. It speaks in all Italian art, which learns, teaches, and perpetuates it, no matter whether it be classic or Christian art. In the Museum at Parma is a bronze hand, dug up with other antiquities at Valleja, of which the fingers are curved inward toward the thumb, with that play of the pantomimic muscles by which the Italian of to-day conveys the idea of fingering money, and which one finds impossible to Anglo-Saxon fibre. In the fragment of an old fresco on the outer wall of the church of Santo Stefano at Venice are two hands held up in the vivacious play of argument, as Italians argue. The *facchini*, who *loaf* every day under the shadow of this wall, make the same gesture as they dispute together, and the artist who painted the saint's hands in the fresco had only to copy the commonest life about him to give the most earnest and vivid effect to his picture. These habits of dramatic dumb-show are not merely forms of individual demonstration, but are the medium in Italy of communicating ideas common to all, and are something as intelligible as language itself. They are the natural utterance of a race which not only finds nothing shocking or vulgar in exuberance of manner, but to which the contrary is cold, dull, and hateful. If possible, we avoid a scene. If possible, the Italian makes one. He seems to find a wonderful zest in the play of his passions. He loves the conflict of emotion, and riots upon the sensations evoked by dispute. Let him be heated with anger,—it is as good as to be moved with joy. To talk rapidly and loudly, to gesticulate furiously, and to express himself with a tempest of his whole person, is his idea of conversation. There is a surface of varnished quiet, which, if he be of gentle breeding, he is apt to present to the stranger; but this is an abnormal state which it bores him to persevere in. With the first impulse of real feeling the varnish cracks away from him, and he bursts forth into passionate demonstration. It is little matter how trifling the affair in hand is; he puts his whole soul into it, if he touches it at all. It may be the Italian unity; it is possibly a question of sixpence, but for the moment it is quite the same to him. No doubt there are exceptions among the Italians to this general type of character, and a quiet, undemonstrative Italian is, like an amiable Englishman, the most delightful person in the world—if you can find him.

The Italian writer of comedy is happy not only in the mobile and dramatic audience for which he writes, but he is peculiarly blest in the society which he describes. The delight which the emotional Italian nature finds in the vivid fables of the stage is hardly to be marred by perception of dramatic excesses which we call theatrical, but in which the more fervid spectator of the South hears only the echo of his own extravagance; and the dramatist may err (according to our colder nations) very far upon the side of exaggeration and romance in his situations and circumstances, without reaching improbability or sacrificing verisimilitude. It is his fortune to celebrate contemporary life, in which love is still made according to the rules of love-making in the old *capa y espada* comedies of the Spanish, with all the picturesque accessaries of confidants, stolen interviews under balconies by moonlight, bribed serving-maids, and the illicit exchange of many *righe di biglietto*; and when he does not care to give his comedy the charm of the jealous difficulty and mystery with which such courtship is invested, he may still copy from Italian married life the pleasant interest of intrigue. In the meanest exigency of his art he is befriended by the characteristics of Italian society, as well as aided by its structure in the conduct of plot and persons. That free-spoken valet and that loquacious and pert maid, who are so dear to his art, and are such odious monsters in English comedy, may be drawn from life in Italy, where there is either very great equality of feeling, or the prefect security of rank which permits freedom in the intercourse of the different classes, and where these convenient persons of the stage actually proffer advice or approval to those socially above them. In the publicity of private life (if the paradox may be pardoned) under skies so lovely that the shelter of a roof and walls is impris-onment, in the promenading at established hours and in certain places, in the idling at *cafés*, and in the thronging to the theatres and other places of amusement, the lazy gossiping on the streets, and the eternal craving either to hear or tell some new thing, this favored dramatist finds the incident, the movement and lightness which his art demands, and which no other life affords so well. Nay, in Italy, where one witnesses the keen interest of crowds in the affairs of others, and the profusion and freedom of comment which the smallest event calls forth in this out-of-doors society, the chorus of the comic opera acquires a sort of truthfulness and probability, and even the soliloquy (that wretched and stupid scapegoat of sentiments which cannot be expressed in dialogue) does not seem so unnatural and grossly offensive to the Italian playgoer, who has not only the habit of uttering his emotions before his fellow-beings, but of not unfrequently obliging the Devil with them when alone. Many old-world formalities, which we have cast aside, but which serve excellently well to garnish plays, are still in vogue with the Italians, and there is no better comedy than to see the encounter and retreat of two Italian fine-ladies, and hear their protestations of civility, their Pro-tean forms of courtesy, their indefatigable expressions of politeness,—unless indeed it be to witness the same scene between two serving-women, who address each other with a high-flown and exuberant courtliness, which is only equalled by the manner of colored people when they stand upon ceremony. But, above all, the comedy is most at home in Italy, because, though the Italians are immovably fixed in the idea that all persons of English blood, and these persons alone, are *originali*, the originals of Italy far outnumber the originals of any other land. This race has so transparent a civilization, the conventional coating, however showy, is so thin upon it, that all the impulses of human nature in action, with which the drama specially deals, are con-stantly visible. There is, moreover, a curious frankness in its character. As the Italian does not seek to conceal his feelings, but loves to display them, so he is equally ready to discover his peculiar merit or foible, virtue or vice, whatever it may be. He is neither proud nor ashamed: *è fatto così!* Indeed, we fancy that men are more openly good or bad in Italy than elsewhere; and there, easy, tolerant society takes them for just what they are worth, and comedy, copying such primitive types of character, has no need to touch them with paint to make them figures for the stage.[2] But it seems to us that it is just with this opulence of incident, scene, action, publicity of life, and transparency of motive that the subjective art of narrative romance does not care to deal; and we think the play must consequently remain the favorite form of fiction in Italy always,—or if not always, at least till an Italian Cervantes or Le Sage shall arise to paint the contemporary life of his countrymen in a novel.

No doubt it was to these peculiarities of national life and character (which we have so slightly sketched, without thought of presenting a study of Italian society) that the old *commedia d' arte* specially owed its popularity in Italy,—popularity that endured long after culture had pronounced the entertainment rude and puerile, and that survived even Goldoni, whose drama finally banished it from the stage. In this kind of play, for which the author furnished merely the plot and the conduct of the action, and the player supplied the dialogue, the sympathetic, eager, and impatient Italian character must have found something wonderfully pleasing. The spectator had always the shock of novelty, and the spur of freshest expectation, while following the improvisations of the actor, and even the keener satisfaction of immediately and visibly furnishing his inspirations, at times. Among no other people could the *commedia d' arte* have been possible so long, and perhaps this flavor of exclusive ownership endeared its possession to the Italians. In spite of its inherent defects, and the gross abuses to which it must have been subject, it required a supreme dramatic genius to supplant it in the affections of the people, by plays in which the beautiful had perfecter form. The dramatists who preceded Goldoni, Gigli, Martelli, Amenta, Maffei, and Faggiuoli, though gifted and learned men, friends of the classic and the French drama, had not the cunning to prevail against the *commedia d' arte*, and the great Venetian found it in full possession of the Italian stage. And how wisely Goldoni temporized with it, and treated with it while preparing its ruin, and how far he won over its friends by borrowing its own attractions, let any one who will know read that delightful autobiography of the friendly, amusing, earnest old play-wright, and those delicious comedies in which constantly recur the standard masks of the *commedia d' arte*: Pantolon dei Bisognosi, sturdy, humorous, and upright Venetian merchant; Il Dottore, learned professor of Bologna, with the wine-stain on his countenance in memory of that remote jurisconsult of the university from whom he was first taken;

---

[2] Since these speculations were put on paper, we have read with singular pleasure, in the Preface to *L' Ultimo Barone*, by Dall' Ongaro, a corroboration of the opinion expressed of Italian character in this respect. The author says: "*I feel sure we Italians have preserved, far more than any other people, the characteristic lineaments impressed by nature and tradition.*"

Arlecchino Bergamasco, stupid rogue and glutton; Brighella, astute rogue and *imbroglione*, and Bergamasco; Columbina, their fellow-servant; and all that company of familiar and pleasant people. One will hardly weary anywhere, we think, of reading these plays, and if one has the fortune to read them in Venice, by the light of such knowledge as he can hardly refuse to have of the living people around him, we believe he shall find it impossible to drowse over them, even on a summer afternoon, when it blows sirocco, and the very swallow ceases for a little, out of sleepiness, to shriek his joy in the Italian sky. For ourselves, we have never found them tiresome or cloying, but always fresh and racy, faithful, full of gentle wit and sweet-blooded humor, easy movement, and blameless delight. And when in Venice the players have relieved our fancy of the care of situation and effect, this delight of perusal has passed into a rapture of seeing and hearing which the acting of no other plays has given. They depict Venice of the last century; but Venetian life must always remain the same in so many things, must always retain so many peculiar and charming features, that the plays of Goldoni still form a picture of the Venetian life about us; a picture so light and graceful, so true in color, so abundant in masterly and exquisite touches, that to praise them enough tempts us past the bounds of sober criticism.

It is interesting and curious evidence of the many-sided perfection of a beautiful work, and of how genius builds better than it knows, that these comedies, written expressly with a view to effect upon the stage, afford that pleasure in their perusal to which we have alluded. Never did author write so exclusively and solely for the theatre as Goldoni. He had, indeed, a new Italian theatre to create, and he set about his task in the most business-like manner, as genius always does. His experience of players began very early, when he ran away from school with a band of strollers; and when he began to write comedies, he attached himself to a company of comedians, and, studying the capacity of the actors, kept them in view as well as the persons of the drama while writing his plays. But he was also at the same time a diligent student of human nature, an observer of manners and the world, and a keen discerner of the springs of action; and he was far too great a master to subordinate the incident and action of the play to the effect to be produced by any certain actor. He seems to have adapted the actor to the part, as far as possible, and to have striven to cultivate his power in every case to sustain it, instead of adapting the part to the actor. He cast his own plays, and himself took the brunt of all the green-room angers and jealousies; and he relates in his *Memorie* how he met and overcame the difficulties he had to encounter in his peculiar method of writing comedy, with a cheerful humor, and a graphic description of the character, as enjoyable in another way as his easy, genial, and good-natured comedies themselves.

Goldoni has been called the Menander of Italian drama, and indeed the Venice of Goldoni's time must have been very like the Athens of Menander's. Political conditions prescribed domestic and social life as the sole theme for both; and we are slow to believe that the Greek in the plays now lost irrevocably could within this range have been greater than the Venetian has proven himself in the comedies which we trust shall remain to us forever. For his pleasant and friendly genius, Comedy lived everywhere in Venice: danced and capered before him through the carnival; walked with him in the gay Piazza; talked with him behind her mask at the Ridotto; sat and gossiped with him at the *café*; beckoned him down the narrow streets, and led him into cool little, many-balconied courts, where the neighbors chatted and disputed from window to window; made the fishwives and lace-makers of Chioggia quarrel for his delight; drew aside secret curtains, and showed him giddy wives and fickle husbands, old-fogy fathers bent on choosing husbands for their daughters, and merry girls laughing with love at locksmiths; pointed him out the lovers whispering at the lattices, and the old women mumbling scandal over their *scaldini*. And with his perfect fidelity and truth to this various life Goldoni wrote, in an age of unchaste literature, plays which a girl may read with as little cause to blush as would be given by a novel of Dickens. At a time when in England only the tedious Richardson wrote chaste romances, Goldoni produced plays full of decent laughter, of cleanly humor and amiable morality, in that Venice which we commonly believe to have been Sodomitic in its filth and wickedness. Either her corruption of that time has been grossly exaggerated, or her unfaithful women and rakish men had a curiously simple taste for a drama in which love was virtuous, vice confounded and put to shame, and domestic peace and affection held up to envy and admiration. Thanks to the purity of this great poet, who was also a good husband, a true friend, and upright man, the Italian drama still abides by the laws of decency, and the coarse sops which actors on our own stage throw to the pit are licenses almost unknown upon the Italian scene.

After the age which had given Alfieri as well as Goldoni to the world, there was a pause in the progress of the Italian drama. The immediate successors of the latter were writers whose works are not now represented on the stage, and whose names have no celebrity. Among those who followed him at greater distance is Alberto Nota, a prolific but not very entertaining writer of plays, in which the manner of the great master is imitated, and his inspirations freely borrowed. Dall' Ongaro, in the preface to his *Fasma*, says Nota is to Goldoni what Terence is to Menander,—a copy and an adaptation. His plays are no longer acted nor reprinted, but may be sometimes found in old editions and voluminous repose at the second-hand book-stalls. A far more amusing and original writer, in whom the influence of Goldoni's happiest manner is visible, is Augusto Bon. He was himself a player, and he wrote, like Goldoni, with an immediate view to effect upon the stage; but his efforts lack the unconscious perfection of the master's, and are better seen than read. His most popular comedies are "Ludro and his Great Day's Work," "Ludretto" (little Ludro, Ludro's servant), "The Marriage of Ludro," and "The Death of Ludro." These are all in the Venetian dialect, and abound in racy humor and telling hits. Bon himself represented his Ludro while he lived, and the plays live after him in the delight of the Venetian public. We have seen "Ludro and his Great Day's Work" played to an audience in Venice which it shook from one jest and situation to another with never-dying laughter. The great day's work consists in uniting two lovers whom their fathers kept asunder, punishing a greedy old creditor, and relieving a debtor, and such like commendable actions on the part of Ludro, who is a money-lender, and the agent of everybody in a tight place, be it in love or in debt. There is a touch of pathos in the play, as there is in every genuinely humorous thing, for Ludro, who has the worst reputation of rascal, usurer, and *imbroglione*, is at heart a very good fellow, and sincerely tries to serve others while helping himself. His true character comes out only at the end of the play, when the others do him a tardy and grudging justice. Dickens, in the character of Pancks, who holds the reader of "Little Dorrit" so long in doubt, has produced a like effect in art.

But, after all, we fancy that, though the plays of Bon still keep their hold upon the public favor, the taste for reproductions of the Goldonian drama has passed away. In truth, the vein which Goldoni wrought he exhausted. Within the scope of his peculiar genius, and the bounds set him by political and social circumstances, he touched every theme and painted every character that could be turned into matter of airy and gracious comedy. His plays must always give delight, and they will probably be acted as long in Italy as Shakespeare's among ourselves, though the public forgets and neglects his imitators. The loves of his Florindo and Rosaura,—invariable names and Protean characters,—must always charm by their infinite variety and naturalness. The liar Lelio and the scandal-monger Marzio, no less than Pantolon, Il Dottore, Arlecchino, and Brighella, have the perennial fascination of the vices and virtues they embody. May the Count from the mainland (through whom alone could patrician follies be touched in jealous, aristocratic Venice) live forever! And as for the old-maiden aunt who always attributes her pretty niece's lovers to herself, and will be the foremost *civetta* among the young ladies; as for the young ladies themselves, with their sweet fears of papa Pantolon, their covert flirtations, sly billets, and masquerading escapades; as for the despotic mothers-in-law and jealous wives and husbands; as for the absurd old suitors made to put up at last with the maiden aunts; as for all the good mothers, tender fathers, and happy spouses, the reformed rakes, baffled seducers, and unmasked hypocrites; as for the whole tribe of pert serving-maids, talkative gondoliers, and waiters at *cafés*, and the pleasant generation of *cavalieri serventi*, gamblers, misers, doltish and cunning menials, pompous doctors, high-and-low-bred rogues, the antiquaries, apothecaries, advocates, usurers,—all characters and figures that swarm through those vivid and various scenes,—who that has ever known them would be willing to let them die? For our own part, we had as lief part with the Pendennises out of Thackeray; and these beloved people of comedy have taken place in our heart with Gil Blas and Sancho Panza, in the honest and improving company of Lazarillo de Tormes.

Recent Italian comedy is of a character as different from that of Goldoni as the present age is different from Goldoni's period. The scope of the modern drama is in another direction, and if its aim be not really higher, there is greater nobility in its tone, and it deals less with peculiar characters copied from life than with exceptional situations, which develop traits in men who have no very striking peculiarity to distinguish them from their fellows, while it seeks to enforce, not a moral for a special emergency, but a loftier code of morality for the whole conduct of life. This drama has been of slow growth, but its roots are all in the soil of this century of thoughts and revolutions; its blossoms have been put forth hardily in inclement seasons, and its fruit tastes often of the acrid and bitter experiences of men who cannot forget that they have suffered, and that those whom they seek to amuse have suffered with them. There is scarcely a play, of all those we have seen and read, but has some covert political allusion, or sparkles with outspoken scorn and hatred of the nation's oppressors, according as it was written before or after the time which emancipated speech among the Italians. The patriotic flavor seldom spoils the taste of the whole play by excess; it remains commonly a hint that the poet has lived and felt, and is not a *codino*; but in respect of this feature alone it differs by the widest variance from the Goldonian comedy. Goldoni contented himself with themes purely domestic and social, and if by chance he ever touches a foible of the patricians, he does it by subterfuge, and with a sort of reverence still, while he never mentions the government of St. Mark but with ardent respect and veneration. There is no doubt that Goldoni was greater within his limited range than any of his successors, with their extended liberty, have proved, and there is no doubt that he was cramped in it. Not that a man of genius must needs wish to mix all his thoughts with a tincture of politics, but that the fact that genius cannot utter everything it will, when and how it will, depresses it, and the contrary exalts it. We fancy, however, that, as liberty becomes a habit in Italy, the comedy will lose its political flavor altogether, and that the laughing mask will utter patriotic appeals only in special danger. As yet it is well for every public voice to remind Italians that their battle is only half won, and that without vigilance all may be lost again.

The modern spirit to which the comedy owes its political tints makes itself known also in the social ethics of the plays, and in the presence of certain characters common to nearly all, and in that degree conventional, like the old masks. We of the New World, we

> "New men that in the flying of a wheel
> Cry down the past,"

are somewhat prone to think ourselves sole patrons of the virtue that derides the pretensions of rank, and declares that merit is, and remains, the only true distinction. But the new Italian comedies teach democracy in as many persons as can be made to inculcate it. Mere blood has as little honor on the stage as off it in Italy, where it is at singular discount. In the plays it is apt to be found in the villains, the tedious old women, and the befooled papas, while honor dwells in the bosom of some young man of genius,—inventor, poet, or artist,—who is, in the nature of things, ardently attached to some beautiful and gifted girl of humble station, or, at the worst, to some noble lady disdainful of her nobility. But blood is not always banished from generous natures. It is sometimes suffered to appear in the person of the young count or marquis of no means whatever, of obscure and uncertain lodgings, many debts and doubts, good heart and amiable temper. He is the friend of the poor young man of genius, whose poverty he shares and whose aspirations he pities. His story is familiar to us. In his green youth he loved one who rejected him for a richer suitor, and being blighted, he displays a dry and pleasant wit in the second or third act when he meets this lady, who has found out her mistake, and would not refuse to mend it, being now a widow. He is not at all caustic with her; he tells her, with a cool, agreeable persiflage, that the past is past, but that they two may still unite in making happy two younger and better people, the inventor (or artist or poet) and his betrothed. No doubt there is good in store for this nobleman before the curtain falls, and one does not hate him for the misfortune of noble birth, and the people in the pit are friends with him. They are glad to have him snub, as a real nobleman may snub, the *parvenus*; and how they applaud when he unmasks the villain of the play, doubly foiled in his failure to injure the poor young man of genius and to dishonor his betrothed!

Without gallantries which pass between silly wives and guilty lovers, these comedies certainly are not. But it is noticeable in all, that a modern and decent destiny tends to defeat the seducer and put him to shame, while the husband and wife whom he has sought to injure triumph over him. Commonly, the sentiment of the new comedy is good and sound in every respect. It is Vice, the abominable, who gets laughed at; and the worldly, witty, and elegant rake and the pensive and fascinating adulteress (more sinned against, both, than sinning) are figures which scarcely appear in these honest scenes. Indeed, the morality which banishes them is most pointed, and is perhaps insisted upon a little tediously at times. It has happened in one or two comedies that an erring wife or husband, after a long and bitter repentance, is forgiven and made happy; but this is an amiable weakness of sentiment which may surely be pardoned now and then to plays commonly so sound. It is to be hoped that the drama derives the inspirations of its elevated morality from the ameliorated sentiment of Italian civilization; and no doubt it must react beneficially upon society. At any rate, virtue is now the ruling passion of the comedy, and in the plays she sometimes fixes her abode in bosoms which have been supposed incapable of her. Ciconi has written a comedy to show that there are *White Flies* even among ballet-dancers and their handmaids, and our friend the count (rich for the nonce) rewards the *ballerina's* purity with matrimony. We are sorry to make known to a land of newspapers, that, in dramas in which the morals of such characters have been reformed, the journalist (who is almost a standard *persona dramatis*) is nearly always a most

desperate and venal scamp,—a regular *birbante matricolato*. He is a pleasant
scamp enough, with an easy and amusing humor, so that, if one had not the
evidences of one's senses, it would be hard to believe him guilty of such
meannesses as he commits. But this unconscionable and attractive rogue
does nothing but take money for puffs, and write down the plays of young
poets who do not fee him, and attack the actresses and dancers who reject his
advances. He seems withal to move in decent society, and fine ladies laugh at
his jokes, which, like those of journalists everywhere, are pointed and
brilliant.

In these new comedies, however, which touch modern life at every salient
point, and take off fac-simile impressions of the prominent features of society, there is an anomalous absence of all ridicule of the priesthood. In Italy
the priests are doubted and misliked by all but the women and the old-
womanish men, and as a man and king the visible head of the Church is
execrated. Wherever there is freedom of the press and of speech, caricatures
of the Pope, of the bishops and priests, swarm in the windows of the print-
shops; the political journals find them convenient texts for innumerable articles; half of the popular wit and wisdom, whether proverbial or impromptu,
deals with the priests and monks. Few pencils which can make the line of
beauty have failed to draw the fair round belly of canonico or bishop. The
mysterious cousins and nieces of the clergy are found in the comic papers;
and the eating and bibbing of the ecclesiastics is the refuge of every talker
hard pushed for a comparison of gluttony. Yet, with all this ridicule, distrust,
and despite, the priests are never dragged upon the stage to awaken popular
laughter by the spectacle of their faults and their sins. There is but one
recent comedy (the *Troppo Tardi* of Ciconi) in which an ecclesiastic appears
for other than mere mechanical purposes, and in this case he is made absurd
rather than odious. The explanation of this anomalous absence must be
looked for in an anomaly of the national character. The Roman Church,
though its temples are deserted by all young and thoughtful men, although
its ministers are doubted and its crimes are abhorred, is yet most powerful in
its hold upon the affections of the Italian people. All forms, vessels, and
symbols significant of its spiritual character are revered, and the belief that
bad men, rather than any inherent vice of the Church, are to blame for its
errors, forms a protection to these guilty agents against a public and degrad-
ing humiliation as a class which would also bring shame upon the Church.
The satire of the journals is more or less personal; their caricatures of the
priesthood are individual portraits. But if a priest were brought upon the
stage for scoffing or despite, the offence would cease to be personal, and
would be an attack upon religion. This, to their honor, the Italians have
never suffered. The very dress of the priests, however well it be known to
cover multitudes of sins in real life, is too dear to the people by association
with the most solemn scenes of life ever to be introduced in the theatre as the
garb of an abominable or contemptible character. Above all, the Church and
its ministers are sacred to the women,—the wives, sisters, and daughters of

the auditors who decide the fate of plays,—and as no degradation in Italy could be so public, general, and complete, in the eyes of all classes and persons, as the ridicule of the theatre, the common good feeling spares it to the priests, who as an order are certainly not bad solely by their own volition, and who represent a Church which is odious only through the delinquencies of a part of their number.

Among the writers of recent Italian comedy (at some of the characteristics of which we have just glanced), the most popular are Teobaldo Ciconi, Paolo Ferrari, and Paolo Giacometti; but after these come others of no less talent, who have either not written so much, or have failed to hit the popular humor so skilfully. Such are Castelvecchio, Gualtieri, Fortis, Botto, and Dall' Ongaro. The latter (who was born under Austrian rule in Istria, and now lives in exile at Florence) has without doubt more poetical genius than any living Italian dramatist; but perhaps it is the very quality of his genius which makes him less successful than inferior men in the vivid and immediate effects of the theatre. His plays are full of poetic feeling; his themes are chosen according to a theory which he develops in the paper of which we have quoted the title at the head of this article. Believing that the theatre should not merely amuse the people, but should seek to touch their better nature, and exalt their tastes and ideas, he turns to history for his plots, and preferably to Italian history; and holding, moreover, that the form best expressive of modern feeling is that middle species of play between the tragedy and comedy, which the Italians call *dramma*, he is sparing of the comic element, and appeals rather to the sensibilities of his audience than to its laughter. "The drama," he says, "is represented before a public, multiplex, numerous, composed of heterogeneous elements. As a work of art, it must offer the æsthetic qualities which render it accessible to all; as a means of social education, it must exclude every narrow and intolerant doctrine, it must appeal to the grand and general principles admitted in all religions, and graven in indelible characters on the living tablets of the human heart . . . . . . The audience, susceptible in the mass to the same emotions, is *people*, not individuals, and is to be collectively educated and affected for vice or for virtue." These views, he thinks, will hardly please the generation of men who are ashamed of feeling, and "who would not shed tears lest they displace the quizzing-glass in wiping them away. Theirs is French taste, come down from the courts. The *beau monde* has wished to laugh at every cost. But the deeps of the human heart are always the same. A day will come when it will be said to the poet: 'Can you no longer touch the chord of feeling? Make us weep!' " The man proposing to himself the scope here indicated will write plays dear to the heart of the scholar, the thinker, the lover of men; and such are the plays of Dall' Ongaro. But if the rarity of their representation is a test of the practicality of the poet's theory, we must believe that the public or the theatre is not yet prepared to receive it without modification. Dall' Ongaro's most popular piece is *Il Fornaretto*, a drama founded on one of the most pathetic incidents of Venetian history. The hero is the poor baker-boy, who, having picked up the sheath of a knife afterwards found in the heart of a murdered patrician, was condemned on evidence of the possession of the sheath, and guiltlessly suffered death for the assassination. The real assassin confessed the crime afterwards, whereupon it was ordered, and always observed by the Ten, that, before sentence of death should be passed on a culprit, one of their number should cry out to the rest, "*Ricordatevi del povero Fornaretto!*" This play has noble and exalted scenes, but we think it has won its hold upon popular affection in Venice chiefly because it deals with a cruel wrong done to one of the people; and its success is that of a tragedy in the English sense, not that of a drama, and far less that of a comedy. In his *Bianca Cappello*, Dall' Ongaro has failed to win in equal degree the popular favor, because, though the subject is equally patriotic and familiar, it appeals less to popular sympathies, which no dignity of treatment can compel. The poet's latest dramatic work is an exquisitely graceful restoration to living literature of one of Menander's comedies, of which only the plot had remained. The Greek called the play *Phasma*, and the Italian, adopting the title and the plot, has supplied from his imagination the characters, situations, and dialogue; promising that, if ever the true Menander be discovered, he will burn his own in expiation,—which would inflict upon literature, we think, a loss as great as it suffered from the Greek orthodoxy which burnt the first *Phasma*.[3] The comedy has met with success upon the stage, but we fancy it is better to read it than to see it played. It is a poem with passages of gentle humor and feeling, and an interest sufficiently eager, without being intense, springing from the unhappy mother's penance for her fault, and from loves of which the fortunate termination may be foreseen.

We speak first of Dall' Ongaro, because we wish to render homage to his earnest and exalted genius before denying him a high place among writers of recent comedy. He is so well known to readers of modern Italian literature as a poet and a writer of singularly clear and delightful prose, that we need hardly celebrate him here. It is mere justice to say, however, that, if his plays are not so popular as those of others in the theatre, they read far better, and that, if he has not directly influenced the drama, the ethics of the modern drama, as he expounds them, have, with some modifications, influenced the recent dramatists in a remarkable degree.

---

[3] The following is the plot of *Phasma*, as invented by Menander, and adopted by Dall' Ongaro.

"*Phasma* is the title of a comedy by Menander, in which a woman, married to a widower having an adolescent son by a former wife, kept a natural daughter of her own in an adjoining house, and found frequent occasion of seeing her, without knowledge of her husband or others. She had secretly perforated the wall between the two houses, and arranged as an oratory the room through which the communication was made, concealing the private door with flowers and votive garlands; and so, with the pretext of celebrating sacred rites, she was wont to call her daughter to her and converse with her. By chance the youth, her step-son, once caught sight of the maiden, and, at the aspect of her great beauty, remained confounded as by a supernatural apparition. Hence the name of the comedy. But the truth appearing, little by little, the youth burned with such ardent love for the maiden that nothing would cure him but giving him her to wife. So, with the great joy of the mother and the lover, and with the consent of the father, the nuptials were solemnized, with which the comedy ends."—Elio Donato's comments on Terence.

Riccardo Castelvecchio is the pseudonyme of a writer who has contributed several successful plays to the dramatic literature of the time, of which the best is *La Donna Romantica*. He is a Venetian, we believe, or at least Veneto, and some of his comedies are in his native dialect,—a tongue which lends itself most gracefully and effectively to the drama; but Castelvecchio has no claim, either by reason of his quantity or quality, to rank with the first of the modern dramatists. Professor Botto, a Genoese, is the author of a most charming and popular comedy called "Genius and Speculation," which is eminent for its fidelity to modern Italian life and feeling, and worthy of the success it has met. Fortis is by birth a Triestine, and a Jew. He lived many years in Padua, where he embraced Christianity; but for some offence a journal which he published in that city was suppressed and himself exiled. He is now editor of the *Pungolo* of Milan, one of the ablest political journals of Italy, and his portrait, in some form of caricature, may be seen any week in the Milanese comic papers. His best play is "Industry and Speculation, or Heart and Art."

Luigi Gualtieri is a dramatist of much versatility, and his plays enjoy a greater degree of favor than those of the writers just named. They vary in quality from very good to very bad indeed; he calls himself, in comparison with Ferrari, "*pittoraccio di scenarii*," and "*sovvertitore, se fosse da tanto, di ogni regola e nemico d'ogni scuola.*" Many of his comedies will bear out this unsparing judgment, but others will win for him the homage paid to a more careful artist than the scene-painter, and, if they show him an enemy of schools, will prove him a friend of art. He has more drollery than any of his contemporaries, and he has the gift, most rare among Southern writers, of touching the heart through the simplest and most natural sympathies. One of his pleasantest comedies is *Lo Spiantato* (a racy word, which, if Done-up will not serve, we must translate by circumlocution, signifying the pennilessness of the spendthrift), of which the hero is worthy of a place in our affections with Dick Swiveller, F. Bayham, and other unlucky and worthless favorites; though the tone of burlesque exaggeration running through the character reminds of Dickens rather than of Thackeray. *Lo Spiantato*, having spent a large patrimony, is living by his wits very slenderly, when a dying brother, whom he has not seen for many years, bequeathes to his care an only daughter. This poor young girl is herself the bearer of her father's last wish, and comes to her uncle, whom she expects to find living in luxury, but whom she finds in utter poverty, and just on the point of going out to fight with a nobleman whom he has insulted in his cups. He receives her with tenderness and embarrassment, and, deeply touched by the sense of her helpless dependence, he resolves for her sake to seek to better his fortunes. He is a man of honor, however, and this duel must be fought, or honorably withdrawn from. Arrived at the rendezvous, he proclaims to his antagonist that he has not come to kill him, but to make him his partner in a grand social discovery, involving the abolition of the duel. The duel is not a question of right and wrong,—it is a question of marksmanship. "If the question of honor, of fame, of right, consists in hitting or being hit, what prevents each of us from getting behind a tree, and firing with greater coolness and precision? If you hit my tree, I ask your pardon; *vice versa*, if I hit yours, I expect you to apologize. Behold the grand discovery: to fight without exposing life, sacred interests, the affections of the heart, and family ties!" His enemy responds: "I will not fight with a humanitarian genius like yourself; and if ever I wished to do so, the very trees would shield you." They shake hands, and the *Spiantato* returns gayly to his friends. Full of the best resolutions to go to work and prosper for his niece's sake, he proclaims a fresh discovery: "I have found out the word,— Assurance, ... behold the grand word of the epoch! life-assurance, fire-assurance, assurance against hail-storms and shipwrecks. How many things there are in the world to be assured! I will assure everything: husbands against the fickleness of their wives; young ladies against single life; the body from disease: yes, I am the grand universal assurer!" He accordingly establishes assurance-companies of every sort, plunging at the same time into various speculations, and pursuing many other callings. He practises mesmerism and dentistry; he opens a herald's office, and a matrimonial bureau; he becomes a charlatan of the most unscrupulous, but he remains good-hearted, tenderly fond of his niece, and devoted to that daughter of his landlady who, in the days of his want, gave him shelter and loved him. He is at last rescued from a career of disgraceful prosperity by the young banker who marries his niece, and gives him a place for the legitimate exercise of his ingenuity and enterprise, and the play ends with his marriage to the faithful Lucietta. The plot is slender, it has many improbabilities and exaggerations, and the comedy sometimes tends to farce, but is full of harmless fun and genuine feeling. The charlatanry of the herald is amusing, and smacks of the daring of charlatans dear to literature and humanity, like Dr. Sangrado and the heroes of Spanish books of roguery. "I put out my sign," says the ingenious cavalier Belindo,—"I put out my sign: Heraldic Bearings traced anew, and Genealogical Trees compiled; Antique Origins and Titles of Nobility vindicated. Well, a flood of citizens is precipitated into my office. 'Sir, my name is Aurelio.' 'Sir,' I reply, 'you descend from Marcus Aurelius, Roman emperor.' An unfathomably rich banker is called by the sport of chance *Poveri* (poor); he wishes to be noble at any cost. Observe my ingenuity! 'The poor eat *polenta*' (hasty-pudding), said I; 'the *Polentas* are an ancient family of Ravenna; henceforth you are a kinsman of Francesca da Rimini!' Would you credit it? These people not only pretended to believe me, but ended by convincing themselves." As for the society to insure husbands against the fickleness of their wives, the jealous spouse pays down a certain premium, whereupon the company "assumes the following grave obligations: 1. To maintain a strict surveillance through its agents, who are clerks, chamber-maids, milliners, dress-makers, hair-dressers, and *concierges*, and who will receive a stipend from the company to watch the wives confided to the company's police; 2. As husbands are always the last to know such trifles, it will be very easy for our agents to discover intrigues by minutely following all the steps of the *surveillée*, listening to all the current rumors, and getting into everybody's confidence. The husband will be notified, and even conducted to assist at flagrant cases of flirtation,—and then, separation and retribution. But he may always rest quietly, as he will receive every month from the company a full report of all his wife's doings and sayings, which he can compare with his own observation. The company's regulations will be published, and society will thus be reformed; for wives, afraid of being subjected to the operation of these rules, will then of their own accord renounce all ideas—*extra domum, extra civitatem.*"

Of character and feeling wholly opposite to *Lo Spiantato* is *L'Abnegazione* of Gualtieri. In this play the Countess Ersilia Beregnardo, at Milan, receives from her lover, the Marquis Sforza, at Genoa, a business letter intended for her husband, who at St. Petersburgh receives from the Marquis the letter meant for his wife, in which a guilty love is spoken of. The lover, in a moment of fatal confusion, has placed the wrong address upon each letter. Apprised of his error by the Countess, he hastens to her at Milan, briefly anticipating the return of the Count, and while he urges the sinful wife to fly with him from her husband's anger, the Countess's *protégée*, a poor young girl named Ersilia, appears. Struck by the name, the Marquis resolves upon a bold hazard, in order to save the Countess from exposure and infamy. He will feign that this letter was meant for the *protégée*, with whom he will pretend to have been in love; and, to give character of sincerity to the pretence, he will offer her his hand and marry her. All this takes place at once, and the Count returns to find the Marquis accepted by Ersilia, who has long loved him timidly in secret, and who is only too glad to believe that the love-letter was meant for her. But being really ignorant of the character of the letter, the poor child betrays herself when, confronted by the Count alone, she reads its allusions to a guilty passion. The old Count pities her, but, satisfied that the world will never know his disgrace, he leaves this victim of others' wrong, and returns to his post at St. Petersburgh. Stunned and crushed by this blow to her hopes, Ersilia, out of regard to the Countess, (who, whatever her sins, has always been a gentle and loving benefactress to her,) still resolves to accept the life of abnegation before her, and, in her own desolation, spare the ruin and shame of others. It seems to us that the ensuing scene is written with peculiar pathos, delicacy, and dignity.

"*THE MARQUIS AND ERSILIA.*

"*Marquis (aside).* The Count is gone; do I dare to ask her! (*Aloud.*) Ersilia—
"*Ersilia.* It is you, sir?
"*Mar.* You have spoken with the Count.—Well?
"*Ers.* He will hold himself paid, sir, if you wed me.
"*Mar.* Then he did not believe—
"*Ers.* And who that read this letter would believe it meant for *me*? The Count did not do me this cruel wrong.
"*Mar.* Then all is discovered?

"*Ers*. No,—all is hidden, appearances are saved; and that for you of the great world is enough.

"*Mar*. We have done you grievous wrongs—

"*Ers*. What do you say, my lord marquis?

"*Mar*. But I will never come to disturb your peace. You will have your palace in the city, and in the country. You will dispose as you please of my riches, of my servants,—we will live apart,—nay, distant from each other.

"*Ers*. It is the Countess who imposes these conditions?

"*Mar*. It is delicacy which imposes them; but if you prefer to live with me, in a pure intimacy,—as friends,—as brother and sister—

"*Ers*. Nay, I would rather express a wish—

"*Mar*. Which is?

"*Ers*. That at all times and places you seek to shun my presence.

"*Mar*. You hate me, then, so much?

"*Ers*. (*in a troubled voice*). No, not hate. But your presence must give me great pain.

"*Mar*. And you wish this?

"*Ers*. Yes.

"*Mar*. May I not hope that time will lessen this aversion for me?

"*Ers*. Never, sir.

"*Mar*. You will at least permit me to write you now and then of whatever concerns us both?

"*Ers*. You are master.

"*Mar*. Not master. Rather a man whom you must pardon many injuries.

"*Ers*. What injuries, my lord? I have found the means of repaying the good which my benefactress has done me and my family. I have spared this house a tragedy, for if this marriage did not take place, the Count would seek your life.

"*Mar*. The Count said this? (*Angrily.*) He believes that I marry you out of fear?

"*Ers*. No, sir,—to save a woman's reputation. He believes you sufficiently punished by this marriage with an humble daughter of the people,—who, however, far better than a great lady, will know how to preserve stainless the name of your noble family.

"*Mar*. (*touched*). Your hand, lady. (*Takes her hand with transport.*)

"*Ers*. O no! not here, but before the world,—there, where all is a lie,—there, where you must hide tears under smiles, indifference under the guise of love, the heartbreak beneath a show of happiness,—there you shall be my husband,—but here, a stranger."

The marriage takes place, and the separation; Ersilia's sole memento of her husband remaining the fatal, guilty letter, to torment her and turn to anguish the love which she cannot overcome. The Marquis, living abroad, is at one time suddenly called home by a letter, declaring that his wife has hastily left her retirement to visit a lover. He finds her just returned from St. Petersburgh, whither she had gone at the old man's secret prayer to close the dying eyes of the Count, her adoptive father, the man whom her husband has irreparably wronged. Touched with remorse and shame the Marquis renounces suspicions which he, of all men, has least right to feel; but again his jealousy is roused when he finds his wife weeping over a letter. He asks to see it; she falters; he wrings it from her,—it is his own guilty letter to the Countess! At last, through many trials and sufferings, these people find out that they are hopelessly in love with each other. Ersilia learns that her husband has never seen the Countess since their marriage; she forgives him, and they are reconciled.

It seems scarcely possible that the same pen which produced this exquisite drama, with its careful plot, its pure and exalted feeling, and its effective scenes, should also have written a melodrama so wild and chaotic as the "Shakespeare" of Gualtieri. In this astounding play the Swan of Avon is taken up as he holds horses at the door of the theatre, and made scene-shifter by a famous actress (*sic!*) of his time. Miss Ariella makes violent love to him, but Shakespeare explains that he can never be hers, having, "at an age when he could not foresee the future, been constrained by family misfortunes and the will of his father to marry a peasant-woman of Stratford, ten years his senior," by whom he has already four children. In the mean time he writes plays and sells the title of authorship to a poetaster, Lord Makensie, for money to support his growing family. One night, however, when "Romeo and Juliet" is to be brought out, and Riccardo Burbage is rather tipsier than usual, Shakespeare himself assumes the part of Romeo, and, in an access of excitement, proclaims himself author of the play. This fires the virgin breast of Queen Elizabeth with the desire to see Sir William, as he is called; but, far from getting on well with him, the Queen offends Sir William, who revenges himself by reading before a literary society patronized by her Majesty a ballad censuring the execution of Mary, Queen of Scots! For this Sir William is cast into prison, where, refusing to offer any apology to the Queen, he finishes the last scene of his *Amleto* just before being led to the block. He is visited by all the players, with Papà Dryden, stage-manager, the poet Ben Johnson, and Lord Suthampton, his patron; who unite in beseeching him to ask the Queen's forgiveness; but he remains the same stubborn, wrong-headed Sir William he has proved throughout the play. Happily the Queen appears at the last moment, as Shakespeare moves to the door of the prison, and exclaims:—

"Stop, Sir William! Elizabeth wished to give you a comedy, or a drama, as you please. It may not be so sublime as your own, but there are happily not so many deaths in it,—not even one. (*Gives him her hand.*)
"*Shakespeare*. Your Majesty—(*kneeling*).
"*Eliz.* She, instead of calling you her court-poet, a title you would disdain, proclaims you poet of the English nation.
"*All.* Long live the Queen! (*Grand picture.*)"

"E perchè no? Gl' Inglesi son tutti originali."
If we may trust Signor Gualtieri, Shakespeare was a most uncomfortable person to meet with in the walks of real life, and, when not quoting his own plays, was always talking a miscellaneous balderdash, which but for the author of this play would hardly have been attributed to him, we think.

The master of the species of biographic drama in which Gualtieri has so egregiously failed with his Shakespeare is Paolo Ferrari, born at Modena, and now living at Milan, the great literary capital of the new Italian kingdom. His plays are only twelve or thirteen in number: five are farces, four are comedies of society, and three biographic dramas. These latter are "Dante at Verona," "Satire and Parini," and "Goldoni and his Sixteen New Comedies." The Goldoni is unquestionably the best of all the author's works, and is eminent for biographical truth and fidelity to Goldoni's character, while it does not lack ease of action, nor larger artistic truth to life. The incidents of Goldoni's career, around which the play is lightly built, are well known to the reader of his autobiography. In 1748, the company Medebac of Venice brought out for Goldoni one of the most excellent and popular of his comedies, which had a success so great as to rouse into active malignity all the enemies of the poet and of the new kind of comedy which he had introduced. Goldoni's play was called *La Vedova Scaltra* (The Sly Widow), and his enemies responded at a rival theatre with *La Scuola delle Vedove* (The School for Widows), in which Goldoni, his comedy, and his ideas were scurrilously ridiculed. As in *La Vedova Scaltra* an English lord was introduced, the rival dramatist employed the same character to cast despite upon the English and the Protestants generally. In rejoinder to this lampoon, Goldoni wrote and printed an Apology for his *Vedova*, in which he replied to the criticisms of his opponents, and severely blamed the ridicule cast upon the Protestants. This Apology was sent to the press and published without the permission of the government, leaving it optional with St. Mark to suppress it or not. It caused great excitement in the gossip-loving capital, and Goldoni was in danger of prison or exile, unless he himself withdrew the Apology. He stood by it manfully, however, and so completely won the day, that the *Scuola delle Vedove* was suppressed, and the marked censure of the Republic uttered against it. Elated by this success, Goldoni promised his comedians sixteen new comedies for the following year,—a year which he declares to have been so terrible for him that he never could remember it without horror. With this promise the play of Ferrari ends, for he has to deal with the causes that led to the production of the comedies, rather than subsequent events. Goldoni, his wife, and two foolish, pompous Spaniards (father and son), who vainly pay her their court, Zigo (a poetic rival of Goldoni), two false friends, the Medebac comedians, and the noble Grimani, friend to Goldoni, are the characters of the play, and its incidents those indicated. The best scenes are those in which the animosities, jealousies, and rivalries of the players are ridiculed. These are nearly all persons whose characteristics Goldoni has himself described in his Memoirs: the modern dramatist has but grouped them and placed them in action. The scene in which the jealous prompter is obliged to read to his own wife the stage directions for her love-scene with another actor, whom he madly hates, is a masterpiece in its way, and irresistibly amusing. But the equable humor of the whole comedy makes it unusually difficult of quotation, and a matter of regret that our present office is not that of translating one comedy, instead of noticing many. There is great spirit and fidelity to types of Venetian character in the different persons,—especially Grimani and Bartolo his gondolier,—and the play revives that old, mad, pleasure-loving world of masquerades and adventures in Venice of Goldoni's time, with charming effect.

"Dante at Verona" is the dramatization of that episode of the poet's life, when he visited in exile the court of Can Grande. We fear that it derives its chief interest from the fact that Dante is the hero, and certainly the drama's best passages are those the author puts into his Dante's mouth from the *Divina Commedia*. The poet embodies the aspiration for Italian unity, and dreams of a restoration of the Roman Empire under an Italian prince, Can Grande, while around his central figure and great purpose are grouped all the wavering fears, selfish interests, and petty and ignorant ambitions which made his dream impossible of realization. Can Grande, figured as a noble and princely soul, has a mind sufficiently large to grasp the magnificence of Dante's idea; but just as he has fully determined to attempt the reconstruction of the empire, news comes that his signorial arms have been torn down and trampled on by the Guelphs of some provincial town, and the spirit of blind feudal and partisan pride sweeps over him, quenching his high ambition, and he leaves all to go in person and avenge the insult. Dante then retires to Ravenna. This play was written some years before the late war of Italian independence, when Italy was entering on a state of transition similar to that of Dante's time, and the author declares that in the picture of another age he wished to mirror the present. Happily for the world, Victor Emanuel was no Can Grande, and Italy may yet be wholly united under him. In this play, Dante is drawn as that figure of sorrowful majesty which we know, but Ferrari has given a certain warmth and life to a conventional idea, and you feel all the bitterness of the poet's exile, and his troubles and small vexations sting you. The adaptation of lines from the *Commedia* to exigencies of the play is never violent, and is often very felicitous. The writer constantly betrays careful study of history and of human nature, and the life of an old signorial court, with its rude luxuries and magnificence, its turbulence and factions, its *condottieri*, its politicians and intriguers, its buffoon and its gross humors and amusements, is finely and vividly depicted.

Another comedy of the biographic sort is the "Satire and Parini," of which the scene is laid in Milan, about the middle of the last century. Parini was a famous satirist of that time, who scourged the follies and vices of the Lombard aristocracy; and making him his protagonist, the author shows the benefits on society of elevated, impersonal satire, as contrasted with the disorganization produced by the lampoons which were contemporaneously so popular in Milan. Ferrari ridicules in this comedy, among other things, a certain learned society called the *Enormi*, whose president held his place by right of descent, and was a miracle of pompous ignorance and stupidity. Academies of this kind are still to be found in Italy; but they were once the rage, and their erudite members amused themselves with incredible extravagances and puerilities. The Academy of the *Sibillone*, for instance, used to "place a child in the chair, who replied with a single word of hazard or caprice to the problem proposed. The academicians then maintained, in long harangues, that this word exactly solved the problem." Unhappily, the comedy "Satire and Parini" is in rhyme,—a lapse of taste which still seems to please in the Italian theatre.

In his Preface to this comedy, Ferrari is at the pains to disclaim the purpose attributed to him by destructive flattery and unfriendly critics, of restoring Goldoni. He says in clear words which must win the gratitude of every young writer who has been troubled in his study of the masters by the shallow criticism always more or less in vogue: "I venerate and study Goldoni,—not to imitate him, but to learn how to imitate nature. . . . . *Genius cannot be repeated*; and at any rate, I know well how different must be the art proper for a tranquil age like the past, from the art suited to a stormy age like the present." The defence is sound and just. Ferrari wishes he might resemble Goldoni in his conduct of the drama, which may be legitimately imitated, while he denies his wish to ape him in his æsthetic conceptions. And there all originality begins! He is the only dramatist of our time wholly worthy to succeed Goldoni,[4] and he has indeed learned from Goldoni to do more than Goldoni knew. Ferrari's dialogue is lively and witty, the situations of his plays are good, with many well-contrived surprises, and full of genial humor. But all which he shares with his master is of the nineteenth, and not of the eighteenth century, and so Ferrari is original.

His last play is *La Donna e lo Scettico*, to which its own merit and the rendering of Ristori is now giving the greatest popularity in Italy. The title ("Woman and the Sceptic") sufficiently suggests the scope of the drama, and the wish to teach the good through the beautiful is noticeable in all Ferrari's plays; though he wisely refuses to make his moral the first thing, knowing that the poet who does this abdicates his superiority to the moralist, without winning the moralist's applause. While modern Italian life finds due representation in his comedies, the bent of Ferrari's genius is evidently toward the kind of play which we have styled the biographic drama. In this he seems to find scope, and pleasure, and success. It is a species of comedy of which the Italians are extremely fond, and its excellence must be in part judged by its popularity. The lives of literary men, which Ferrari and his imitators chiefly celebrate, do not often afford the sharply-cut incidents and vivid events which the dramatist wishes, and his invention, unless most skilfully employed, must offend an audience acquainted with the biographic facts and mislead one ignorant of them. This drama is materially different from the historical play. There, events interest you in the hero; here the hero interests you in

---

[4] "I have found," says Ristori in a recent letter to a friend at Paris, "a new poet, who has written me a new comedy in which everybody is not always laughing. It is called 'Woman and the Sceptic,' and gives me the whole range of feeling; I play it with delight. The poet's name is Paolo Ferrari,—a worthy heir of Goldoni."

events. The worst that can be said of the biographic drama is that it is subjective; the best is that it pleases.

Paolo Giacometti is a writer who has carried it to excess, and who has succeeded in winning a wide popularity in Italy. He is the author of some forty dramas, of which nearly half are biographic. No career which offers any salient point on which to hang a play seems to be safe from this voluminous and unscrupulous writer. Those who recall the name of Lucretia Maria Davidson—a gifted and precocious American girl, whose facile verse won her even the difficult praises of the London Quarterly, and whose premature death consigned her to the limbo of books on literary biography—will be puzzled to know how her life could possibly be made to serve the purposes of drama. Nevertheless, the Cavaliere Giacometti has made a *dramma storico* of her career, which we have read not wholly without profit, we trust, and certainly not without amusement. In this play, we learn from the lips of the good Abbé Villars (who keeps an *Istituto* for young ladies in the State of Pennsylvania), that "the English are more civilized than the Americans, and they ought to be so, for they came first into the world: their wrong was in not knowing how to civilize us. Enough! George Washington has kindled here his beacon-fire, and I think they have beheld it beyond the sea! And his friend and mine, Benjamin Franklin, has had the daring to civilize the lightnings. Although the period of our existence on the geographic chart numbers only some three hundred and twenty years, *we are no longer those hideous savages we once were!*" No one who reads this will be surprised to learn further from the play that American citizens commonly bear the title of Sir, and cherish a deep-seated hostility to enlightenment of all kinds, and literature in particular, or that the death of Miss Davidson resulted partly from an unhappy attachment for a famous English poet (Sir Giorgio Dorsey, travelling in America for the purpose of kissing the tomb of Washington), which she concealed that it might not divide him from a friend to whom he was betrothed. It would be, of course, unjust to judge this play, and others of its class, by absurdities not palpable to the Italians. It has very great merit of a certain kind, and is played to tearful audiences in Italy. Giacometti never writes comedies, properly speaking; where he does not select some passage of biography, he takes a subject destitute of comic interest, and appends a dramatic sentimentality, or a dramatic sarcasm. It must be said to his credit that his aim is always lofty and pure; in none of the many plays which we have read, in search of something to praise, have we found one objectionable passage, nor any immoral tendency masked under a show of virtuous purpose. We must ascribe to him unaffected conscientiousness, extreme infelicity in the choice of subjects, utter ignorance of Anglo-Saxon life (which he is fatally fond of depicting), perfect mastery of stage effects, superfluous sentiment, and the art of writing the most unreasonably successful plays in the world; he is moreover original—by mere virtue of mediocrity.

The life of Teobaldo Ciconi is one of those lives which give the author (as in the case of Theodore Winthrop) so deep a hold upon the sympathy of his readers as almost to annul in them the faculties by which art is judged apart from the artist. We attribute to this, at least, part of the popularity, or rather affection, which he enjoys. He was born, like Aleardo Aleardi, Dall' Ongaro, and a large number of other Italian poets of the day, under Austrian rule, and his story embraces the usual romance of lofty aspirations duly snubbed with exile. Ciconi was a native of the Friuli, and studied law at the University of Padua, where he took a degree. We believe he never practised the profession of advocate; he early devoted himself to dramatic literature, in which he won great success, translating from the French, besides producing a great many original plays. When the war of independence broke out, in 1859, he entered the ranks of the Italian army as volunteer, and fought bravely throughout that struggle—to die of consumption at Milan in 1863, while yet quite young. He was a man who had cordial friends while he lived, and no one can look upon the likeness of his face without sympathy and tenderness, it is so sad and so winning.

Ciconi was as true to the spirit of his age in letters as in politics, and his comedies unite many of the best characteristics of the modern school. He is, perhaps, superior to Ferrari in the art of lightly sketching slight latter-day people of the world, and he is happiest when dealing with men and women of *buon genere*. But in these sketches there is now and then a hardness of spirit which makes you regret that the author chose to do them, though the hardness contributes to the excellence of the work. Ciconi's dialogue is like that of Charles Reade in "Peg Woffington,"—quick, poignant, glittering, and witty, and many of the people in his comedies are like those in Thackeray's novels,—granting the radical differences of Italian and English life. For the rest he seems to have been more affected by the French dramatists than any of his Italian contemporaries, though at last his own heart seems to have echoed the cry of other men's,—"Can you no longer touch the chord of feeling? Make us weep!" In one of his latest plays he has dealt with the saddest problem which vexes the world,—that of the lost woman,—and which Dall' Ongaro says he has solved in a manner more Christian and human than that of the French authors. It is a singular drama, and is more like the fantasy of a German brain, than the product of the practical, undreamy Italian mind. It is called *La Statua di Carne*, and the living statue is a beautiful, gifted, and wicked girl, who chances to bear a wondrous resemblance to the young wife of Count Santa Rosa. This wife was an humble seamstress, to whom the Count, sick of being loved for his rank and wealth, had never revealed his true character; her devotion in his supposed poverty restored him to faith in God and men, and her early death left him heir to a life-long sorrow. He goes to America, renouncing his identity, and allowing himself to be thought dead by all but one faithful friend. This friend, meeting Noemi, is struck by her strange resemblance to Maria, the Count's dead wife, and writes to him; the Count instantly quits Boston, and repairs to Milan, where he finds Noemi one of the most reckless and boisterous spirits at a pleasant but wicked little supper. The Count, too, sees the likeness remarked by his

friend, and, with no thought but of his wife in his heart, he offers this beautiful and heartless wanton his protection, and places all his wealth at her
disposal, on condition that she will assume the name of Maria, and live in the
room where his wife died. Two hours each day she is to sit before him while
he gazes upon the features endeared to him by eternal loss; at all other times
she may go where she will, and do what she will. At first Noemi finds this
merely tedious; then, piqued by the persistent coldness and indifference of
her protector, she tries her arts upon him; failing, she is moved by his fidelity
and devotion to his dead wife, and for the first time she believes in love, and
loves. Her truth and love are now put to proof, they sustain it, and the Count
ends by wedding her. Such is the outline of the play, which has certainly a
fantastic charm; but whether it solves the problem of the social evil may
reasonably be questioned. The reformation so peculiarly effected by Count
Santa Rosa must, we fear, be regarded as exceptional,—though no one need
for that matter refuse to recognize the great truth inculcated by the drama:
that lost faith can only be recovered through suffering, and that love cannot
begin where there is no faith.

In what the eloquent critic, so often quoted, calls Ciconi's last and best
comedy, "The Only Daughter," the author deals with better human nature
than usual. The humor and events of the whole play turn upon the imbecile
fondness of rich parents for their only, spoiled child, to whom they have
given a young man of spirit for a husband, just as they would have given her
anything else she asked for. As the husband is never permitted to control his
wife in anything nor to have any voice concerning her, he has sunk to the
place of an unsalaried servant in his father-in-law's house, when his friend
Ippolito returns from the acquisition of wisdom in America,—where all the
disappointed lovers and adventurous spirits of modern Italian comedies always go. He inspires the husband to assert himself, and Alfredo's self-
assertion ends in a separation from his wife; the friends quit Milan together,
take service in the Italian army, and re-enter the city with the triumphal army
of Victor Emanuel. Meantime, the father-in-law has taken a new house, and
the friends, without his knowledge or their own, are billeted upon him. Alfredo's wife returns from the opera at night, finds her husband and seeks to
be reconciled with him,—for she has secretly adored him ever since he refused to be her slave, and has nearly broken her heart for him in his absence.
The Count Paride, of whom Alfredo has been jealous, and who once refused
to fight him on the pretence that they were not equals, is put to open shame
before the husband and wife reconciled; he furiously challenges Alfredo, and
is answered that a man who has spent his time in fashionable dawdling during
that glorious war is not the equal of a soldier who has fought for his country.
Ippolito gently adds, "Better by the door than through the window, Count,"
and shows him out, while virtue and happiness triumph in the re-union of
Alfredo and Elena. Ippolito is a character exquisitely drawn, and altogether
delightful. His brilliant and crisp surface of wit commands your admiration,
and his really kind, friendly and honest heart wins your liking. He has had a

love-affair in his first youth with a singer at Verona, who reappears in this play as the pretty widow of a rich marquis. The passages in which they rehearse their former loves are the wittiest and best in the play,—and for sparkle of easy natural repartee have seldom been excelled. Ciconi seems to have wished in this play to hold up before Italian society a picture of some of its faults, and of the simple manliness that may overcome them. There is sufficient license in parts of the dialogue, but the meaning, as well as the declared intention, is good; and certainly the play is very pleasing.

The comedies of Ciconi are many, and they are all popular, but the two particularly mentioned are the best liked,—which is to say, they are the best. If the author had lived, he would hardly have turned his attention to the historical or sentimental drama, for either is alien to his genius, but he would probably have continued to write his graceful comedies of society, growing better-natured as he grew older. It is the fault of the fine world which he drew so faithfully, that his characters are often so hard, and his words of such bitter persiflage. It cannot be said that he has ever by precept or tendency done conscious wrong to principles which neither men nor literature can violate without degradation.

Like praise may be bestowed upon all recent Italian comedy, in which there is seldom verbal licentiousness, and never the badness of heart which turns the high and the pure into ridicule. The French dramas, for which the repeated invasions of Italy by French ideas had made way, have been well-nigh banished from the stage by the naturally healthy taste of the Italians, fostered and developed by the native dramatists. The merit of writers who have thus succeeded in exiling productions which have great and undeniable attractions for play-goers, stands proved by the fact. All efforts to please innocently must be made with uncommon skill and genius; he who appeals from lust to taste must be master of most persuasive eloquence. The Italians have reason to be proud of the drama which makes this appeal, and the student of Italian life must turn to this drama for that knowledge of society which he would look for vainly in the contemporary romance of Italy. The only novels, as we have said, which are worth reading, are historical; but in the comedies are fairly reflected many of the most interesting features of modern Italian life and thought. You see there a state of society in which all things seem in transition: the old traditions of rank are disputed; suspicion is not only cast upon social prejudices, but well-known and time-honored social vices are openly disgraced; the dignity of man is asserted, the purity of woman is defended, the sanctity of all family ties is honored. Whatever is best in modern doubt works there to the triumph of faith and virtue. In fine, the Italians have a genuine drama, which they may cherish without loss of self-respect. The defects of this drama cannot be denied, however. With all its freedom, its range is narrow, and the life it represents is too exclusively that of the best society; and while it has no exotic growth, it lacks the exquisite raciness of the Goldonian comedy. But, with all its defects, it must be acknowledged that we have nothing to compare with it in English literature. It seems, like the society which it reflects, to be in a state of development and transition, and it is reasonable to suppose that it will enlarge its scope with changing conditions till, like society, it includes and acknowledges all phases of national life.

"The moment," says Dall' Ongaro, in his admirable essay on the drama, "is propitious for the dramatic art. . . . . . Liberty of speech has brought into existence new elements, new ideas, new feelings. . . . . . Liberty has emancipated us not only from the yoke of our tyrants, but has freed us from the moral chains of bigotry, academic and official. The True and the Beautiful! behold the law, behold the evangel of Art! For the rest, any form is good, if it speaks to the heart and moves it. Yet I shall not cease to repeat to the young Italian poets, Write for the Theatre,—that is, for the People. Do not leave this noble office to court buffoons and flatterers of the worst instincts of the vulgar. Write for the people, the whole people, the united people, met before you, your judge, your inspiration, your aspiration. Put yourself in communication with it, live its life, make yourself *populace*,—not to flatter its ignoble passions, but to lift it to the serene region of the ideal, to teach it consciousness of its worth, to show it how is lost, how is won, and, above all, how is preserved, the greatest of all good, the most sacred of all rights, Liberty!"

[*North American Review*, October 1864]

8

Drum-Taps.[1]

WILL saltpeter explode? Is Walt Whitman a true poet? Doubts to be solved by the wise futurity which shall pay off our national debt. Poet or not, however, there was that in Walt Whitman's first book which compels attention to his second. There are obvious differences between the two: this is much smaller than that; and whereas you had at times to hold your nose (as a great sage observed) in reading "Leaves of Grass," there is not an indecent thing in "Drum-Taps." The artistic method of the poet remains, however, the same, and we must think it mistaken. The trouble about it is that it does not give you sensation in a portable shape; the thought is as intangible as aroma; it is no more put up than the atmosphere.

We are to suppose that Mr. Whitman first adopted his method as something that came to him of its own motion. This is the best possible reason, and only possible excuse, for it. In its way, it is quite as artificial as that of any other poet, while it is unspeakably inartistic. On this account it is a failure. The method of talking to one's self in rhythmic and ecstatic prose is one that surprises at first, but, in the end, the talker can only have the devil for a listener, as happens in other cases when people address their own individualities; not, however, the devil of the proverb, but the devil of reasonless, hopeless, all-defying egotism. An ingenious French critic said very acutely of Mr. Whitman that he made you partner of the poetical enterprise, which is perfectly true; but no one wants to share the enterprise. We want its effect, its success; we do not want to plant corn, to hoe it, to drive the crows away, to gather it, husk it, grind it, sift it, bake it, and butter it, before eating it, and then take the risk of its being at last moldy in our mouths. And this is what you have to do in reading Mr. Whitman's rhythm.

At first, a favorable impression is made by the lawlessness of this poet, and one asks himself if this is not the form which the unconscious poetry of American life would take, if it could find a general utterance. But there is really no evidence that such is the case. It is certain that among the rudest peoples the lurking sublimity of nature has always sought expression in artistic form, and there is no good reason to believe that the sentiment of a people with our high average culture would seek expression more rude and

[1] Walt Whitman's "Drum-Taps." New York. 1865.

48

formless than that of the savagest tribes. Is it not more probable that, if the passional principle of American life could find utterance, it would choose the highest, least dubious, most articulate speech? Could the finest, most shapely expression be too good for it?

If we are to judge the worth of Mr. Whitman's poetic theory (or impulse, or possession) by its popular success, we must confess that he is wrong. It is already many years since he first appeared with his claim of poet, and in that time he has employed criticism as much as any literary man in our country, and he has enjoyed the fructifying extremes of blame and praise. Yet he is, perhaps, less known to the popular mind, to which he has attempted to give an utterance, than the newest growth of the magazines and the newspaper notices. The people fairly rejected his former revelation, letter and spirit, and those who enjoyed it were readers with a cultivated taste for the quaint and the outlandish. The time to denounce or to ridicule Mr. Whitman for his first book is past. The case of "Leaves of Grass" was long ago taken out the hands of counsel and referred to the great jury. They have pronounced no audible verdict; but what does their silence mean? There were reasons in the preponderant beastliness of that book why a decent public should reject it; but now the poet has cleansed the old channels of their filth, and pours through them a stream of blameless purity, and the public has again to decide, and this time more directly, on the question of his poethood. As we said, his method remains the same, and he himself declares that, so far as concerns it, he has not changed nor grown in any way since we saw him last:

> "Beginning my studies, the first step pleased me so much, The mere fact, consciousness—these forms—the power of motion, The least insect or animal—the senses—eye-sight; The first step, I say, aw'd me and pleas'd me so much, I have never gone, and never wish'd to go, any further, But stop and loiter all my life to sing it in ecstatic songs."

Mr. Whitman has summed up his own poetical theory so well in these lines, that no criticism could possibly have done it better. It makes us doubt, indeed, if all we have said in consideration of him has not been said idly, and certainly releases us from further explanation of his method.

In "Drum-Taps," there is far more equality than in "Leaves of Grass," and though the poet is not the least changed in purpose, he is certainly changed in fact. The pieces of the new book are nearly all very brief, but generally his expression is freer and fuller than ever before. The reader understands, doubtless, from the title, that nearly all these pieces relate to the war; and they celebrate many of the experiences of the author in the noble part he took in the war. One imagines the burly tenderness of the man who went to supply the

> "———lack of woman's nursing"

that there was in the hospitals of the field, and woman's tears creep unconsciously to the eyes as the pity of his heart communicates itself to his
reader's. No doubt the pathos of many of the poems gains something from
the quaintness of the poet's speech. One is touched in reading them by the
same inarticulate feeling as that which dwells in music; and is sensible that
the poet conveys to the heart certain emotions which the brain cannot
analyze, and only remotely perceives. This is especially true of his inspirations from nature; memories and yearnings come to you folded, mute, and
motionless in his verse, as they come in the breath of a familiar perfume.
They give a strange, shadowy sort of pleasure, but they do not satisfy, and
you rise from the perusal of this man's book as you issue from the presence
of one whose personal magnetism is very subtle and strong, but who has
not added to this tacit attraction the charm of spoken ideas. We must not
mistake this fascination for a higher quality. In the tender eyes of an ox
lurks a melancholy, soft and pleasing to the glance as the pensive sweetness
of a woman's eyes; but in the orb of the brute there is no hope of expression, and in the woman's look there is the endless delight of history, the
heavenly possibility of utterance.

Art cannot greatly employ itself with things in embryo. The instinct of the
beast may interest science; but poetry, which is nobler than science, must
concern itself with natural instincts only as they can be developed into the
sentiments and ideas of the soul of man. The mind will absorb from nature
all that is speechless in her influences; and it will demand from kindred mind
those higher things which can be spoken. Let us say our say here against the
nonsense, long current, that there is, or can be, poetry *between the lines*, as is
often sillily asserted. *Expression* will always suggest; but mere *suggestion* in art
is unworthy of existence, vexes the heart, and shall not live. Every man has
tender, and beautiful, and lofty emotions; but the poet was sent into this
world to give these a tangible utterance, and if he do not this, but only give
us back dumb emotion for dumb emotion, he is a cumberer of the earth.
There is a yearning, almost to agony at times, in the human heart, to throw
off the burden of inarticulate feeling, and if the poet will not help it in this
effort, if, on the contrary, he shall seek to weigh it and sink it down under
heavier burdens, he has not any reason to be.

So long, then, as Mr. Whitman chooses to stop at mere consciousness, he
cannot be called a true poet. We all have consciousness; but we ask of art an
utterance. We do not so much care in what way we get this expression; we
will take it in ecstatic prose, though we think it is better subjected to the laws
of prosody, since every good thing is subject to some law; but the expression
we must have. Often, in spite of himself, Mr. Whitman grants it in this volume, and there is some hope that he will hereafter grant it more and more.
There are such rich possibilities in the man that it is lamentable to contemplate his error of theory. He has truly and thoroughly absorbed the idea of
our American life, and we say to him as he says to himself, "You've got
enough in you, Walt; why don't you get it out?" A man's greatness is good for

nothing folded up in him, and if emitted in barbaric yawps, it is not more filling than Ossian or the east wind.

[*Round Table*, 11 November 1865]

9

Concerning Timothy Titcomb.[1]

SINCE the "Country Parson" has been called a prose Tupper, there is, unhappily, nothing left within the whole range of epigram for the characterization of "Timothy Titcomb." The situation is perhaps inevitable, but it is not the less desperate. No doubt a future age, should his work descend to posterity, will have the courage and wisdom to express in some comprehensive phrase a sense of their quality; for the present we can only hope to suggest their nature vaguely and unequally.

Fortunately, a great number of readers have already some idea of our author. He has written a good many books, which have had large sales. He has a wide reputation as poet and novelist; and it seems to us he has done his best things in these characters. As a lecturer he is quite as well known, and in the volume before us he publishes the lectures which he has written and delivered during the last six or seven years. These are nine in number, and of such quantity and quality that it exalts our respect for the national sweetness and patience when we consider that they must have each been delivered to popular assemblies at least a score of times.

It might not be without a measure of sadness, however, that we considered this, for the fact suggests uncomfortable ideas of the facility of literary success in this country, and goes far to prove that reputation is the only thing still to be had cheap among us; that while overcoats, butter and eggs, rents and fuel, are exorbitantly dear, fame, like consolidated milk, is within the reach of the humblest resources. But it would be unjust to the public to judge it by what it endures rather than what it likes; and it is doubtful whether the popularity of such writers and lecturers as Mr. Holland is other than apparent. A slovenly and timorous criticism has been the bane alike of readers and of writers, and an order of mind has been allowed to flourish up into a thistly rankness in our literature fit only to browse donkeys. But we doubt greatly whether most people have any genuine appetite for the growth, and we question if even among those to whom harsh dispraise of Mr. Holland would come with almost the shock of a personal affront, there has not sometimes been a suspicion that he was heavy and trite. It would be

---

[1] "Plain Talks on Familiar Subjects. A Series of Popular Lectures. By J. G. Holland." New York: Charles Scribner & Co. 1866.

difficult, certainly, to find anything in these popular lectures which is not dull if new, or old if good. The lecturer himself has sometimes a sense of this, and once expresses the belief that a great deal he has been saying must seem to his audience like the recitation of a schoolroom. We must do him the justice to say, however, that this concession is made in a moment of rare consciousness, and that, for the most part, he rehearses his commonplaces with a dignified carefulness and a swelling port of self-satisfaction inexpressibly amusing. He does not wonder, this eloquent lecturer, he is "smitten with wonder," he says, when he thinks "of the power which bold assumption has in the world," though we suspect that he is merely smitten with wonder that he should have thought of the tremendous fact; and he might have marvelled at his hearers for submitting to his own pretence of having something wise and novel to tell them. He loves to say "Now, mark you," when there is nothing to mark, and is fond of the sort of metaphor which, like bear's meat, grows as you chew upon it, and can neither be swallowed nor ejected. Nothing daunts him, and he does not hesitate to electrify you with the idea, for example, "that hate is not so good a motive as love, and, thank God! it is not so powerful a motive as love!"

Throughout these lectures Mr. Holland patronizes the good, the true, and the beautiful. He encourages these amiable abstractions, and tries to keep up their spirits by a constant testimony to their good behavior. He is also friendly to the domestic and public virtues; but the great object of his philanthropic condescension is the Christian religion. He cannot say enough in favor of its many winning and useful qualities; and if he sometimes suspects that his platitudes on other subjects might seem like the recitations of schoolboys, he has every reason to believe that his attitude toward our common faith is that of a pedagogue. He wishes to bring this faith out and have its merit recognized, and will never give up his protégée, even though people should think his constancy unfashionable. Religion he finds lamentably absent from politics and society, and, above all, from fashionable literature. He does not find Thackeray Christian, even when he takes "into account the sulphurous satire which he points with such deadly fire at the very society which makes him fashionable;" and he objects to the pen of Charles Dickens that, although "thrilling to its nib with the genius which inspires it, he has never written, in good, honest text, the name of Jesus Christ." The rebuke of worldly-mindedness and vanity and uncharitableness which breaks forth from Thackeray, the unfailing advocacy of the cause of the despised, the poor, and the prisoner in the novels of Charles Dickens, prove nothing of their love of Christianity, because the *name* of Christ is not in their works. Does Mr. Holland wear a crucifix about him? Kingsley, although a traitor to the cause of popular reform, and the inventor of the odious muscular piety of second-rate modern fictions, is Christian, because he calls on the name of the Lord; and Ruskin, who has lately discovered the divine beauty of slavery, is likewise a Christian for the like reason. Mrs. Browning, also, is a Christian writer; and whereas fashionable unchristian writers are doomed to perish, our lecturer is led to the anticlimax of saying: "The earth is not broad enough, the earth is not deep enough, to bury Mrs. Browning in."

It may be objected to the censure of such writers as Mr. Holland that, granting their popularity to be factitious, they do a great deal of good to commonplace people; that they reach a large class of hearers and readers who could not be reached by men of genius; that they act as smoked glasses for the weak vision that would else turn away from thought, or, regarding her, would be dazzled to death by her aspect. We desire to give Mr. Holland's admirers and apologists the benefit of this doubt.

[*Nation*, 23 November 1865]

10

Our Mutual Friend.[1]

DIVIDING prose fictions into the two classes of novel and romance, with the theory that the novel is a portraiture of individuals and affairs, and the romance a picture of events and human characteristics in their subtler and more ideal relations, we believe we are right in saying that Mr. Dickens is not at all a novelist but altogether a romancer. The novelist deals with personages, the romancer with types. Thackeray, the greatest of novelists, has given us characters which have such absolute and perfect personality that we know them as we know Smith and Jones. Dickens, the first of living romancers, gives us types by which we can characterize all the qualities of our acquaintance. Pendennis, Clive Newcome, Blanche Amory, Becky Sharpe, are faultless likenesses of individual life in the world; Micawber, Mr. Pecksniff, Harold Skimpole, Mrs. Nickleby, are images of cheerful haplessness, hypocrisy, amiable, irresponsible selfishness and folly, which exist at large in human nature. We are far from thinking the novelist's art less than the romancer's; only we do not think it more. You do homage to the exquisite, reproachless fidelity of Thackeray, while you marvel at the creative power of Dickens. You know that Micawber and Pecksniff are individually impossibilities, but you constantly find men who remind you of them. When you go to London you feel it not unlikely you may meet Fred Bayham; but who ever expected to encounter Dick Swiveller in any particular locality? Mr. Dickens's people are essentially types, not persons; and though they have, by the sovereign laws of art, a right to individual existence in the books where we find them, yet if we attempt to translate them into real life, as we do Becky Sharpe and Arthur Pendennis, they lose all organic propriety, and dissolve into traits and resemblances.

Believing in romance's office to produce images of universal truth and value, we have slight patience, and less sympathy, with the criticism which accuses Mr. Dickens of exaggeration; and we have no blame for his last book because most of its people are improbable. So long as they are not moral impossibilities, we cannot think them exaggerations except in the sense that Lear and Othello are exaggerations; and we are rather surprised that critics who have observed the Shakespearian universality of Mr. Dickens's feeling,

---

[1] "Our Mutual Friend." By Charles Dickens. Philadelphia: T. B. Peterson & Brothers.

have not been struck with the Shakespearian universality of his art. We find that it will be useless to condemn Mr. Dickens for Wegg and Podsnap, unless we condemn Shakespeare for Falstaff and Pistol, and Cervantes for Sancho Panza. It is even idler to object that Mr. Dickens places his physically impossible characters among us in our own day; for they certainly represent present longings, interests, and delusions, though nobody has seen their whole likeness in life. Cervantes made his knight to live in his own day; it was impossible that he should exist then in geographical and political Spain, but nevertheless he did exist then in the spirit of most Spaniards.

Whether Mr. Dickens has given us new types in his new work, is to us the most interesting question in regard to it, for we count the management of plot as comparatively unimportant in his fictions, and only value it as it develops his characters. If the plot is one in which a fitting part falls to each character, we think it successful, no matter what gross improbabilities it may involve as a scheme of action: it has to preserve in the characters consistency and harmony, and nothing more.

Some of the people in "Our Mutual Friend" must inevitably remind the reader of former creations by the same master. In Mr. Podsnap we have Mr. Bounderby, of Coketown, removed to London, and greatly enlarged and improved. Bounderby was exceptional in his former career; and, though we might meet his like at rare intervals, he was not of great use to epithet; but, as Podsnap, he becomes of universal acceptance. Podsnap is a word to be used for ever to name an otherwise unspeakably odious order of human creature, and the world will receive gratefully the author's suggestion of Podsnappery as a fit term for the thinking and doing of this kind of human creatures. Still, however, Podsnap is scarcely more than a more practicable Bounderby, and we cannot salute him as a novel type. In like manner, we have had earlier acquaintance with Lady Tippins, and knew that gray enchantress in "Dombey and Son" as Cleopatra. Lady Tippins, indeed, is less vulgar, and less a fool than Cleopatra; but she has much of her manner, and, with Major Bagstock for company instead of the young men Wrayburn and Lightwood, we suspect would do and say the same things that Cleopatra did. Rogue Riderhood, again, who gets his living by the sweat of his brow, is too nearly related to the honest tradesman in "The Tale of Two Cities" to be of great original value, and his daughter Pleasant, slightly as she is sketched, is more admirable as a creation. As for Lizzie Hexam, though her part is dwelt on a great deal, she fails to interest us, and we think her selfish, mean-souled brother an infinitely better work of art. One of the least natural characters in the book is one which was quite possibly copied from life, and one on which the author has unmistakably bestowed great pains—that of the doll's dressmaker, Miss Jenny Wren. The other women are all admirable in their way. Bella Wilfer is delicious; but it would be hard for any reader to say where he left off disliking her for a pert and selfish little wretch and began liking her for the sweetest and best of lovely women; for long before her furious outburst against Mr. Boffin, the most bewitching goodness had been visible in her most bewitching badness. Her mother is almost as great a fool, pure and simple, as Mrs. Nickleby, which is the highest praise we can pronounce, unless we add that her folly is of quite a different sort—a serious and stately idiotcy perfectly unique. Miss Podsnap is the very soul of bashful, nervous sincerity and artlessness, with only enough of the common mother of our race to make her frantically vindictive under the torture of polite attentions at her birth-day party. Mrs. Lammle would have been better managed by Thackeray, as, indeed, would the whole episode of the Lammles have been. But who besides Mr. Dickens could have so perfectly presented Mrs. Milvey and all her good, energetic little life by merely the virtue of that emphasis, recurrent and capricious, she bestows on her words?

The hero of the romance, if John Harmon be its hero, is a mere hinge on which the plot works, and, as a man, is utterly uninteresting. Neither does Mr. Boffin convey the impression of consistent character, and we cannot believe him fitted to play the part assigned him in Harmon's prolonged and clumsy *ruse*.

Eugene Wrayburn has a slight but genuine value in representing the sort of purposeless, graceful *ennui* which, no doubt, largely exists among well-educated and well-bred young men in England, but which our late war has terribly abolished among them here—for ever, let us hope. The author cures Wrayburn by that attempted murder, which the reader knows, and afterwards we find him so full of true and noble stuff that we are sorry not to have seen more of him. Bradley Headstone, as a study of murderous human nature, is not so good as other like studies by the author; but he is excellent as showing how barren and stony the mere culture of the mind leaves the soul, especially when this culture is not wide and deep enough to make the mental principle distrust its own infallibility. Mr. Alfred Lammle is not successful, it seems to us, though the author has taken pains to mark his devilishness with white dints in the nose, so that it may be recognized at all times; but Fascination Fledgeby is finely done, and admirably punished at last with the sort of retribution which the reader had instinctively longed for. It is curious with what skill Mr. Dickens manages beatings so as to lift them out of the province of farce and pantomime, and make them felicitous points of the drama, on which ladies and children may look "with cheerfulness and refreshment." There is an exquisite enjoyment to the reader in the thrashing which Nicholas Nickleby gives Squeers the schoolmaster, which we find also in the caning of Mr. Fledgeby under quite different circumstances; while we look with just as keen a relish on Sloppy dropping Mr. Wegg into the slush and garbage of the scavenger's cart. Not but that we have a high opinion of Mr. Wegg as a character. Indeed, we think him, altogether, the most original and successful character in the book; that mean and doggish sagacity which leads him to suspect a secret value in himself because some one seems to need him, and his wretched, groveling purpose not to let himself go cheap, though he could not say why he should be worth anything, are traits of human nature embodied in him with faultless art. His different bargains with Mr. Boffin are evidence of marvellous subtlety and keenness in the author's study of men; while Wegg's envy of Mr. Boffin's wealth, his sense of deadly injury received through the benefits bestowed on him, and his resolution to ruin his benefactor in return for them, are consequences resulting so naturally from existing tempers and relations that the reader may be slower than he should to discern the unique art with which they are made to appear. In fine, Wegg seems to have been not only born, but to have lost his leg, in order to be fitted perfectly for the part he plays in this book.

Mr. Dickens, in the postscript to his romance, says when he devised the story he foresaw the likelihood that a class of readers and commentators would suppose that he wished to conceal what he really tried to suggest— that is, the common identity of John Harmon and John Rokesmith. Impression of this sort, it must be confessed, was more creditable to Mr. Dickens's prophetic qualities than complimentary to his readers, among whom such a mistake was presumably possible. We think that, to people of very ordinary perspicacity and very moderate acquaintance with fiction, this part of the plot was visible from the beginning, though it does not seem to us very ingenious. Indeed, we find the plot scarcely to have even the secondary excellence which we would have demanded, for it appears to offer the different characters slight opportunity for consistent development, and it ends like a Christmas pantomime, with a most boisterous distribution of poetical justice. The motives assigned to the personages are rarely sufficient to account for their actions, and they all act parts which have little or no coherence or propriety. Indeed, the reader, after passing through the painful scenes of John Rokesmith's dismissal and year-long enmity with the Boffins, angrily resents the explanation offered him that John Rokesmith and Mr. Boffin were only making believe in order to prove Bella's devotion to the utmost— resents the explanation as a weak refuge from the events invented after their occurrence. In a young writer the device would be pronounced a puerile invention, and it has not even the justification of Mr. Boffin's long delusion of Mr. Wegg, for that brings out all the despotic baseness of Wegg's character; while John Harmon's *ruse* leaves us no better acquainted with him than we were before, but rather disposed to like him less than before. The main plot of the book scarcely seems to concern the other characters who figure in different episodes of slender coherence; and one vainly asks himself at the end what any of them has done to help the story forward, though he would be loth to lose any of them from the book.

Whether the reader will think that Mr. Dickens has improved upon his former works in the present one, or has fallen below them in excellence, will greatly depend upon whether he can read him now with that eager sympathy which he gave to the perusal of his romances in other days. Men are prone to think (even when they are not very old men) that the pleasure and excellence of these days are not at all comparable to the pleasure and excellence of other days; and though "Our Mutual Friend" may be intrinsically as good as "David Copperfield," it is scarcely possible that any old-established admirer of "David Copperfield" should allow it. To him who read of the courtship in the latter book when he was himself first in love, and who reads of the courtship in the former book after having lived through the champagne of life, Dora must be infinitely more bewitching and lovable than Bella. So, if you please, the present writer would rather have the opinion of some intelligent person newly experienced in Mr. Dickens's former romances—if that person exists; and he would care more for the judgment of eighteen or twenty years than thirty or forty, in the matter. We think this ideal critic would pronounce that he found this last romance as full of generous interest as any earlier one; that he found in its pages the same intimate friendship with the nature of fields and woods and the nature of docks and streets; the same warm-blooded sympathy with poverty and lowliness; the same scorn of solemn and respectable selfishness, and of mean and disreputable cunning; the same subtle analysis of the motives and feelings and facts of crime; the same exuberant happiness in love and lovers; the same comprehension of what Carlyle calls "inarticulate natures;" the same gay, fantastic humor; the same capricious pathos. As to the manner, it should scarcely seem the old manner, though the critic could not tell where it departed from it; and for the style, could that ever have been more luminous, flexible, felicitous?

[*Round Table*, 2 December 1865]

11

Literary Criticism.

A very common, but very unjust and harmful, misapprehension exists as to the office and the object of literary criticism. By some curiously irrational process the notion obtains here and there that spleen, personal liking or animosity, a bad temper, a bad digestion, a chronic tendency to fault-finding—anything but the love of truth and justice and an honest devotion to the cause of pure literature—inspire all fearless criticism. In accordance with this view, the critic himself is supposed to be perpetually suspended, somewhat like Mahomet's coffin in mid-air, between the author and the reader, enjoying neither the pleasure of communicating on the one hand nor the pleasure of receiving on the other.

Very obviously, however, such misconceptions of the aim and the character of independent criticism belong only to the ignorant or unreflecting. True criticism, indeed, is the function and the natural habit of every intelligent and candid mind—which, accordingly, is probably the reason why the ignorant and dishonest always feel annoyed and alarmed at its appearance. Criticism implies in its very derivation and signification judgment, discernment, sifting, separating good from bad, the wheat from the chaff. True criticism, therefore, consists of a calm, just, and fearless handling of its subject, and in pointing out in all honesty whatever there is hitherto undiscovered of merit, and, in equal honesty, whatever there has been concealed of defect. This function is entirely distinct from the mere trade-puff of the publisher, the financial comments of the advertiser, or the bought-and-sold eulogium of an ignorant, careless, or mercenary journalist. It is equally removed from the wholesale and baseless attacks of some rival publication house, or from the censure which is inspired by political, personal, or religious hatred. So commonly, however, especially in America, is this high function of literary criticism degraded to base uses that we can hardly wonder at the popular incredulity as to its aim and scope. The dignified title of criticism applied to the "book notices" and "literary reviews" of ordinary American periodical literature is simply a misnomer. In the majority of cases the fault lies purely in the ignorance and incapacity of the person to whom this work miscalled "criticism" is assigned—in his lack of discernment; in his inability to see wherein a good book is good or where a bad book might have been better. This department of American journalism is usually considered among the least important, and, accordingly, is almost invariably done the worst. But, when ignorance or negligence do not account (as they will in most cases) for faulty criticism, some worse cause must be assigned, as, for example, a weak good-nature, anxious not to hurt the author's feelings or the publisher's profits; sordid praise purchased at so much a column, like tape bought by the yard; partisan feeling, envy of a rival, personal dislike, ecclesiastical terror, or mean malevolence of any sort. Criticism is often perverted from being a stern and responsible duty to serve some private feeling or end, to act as a cloak for some entirely alien purpose. Accordingly, our American people, including in a somewhat pardonable confusion of ideas all sorts of "book noticing" under the head of literary criticism, have been much inclined to follow Byron's advice in "English Bards," and to believe

> —"an epitaph,
> Or any other thing that's false, before
> You trust in critics."

The same willful dishonesty of purpose—but still more shameful in degree—is sometimes to be found not only in notices of publications, but even in some pretended homilies on the nature of criticism in general. For example, the New York *Observer*, one of the religious weeklies (and, by the way, the poorest of them all), discoursed nominally, of late, on "American criticism." Its object could not have been to aid the cause of "American criticism," because side by side with its editorial were two full columns of indiscriminate and unqualified puffs of recent publications. There was not a line of painstaking "criticism" in the whole mass—the only virtue of the nearly twenty different book notices crowded into two columns being their necessary brevity. It is simple charity to suppose that the practical example under that general subject of criticism which this "religious" paper artfully pretended to think so important as to demand the use of its leading editorial column, was assigned to its worst writer, and that even he merely glanced at the title-page and table of contents of the volumes reviewed.

Honest criticism is at once the attribute and the indication of an educated and refined literary taste. It is the impulsive act of an accomplished mind. An intelligent man is "nothing if not critical." It is only a canon of common experience that the more one is versed in his subject and the deeper he has progressed therein, the more natural and voluntary it is to exercise the critical faculty. Indeed, the thing unnatural would be *not* to criticise—the mere fact, meanwhile, that one man has observed, heard, read, reflected, more than another making his views all the more valuable. And when such almost unconscious and certainly unavoidable exercise of discernment between the good and bad, the false and the true, the sincere and the sham, is honestly and loyally put into print for general perusal, though the pride of the author reviewed be punctured a little, pray is not the public the gainer?

A common question asked of independent critics is, why they point out blemishes more assiduously than merits? The answer is obvious. There are enough people who are anxious to do the agreeable half of the task, and enough, too, who are ready to hide the disagreeable. The author and all his friends, the publisher and all his friends and patrons and dependents, are quite willing to point out excellences. The easy-going negligence of ordinary editors and writers of "notices," the very fear of the critic lest, by attack, his own ignorance and superficial perusal shall provoke exposure in return— these, and all the other causes already enumerated in this article, conspire to make it sure that the excellences of any book will have a better chance of celebration than its faults will run of exposure. Whatever is meritorious is likely to gain due honor and credit in our age of general reading and discussion and our avidity for amusement; the only fear is lest faults shall be deliberately concealed and errors in thought, fact, style, or language passed by which will impede the progress of American literature. People who beherald every new book with eulogistic bravado, and, after its appearance, bespatter it with indiscriminate and senseless praise, need not plume themselves on their performance. It is the pleasantest thing in the world not to offend by plain speech, and flattery is easy enough to use if one will condescend to use it. But why should those who belaud everything in the way of publications find fault with the genuine critic, who sets himself to the honest, painstaking labor of finding what is faulty in a book, and pointing it out to the author and to all authors and readers, for the benefit of all? This is a more onerous and ungracious task to perform than the other, but it is infinitely more valuable to the cause of American literature.

[*Round Table*, 27 January 1866]

12

[Slavery in M. L. Putnam's Novel]

Fifteen Days. An Extract from Edward Colvil's Journal.
Boston: Ticknor and Fields.

THIS is a work of fiction, in which the passion of love, so far from being the prime motive, as in other fictions, does not enter at all. The author seeks to reach, without other incident, one tragic event, and endeavors to make up for a want of adventure by the subtile analysis of character and the study of a civil problem. The novelty and courage of the attempt will attract the thoughtful reader, and will probably tempt him so far into the pages of the book, that he will find himself too deeply interested in its persons to part from them voluntarily. The national sin with which the author so pitilessly deals has been expiated by the whole nation, and is now no more; but its effects upon the guilty and guiltless victims, here alike so leniently treated, remain, and the question of slavery must always command attention till the question of reconstruction is settled.

In "Fifteen Days" the political influences of slavery are only very remotely considered, while the personal and social results of the system are examined with incisive acuteness united to a warmth of feeling which at last breaks forth into pathetic lament. Is not the tragedy, of which we discern the proportions only in looking back, indeed a fateful one? A young New-Englander, rich, handsome, generous, and thoroughly taught by books and by ample experience of the Old World and the New to honor men and freedom, passes a few days in a Slave State, in the midst of that cruel system which could progress only from bad to worse; to which reform was death, and which with the instinct of self-preservation punished all open attempts to ameliorate the relations of oppressor and oppressed, and permitted no kindness to exist but in the guise of severity or the tenderness of a good man for his beast; which boasted itself an aristocracy, and was an oligarchy of plebeian ignorance and meanness; which either dulled men's brains or chilled their hearts. In the presence of this system, Harry Dudley lingers long enough to rescue a slave and to die by the furious hand of the master,—a man in whose soul the best impulse was the love he bore his victim, and in whom the evil destiny of the drama triumphs.

From the conversation of Harry and the botanist, his friend, the author retrospectively develops in its full beauty a character illustrated in only one phase by the episode which the passages from Edward Colvil's journal cover, while she sketches with other touches, slight, but skilful, the people of a whole neighborhood, and the events of years. Doctor Borrow, the botanist, is made to pass, by insensible changes, from a learned indifference concerning slavery to eloquent and ardent argument against it, and thus to present the history of the process by which even science, the coldest element of our civilization, found itself at last unconsciously arrayed against a system long abhorrent to feeling. In the Doctor's talk with Westlake, we have a close and clear comparison of the origin and result of the civilizations of New England and the South, the high equality of the North and the mean aristocracy of the Slave States, and the Doctor's first perfect consciousness of loving the one and hating the other. The supposititious Mandingo's observations of the state of Europe at the time of opening the African slave-trade form a humorous protest against judgment of Africa by travellers' stories, and suggest more than a doubt whether the first men-stealers were better than their victims, and whether they conferred the boon of a higher civilization upon negroes by enslaving them. But the humor of the book, like its learning, is subordinated to the story, which is imbued with a sentiment not wanting in warmth because so noble and lofty. The friendship of Colvil and Dudley is less like the friendship between two men, than the affectionate tenderness of two women for each other; and the character of Dudley in its purity and elevation is sometimes elusive. The personality of Colvil is also rather shadowy; but the Doctor is human and tangible, and the other persons, however slightly indicated, are all real, and bear palpable witness, in their lives, to the influences of that system which, though cruel to the oppressed, wrought a ruin yet more terrible in the oppressor.

[*Atlantic Monthly*, July 1866]

13

[Charles Reade's Remarkable Novel]

Griffith Gaunt; or, Jealousy. By Charles Reade. With
Illustrations. Boston: Ticknor and Fields.

IN discussing the qualities of this remarkable novel before the readers of
"The Atlantic Monthly," we shall have an advantage not always enjoyed by
criticism; for we shall speak to an audience perfectly familiar with every detail
of the story, and shall not be troubled to *résumer* its events and characters.
There has been much doubt among many worthy people concerning Mr.
Reade's management of the moralities and proprieties, but no question at
all, we think, as to the wonderful power he has shown, and the interest he has
awakened. Even those who have blamed him have followed him eagerly,—
without doubt to see what crowning insult he would put upon decency, and
to be confirmed in their virtuous abhorrence of his work. It is to be hoped
that these have been disappointed, for it must be confessed that, in the
dénouement of the novel, others who totally differed from them in purpose
and opinion have been brought to some confusion.

It is not as a moralist that we have primarily to find fault with Mr. Reade,
but as an artist, for his moral would have been good if his art had been true.
The work, up to the conclusion of Catharine Gaunt's trial, is in all respects
too fine and high to provoke any reproach from us; after that, we can only
admire it as a piece of literary gallantry and desperate resolution. "C'est
magnifique; mais ce n'est pas la guerre." It is courageous, but it is not art. It
is because of the splendid *elan* in all Mr. Reade writes, that in his failure he
does not fall flat upon the compassion of his reader, as Mr. Dickens does with
his "Golden Dustman." But it is a failure, nevertheless; and it must become a
serious question in æsthetics how far the spellbound reader may be tortured
with an interest which the power awakening it is not adequate to gratify. Is it
generous, is it just in a novelist, to lift us up to a pitch of tragic frenzy, and
then drop us down into the last scene of a comic opera? We refuse to be
comforted by the fact that the novelist does not, perhaps, consciously mock
our expectation.

Let us take the moral of "Griffith Gaunt,"—so poignant and effective for
the most part,—and see how lamentably it suffers from the defective art of
the *dénouement*. In brief: up to the end of Mrs. Gaunt's trial we are presented
with a terrible image of the evils that jealousy, anger, and lies bring upon
their guilty and innocent victims. Griffith Gaunt is made to suffer—as men in
life suffer—a dreadful remorse and anguish for the crimes he has committed

and the falsehoods to which they have committed him. A man with a heart at first tender and true becomes a son of perdition, utterly incapable of tenderness and truth,—consciously held away from them by ever-cumulative force. The spectacle is not new,—it is old as sin itself; but it is here revealed with the freshest and most authentic power, and with a repelling efficacy which we have seldom seen equalled in literature. Mrs. Gaunt justly endures the trouble brought upon her by pride and unbridled bad temper, and unavoidably endures the consequences of another's wrong. Mercy Vint is a guiltless and lovely sacrifice to both almost equally.

What is the end? Mercy Vint is given in marriage to the honestest and faithfulest gentleman in the book, whose heroism we admire without envying. But in any case so good a woman would have achieved peace for herself, and it is at some cost to our regard for her entirety that we consent to see her rewarded by being made a nobleman's wife and the mother of nine children. In this character she lives a life less perfect and consequent than she might have led in a station less exalted, but distant from the circles in which she could not appear at the same time with the man who had infamously wronged her without exciting whispers painful to herself and embarrassing to her husband. Indeed, there seems to be rather more of vicarious expiation in her fate than the interests of population and of "young women who have been betrayed" have any right to demand.

Mrs. Gaunt fully expiates her error before her trial ends. But how of her husband? Mr. Reade seems to like his Griffith Gaunt, who is not to our mind, and who is never less worthy of happiness than at the moment when his wife forgives him. It is not that he is a bigamist and betrayer of innocence that his redemption seems impossible through the means employed; but how can Catharine Gaunt love a coward and sneak, even in the wisdom which a court of justice has taught her? This furious and stupid traitor is afraid to appear and save his wife lest he be branded in the hand; and we are to pardon him because, at no risk to himself, he gives the worthless blood of his veins to rescue her from death. If the fable teaches anything in Griffith Gaunt's case, it is this: Betray two noble women, and after some difficulty you shall get rid of one, be forgiven by the other, come into a handsome property, and have a large and interesting family. If the reader will take the fate of Griffith Gaunt and contrast it with that of Tito Melema, in "Romola," he shall see all the difference that passes between an artificial and an artistic solution of a moral problem.

Defective art is noticeable in the minor as well as the principal features of the *dénouement* of Griffith Gaunt. There is the case of the unhappy little baby of Mercy. It is plain that the infant is a stumbling-block in its mother's path to Neville Cross; but we have scarcely begun to lament its presence, when it is swiftly put to death by a special despatch from the obliging destiny of the *dénouement*. The event is a coincidence, to say the least, and is scarcely less an operation than the transfusion of blood by which Griffith Gaunt and his wife are preserved to a long life of happiness. But this part of the work is full of wonders. The cruel enchantments are all dissolved by more potent preternatural agencies, and a superhuman prosperity dwells alike with the just and the unjust,—Mrs. Ryder excepted, who will probably go to the Devil as some slight compensation for the loss of Griffith Gaunt.

But if the conclusion of the fiction is weak, how great it is in every other part! The management of the plot was so masterly, that the story proceeded without a pause or an improbability until the long fast of a month falling between the feasts of its publication became almost insupportable. It was a plot that grew naturally out of the characters, for humanity is prolific of events, and these characters are all human beings. They are not in the least anachronistic. They act and speak a great deal in the coarse fashion of the good old times. Griffith Gaunt is half tipsy when Kate plights her troth to him; and he is drunk upon an occasion not less solemn and interesting. They are of an age that was very gallant and brutal, that wore gold-lace upon its coat, and ever so much profanity upon its speech; and Mr. Reade has treated them with undeniable frankness and sincerity. Mercy Vint alone seems to belong to a better time; but then goodness and purity are the contemporaries of every generation, and, besides, Mercy Vint's puritan character is an exceptional phase of the life of the time. It is admirable to see in this fiction, as we often see in the world, how wise and refined religion makes an ignorant and lowly-bred person. As a retrospective study, Griffith Gaunt cannot be placed below Henry Esmond. As a study of passions and principles that do not change with civilizations, it is even more excellent. Griffith Gaunt himself is the most perfect figure in the book, because the plot does not at any period interfere with his growth. We start with a knowledge of the frankness and generosity native to a somewhat coarse texture of mind, and we readily perceive why a nature so prone to love and wrath should fall a helpless prey to jealousy, which is a thing altogether different from the suspicion of ungenerous spirits. It is jealousy which drives Griffith to deceive Mercy Vint, for even his desolation and his need of her consoling care cannot bring him to it, and it is only when his triumphing rival appears that this frank and kindly soul consents to enact a cruel lie. The crime committed, there is no longer virtue or courage in the man, and we see without surprise his cowardly reluctance to do the one brave and noble thing possible to him, lest he be arrested for bigamy. The letter, so weak and so boisterous, which he gives Mercy Vint to prove him alive before the court, is in keeping with the development of his character; and it is not unnatural that he should think the literal gift of his blood to his wife a sort of compensation and penance for his sins against her. The wonder is that the author should fall into the same error, as he seems to do.

The character of Kate Gaunt is treated in the *dénouement* with a violence which almost destroys its identity, but throughout the whole previous progress of the story it is a most artistic and consistent creation. From the beautiful girl, so virginal and dreamy and insecure of her destiny in the world, with her high aspirations and her high temper, there is a certain lapse to the handsome matron united with a man beneath her in mind and spirit, and assured of the commonplace fact that in her love and duty to him is her happiness; but as Love must often mate men and women unequally, it is perfectly natural that Love in her case should strive to keep his eyes shut when no longer blind. Great exigencies afterwards develop her character, and it gains in dignity and beauty from her misfortunes, and we do not again think compassionately of her till she is reunited with Griffith. In spite of all her faults, she is wonderfully charming. The reader himself falls in love with her, and perhaps a subtile sense of jealousy and personal loss mingles with his dissatisfaction in seeing her given up again to her unworthy husband. She should have been left a lovely and stately widow, to whom we could all have paid our court, without suffering too poignantly when Sir George Neville finally won her.

[*Atlantic Monthly*, December 1866]

14

[Lowell's Biglow Papers]

The Biglow Papers. Second Series. Ticknor and Fields.

"You kin spall an' punctooate thet as you please," says Mr. Biglow in sending to the editor of the Atlantic the last of the Biglow Papers; "I allus do, it kind of puts a noo soot of close onto a word, this ere funattick spellin' doos, an' takes 'em out of the prissen dress they wair in the Dixionary. Ef I squeeze the cents out of 'em, it 's the main thing, and wut they wuz made for; wut's left 's jest pummis." Whereby, we fear, Mr. Biglow may give the impression that it is not a dialect in which he writes his poems, but a language which he misspells and perverts by caprice or through ignorance, and thus discredit something of Mr. Lowell's exquisite introductory discourse. The feeble critic-folk who have gravely made our great humorist responsible for the clownish tricks in orthography of Artemus Ward, Josh Billings, and the like, scarcely needed to have such a doubt added to the confusion born in them.

After all, however, Mr. Biglow's carelessness and their dulness cannot greatly trouble the larger number of Mr. Lowell's admirers, who perceive the perfect art and lawful nature of his quaintest and most daring drollery. At the door of Mr. Thackeray must lie the charge of bastardy in question, for he was the first to create the merry monsters now so common in literature. In Charles Yellowplush, he caricatured the man of a certain calling, and by the rule of unreason gifted him with a laboriously fantastic orthography; and Artemus Ward and Nasby are merely local variations of the same idea. The showman and the confederate gospeller make us laugh by their typographical pleasantry; they are neither of them without wit; and for the present they have a sort of reality; but they are of a stuff wholly different from that of Hosea Biglow, who is the type of a civilization, and who expresses, in a genuine vernacular, the true feeling, the racy humor, and the mother-wit of Yankee-land. His characteristic excellences are likely to survive for a long time the dialect which gives them utterance, though this is by no means evanescent; for Hosea Biglow is almost as much at home now in the rural speech of Northern Ohio, Indiana, and Illinois, as in that of New England. Yet his dialect must one day cease to be spoken; and when posterity read him, as Englishmen do Burns, for the imperishable quality of his humor and sentiment, we fear that they will be somewhat puzzled to recall the immortal name of Petroleum V. Nasby, to whom he resigns the office of political satire.

Alas! has the king really abdicated? Then let us have a republic of humor, and make each one his own jokes hereafter. As for Nasby, he is not of the blood. He is wittier and better-hearted than Artemus Ward, and he has generosity of purpose and elevation of aim, but he is only a moralized merry-andrew; whereas one may lift his glance from the smiling lips of the Yankee minstrel, and behold his honest eyes full of self-respectful thought, and that complement of humor, pathos,—without which your jester is but a sorry antic. He himself hardly knows whether his next word is to be in shower or shine. But how sovereignly he passes from one mood to the other, or then gives us a strain mixed of both,—an interfusion of delight and pain, such as we feel in reading that perfect poem explaining to the public his long silence! It is his great art to lift us above the parties and persons he satirizes, and confront us with their errors; and if his wit seems to play with any theme too long, there is some surprise awaiting us like that which, in the "Speech in March Meetin'," turns us from the droll aspects of Mr. Johnson's defection to the thrilling and appealing spectacle of a nation's life, love, and hope possibly lost in the neglect of a Heaven-given occasion:—

> "I seem to hear a whisperin' in the air,
> A sighin' like of unconsoled despair,
> That comes from nowhere an' from everywhere,
> An' seems to say, 'Why died we? warn't it, then,
> To settle, once for all, that men wuz men?
> O, airth's sweet cup snetched from us barely tasted,
> The grave's real chill is feelin' life wuz wasted!
> O, you we lef', long-lingerin' et the door,
> Lovin' you best, coz we loved Her the more,
> That Death, not we, had conquered, we should feel
> Ef she upon our memory turned her heel,
> An' unregretful throwed us all away
> To flaunt it in a Blind Man's Holiday.' "

There never was political satire so thoroughly humane as Hosea Biglow's; there never was satire so noble before. The purpose is never once degraded; and where the feeling deepens, as in the passage we have quoted, the dialect fades to an accent, and the verse of the supposed rustic is, as his prayer would be, in speech natural, pure, solemn, and strong. It is always strong. It would be hard to find a weak line, or a line of wandering significance, in the whole book; and the reader who threw a word away would find himself a thought the poorer. We shall not repeat here the cheapened phrase of compliment, which seems more flimsy and unreal than ever in its application to the robust life of such poetry. If we do not find fault, it is because we see everything to admire, and nothing to blame. Quick, sharp wit, pervading humor, trenchant logic, sustained feeling,—well, we come to the poverty of critical good-nature in spite of ourselves, and it is a satisfaction to know that the reviewed can suffer nothing from it, but will remain as honestly fresh, original, and great as if we had not sought to label his fine qualities.

It is not as mere satire, however, that the Biglow Papers are to be valued. The First and Second Series form a creative fiction of unique excellence. The love for nature, so conspicuous in these later poems, is of the simplest and manliest expressed in literature. The four seasons are not patronized, nor the reader bored; but we enjoy the very woods and fields in Hosea Biglow's quaintly and subtly faithful feeling for them. They are justly subordinate to him, however, and we are not suffered to forget Mr. Lowell's creed, that human nature is the nature best worth celebrating. The landscape is but the setting for Jaalam,—shrewd, honest, moral, angular,—Hosea Biglow munici-palized. The place should be on the maps, for it has as absolute existence as any in New England, and its people by slight but unerring touches are made as real. For ourselves, we intend to spend part of our next vacation at Jaalam, and shall visit the grave of the Reverend Homer Wilbur, for whose character we have conceived the highest regard, and whose death we regret not less keenly than Hosea Biglow's resolution to write no more. It would have been a pleasure—which we shall now never enjoy—to enter the study of the good minister, and tell him how thoroughly we had learned to know him through his letters introducing Mr. Biglow's effusions, and how we had thus even come to take an interest in Jaalam's shadowy antiquities. We should have esteemed it a privilege to have his views of the political situation; and if we had turned to talk of literature, we should have been glad to hear an admirer of the classic Pope give his notion of the classic Swinburne.

Somewhere in the South, Birdofredum Sawin must be lingering,—the most high-toned and low-principled of the reconstructed. In his character Mr. Lowell has presented us with so faultless an image of what Pure Cussed-ness works in the shrewd and humorous Yankee nature, that we hope not even the public favor shall prevent his appearance as an original Union man. The completion of the ballad of "The Courtin'" is a benefaction very stimu-lating to desire for whatever the author has not absolutely refused to give us.

As for the Introduction to this series of the Biglow Papers, the wonder is how anything so curiously learned and instructive could be made so deli-cious. Most of us will never appreciate fully the cost of what is so lightly and gracefully offered of the fruit of philological research; but few readers will fail to estimate aright the spirit which pervades the whole prologue. Mr. Lowell pauses just before the point where those not sharing the original enthusiasm might be fatigued with the study of words and phrases, and yet possesses his reader of more portable, trustworthy knowledge of American-isms than is elsewhere to be found. The instances of national and local hu-mor given are perfect; and Mr. Lowell's reserve in attempting to define American humor—which must remain, like all humor, an affair of percep-tion rather than expression—might teach something to our Transatlantic friends, who suppose it to be merely a quality of exaggeration. We enjoy, quite as well as even the discreet learning of this Introduction, such glimpses as the author chooses to give us of his purpose in writing the Biglow Papers, and in adopting the Yankee dialect for his expression, as well as of his methods of studying this dialect. Some slight defence he makes of points assailed in his work; but for the most part it is effortless, familiar talk with his readers, always significant, but persistent in nothing, and in tone as full and rich as the best talk of Montaigne or Cervantes.

[*Atlantic Monthly*, January 1867]

15

[Melville's Battle-Pieces]

Battle-Pieces and Aspects of the War. By Herman Melville.
New York: Harper and Brothers.

Mʀ. Melville's work possesses the negative virtues of originality in such degree that it not only reminds you of no poetry you have read, but of no life you have known. Is it possible—you ask yourself, after running over all these celebrative, inscriptive, and memorial verses—that there has really been a great war, with battles fought by men and bewailed by women? Or is it only that Mr. Melville's inner consciousness has been perturbed, and filled with the phantasms of enlistments, marches, fights in the air, parenthetic bulletin-boards, and tortured humanity shedding, not words and blood, but words alone?

Mr. Melville chooses you a simple and touching theme, like that of the young officer going from his bride to hunt Mosby in the forest, and being brought back to her with a guerilla's bullet in his heart,—a theme warm with human interests of love, war, and grief, and picturesque with greenwood lights and shadows,—and straight enchants it into a mystery of thirty-eight stanzas, each of which diligently repeats the name of Mosby, and deepens the spell, until you are lost to every sense of time or place, and become as callous at the end as the poet must have been at the beginning to all feeling involved, doubting that

"The living and the dead are but as pictures."

Here lies the fault. Mr. Melville's skill is so great that we fear he has not often felt the things of which he writes, since with all his skill he fails to move us. In some respects we find his poems admirable. He treats events as realistically as one can to whom they seem to have presented themselves as dreams; but at last they remain vagaries, and are none the more substantial because they have a modern speech and motion. We believe ghosts are not a whit more tangible now that they submit to be photographed in the sack-coats and hoop-skirts of this life, than before they left off winding-sheets, and disappeared if you spoke to them.

With certain moods or abstractions of the common mind during the war, Mr. Melville's faculty is well fitted to deal: the unrest, the strangeness and solitude, to which the first sense of the great danger reduced all souls, are reflected in his verse, and whatever purely mystic aspect occurrences had seems to have been felt by this poet, so little capable of giving their positive likeness.

The sentiment and character of the book are perhaps as well shown in its first poem as in any other part of it. Mr. Melville calls the verses "The Portent (1859)"; but we imagine he sees the portent, as most portents are seen, after the event portended.

> "Hanging from the beam,
>   Slowly swaying (such the law),
> Gaunt the shadow on your green,
>   Shenandoah!
> The cut is on the crown
> (Lo, John Brown),
> And the stabs shall heal no more.
>
> "Hidden in the cap
>   Is the anguish none can draw;
> So your future veils its face,
>   Shenandoah!
> But the streaming beard is shown
> (Weird John Brown),
> The meteor of the war."

There is not much of John Brown in this, but, as we intimated, a good deal of Mr. Melville's method, and some fine touches of picturesque poetry. Indeed, the book is full of pictures of many kinds,—often good,—though all with an heroic quality of remoteness, separating our weak human feelings from them by trackless distances. Take this of the death of General Lyon's horse a few moments before he was himself struck at Springfield,—a bit as far off from us as any of Ossian's, but undeniably noble:—

> "There came a sound like the slitting of air
>   By a swift sharp sword—
> A rush of the sound; and the sleek chest broad
>   Of black Orion
> Heaved, and was fixed; the dead mane waved toward Lyon."

We have never seen anywhere so true and beautiful a picture as the following of that sublime and thrilling sight,—a great body of soldiers marching:—

> "The bladed guns are gleaming—
>   Drift in lengthened trim,
> Files on files for hazy miles
>   Nebulously dim."

A tender and subtile music is felt in many of the verses, and the eccentric metres are gracefully managed. We received from the following lines a pleasure which may perhaps fail to reach the reader, taking them from their context in the description of a hunt for guerillas, in the ballad already mentioned:—

> "The morning-bugles lonely play,
>   Lonely the evening-bugle calls—
> Unanswered voices in the wild;
>   The settled hush of birds in nest
>   Becharms, and all the wood enthralls:
>   Memory's self is so beguiled
>   That Mosby seems a satyr's child."

He does so; and the other persons in Mr. Melville's poetry seem as widely removed as he from our actual life. If all the Rebels were as pleasingly impalpable as those the poet portrays, we could forgive them without a pang, and admit them to Congress without a test-oath of any kind.

[*Atlantic Monthly*, February 1867]

16

[Henry Wadsworth Longfellow]

1. *The Poetical Works of Henry Wadsworth Longfellow.*
Revised Edition. Boston: Ticknor and Fields. 1866. 4
vols. 16mo.
2. *The Prose Works of Henry Wadsworth Longfellow.*
Revised Edition. Boston: Ticknor and Fields. 1866. 3
vols. 16mo.

THE publication of a complete and uniform edition of Mr. Longfellow's
Works is an event which suggests to us not so much question as
acknowledgment of his excellence, and we have here rather to celebrate a
fame already assured than to enter upon a critical analysis of his poetry. It is
yet too soon to measure the whole obligation of American letters to him, and
it seems somewhat late to reason minutely of the fact of his genius. We doubt
if criticism be the hazel wand that points to the hidden sources of the living
springs; but even if it were so, we should think it rather idle to flourish it with
an air of divination over clearness and sweetness that long ago sparkled into
the sun. It is not necessary to dwell upon Mr. Longfellow's delicate and
beautiful feeling,

> "As pure as water and as good as bread,"

or his exquisite intellectual refinement, which has troubled shallowness before now with doubts of his original power. Nor is it possible for our time to
determine accurately the greatness of this original power, or to separate it
from the manifold acquirements interwoven with it. Enough that the whole is
admirable, and that the quickening faculty is unmistakable.

There is something, indeed, in all the aspects of these familiar poems that
appeals to us in proof of the purely creative and poetical nature of Mr.
Longfellow's mind. It is very noticeable how large is the proportion of his
dramatic and narrative pieces, and how, when obeying his own instincts, he
seems always to have chosen the literary form faithfulest to life, which is
primarily a story and not a sermon or a lecture. Consciousness of the truth
that only the art which recounts can fully and lastingly interest all men, is
dominant in him; yet he is not entirely free from the lingering superstition,
come down to us from the artistic depravity of the last century, that poetry
can teach by appealing to the logical faculties instead of the imagination. So,
while his longer poems are all sustained by the recital or exhibition of events,
and by far the greater number of his shorter pieces have something of drama
or narrative in them, and of course point their own moral, he has himself
sometimes "moralized his song," and given us didactic verses, which have
among his other poems about the same relative value that his occasional

criticisms have among his travel-sketches and prose romances. Mr. Longfellow has unerring perceptions as regards his own work, but he has not the exegetic nor the critical temperament. It is the creative habit of his mind not to consider things as in themselves beautiful or ugly, but rather as elements from which a beautiful effect may or may not be produced. Wherever he has to assemble, and narrate, or present, he is charming, and master of his reader. When he has to declare or to decide, he betrays the poet's strangeness to the office of the preacher and the critic, and fails of his wonted effect.

We do not mean, then, great praise of the didactic poems of Mr. Longfellow when we say that they please us better than most other poems of the kind: for of all that he has written, they alone seem to us wanting in original thought. They have, however, such a characteristic manner and music, that they have always enjoyed a very undue share of association with his name. As a poet's poorest is easiest to be copied, Mr. Longfellow's didactic vein has been wrought by imitation and repetition till its original product has been made tedious to many, and question of the value of all his work has been mooted by critics in the country where Mr. Swinburne has become great. The fatality is not a strange one;

"All can raise the flowers now,
    For all have got the seed";

"And now again the people
    Call it but a weed,"—

laments another master of our time, whom this fatality has befallen. Yet it is only an annual flower that ripens seeds for thieves to steal, and, as we have hinted, not the gardener's best. There is little danger that perennials like the "Evangeline" and "The Golden Legend" shall be generally cheapened by reproduction, or that "Hyperion" and "Kavanagh" shall cease to be sole in their beauty.

Of these, and of all the principal works of Mr. Longfellow, it is remarkable how they continue to hold the first place in the kinds of literature to which they belong. The "Hiawatha," indeed, is unique, whatever its absolute merit may be, or its worth as compared with that of the other poems of its author, or of contemporary poets. For ourselves, we are inclined to rate it high, because of its courage and truth. It is not a copy of Indian life, but it is better than a copy, for in dealing with the life of an untamable race in the light of its own wild beauty of legend and custom, the poet works in a spirit of the highest fidelity to art. He does not portray savage squalor and brutality and vileness, as Greek art would not reproduce the ugliness that was unquestionably commoner than beauty among Greek men and women. The result is a reproduction of Indian life, none the less typical because idealized, and infinitely better than all other pictures of it. The "Hiawatha" leaves the Indians to the reason as it found them, savages; but it restores them to the fancy, and it annihilates at once the conventional Redman of the novelists, and the Varmint of the borderers, rehabilitating the shadowy past of our primeval wilderness with a poetic, simple, natural, sylvan life.

In like manner "The Courtship of Miles Standish" restores an image of Puritan days, less austere and gloomy than those Hawthorne has given, but not less fascinating, and not, we believe, less faithful; while it is again in its conception a poem as original as the "Hiawatha" or the "Evangeline." This last, which we think the best of all Mr. Longfellow's poems, if not the best poem of our age, is to be prized for many different reasons that will suggest themselves to the reader, but for none more, it seems to us, than for its creative gift of living human interest to unstoried places. The beings of the poet's fancy, who are akin to us in faith, in time, and capacity of suffering and enjoyment, traverse vast silent spaces of continent with scarce a memory of our race, and leave them articulate and full of association. It is not much that everywhere in French Canada the traveller should look to see Evangeline, and Gabriel Lajeunesse, and Basil the Blacksmith, and Father Felician, in the quaint towns of dormer-windowed cottages and among the picturesque peasants in the fields; but it is much that, wherever he goes upon the great rivers of the West, his reveries should be full of them only, and that the poem should chant its music in his ear, till it breathes away all the present, and makes him contemporary and companion of the exiles who rowed their cumbrous boat

> "far down the Beautiful River,
> Past the Ohio shore, and past the mouth of the Wabash,
> Into the golden stream of the broad and swift Mississippi."

It is much that one poem should have so peopled these scenes that the mind seeks there no other presences than those it suggests.

"Kavanagh," in dealing with the New England village-life of our own time, or of the transitional period that passed with the introduction of railways, is also very successful. Indeed, it seems to us as yet quite unapproached, by the multitude of New England romances that have followed it, in a certain delicate truthfulness, as it is likely to remain unsurpassed in its light humor and pensive grace. In "Kavanagh," and in the poems mentioned, as well as many shorter poems, Mr. Longfellow has responded to a very natural and evident longing of the popular heart for something like recognition of the national place and home in literature, while at other times he has been true to as genuine an impulse of our complex Americanism, where he has dealt with the beautiful remote from us in everything but sympathy.

The whole English-speaking world, and great part of Continental Europe, have naturalized and translated his poetry; yet we feel so deeply his intense nationality that we find it hard to consider his work except as related to our growth in the best forms of civilization. Although our poetic literature did not actually begin with him, he is nevertheless to be accounted first among those who enlarged and enriched it, and lifted it from a conceited provincialism into a generous universality. He had faith from the beginning in the native sense of beauty which underlies all our busy, shrewd, hard civilization, and which makes us as a people at this moment the foremost in the world in appreciation of letters which appeal to the sentiment and the imagination. He in greater degree than any other has discerned that our separation from the past affords vantage-ground on which we may enjoy it undisturbed; that we are indeed its absolute heirs, with a possession untroubled by the mortmains that sadden and confuse the modern life of Europe. From a consciousness of this kind came "The Golden Legend," where the old picturesque, superstitious, mystical, devoted spirit of mediæval days breathes again in an atmosphere which it never darkened, and in which the corporeal decay of dead errors and obsolete good has not left a taint of pestilence. Above all, in this sentiment is written the lovely romance of "Hyperion,"—a book which it is hard to mention without some expression of delight in its style. Its prose, vibrant, harmonious, sustained, has not too often a rhythmic character, though it is the prose of a poet, and is full of poetic imagery and that kind of metaphor which flows naturally into verse. It has sometimes the movement of imaginative German prose; yet it is always pure English. At other times, for uncloying sweetness of tone it deserves to match with the Italian of Boccaccio, while its numerous briefer periods give it a variety which the work of the elder master has not. After the first perusal of the book the reader is so taken with its music, that to open it at any place is to yield to a delicious fascination. There is in the perfect adaptation of the style to the subject a felicity equal to that which associates a poetic thought with its appropriate measure: there is nothing to be forgiven, there is everything to be enjoyed. But it is another value of the book which we wish to note here in the fact that, while none of its scenes are laid in America, its inspiration and its chief person are wholly and immutably American. The romance is colored and perfumed through and through with the literature and life of Europe, yet it comes from the heart of Americanism, and none but Americans can appreciate its sentiment thoroughly; for in Paul Flemming is embodied the affection for the historic and the traditional which is the genuine fruit of our soil, and which contrasts so vividly with the indifference of Europeans themselves to such things. "It often astonishes me," says the Baron to Flemming, "that, coming from that green world of yours beyond the sea, you should feel so much interest in these old things,—nay, at times seem so to have drunk in their spirit as really to live in the times of old. For my part, I do not see what charm there is in the pale and wrinkled countenance of the past, so to entice the soul of a young man." The puzzled Baron speaks for the polite Europe of every traveller's acquaintance. In another place our author had already spoken for the America thus addressed: "I, too, have been a pilgrim of Outre-Mer, for to my youthful imagination the Old World was a kind of Holy Land";—in which sense all Americans are pilgrims of Outre-Mer as certainly as they are generous and refined.

There was early a revolt in Mr. Longfellow's mind against the theory once cherished, of a native literature corresponding to American geography and natural history; and he was one of the first to ridicule conceptions that have since become the laughing-stock of criticism. This poet, so essentially of our time and country, and with so great innate power, has always felt that beauty, from whatever source it came, was as little to be shut out of our hearts as the races of men seeking homes and citizenship among us were to be refused by our polity; and he has delighted us with charms won from the poets of all times and countries, though chiefly from those he seems to have loved most,—the German romantic poets. With these, indeed, he had a natural affinity, the reason for which appears to the student in the fact that modern German romance was largely English in its inspiration. The poets of this school wrought in the ways that have amplified all modern literatures. The springs of Italian song, from which the wells of our English were so long and often filled, from Chaucer's time to Milton's, had been enriched by their course through Greek and Latin soil, and the Germans, in their turn, drank from what was best in English letters. But Mr. Longfellow, in drawing so deeply as he has done from German romance, has not only brought us back something of our own again, but has also introduced new elements with it. Some delicate graces of peculiarly German poetry are through his influence as much at home among us as the Christmas-tree, and their popularity has greatly helped us toward the knowledge that in vague suggestion and subtle sentiment is a charm that wins the heart of downrightness and reality. A great poet educates his nation by developing its original capacities for intellectual pleasure; and Mr. Longfellow's success in imbuing Americans with a feeling for unfamiliar effects in literary art, contemporaneous with much laborious failure on the part of others to accustom our taste to those peculiarities of the German mind which they have admired, is proof of his finer perception and wiser judgment. We remain almost wholly unaffected by efforts to infuse a liking for any characteristics of German literature except those which Mr. Longfellow has brought us from the poets.

Somewhat curiously contrasting with the earnest and often pensive cast of our author's best work, and the unpalliated moralization of his poorest, is a quality we note in him, and find very rare among later writers of the English tongue,—whom, indeed, he resembles little in any way. This is a certain beautiful gayety, which is to humor somewhat as the bouquet is to the body of wine. It is an effect that seems to have its spring rather in the poet's heart than brain, and it pleases through mere will of pleasing. It is the breath of the airiest talk, a grace of the social Continental life, the last and least definable charm of perfect culture and maturity. It appears among the poems chiefly in "The Golden Legend," where it seems to be the poet's own nature playing irrepressibly through the story, and in the Interludes of "The Wayside Inn," where he speaks familiarly with the reader. We find it in "Kavanagh," though that is on the whole a pensive book, and sometimes also in

"Hyperion." But this mature grace struck us most of all in the author's first book, "Outre-Mer."

It is only one of many flavors of ripeness in his earlier productions. Indeed, it appears to us that his art never betrays the crudeness or imperfection of essay. It was excellent in the beginning, and its last exercise is singularly like its first. He has had from the beginning but one manner. In his latest books we are aware of the same magic that charmed us of yore, and we discern that this *goldene Zeit die nicht rostet* is not an *ewige Jugend* only when we contrast such poems as "The Bridge" and "The Bridge of Cloud," which have all the pathetic difference of youth and age in their likeness. The poet keeps throughout the grace and subtile power of the past; he keeps all that was ever his own, even to the love of profuse simile, and the quaint doubt of his reader implied by the elaborated meaning; and he loses only the tints and flavors not thoroughly assimilated or not native in him. Throughout is the same habit of recondite and scholarly allusion, the same quick sympathy with the beautiful in simple and common things, the same universality, the same tenderness for country and for home. Over all presides individuality superior to accidents of resemblance, and distinguishing each poem with traits unmistakably and only the author's; and the equality in the long procession of his beautiful thoughts never wearies, but is like that of some fine bass-relief, in which the varying allegory reveals one manner and many inspirations.

Together with this peculiar artistic equality in the poems of Mr. Longfellow is a spiritual maturity, which the reader cannot fail to notice. As there never has been anything unripe or decrepit in this master's art, so there never has been anything crude or faltering in his devotion to greatness and purity in life. His work is not the record of a career beginning in generous and impossible dreams, and ending in sordid doubt and pitiful despite; nor the history of a soul born to spiritual poverty, and working at last into tardy hopes and sympathies which scarcely suffice to discharge the errors of the past. These books tell of a soul clothed at once in humane affections and divine aspirations, of a poetic nature filled with conscious and instinctive reverence for the supreme office of poetry in the world. They form, indeed, so perfect a biography of the author, that, if one knew nothing of his literary life, here one might read more than could otherwise be told of its usefulness and beauty. Here is the story of blithe acquaintance with Latin lands and literature, and the exultation of a young man's heart and brain in their ancient scenes and ever-youthful songs; here is hinted, in a strain graver, but not less sweet, and even more enthusiastic, friendship with German romance, old and new, life in the home of sentiment, and growth in learning as graceful and easy as it is wide; here is the half-pensive serenity of the studious poet as he turns the key upon his books, and saunters forth into the green by-ways and elmy streets of the New England life about his gates. This poet is the traveller of the wide realm of thought, the world of imagination; he has touched at all the sunny Mediterranean and Adriatic ports; all the French and Spanish coasts are known to him; he brings wealth from the frozen Scandinavian lands as rare as the ivory set in the beryl of the immemorial icebergs; he gathers flotsam from the bays and inlets, the lakes and rivers of home. Full of the world, he transmutes his large experience and far-brought learning into the poems we know, with a secure and patient art that malice or envy never could mar, and that has never acknowledged enmity with any man. Indeed, the silence of all these books concerning things that usually embitter poet's lives is not their least significant comment upon the author's wisdom and good-heartedness. His growing fame did not fail to create him foes; but if few poets have been more repeatedly assailed than he, none has been so willing to leave his defence entirely to time.

It is, of course, not the poet's merely literary life that is recorded in his books. He who touches the hearts of others must write from his own, and doubtless the songs of a true poet preserve the memory, not only of all the events, but of all the moods of his life. They must needs commemorate his sacredest and inmost experiences,—his joy and his sorrow, his loss and his gain, the love dear and the death sore to him,—and thus again form his truest biography. But the hospitality that invites the whole world home is exquisitely proud and shy, and its house is built like those old palaces in which a secret gallery was made for the musicians, and gay or plaintive music from an invisible source delighted the banqueting guests. The poet's courteous guests will be decently content with their pleasure, and may not seek to know the hidden impulse of his songs. We could not, indeed, inquire too curiously without self-betrayal; for if this poet's songs are the history of his inner life, are they not equally history of the lives of us who have grown to be men and women since he began to sing?

It is certainly one of the great privileges of a beloved poet to have his thoughts so interwoven with his readers' days, that, looking back, they seem not so much to have read his work as to have lived it, and that they largely recall themselves, remembering what and where they were, and how they fared when they first read such and such a poem of his. Perhaps it will be one of the compensations of the future which the poet shall inherit, that those whom he has delighted shall pay him, in language purged alike of flattery and of shame, the homage of their entire gratitude. There is an inadequate longing in every one who approaches a poet's presence to declare something of this obligation, and to confide a sense of identified sympathies. But the occasion tricks poet and admirer alike, and slips away, and nothing has been said. The confidence too sacred to be shared with a third, which was to have celebrated the intimacy established in many years of silent communion, is destined not to be uttered; and each reader must be content to express only that which may be spoken without awkwardness in the acclaim of a common voice.

As we submit ourselves to some such condition here, we are sensible how small part all that we have written is of the tribute due the master whose greatness has tended to the goodness and happiness of men in so potent and fine a degree that he has not only made the world wiser and pleasanter, but has not added a word's weight to the bitterness and evil of any soul in it.

[*North American Review*, April 1867]

17

Mr. Longfellow's Translation of the Divine Comedy.

IN our first article on this translation we half promised ourselves the pleasure of comparing the different versions of certain passages with that of Mr. Longfellow; but we intended this to be rather in witness of the fidelity than of the beauty of Mr. Longfellow's work. The sense of this beauty must be left to the English reader; if he does not find the work pleasing in itself as an English poem, he cannot be expected to like it, and he could not be blamed if he preferred the fidelity of an interlinear, literal prose translation before all that Mr. Longfellow has achieved. The difficult problem which our translator proposed himself remains unsolved if, with his perfect loyalty to his original, he has not united poetic perceptions and sympathies far transcending the scholar's faculty. We believe he has done this, and we accept the result of his labors as a solution of the problem. We think his translation incomparably the best that has been made. Whether it is the best that can be made, remains for proof. Man is so constituted that probably every one of Mr. Longfellow's Italian-reading critics will feel that he could better it if he would, and will probably reserve his effort for that moment of leisure when mortals purpose to amend themselves.

There is abroad, together with the schoolmaster who half educates the popular mind, a shrewd doubt whether a poet of Mr. Longfellow's supposed essential gentleness and sweetness could possibly translate a poet of Dante's supposed essential ruggedness and fierceness. Somehow, people have been taught to look upon Dante as a monster of extraordinary force and activity, who is for ever doing prodigies of vigor; like a statue of the worst Renaissance period all tense with muscular action, whatever mood it represents. We need not pause to combat this notion, or the doubt born of it, further than to explain that in passages of peculiar force Mr. Longfellow's task must have been simplified, for he had there merely to give the exact equivalent of the Italian in a language of superior directness and compactness. It is probable that the translator's patient and exquisite art was as severely tasked to render lines of narrative, of description, and of argument as the fiercest outburst of his author's wrath or scorn. There is also quite as much of scholarly skill and poetic sympathy demanded by the softer and more lyrical moods of Dante as by his dramatic strokes. In the nineteenth canto of the "Purgatorio" is that song of the siren to translate which, as Mr. Longfellow has translated it, must be, as we think, a costlier triumph than any six of the "strongest" lines in the "Inferno:"

> " 'Io son,' cantava, 'Io son dolce Sirena,
>   'I am,' she sang, 'I am the siren sweet,
>   Che i marinari in mezzo il mar dismago,
>   Who mariners amid the main unman,
>   Tanto son di piacere a sentir piena.
>   So full am I of pleasantness to hear.
>   Io trassi Ulisse del suo cammin vago
>   I drew Ulysses from his wandering way
>   Al canto mio; e qual meco s' ausa
>   Unto my song, and he who dwells with me,
>   Rado sen parte, sì tutto l'appago.
>   Seldom departs, so wholly I content him.' "

A siren's song, indeed, and a perfect echo of the meaning and the music of the Italian! Is it not amusing after this to read it in Cary's translation?

> " 'I,' thus she sang,
>   'I am the Siren, she who mariners
>   On the wide sea are wildered when they hear:
>   Such fulness of delight the listener feels.
>   I from his course Ulysses by my lay
>   Enchanted drew. Whoe'er frequents me once
>   Parts seldom; so I charm him, and his heart
>   Contented knows no void.' "

How Mr. Longfellow meets the complex difficulties of his work will be seen, we think, in an extract from the episode of Ugolino, where there is a fusion of the qualities of picturesqueness and drama which form so great a part of Dante's genius. The reader recalls how Ugolino, relating to the poet his imprisonment in the Tower of Famine, breaks forth:

> "Cruel, indeed, art thou, if yet thou grieve not,
>   Thinking of what my heart foreboded me,
>   And weep'st thou not, what art thou wont to weep at?
> They were awake now, and the hour drew nigh
>   At which our food used to be brought to us,
>   And through his dream was each one apprehensive;
> And I heard locking up the under door
>   Of the horrible tower; whereat, without a word,
>   I gazed into the faces of my sons.
> I wept not, I within so turned to stone;
>   They wept; and darling little Anselm mine
>   Said, 'Thou dost gaze so, father, what doth ail thee?'
> Still not a tear I shed, nor answer made
>   All of that day, nor yet the night thereafter,

Until another sun rose on the world.
As now a little glimmer made its way
  Into the dolorous prison, and I saw
  Upon four faces my own very aspect,
Both of my hands in agony I bit;
  And, thinking that I did it from desire
  Of eating, on a sudden they uprose,
And said they: 'Father, much less pain 't will give us
  If thou do eat of us; thyself didst clothe us
  With this poor flesh, and do thou strip it off.'
I calmed me then, not to make them more sad;
  That day we all were silent, and the next.
  Ah! obdurate earth, wherefore didst thou not open?
When we had come unto the fourth day, Gaddo
  Threw himself down outstretched before my feet,
  Saying, 'My father, why dost thou not help me?'
And there he died; and, as thou seest me,
  I saw the three fall one by one, between
  The fifth day and the sixth; whence I betook me,
Already blind, to groping over each,
  And three days called them after they were dead;
  Then hunger did what sorrow could not do."

Turning from this to the different English versions of the same lines, it is hard to see where any in any part equals it, while in their entirety it is quite idle to compare them. The last terzines:

"Quivi morì, e come tu mi vedi
  Vid' io cascar li tre ad uno ad uno
  Tra 'l quinto dì e 'l sesto; ond' io mi diedi
Già cieco a brancolar sovra ciascuno,
  E tre dì gli chiamai, poich' e' fur morti:
  Poscia più che'l dolor potè il digiuno,"

are thus translated by Cary:

            "There he died; and e'en
Plainly as thou seest me saw I the three
Fall one by one 'twixt the fifth day and the sixth:
Whence I betook me, now grown blind, to grope
Over them all, and for three days aloud
Called on them who were dead. Then fasting got
The mastery of grief."

Mr. Ford, who has rendered this episode well and with a due sense of its beauties, must say for his rhyme's sake,

"I did not weep, turned marble in my woe;"

> "Frantic with grief I bit my hands, and they
> Deeming that hunger made me furious grow;"

> "Then hunger, more than sorrow, finished all;"

missing in each line, and throughout the whole, some delicate meaning and subtle grace which Mr. Longfellow gives us.

> "Three days upon the dead my cries resound,
> Then grief no longer could with hunger cope,"

sings Mr. Brooksbank, who seems to have here an eye rather to the title of Dante's whole work than his local meaning.

Mr. Cayley is brought by his *terza rima*, if nothing worse, to the horrible pass below:

> "Then did I both my hands for fury gnaw.
> But they perceiving me, rose up amain,
> Believing I had done so for my maw."

The version of this episode by Mrs. Ramsay is one of the most pleasing of the rhymed translations, and is rather faithful, but the strong figure,

> "Tu ne vestisti
> "Queste misere carni e tu ne spoglia,"

is paraphrased,

> "From thee we had
> These wretched bodies; take them back again;"

and throughout the version there is sacrifice of light and delicate meanings in which there is much Dante lost.

Mr. Wright's translation is bad, almost of course—so bad that we must give the whole of it if we would give a full sense of its absurdity. Happily this is not necessary.

> "Thou gav'st us birth,"

say the children, in language suited to their delirious state, and otherwise his translation is weakened, inflated, and distorted.

Not one of these translators, however free with the original, has won a grace beyond the reach of Mr. Longfellow's fidelity; but all fall as far below him in beauty of diction and poetic dignity as they do in loyalty to Dante. On comparing the version of our translator with that of Mr. Rossetti, who has proceeded upon the same principle of perfect literality and line-for-line rendering, it is very remarkable that in the whole thirty-six verses cited only one verse should be found the same in both versions. Mr. Longfellow is uniformly more faithful than Mr. Rossetti, and that he is more artistic and spirited, we suppose no one will deny who looks at the work of both. We do not quote Mr. Rossetti's version of this passage; but we can equally well exhibit the difference between his performance and that of Mr. Longfellow in the episode of Francesca:

LONGFELLOW.

" 'Sitteth the city, wherein I was born,
    Upon the sea-shore where the Po descends
    To rest in peace with all his retinue.
Love, that on gentle heart doth swiftly seize,
    Seized this man for the person beautiful
    That was ta'en from me, and still the mode offends me.
Love, that exempts no one beloved from loving,
    Seized me with pleasure of this man so strongly
    That, as thou seest, it doth not yet desert me;
Love has conducted us unto one death;
    Caïna waiteth him who quenched our life!'
    These words were borne along from them to us.
As soon as I had heard those souls tormented,
    I bowed my face, and so long held it down
    Until the Poet said to me, 'What thinkest?'
When I made answer, I began: 'Alas!
    How many pleasant thoughts, how much desire,
    Conducted these unto the dolorous pass!'
Then unto them I turned me, and I spake,
    And I began: 'Thine agonies, Francesca,
    Sad and compassionate to weeping make me.
But tell me, at the time of those sweet sighs,
    By what and in what manner Love conceded,
    That you should know your dubious desires?'
And she to me, 'There is no greater sorrow
    Than to be mindful of the happy time
    In misery, and that thy Teacher knows.
But, if to recognize the earliest root
    Of love in us thou hast so great desire,
    I will do even as he who weeps and speaks.
One day we reading were for our delight
    Of Launcelot, how Love did him enthrall.
    Alone we were and without any fear.
Full many a time our eyes together drew
    That reading, and drove the color from our faces;
    But one point only was it that o'ercame us.
When, as we read of the much-longed for smile
    Being by such a noble lover kissed,
    This one, who ne'er from me shall be divided,
Kissed me upon the mouth, all palpitating.

Galeotto was the book and he who wrote it.
That day no farther did we read therein.'
And all the while one spirit uttered this,
The other one did weep so that, for pity,
I swooned away as if I had been dying,
And fell, even as a dead body falls."

ROSSETTI.

" 'The territory I was born in sits
Upon the shore whereat the Po descends,
To be at peace, he and his followers.
Love, which takes quickly to the gentle heart,
Took *him* for the fair person which was reft
From me, and still the mode offendeth me.
Love, which excuses no beloved from love,
Took me so strongly of the cheer of him
That, as thou seest, yet it leaves me not.
Love brought us unto one the self-same death:
Him who in life destroyed us Caïna waits.'

These words were proffered unto us by them.

When I had hearkened those offended souls,
I bent my face, and held it down so long
As till the Poet said to me, 'What think'st?'

'Alas!' when I responded, I began,
'How many tender thoughts, how much desire,
Brought these along unto the woful pass!'

Then I turned round to them, and spoke myself,
And I began: 'Francesca, these thy pains
Make me to weep, mournful and pitying.
But tell me,—at the time of the sweet sighs,
Whereat and in what way did love concede
That you your dubious longings recognized?'

And she to me: 'There is no greater grief
Than to remember one of happy time
In misery: and this thy tutor knows.
But, if thou hast desire so powerful
To be acquainted of our love's first root,
Like him will I do who doth weep and speak.
Reading we were one day, for our delight,
Of Lancelot, how love constrained him:
We were alone, with no suspiciousness.
More than one time that reading struck our eyes
Together, and discolored us in face:

But it was only one point conquered us.
When as we read about the longed-for smile,
How by so great a lover it was kissed,
This one who from me ne'er shall be disjoined,
Trembling all over kissed me on the mouth.
A Galahalt was the book, and he that writ:
Further that day we read in it no more.'

Meantime, as the one soul was saying this,
The other wept so that, for pitying,
I failed at heart, as though I should have died;
And down I fell as a dead body falls."

The sincerity of Mr. Rossetti's wish to accurately reproduce Dante is not less questionable than his failure to do so, and it appears to us that his version wants metrical grace in the same degree that it wants literality. After allowing him all the praise that can justly be given him, the need of such a version as Mr. Longfellow's, which preserves in a strong and perfectly coherent poetic feeling all Dante's meaning, is undeniable. Mr. Rossetti sometimes mistranslates, but his chief disqualification is that he is no poet—has not even a good ear for rhythm.

At first glance the reader feels a certain dissatisfaction with Mr. Longfellow's translation of the inscription on the gate of hell; and after many readings we confess that we cannot escape the unpleasant impression of the phrase "city dolent," though we perceive the advantages of preserving the musical change from dolent to dole and dolorous in succeeding lines. Let the reader, however, take these lines and compare them with the original, and then with the wild and sometimes ludicrous versions of others, and he will discern their exceeding skilfulness and their unquestionable superiority:

LONGFELLOW.
"Through me the way is to the city dolent;
    Through me the way is to eternal dole;
    Through me the way among the people lost.
Justice incited my sublime Creator,
    Created me divine Omnipotence,
    The highest Wisdom and the primal Love.
Before me there were no created things,
    Only eterne, and I eternal last.
    All hope abandon, ye who enter in."

ROSSETTI.
"Through me you pass into the grieving realm;
    Through me you pass into the eternal grief;
    Through me you pass among the kin that's lost.
Justice impelled my Maker, the All-High;
    The Puissance Divine created me,

The supreme Wisdom and the primal Love.
Before myself created things were not,
　　Unless eternal—I eternal last.
　　Leave off all hope, all ye who enter in."

FORD.

"By me is reached the city doomed to grieve;
　　By me the grief that must eternal prove;
　　By me the people lost beyond reprieve.
Justice my mighty Maker first did move;
　　Omnipotence Divine my structure rear,
　　The supreme Wisdom and the primal Love.
Save things eternal none created were
　　Prior to me: eternal I remain:
　　Despair for ever, ye who enter here."

WRIGHT.

"Through me ye enter the abode of woe;
　　Through me to endless sorrow are ye brought:
　　Through me amidst the souls accurst ye go.
Justice did first my mighty Maker move;
　　By power Almighty was my fabric wrought,
　　By highest Wisdom and by primal Love.
Ere I was formed no things created were
　　Save those eternal—I eternal last:
　　All hope abandon, ye who enter here."

CAYLEY.

"Through me ye pass into the city of woe;
　　Through me ye pass eternal woes to prove;
　　Through me among the blasted race ye go.
'Twas Justice did my most high Maker move,
　　And I have been the work of power Divine,
　　Of supreme Wisdom and of primal Love.
No creature has an elder date than mine
　　Unless eternal, and I have no end.
　　O ye that enter me, all hope resign."

It is not worth while to give the versions of Mrs. Ramsay, of Thomas, and of Brooksbank, or to comment upon the quality of the different versions above, further than to note the exceeding badness of Mr. Rossetti's, which is no more literal than some of the rhymed versions, and yet has all the awkwardness of mere literality.

We are sensible of the injustice of criticism which compares part with part, for it necessarily fails of conveying an idea of the whole in either case; but it is the only means of comparative criticism possible in the limited space of a newspaper, and Mr. Longfellow suffers equally with the rest. We must do a kindred injustice to our translator when we attempt to represent, by means

of extracts, the absolute value of his work. The best to be said of it is that it is
certainly Dante. After that, every one must acknowledge that it has a delightful music, and a fresh original quality in the English so resolutely faithful to
the Italian. There is remarkably little inversion, and not one inversion that
need obscure the sense for a moment, though the sense is often hard in itself,
or at other times is so simple that the reader's own unwillingness to accept
the plainest purport of the words as Dante's meaning makes difficulty for
which he is tempted to blame the translator. There is in Mr. Longfellow's
work an occasional excess of literality, as in the line,

> "If were the King of the Universe our friend,"

and the diction is now and then disagreeably characterized by the use of
words like *antelucan* and *serotine*, which translate Dante into the English dictionary rather than the English language. But these are blemishes extremely
rare in a performance that wins greater liking and honor the more closely it
is studied and examined. To whatever part of the poem we turn, it seems to
us that the translator has been equal to his most difficult task, and we should
hardly know which part of his version to praise most. We have already let it
praise itself, so far as quotation can go, in the passages quoted from the
"Inferno;" but we think neither of these is finer than the description of the
Wood of Thorns, or the story of Ulysses, or the scenes of grotesque horror
about the lake of pitch, or the canto telling of Cavalcanti and Farinata.

The present version of the "Purgatorio" is exquisitely responsive to the
spirit of the original; less sombre than that of the "Inferno," but not less
beautifully solemn and grand. The sublime picturesqueness of the poem is
felt as in the Italian itself, and we perceive how, in such a passage as this
describing the approach of the celestial pilot, the translator has shared the
exaltation of his original:

> "And lo! as when, upon the approach of morning,
>   Through the gross vapors Mars grows fiery red
>   Down in the West upon the ocean floor,
> Appeared to me—may I again behold it!—
>   A light along the sea so swiftly coming,
>   Its motion by no flight of wing is equalled;
> From which, when I a little had withdrawn
>   Mine eyes, that I might question my Conductor,
>   Again I saw it brighter grown and larger.
> Then on each side of it appeared to me
>   I knew not what of white, and underneath it
>   Little by little there came forth another.
> My master yet had uttered not a word
>   While the first whiteness into wings unfolded;
>   But when he clearly recognized the pilot,
> He cried, 'Make haste, make haste to bow the knee!
>   Behold the Angel of God! fold thou thy hands!

Henceforward shalt thou see such officers!
See how he scorneth human arguments,
    So that nor oar he wants, nor other sail
    Than his own wings between so distant shores.
See how he holds them pointed up to heaven,
    Fanning the air with the eternal pinions
    That do not moult themselves like mortal hair!'
Then as still nearer and more near us came
    The Bird Divine, more radiant he appeared,
    So that near by the eye could not endure him,
But down I cast it: and he came to shore
    With a small vessel, very swift and light,
    So that the water swallowed naught thereof.
Upon the stern stood the Celestial Pilot;
    Beatitude seemed written in his face,
    And more than a hundred spirits sat within."

Then, how charmingly all the quaintness and tenderness of that description of Dante's meeting with the Countess Matilda beside Lethe is given us, so that the scene affects us like some lovely painting painted when art was a soul and not a mere intelligence:

"And lo! my further course a stream cut off,
    Which, tow'rd the left hand with its little waves
    Bent down the grass that on its margin sprang.
All waters that on earth most limpid are
    Would seem to have within themselves some mixture
    Compared with that which nothing doth conceal,
Although it moves on with a brown, brown current
    Under the shade perpetual, that never
    Ray of the sun lets in, nor of the moon.
With feet I stayed, and with mine eyes I passed
    Beyond the rivulet, to look upon
    The great variety of the fresh May.
And there appeared to me (even as appears
    Suddenly something that doth turn aside
    Through very wonder every other thought)
A lady all alone, who went along
    Singing and culling floweret after floweret,
    With which her pathway was all painted over.
'Ah, beauteous lady, who in rays of love
    Dost warm thyself, if I may trust to looks,
    Which the heart's witnesses are wont to be,
May the desire come unto thee to draw
    Near to this river's bank,' I said to her,
    'So much that I may hear what thou art singing,
Thou makest me remember where and what
    Proserpina that moment was when lost

> Her mother her, and she herself the Spring.'
> As turns herself with feet together pressed
> And to the ground, a lady who is dancing,
> And hardly puts one foot before the other,
> On the vermilion and the yellow flowerets
> She turned towards me, not in other wise
> Than maiden who her modest eyes casts down;
> And my entreaties made to be content,
> So near approaching, that the dulcet sound
> Came unto me together with its meaning.
> As soon as she was where the grasses are
> Bathed by the waters of the beauteous river
> To lift her eyes she granted me the boon.
> I do not think there shone so great a light
> Under the lids of Venus, when transfixed
> By her own son beyond his usual custom!
> Erect upon the other bank she smiled,
> Bearing full many colors in her hands."

 The beautiful mysticism of the ensuing canto, delighting with every sweet sight and sound, is a pleasure which we leave untouched to the reader's enjoyment, as we must leave a thousand other pleasures in the poem. Here at last that much suffering reader will find Dante's greatness manifest, and not his greatness only, but his grace, his simplicity, and his affection. Here he will find strength matched with wonderful sweetness, and dignity with quaintness—Dante of the thirteenth century and Dante of eternity. There has been no attempt to add to or take from this lofty presence. Opening the book we stand face to face with the poet, and when his voice ceases we may well marvel if he has not sung to us in his own Tuscan. "I suppose," said Blake, when questioned of the language used by the spirit of a great poet in converse with him, "I suppose that he spoke in his native tongue, but it sounded to me like the most noble English."

[Nation, 20 June 1867]

18

[De Forest's Miss Ravenel]

Miss Ravenel's Conversion from Secession to Loyalty. By J.
W. De Forrest. New York: Harper and Brothers.

THE light, strong way in which our author goes forward in this story from the
first, and does not leave difficulty to his readers, is pleasing to those
accustomed to find an American novel a good deal like the now extinct
American stage-coach, whose passengers not only walked over bad pieces of
road, but carried fence-rails on their shoulders to pry the vehicle out of the
sloughs and miry places. It was partly the fault of the imperfect roads, no
doubt, and it may be that our social ways have only just now settled into such
a state as makes smooth going for the novelist; nevertheless, the old stage-
coach was hard to travel in, and what with drafts upon one's good nature for
assistance, it must be confessed that our novelists have been rather trying to
their readers. It is well enough with us all while the road is good,—a study of
individual character, a bit of landscape, a stretch of well-worn plot, gentle
slopes of incident; but somewhere on the way the passengers are pretty sure
to be asked to step out,—the ladies to walk on ahead, and the gentlemen to
fetch fence-rails.

Our author imagines a Southern loyalist and his daughter sojourning in
New Boston, Barataria, during the first months of the war. Dr. Ravenel has
escaped from New Orleans just before the Rebellion began, and has brought
away with him the most sarcastic and humorous contempt and abhorrence of
his late fellow-citizens, while his daughter, an ardent and charming little
blonde Rebel, remembers Louisiana with longing and blind admiration. The
Doctor, born in South Carolina, and living all his days among slaveholders
and slavery, has not learned to love either; but Lillie differs from him so
widely as to scream with joy when she hears of Bull Run. Naturally she
cannot fall in love with Mr. Colburne, the young New Boston lawyer, who
goes into the war conscientiously for his country's sake, and resolved for his
own to make himself worthy and lovable in Lillie's blue eyes by destroying
and desolating all that she holds dear. It requires her marriage with Colonel
Carter—a Virginia gentleman, a good-natured drunkard and *roué* and soldier of fortune on our side—to make her see Colburne's worth, as it requires
some comparative study of New Orleans and New Boston, on her return to
her own city, to make her love the North. Bereft of her husband by his own
wicked weakness, and then widowed, she can at last wisely love and marry
Colburne; and, cured of Secession by experiencing on her father's account

95

the treatment received by Unionists in New Orleans, her conversion to loyalty is a question of time duly settled before the story ends.

We sketch the plot without compunction, for these people of Mr. De Forrest's are so unlike characters in novels as to be like people in life, and none will wish the less to see them because he knows the outline of their history. Not only is the plot good and very well managed, but there is scarcely a feebly painted character or scene in the book. As to the style, it is so praiseworthy that we will not specifically censure occasional defects,—for the most part, slight turgidities notable chiefly from their contrast to the prevailing simplicity of the narrative.

Our war has not only left us the burden of a tremendous national debt, but has laid upon our literature a charge under which it has hitherto staggered very lamely. Every author who deals in fiction feels it to be his duty to contribute towards the payment of the accumulated interest in the events of the war, by relating his work to them; and the heroes of young-lady writers in the magazines have been everywhere fighting the late campaigns over again, as young ladies would have fought them. We do not say that this is not well, but we suspect that Mr. De Forrest is the first to treat the war really and artistically. His campaigns do not try the reader's constitution, his battles are not bores. His soldiers are the soldiers we actually know,—the green wood of the volunteers, the warped stuff of men torn from civilization and cast suddenly into the barbarism of camps, the hard, dry, tough, true fibre of the veterans that came out of the struggle. There could hardly be a better type of the conscientious and patriotic soldier than Captain Colburne; and if Colonel Carter must not stand as type of the officers of the old army, he must be acknowledged as true to the semi-civilization of the South. On the whole he is more entertaining than Colburne, as immoral people are apt to be to those who suffer nothing from them. "His contrasts of slanginess and gentility, his mingled audacity and *insouciance* of character, and all the picturesque ins and outs of his moral architecture, so different from the severe plainness of the spiritual temples common in New Boston," do take the eye of peace-bred Northerners, though never their sympathy. Throughout, we admire, as the author intends, Carter's thorough and enthusiastic soldiership, and we perceive the ruins of a generous nature in his aristocratic Virginian pride, his Virginian profusion, his imperfect Virginian sense of honor. When he comes to be shot, fighting bravely at the head of his column, after having swindled his government, and half unwillingly done his worst to break his wife's heart, we feel that our side has lost a good soldier, but that the world is on the whole something better for our loss. The reader must go to the novel itself for a perfect conception of this character, and preferably to those dialogues in which Colonel Carter so freely takes part; for in his development of Carter, at least, Mr. De Forrest is mainly dramatic. Indeed, all the talk in the book is free and natural, and, even without the hard swearing which distinguishes the speech of some, it would be difficult to mistake one speaker for another, as often happens in novels.

The character of Dr. Ravenel, though so simple, is treated in a manner invariably delightful and engaging. His native purity, amiability, and generosity, which a life-long contact with slavery could not taint; his cordial scorn of Southern ideas; his fine and flawless instinct of honor; his warm-hearted courtesy and gentleness, and his gayety and wit; his love of his daughter and of mineralogy; his courage, modesty, and humanity,—these are the traits which recur in the differing situations with constant pleasure to the reader.

Miss Lillie Ravenel is as charming as her adored papa, and is never less nor more than a bright, lovable, good, constant, inconsequent woman. It is to her that the book owes its few scenes of tenderness and sentiment; but she is by no means the most prominent character in the novel, as the infelicitous title would imply, and she serves chiefly to bring into stronger relief the traits of Colonel Carter and Doctor Ravenel. The author seems not even to make so much study of her as of Mrs. Larue, a lady whose peculiar character is skilfully drawn, and who will be quite probable and explicable to any who have studied the traits of the noble Latin race, and a little puzzling to those acquainted only with people of Northern civilization. Yet in Mrs. Larue the author comes near making his failure. There is a little too much of her,—it is as if the wily enchantress had cast her glamour upon the author himself,— and there is too much anxiety that the nature of her intrigue with Carter shall not be misunderstood. Nevertheless, she bears that stamp of verity which marks all Mr. De Forrest's creations, and which commends to our forbearance rather more of the highly colored and strongly-flavored parlance of the camps than could otherwise have demanded reproduction in literature. The bold strokes with which such an amusing and heroic reprobate as Van Zandt and such a pitiful poltroon as Gazaway are painted, are no less admirable than the nice touches which portray the Governor of Barataria, and some phases of the aristocratic, conscientious, truthful, angular, professorial society of New Boston, with its young college beaux and old college belles, and its life pure, colorless, and cold to the eye as celery, yet full of rich and wholesome juices. It is the goodness of New Boston, and of New England, which, however unbeautiful, has elevated and saved our whole national character; and in his book there is sufficient evidence of our author's appreciation of this fact, as well as of sympathy only and always with what is brave and true in life.

[*Atlantic Monthly*, July 1867]

19

[Literature and Its Professors]

Literature and its Professors. By Thomas Purnell.
London: Bell and Daldy.

A cultivated intellect, a fair degree of shrewd perception, an inviolable conscientiousness, a common sense frankly self-satisfied, are some of the qualifications which Mr. Purnell brings to the discussion of literature as seen in modern journalism, and in the lives of Giraldus Cambrensis and Montaigne,—of Roger Williams, the literary statesman,—of Steele, Sterne, and Swift, essayists,—of Mazzini, the literary patriot.

Many of the conditions of literary journalism alluded to in these essays are unknown in our country, where literature has not yet become merely a trade, and where we cannot see that literary men are sinking in popular esteem, and deservedly sinking, as being no better informed, or better qualified to control opinion, than their non-writing neighbors. We can better understand Mr. Purnell when he speaks of the imperfections and discrepancies of criticism, but are not better able to sympathize with all his ideas. The trouble is not, we think, that "critics who conceive themselves to be men of taste give their opinions fearlessly, having no misgivings that they are right," and "if a book is bad, feel it is bad," without being able to refer to a critical principle in proof, but that many who write reviews have not formed opinions and have not *felt* at all, and have rather proceeded upon a prejudice, a supposed law of æsthetics applicable to every exigency of literary development. A sense of the inadequacy of criticism must trouble every honest man who sits down to examine a new book; and it might almost be said, that no books can be justly estimated by the critic except those which are unworthy of criticism. Upon certain points and aspects of an author's work the critic can justly give his convictions, and need have no misgivings about them; but how to present a complete idea of it, and always to make that appear characteristic which is characteristic, and that exceptional which is exceptional, is the difficulty. Still, criticism must continue: the perfect equipoise may never be attained, and yet we must employ the balance, or nothing can be appraised, and traffic ceases.

It appears to us that criticism would be even more inadequate than it is, however, if, as Mr. Purnell desires, it should have "to do solely with the disposal of the materials, and but incidentally with the quality of the materials themselves." If the German critics whom we are asked to imitate have taught us anything, it is to look through form at the substance within, and to judge that. When criticism was supposed a science, it declared with a mathematical absoluteness that no drama was good or great which did not preserve the unities. Yet Shakespeare has written since, and no critic in the world thinks his plays bad or weak,—thanks, chiefly, to the German criticism, which is an art, and not a science, as Mr. Purnell desires us to think it. In fact, criticism is almost purely a matter of taste and experience, and there is hardly any law established for criticism which has not been overthrown as often as the French government. Upon one point—namely, that a critic should judge an author solely by his work, and never by anything known of him personally—we think no one will disagree with our essayist.

We hardly know how much or how little to value the clever workmanship of these essays, which is characteristic of a whole class of literature in England, though we suspect it has not much greater claim to praise than the art possessed by most Parisians of writing dramatic sketches of Parisian society. It seems to come of a condition of things, rather than from an individual faculty. Still, it is remarkable, and even admirable, though in Mr. Purnell's case it is not inconsistent with dealing somewhat prolixly with rather dry subjects, and being immensely inconclusive upon all important matters, and very painfully conclusive on trivial ones. Our essayist says little that is new of Montaigne, and does not add to our knowledge of Steele, Swift, and Sterne, though he speaks freshly and interestingly of Roger Williams as the first promoter of religious toleration. He requires seventeen pages ("Literary Hero-Worship") to declare that a great poet ought not to be thought great because he is not a great soldier, and *vice versa*; he is neat and cold, and generally doubtful of things accepted, and assured of things doubted,—and, without being commonplace himself, he seems to believe that he was born into the world to vindicate mediocrity of feeling.

[*Atlantic Monthly*, August 1867]

20

[Emerson's Poetry]

May-Day and other Pieces. By Ralph Waldo Emerson.
Boston: Ticknor and Fields.

WE wonder whether those who take up Mr. Emerson's poem now, amid the
glories of the fading summer, are not giving the poet a fairer audience than
those who hurried to hear his song in the presence of the May he celebrates.
As long as spring was here, he had a rival in every reader; for then we all felt
ourselves finer poets than ever sang of the season, and did not know that our
virtue was but an effect of Spring herself,—an impression, not an expression
of her loveliness, which must pass with her. Now, when the early autumn is in
every sense, and those days when the year first awoke to consciousness have
grown so far away, we must perceive that no one has yet been allowed to
speak so well for the spring of our New World as this poet. The very
irregularity of Mr. Emerson's poem seems to be part of its verisimilitude, and
it appears as if all the pauses and impulses and mysterious caprices of the
season—which fill the trees with birds before blossoms, and create the soul
of sweetness and beauty in the May-flowers under the dead leaves of the
woodlands, while the meadows are still bare and brown—had so entered into
this song, that it could not emulate the deliberation and consequence of art.
The "May-Day" is to the critical faculty a succession of odes on Spring,
celebrating now one aspect and now another, and united only by their title;
yet since an entire idea of spring is evolved from them, and they awaken the
same emotions that the youth of the year stirs in us, we must accept the result
as something undeniably great and good. Of course, we can complain of the
way in which it is brought about, just as we can upbraid the New England
climate, though its uncertain and desultory April and May give us at last the
most beautiful June weather in the world.

The poem is not one that invites analysis, though it would be easy enough
to instance striking merits and defects. Mr. Emerson, perhaps, more than any
other modern poet, gives the notion of inspiration; so that one doubts, in
reading him, how much to praise or blame. The most exquisite effects seem
not to have been invited, but to have sought production from his unconsciousness; graces alike of thought and of touch seem the unsolicited gifts of
the gods. Even the doubtful quality of occasional lines confirms this impression of unconsciousness. One cannot believe that the poet would wittingly
write,

"Boils the world in tepid lakes,"

for this statement has, for all that the reader can see to the contrary, the same value with him as that preceding verse, telling how the waxing heat

"Lends the reed and lily length,"

wherein the very spirit of summer seems to sway and droop. Yet it is probable that no utterance is more considered than this poet's, and that no one is more immediately responsible than he. We must attribute to the most subtile and profound consciousness the power that can trace with such tenderness and beauty the alliance he has shown between earth and humanity in the exultation of spring, and which can make matter of intellectual perception the mute sympathies that seemed to perish with childhood:—

> "The pebble loosened from the frost
> Asks of the urchin to be tost.
> In flint and marble beats a heart,
> The kind Earth takes her children's part,
> The green lane is the school-boy's friend,
> Low leaves his quarrel apprehend,
> The fresh ground loves his top and ball,
> The air rings jocund to his call,
> The brimming brook invites a leap,
> He dives the hollow, climbs the steep."

Throughout the poem these recognitions of our kindred with external nature occur, and a voice is given to the blindly rejoicing sense within us when the poet says,

> "The feet that slid so long on sleet
> Are glad to feel the ground";

and thus celebrates with one potent and satisfying touch the instinctive rapture of the escape from winter. Indeed, we find our greatest pleasure in some of these studies of pure feeling, while we are aware of the value of the didactic passages of the poem, and enjoy perfectly the high beauty of the pictorial parts of it. We do not know where we should match that strain beginning,

> "Why chidest thou the tardy spring?"

Or that,

> "Where shall we keep the holiday,
> And duly greet the entering May?"

Or this most delicate and exquisite bit of description, which seems painted *a tempera,*—in colors mixed with the transparent blood of snowdrops and Alpine harebells:—

> "See, every patriot oak-leaf throws
> His elfin length upon the snows,
> Not idle, since the leaf all day
> Draws to the spot the solar ray,
> Ere sunset quarrying inches down,
> And half-way to the mosses brown;
> While the grass beneath the rime
> Has hints of the propitious time,
> And upward pries and perforates
> Through the cold slab a hundred gates,
> Till green lances, piercing through,
> Bend happy in the welkin blue."

There is not great range of sentiment in "May-Day," and through all the incoherence of the poem there is a constant recurrence to the master-theme. This recurrence has at times something of a perfunctory air, and the close of the poem does not seal the whole with any strong impression. There is a rise—or a lapse, as the reader pleases to think—toward a moral at the close; but the motion is evidently willed of the poet rather than the subject. It seems to us that, if the work have any climax, it is in those lines near the end in which the poet draws his reader nearest his own personality, and of which the delicately guarded and peculiar pathos scarcely needs comment:—

> "There is no bard in all the choir,
> Not Homer's self, the poet sire,
> Wise Milton's odes of pensive pleasure,
> Or Shakespeare, whom no mind can measure,
> Nor Collins' verse of tender pain,
> Nor Byron's clarion of disdain,
> Scott, the delight of generous boys,
> Or Wordsworth, Pan's recording voice,—
> Not one of all can put in verse,
> Or to this presence could rehearse,
> The sights and voices ravishing
> The boy knew on the hills in spring,
> When pacing through the oaks he heard
> Sharp queries of the sentry-bird,
> The heavy grouse's sudden whir,
> The rattle of the kingfisher;
> Saw bonfires of the harlot flies
> In the lowland, when day dies;
> Or marked, benighted and forlorn,
> The first far signal-fire of morn.
> These syllables that Nature spoke,
> And the thoughts that in him woke,

Can adequately utter none
Save to his ear the wind-harp lone.
And best can teach its Delphian chord
How Nature to the soul is moored,
If once again that silent string,
As erst it wont, would thrill and ring.

   "Not long ago, at eventide,
It seemed, so listening, at my side
A window rose, and, to say sooth,
I looked forth on the fields of youth:
I saw fair boys bestriding steeds,
I knew their forms in fancy weeds,
Long, long concealed by sundering fates,
Mates of my youth,—yet not my mates,
Stronger and bolder far than I,
With grace, with genius, well attired,
And then as now from far admired,
Followed with love
They knew not of,
With passion cold and shy.
O joy, for what recoveries rare!
Renewed, I breathe Elysian air,
See youth's glad mates in earliest bloom,—
Break not my dream, obtrusive tomb!
Or teach thou, Spring! the grand recoil
Of life resurgent from the soil
Wherein was dropped the mortal spoil."

Among the other poems in this volume, it appears to us that "The Romany Girl," "Voluntaries," and "The Boston Hymn" are in their widely different ways the best. The last expresses, with a sublime colloquiality in which the commonest words of every-day parlance seem cut anew, and are made to shine with a fresh and novel lustre, the idea and destiny of America. In "Voluntaries" our former great peril and delusion—the mortal Union which lived by slavery—is at first the theme, with the strong pulse of prophecy, however, in the mournful music. Few motions of rhyme so win and touch as those opening lines,—

    "Low and mournful be the strain,
    Haughty thought be far from me;
    Tones of penitence and pain,
    Moanings of the tropic sea,"—

in which the poet, with a hardly articulate sorrow, regards the past; and Mr. Emerson's peculiarly exalted and hopeful genius has nowhere risen in clearer and loftier tones than in those stops which open full upon us after the pathetic pleasing of his regrets:—

"In an age of fops and toys,
Wanting wisdom, void of right,
Who shall nerve heroic boys
To hazard all in Freedom's fight,—
Break sharply off their jolly games,
Forsake their comrades gay,
And quit proud homes and youthful dames,
For famine, toil, and fray?
Yet on the nimble air benign
Speed nimbler messages,
That waft the breath of grace divine
To hearts in sloth and ease.
So nigh is grandeur to our dust,
So near is God to man,
When Duty whispers low, *Thou must*,
The youth replies, *I can*.
          . . . . . .
"Blooms the laurel which belongs
To the valiant chief who fights;
I see the wreath, I hear the songs
Lauding the Eternal Rights,
Victors over daily wrongs:
Awful victors, they misguide
Whom they will destroy,
And their coming triumph hide
In our downfall, or our joy:
They reach no term, they never sleep,
In equal strength through space abide;
Though, feigning dwarfs, they crouch and creep,
The strong they slay, the swift outstride:
Fate's grass grows rank in valley clods,
And rankly on the castled steep,—
Speak it firmly, these are gods,
All are ghosts beside."

It is, of course, a somewhat Emersonian Gypsy that speaks in "The Romany Girl," but still she speaks with the passionate, sudden energy of a woman, and flashes upon the mind with intense vividness the conception of a wild nature's gleeful consciousness of freedom, and exultant scorn of restraint and convention. All sense of sylvan health and beauty is uttered when this Gypsy says,—

"The wild air bloweth in our lungs,
The keen stars twinkle in our eyes,
The birds gave us our wily tongues,
The panther in our dances flies."

"Terminus" has a wonderful didactic charm, and must be valued as one of the noblest introspective poems in the language. The poet touches his reader by his acceptance of fate and age, and his serene trust of the future, and yet is not moved by his own pathos.

We do not regard the poem "The Adirondacks" as of great absolute or relative value. It is one of the prosiest in the book, and for a professedly out-of-doors poem has too much of the study in it. Let us confess also that we have not yet found pleasure in "The Elements," and that we do not expect to live long enough to enjoy some of them. "Quatrains" have much the same forbidding qualities, and have chiefly interested us in the comparison they suggest with the translations from the Persian: it is curious to find cold Concord and warm Ispahan in the same latitude. Others of the briefer poems have delighted us. "Rubies," for instance, is full of exquisite lights and hues, thoughts and feelings; and "The Test" is from the heart of the severe wisdom without which art is not. Everywhere the poet's felicity of expression appears; a fortunate touch transfuses some dark enigma with color; the riddles are made to shine when most impenetrable; the puzzles are all constructed of gold and ivory and precious stones.

Mr. Emerson's intellectual characteristics and methods are so known that it is scarcely necessary to hint that this is not a book for instant absorption into any reader's mind. It shall happen with many, we fancy, that they find themselves ready for only two or three things in it, and that they must come to it in widely varying moods for all it has to give. No greater wrong could be done to the poet than to go through his book running, and he would be apt to revenge himself upon the impatient reader by leaving him all the labor involved in such a course, and no reward at the end for his pains.

But the case is not a probable one. People either read Mr. Emerson patiently and earnestly, or they do not read him at all. In this earnest nation he enjoys a far greater popularity than criticism would have augured for one so unflattering to the impulses that have heretofore and elsewhere made readers of poetry; and it is not hard to believe, if we believe in ourselves for the future, that he is destined to an ever-growing reward and fame. He makes appeal, however mystically, only to what is fine and deep and true and noble in men, and no doubt those who have always loved his poetry have reason to be proud of their pleasure in it. Let us of the present be wise enough to accept thankfully what genius gives us in its double character of bard and prophet, saying, when we enjoy the song, "Ah, this is the poet that now sings!" and when the meaning is dark, "Now we have the seer again!"

[*Atlantic Monthly*, September 1867]

21

[J. G. Holland's Feeble Poetic Fancy]

Kathrina: her Life and mine, in a Poem. By J. G. Holland,
Author of "Bitter-Sweet." New York: Charles Scribner
and Company.

LET us tell without any caricature of ours, in prose that shall be just if not
generous, the story of Mr. Holland's hero as we have gathered it from the
work which the author, for reasons of his own, calls a poem.

The petted son of a rich widow in Northampton, Massachusetts, whose
father has killed himself in a moment of insanity, reaches the age of fourteen
years without great event, when his mother takes him to visit a lady friend
living on the other side of the Connecticut River. In this lady's door-yard the
hero finds a little lamb tethered in the grass, and decked with a necklace of
scarlet ribbon, and, having a mind for a frolic with the pretty animal, the boy
unties it. Instantly it slips its tether from his hand, leaps the fence, and runs
to the top of the nearest mountain, whither he follows it, and where, exalted
by the magnificence of the landscape, he is for the first time conscious of
being a poet. Returning to his anxious mother, she too is aware of some
wondrous change in him, and says:

> "My Paul has climbed the noblest mountain height
> In all his little world, and gazed on scenes
> As beautiful as rest beneath the sun.
> I trust he will remember all his life
> That to his best achievement, and the spot
> Nearest to heaven his youthful feet have trod,
> He has been guided by a guileless lamb.
> It is an omen which his mother's heart
> Will treasure with her jewels."

Resolved to give him the best educational advantages, his mother sends
him to Mr. Bancroft's school; or, as Mr. Holland sings, permits him

> "To climb the goodly eminence where he
> In whose profound and stately pages live
> His country's annals, ruled his little realm."

Here the hero surpasses all the other boys in everything, and but repeats his
triumphs later when he goes to Amherst College. His mother lives upon the
victories which he despises; but at last she yields to the taint which was in her

own blood as well as her husband's, and destroys herself. The son, who was aware of her suicidal tendency, and had once overheard her combating it in prayer, curses the God who would not listen to her and help her, and rejects Him from his scheme of life.

In due time he falls in love with Kathrina, a young lady whom he first sees on the occasion of her public reception into the Congregational Church at Hadley. Later he learns that she is staying with the lady whose pet lamb led him such a chase,—that she is in fact her niece, and that she has seen better days. We must say that this good lady does everything in her power to make a match between the young people; and she is more pleased than surprised at the success of her efforts. It has been the hero's idea that human love will fill up the void left in his life by the rejection of God and religion; but he soon finds himself vaguely unhappy and unsatisfied, and he determines to glut his heart with literary fame. He goes, therefore, to New York, and succeeds as a poet beyond all his dreams of success. For ten years he is the most popular of authors; but he sickens of his facile triumph, and imagines that to be happy he must write to please himself, and not the multitude. He writes with this idea, but pleases nobody, and is as unhappy as ever.

Meanwhile, Kathrina has fallen into a decline. On her death-bed she tells him that it is religion alone which can appease and satisfy him; but she pleads with him in vain, till one day, when he enters her room, and is startled by a strange coincidence: the lamb, which led him to the mountain-top and the consciousness of poetic power, had a scarlet ribbon on its neck, and now he finds this ribbon

> "at her throat
> Repeated in a bright geranium-flower!"

Then Kathrina tells him that his mother's spirit has talked with her, and bidden her say to him this:—

> "The lamb has slipped the leash by which his hand
> Held her in thrall, and seeks the mountain-height;
> And he, if he reclaim her to his grasp,
> Must follow where she leads, and kneel at last
> Upon the summit by her side. And more,
> Give him my promise that, if he do this,
> He shall receive from that fair altitude
> Such vision of the realm that lies around,
> Cleft by the river of immortal life,
> As shall so lift him from his selfishness,
> And so enlarge his soul, that he shall stand
> Redeemed from all unworthiness, and saved
> To happiness and heaven."

Whereupon, having delivered her message, Kathrina bids him kneel. It is the supreme moment of her life. He hears his mother's voice, and the voice of the innumerable heavenly host, and even the voice of God repeating her mandate. He kneels, and she bids him pray, and, as before, all the celestial voices repeat her bidding. He prays and is saved.

Such is the story of Kathrina, or rather of Kathrina's husband, for she is herself scarcely other than a name for a series of arguments, with little of the flesh and blood of a womanly personality. We have too much reverence for high purposes in literature not to applaud Mr. Holland's good intent in this work, and we accept fully his theory of letters and of life. Both are meagre and unsatisfactory as long as their motive is low; both must yield unhappiness and self-despite till religion inform them. This is the common experience of man; this is the burden of the sayings of the sage from the time of Solomon to the time of Mr. Holland; and we can all acknowledge its truth, however we may differ as to the essence of religion itself. But we conceive that repetition of this truth in a long poem demands of the author an excellence, or of the reader a patience, all but superhuman.

How Mr. Holland has met the extraordinary demand upon his powers is partly evident from the outline of the poem as we have given it. It must be owned that it is rather a feeble fancy which unites two vital epochs by the incident of the truant lambkin, and that the plot of the poem does not in any way reveal a great faculty of invention. A parable, moreover, teaches only so far as it is true to life; and in a tale professing to deal with persons of our own day and country, we have a right to expect some fidelity to our contemporaries and neighbors. But we find nothing of this in "Kathrina,"—not even in the incident of a young gentleman of fourteen sporting with a lambkin; or in the talk of young people who make love in long arguments concerning the nature and office of genius and the intermediary functions of the teacher. Polemically considered, there is nothing very wrong in the discussions between those metaphysical lovers, and no one need raise the question as to how far Kathrina's peculiar ideas are applicable to the work of genius bearing her name.

> "The greatest artists speak to fewest souls.
> . . . . The bread that comes from heaven
> Needs finest breaking. Some there doubtless are,
> Some ready souls, that take the morsel pure
> Divided to their need; but multitudes
> Must have it in admixtures, menstruums,
> And forms that human hands or human life
> Have moulded."

Such passages, though they add nothing to the verisimilitude of Kathrina's character, help to make her appear consistent in not laughing at a certain weird poem which her lover reads to her. Few ladies in real life, however great a tenderness they might feel for a morbid young poet, could practise Kathrina's self-control, when, depicting himself as a godless youth imprisoned by phantoms "among the elves of the silent land," he sings:

> "Under the charred and ghastly gloom,
>   Over the flinty stones,
> They led him forth to his terrible doom,
> And, plunged in a deep and noisome tomb,
>   They sat him among the bones."

Where, crouching, he beholds, through a "loop" in the wall, "a sweet angel from the skies":—

> "Could she not loose him from his thrall,
>   And lead him into the light?
> 'Ah me!' he murmured, 'I dare not call,
> Lest she may doubt it a goblin's waul,
>   And leave me in swift affright!' "

The question is of the poet himself, immersed in his own gloomy thoughts, and of Kathrina, who could rescue him from them; but she has heard "only a wild, weird story," and her lover is obliged to explain it, and still we are to suppose that she did not laugh. Nay, we are told that she instantly accepted the poet, who exclaims:

> "Are there not lofty moments when the soul
> Leaps to the front of being, casting off
> The robes and clumsy instruments of sense,
> And, postured in its immortality,
> Reveals its independence of the clod
> In which it dwells?—moments in which the earth
> And all material things, all sights and sounds,
> All signals, ministries, interpreters,
> Relapse to nothing, and the interflow
> Of thought and feeling, love and life, go on
> Between two spirits, raised to sympathy
> By an inspiring passion, as in heaven,
> The body dust, within an orb outlined,
> It shall go on forever?"

We have no reason to suppose that this is not thought a fine passage by the author, who will doubtless find readers enough to agree with him, if he should not care to accept our estimate of his whole poem. Nevertheless, we must confess that it appears to us puerile in conception, destitute of due motive, and crude and inartistic in treatment. But we should be unjust both to ourselves and our author, if we left his work without some allusion to its highly embellished style, or, having failed to approve the whole design, refused to notice at all the elaborate ornamentation of the parts. Not to be guilty, then, of this unfairness, let us cull here some of the fanciful tropes and figures which enamel these flowery pages. The oriole is "a torch of downy flame"; the "reiterant katydids rasp the mysterious silence"; a mother's loss and sorrow are "twin leeches at her heart"; the frosty landscape is "fulgent with downy crystals"; Kathrina wears a "pale-blue muslin robe," which the hero fancies "dyed with forget-me-nots"; and the landscape has usually some effect of dry-goods to the poet's eye. We might almost believe that this passage,

> "We touched the hem
> Of the dark mountain's robe, that falls in folds
> Of emerald sward around his feet, and there
> Upon its tufted velvet we sat down,"

was inspired by perusal of Dr. Holmes's ode to "Evening—by a Tailor":—

> "Day hath put on his jacket, and around
> His burning bosom buttoned it with stars.
> Here will I lay me on the velvet grass,
> That is like padding to earth's meagre ribs."

But Mr. Holland's fancy is of a quality which transcends all feigning in others. Whatever it touches it figures in gross material substance, preferably wood or some sort of upholstery. When, however, his hero first stood in Broadway, he seems to have found no fabric of the looms, no variety of plumage, no sort of precious wood or dye-stuff equal to the allegory, and he wreaks himself in the following tremendous hydraulic image:—

> "I saw the waves of life roll up the steps
> Of great cathedrals and retire; and break
> In charioted grandeur at the feet
> Of marble palaces, and toss their spray
> Of feathered beauty through the open doors,
> To pile the restless foam within; and burst
> On crowded caravansaries, to fall
> In quick return; and in dark currents glide
> Through sinuous alleys, and the grimy loops
> Of reeking cellars, and with softest plash
> Assail the gilded shrines of opulence,
> And slide in musical relapse away."

[*Atlantic Monthly*, December 1867]

22

[George William Curtis]

Nile Notes of a Howadji. New York: Harper &
Brothers. 1851.
The Howadji in Syria. By George William Curtis,
Author of "Nile Notes." New York: Harper &
Brothers. 1852.
Lotus-Eating: A Summer-Book. By George William
Curtis. Illustrated by Kensett. New York: Harper &
Brothers. 1852.
The Potiphar Papers. By George William Curtis. New
York: Harper & Brothers. 1856.
Prue and I. By George William Curtis. New York:
Harper & Brothers: 1856.
Trumps. A Novel. By Geo. Wm. Curtis. New York:
Harper & Brothers. 1861.

A very little book often holds a great immortality, and far more than enough
for the daunted critic-folk who have to measure it, and report its dimensions
in their poor lines and inches, but we imagine that it must be the feeling of
every one who presumes to judge a living author, that the author's books,
however numerous do not fully represent him, and that the material for a
perfect consideration of his work is somehow wanting. Plainly, prophecy,
even of a retrospective cast, is no part of our present task and we should
regret to be thought at all inspired or infallible. Yet in venturing to speak of
the above-cited books of Mr. George William Curtis, we feel that we have
safer ground for criticism than contemporaries commonly afford, for Mr.
Curtis has of late so exclusively employed himself with journalism and
politics and lecturing that he has drawn a deep line round the literary work
previously accomplished, which separates it at least from his present if not
from his future, and gives it an unusual degree of completeness. His six
volumes represent in great part the activity of fifteen years, now some time
past, and for good or for bad they have the absolute character which
distinguishes a gift from a promise in literature. We will at once let the reader
into our secret, and say that even if it were not a gift we should think it good,
and to be prized in itself and as something no one else could have bestowed.

The cordial remembrance of pleasure his work has given in other times is
something which many of our readers will share with us, and which will not
perhaps be thought by any a disadvantage in our slight study; for every
literary period has its transient sympathies and susceptibilities, to which all
successful books are largely addressed, and in making a later estimate of their
worth, one could not forget the prime delight they gave without judging
them faintly and ineffectually. Mr. Curtis's characteristic charm and value
appeared in his first book, and are still conspicuous in the "Nile Notes of a

Howadji," though one now feels a want of simplicity there that did not trouble him at twenty. The fault is repaired in subsequent work; but how well that luscious expression, those gaudy alliterations, those vague allusions, those melting hues, that sadness and sweetness of a young poet's spirit, satisfied the utmost desire of the earlier time! Then the senses were so quick that one tasted the rich, sooth quality of the book not with the intellectual palate merely, which it cloys, but with the whole heart and mental body, as it had been a bath. Luxury not perfection that age wanted, and if the Howadji gave it something more and better, it knew it not, and still felt that Egypt whatever it might be in geography, history or philosophy was in reality odors, cadences and colors. It is indeed a singularly pleasing book, and it is one of the best to teach that modern travel is truth rather than facts; for foreign countries are always an ideal realm, in which to the eye of candor the commonest things have a fantastic appearance through the insoluble mystery of conditions; and the most satisfactory traveller is he who contrives to give this fantastic effect again by describing just what he saw and felt, and leaving his reader to enjoy the picture neither more nor less ignorantly than he enjoyed the original. Mr. Curtis was twenty-seven when he published the Nile Notes, and the book was doubtless the fruit of yet earlier years. It suggests this in style and manner, in its redundant hues and tones, in its wonderful use of words, which so often degenerates into play with words. It is prose measured so deliberately that you continually feel its pulsation, and often find it too much for the nerves of middle life. The prodigious excess of alliteration is perhaps not so much to blame, for that is the instinct of our tongue; still its absence is to be noted with relief in the author's very next book, The Howadji in Syria, where the whole atmosphere seems cooler and sharper. The feeling is much the same, but the soul of youth has wreaked itself upon the mystic grandeur and melancholy of Egypt, and has finally indulged that riot of expression which leaves a gifted man's thought clearer for a whole life-time. Within the limits of decency and sanity perhaps it would be well for every young author thus to commit all the literary excesses to which he feels tempted in some early book where they can be forgiven him; for there are dreadful examples of profligacy in some oldsters who having passed a pale and stinted youth, abandon themselves to wantonness of style when it is too late to reform. Carlyle is not quite a case in point, but how well for him if he could have written the life of Schiller long ago as he has now lately written the life of Frederick and *vice versa*!

We do not mean by all this to say the luxury of the Nile Notes is so bad as we paint it, or that the book is not fully redeemed from being merely sensuous. What a voyage up the Nile could suggest to a man of imagination, lively humor, and liberal literature, finds record there, and in that atmosphere of dreams there is veritable Egypt. Yet amid those contours so smoothly rounded, (as if the Sphynx had shoulders of ivory instead of sand-worn granite,) one longs for something rough and angular to clutch; in those graceful draperies, melting from the textures of thought into the misty fabric of dreams, even the fancy feels itself naked and cold at times; in the want of chronological perspective,—greater, we think, than the author intended,—those English people in the Cairene hotels, who are distinguished in the sepulchral Egyptian manner rather by symbols attached to their effigies than by characteristic traits, seem as remote and uncertain as Ramses and Cambyses; the guide in handing his newly-filled chibouque to the tourist in the foreground, places the amber mouth-piece to the lips of Memnon opened to chaunt his sun-rise song in the far-off dawn of time.

Grant all this, and yet how good the book remains,—so original in motive, so fine in temper, so charming, despite its affectations, in effect. If it were divided into lines beginning with capital letters, its studied alliterations would have made it a well-formed poem in Anglo-Saxon times, and it has other charms which make it so like poetry in ours, that we feel it ought scarcely to be read save from the same impulse and in the same moods as poetry. If any one would shame the doubting critic, let him thus read "Under the Palms," or "A Crow that flies in Heaven's Sweetest Air," or parts of "Southward," and "Ultima Thule," or nameable passages in any chapter of the book. Let him read aloud, if he will have the due effect of Mr. Curtis's art, this exquisitely finished bit in which, while some of the author's caprices appear, one knows a touch and brain poetically quick and most sensitively skilful:

"In the Villa Serra di Falco, within sound of the vespers of Palermo, there is a palm beautiful to behold. It is like a Georgian slave in a Pacha's hareem. Softly shielded from eager winds, gently throned upon a slope of green, fringed with brilliant and fragrant flowers, it stands separate and peculiar in the odorous garden air. Yet it droops and saddens and bears no fruit. Vain is the exquisite environment of foreign fancies. The poor slave has no choice but life. Care too tender will not suffer it to die. Pride and admiration surround it with the best beauties, and feed it with the warmest sun. But I heard it sigh as I passed. A wind blew warm from the East, and it lifted its arms hopelessly, and when the wind, love-laden with most subtle sweetness, lingered loth to fly, the palm stood motionless on its little green mound, and the flowers were so fresh and fair—and the leaves of the trees so deeply hued, and the native fruit so golden and glad upon the boughs—that the still warm garden air seemed only the silent, voluptuous sadness of the tree; and had I been a poet my heart would have melted in song for the proud, pining palm."

This beautiful tenderness and delicacy of feeling, and this luxury of expression that delights even in its dulcet excess, are true to the mood if not to the quality of the whole book. Yet its poetry is as frequently of a meditative as of an emotional cast, and it deals—however airily and fantastically—with what takes the thoughts as well as the sentiments, while a very fine and peculiar humor often plays through it. Less fervor and music of phrase would have gone with the same suggestion and speculation in colder years; but to what the East revealed the author listened with a young man's bound-

ing pulse, and a supreme sense of enjoyment, and the secret imparted again
has still the motion of his blood. The book is sensuous, certainly, yet its
poetry is of so pure a source that nothing corrupts in it; not even the poor
Ghawazee, whom it celebrates, and who are suffered to take the heart only
with a kind of abstract passion, though no warmth of color or significance of
expression in their life is unrendered. When the song is moralized, it is not
didactic of set purpose, but of the best civilization working in a nature singularly harmonious and sound, and already obedient amidst its æsthetic luxuries and enjoyments, to that tendency which has given us in Mr. Curtis a
moralist of so winning and new and individual a kind, that the old word
seems not to describe him, though there is none better.

The reader will perhaps realize him best in this character if we speak here
of the charming essays which he has given us from month to month for now
many years,—of those incomparable homilies which are preached from the
"Easy Chair" of Harper's Magazine, and in which there is nothing of ser-
monizing but religion and goodwill. They handle with admirable taste and
breeding, topics of society, literature and the every-day popular life, with an
unfailing honor for elegance, good-manners and hearty sense. There is nowhere else in our journalism so much truth so amiably yet so clearly spoken,
and one does not mind that these papers are a little mannered, they are
essentially so well-mannered. It is that part of morality to be distinguished as
civilization or civility in its wide significance which Mr. Curtis chiefly teaches
from his Easy Chair; and he does it with an art that never lapses or fatigues.
There must be not only brain and heart in those little papers, but a constant
charm of style which shall take the reader in spite of the narrowness of their
limitations. There is a monotony in our barbarities and crises and sensations;
the news from Europe is swiftly suicidal, now we have got the Cable; forty-
nine books out of fifty cannot be safely or significantly mentioned; it is something little short of inspiration which discerns the finely-varying aspects of
events and seizes their lesson.

We fancy that Mr. Curtis, however unconsciously, had also rather the
moralist's than the artist's motive in writing "Potiphar Papers," though these
as mere literary art are more successful than they are likely to be considered
by those who do not take into account the singular difficulties of the performance. New York society is not American society, any more than Boston or
Philadelphia society is so, and to the vast majority of his readers, Mr. Curtis
had not only to depict types but present conditions all-but strange before,
and often too transient for any process less swift than photography. He thus
encountered obstacles unknown to satirists in older societies, and he overcame them so far as to produce scenes bearing intrinsic evidence of fidelity,
and to give us in Mrs. Potiphar and Rev. Cream Cheese, names permanently
descriptive of characteristics, if not of classes. No one knows New York society better than he, and no one in a certain light and incidental way touches it
more effectively. But harm comes to "The Potiphar Papers" in several quite
needless ways. They should never have been united under one name for they

do not form a whole. There is sometimes infirmity as well as sketchiness of handling in the same paper; though this does not make such bad effect as the fact that some of the people not only change their aspects but their characters in the different papers, while they keep their names. In one, Paul Potiphar is said to have a library of book-backs; in another we are asked to believe that he reads and enjoys Thackeray. Moreover, there is on the part of the author too much attitude, too much self-defence, too much consciousness; and a man who has very good eyes of his own will insist, at times, upon looking at New York society through Mr. Thackeray's spectacles, and talking of Major Dobbin, and Becky Sharpe and the Pendennises. It is only the spectacles, however; neither the voice nor the manner is Thackeray's, while the feeling is quite different from his.

If it were not so, how could women love this and the other books of Mr. Curtis so much? They find there not only a most singular purity of thought and fancy, but a cordial and reverent homage, unmixed with patronage or gallantry, rarely offered to their sex. No one deserves better at their hands than he who is so enamored of the idea of womanhood in its inalienable beauty of affection, that he can never draw any woman's character which is altogether heartless and unlovely.

We imagine, too, that women like Mr. Curtis's books for the air of gentle and gracious pedantry that breathes through them. When he talks of books, it is of the finer and friendlier books, of the poems writ in sympathetic ink that only yield their whole meaning to the warmth of the reader's own heart. And when does he not talk of books? No one is more entirely the child of this literary age, in which a single writer has colored the parlance of his whole generation; in which things have come to stand for books, instead of books for things; in which literature has usurped the place of all the other arts, and people see pictures, statues, and architecture only through the medium of print. It is not easy to describe, without grossness or excess, a trait which characterizes so much of his work by fortunate quotation or felicitous allusion; or to say how the all-pervasive literary influences of our epoch seem, at times, to exclude from him every impression that does not come through them. Yet, as you read him, and note how greatly, with all his proper subtlety and discernment, he enjoys the beautiful through the delight it has already given, the truth we suggest is sufficiently plain.

Mr. Curtis's peculiarity in this respect is nearest a fault in "Lotus-Eating," and most a virtue in "Prue and I." It is very curious to look over the former book, and see how much it is the fruit of association and sympathy. He steams up the Hudson, and sees where the Lorelei sang, and Uhland's overpaid boatman crossed on the Rhine; where Rip Van Winkle and Ichabod Crane loitered on their native ground, and Drake's Culprit Fay sinned and suffered. At Catskill, who should appear but the inaccessible maid on the mountain out of the "small sweet Idyl" in the "Princess"? We find that Yarrow is in the neighborhood of Trenton; and that Waller wrote a poem suitable for lovesick singing under windows at Saratoga, Charles Lamb contributing a "Gipsey's Malison" proper to be repeated to old gentlemen gossiping on the piazza of the hotel, and Robert Herrick furnishing a farewell-song for the traveller going away after dinner, and lingering upon a full stomach to catch a strain of the music played to the young people in the hotel-garden. At Lake George, at Nahant, at Newport, what poets are not brought to the rescue?—with something, we own, of the reluctance of drafted men, and occasionally the recklessness and irresponsibility of bounty-jumpers enlisted over and over again in all the corps of the great army of sentiment. We should do the book an injustice, which must affect the author less than his critic, if we failed to recognize, in spite of all this, its essential originality, its unapproached success in throwing around beautiful scenes an atmosphere less crude and arid than that of mere fashion, its peculiarly acute and amiable study of certain phases of American society and character in the light of Old-World travel and intelligence.

In "Prue and I" the quotations have mostly dwindled to here and there a vivid line, or have wholly put off their original form and risen again in graceful and happy allusion; and the emotion of earlier books has been all purified into feeling. It is hard to say just wherein the charm of the work lies. It is in nowise, in whole or in part, strongly actuated. The old book-keeper seems inadequate to his own dreams, and his wife Prue, with her patching and darning, sometimes wears her robe of romance like a fine dress, uneasily. Aurelia is a fine sketch of a pure and lovely woman of society, but is scarce more than a sketch. Titbottom is the chief creation of the book, and yet his substance is not to be closely scanned. One establishes all this, and straightway forgets it as soon as he re-opens the volume, for he finds there a truth to human nature, to himself, that appears better than the invention of situation or character. The three papers which form great part of the book cannot be judged by comparison with anything else, for each is sole of its kind. One thinks of the idea of "Titbottom's Spectacles" as something that perhaps Hawthorne would have chosen; but it is imagined in a temper peculiarly Mr. Curtis's, and is wrought with a fantastic gayety, a frank pathos, and a firm hold upon the allegory entirely characteristic of him. He alone could have written "My Chateaux in Spain," with its pensive satires and longings and regrets, and that strange power of suggestion and association which gathers its airy enchantment most about the reader when he feels himself asked, with the other dream-people, to meet all those famous personages of fiction and history at the triumphal banquet to be given in the Spanish castle. In "Sea from Shore" a like witching fancy plays with the sentiment of universal travel,—with the vague desire and unrest which visit all lands and climes, not omitting even the island of Barataria and the Bohemian coasts, and voyage in all the ships that ever sailed,—till the charming revery appears the only true and probable account of the world. We poorly and awkwardly hint the nature of a book that merits its fortune of being taken to the hearts of all its readers, though it is a fortune so rare as to come to but two or three books in a generation, and not to have attended in equal degree any other of the time of "Prue and I." That sort of personal regard which people have for it, comes to it from the most various experiences and conditions, but of course the young and happy have best loved its pensive tenderness and vague regrets; those who were in their earlier loves and later teens when it appeared could hardly have been persuaded that it was not the most exquisite book ever written; and we have heard of survivors of that time, now growing middle-aged in their first passions, who still think it incomparably beautiful, and give it away upon all occasions of making a present.

The work is as original as it is beautiful, and the workmanship excellent. Indeed, whatever Mr. Curtis does is done from a conscience to which slovenly literature is impossible, and his errors are of excessive, not of defective performance. His prose in "Prue and I" is of the best modern art, studied word by word like verse, balanced, and attuned by a jealous sense—no pomp or formality, but a constant ease and suavity of movement. The book is of a period to which the smoke of an intervening war gives an undue effect of remoteness—a period of uncertain aspiration and suspense and misgiving in politics, just before the transition to hopeful or desperate but always decided action, in which nearly every man prominent among us for any reason took part. Mr. Curtis had already in The Potiphar Papers, made a jest of the young men who sneered at "Uncle Tom's Cabin," and in finding some things ugly and ridiculous besides negros' heels and the long hair of reformers, had unmistakably hinted the direction of his sympathies; but it was still a surprise to learn that there was all along a politician lying hid in that life, refined by knowledge of the best in two worlds, and now lingering somewhat sadly over the delicate sentiment and gentle art with which it had hitherto played—a politician with whom politics were a liberal science and a generous faith. Many men, not yet old, but younger in that time, can recall the pride and delight with which they read that address of his to the youth of some unremembered college; in which he celebrated the irrepressible conflict in Kansas as the sublime opportunity of all Americans to array themselves upon the side of justice and freedom. It was yet merely a question of voting, but many died in battle thereafter because the most were not then brave enough to face the south at the ballot-box. Of course Mr. Curtis did but honor himself, in whatever he said for the right then, but all of that side, who had read his books, and recognized the lofty and noble spirit of them, felt stronger and bolder in his company, and triumphed in such an accession.

Mr. Curtis seems to have a more authentic vocation to politics than any other American littérateur has felt. Other American authors have held office: not to begin with Franklin, there had been Irving minister to Spain, Paulding Secretary of the Navy, Hawthorne Consul at Liverpool; but the first and last of these had merely a political creed and no political life, and the second was in no way great. John Quincy Adams was like those Spanish statesmen who begin their political career with a volume of poems in their hands; with Mr. Curtis, it has been something as it is with such politico-literary Englishmen as Bulwer and Disraeli; but he has had a grander and more unselfish aim than they: he may be classed rather with Hughes in England, with Lamartine in France, and with D' Azeglio in Italy. As he entered upon public life with a higher and purer motive than actuates most men, we suppose that he does not think his devotion unrequited merely because he has never yet attained office. Probably he never promised himself at once the most obvious political success, or he would hardly have remained in New York where the immense antagonistic majorities are to be but slowly affected. He might have been in Congress long ago, by mere change of residence; but he could have been nowhere so useful as where he has been ever since the war. He is a positive influence,—of zeal with knowledge, of ambition for good, of advanced reform without fanaticism—which must be more and more felt. Nothing less than absolute purity and unselfishness of purpose can succeed against the practices and theories which give New York her ugly repute for venal legislation and political corruption. The whole nation has an interest in Mr. Curtis's success in public life, and whatever is best in us must sympathize with him.

We are very far from thinking such a man condescends in espousing politics. There is no one so fine and good among cultivated gentlemen but he has his counterpart among simple and common men in this nation, and none can be better employed than in serving their cause in the government, whether in Congress or out of it. But this service cannot be done with a half heart, and whoever enters upon it in the spirit of a dilettante and a patron, dooms himself to defeat. The waters will go over him, and in their muddy deposits his old age will become as thoroughly fossilized as if he had died before the deluge.

If Mr. Curtis is doing good to politics, we think they have already done good to him even in his literature. We need not praise him as one of the ablest public speakers in the country, and doubtless the first in saying things at once gracefully and forcibly; but we wish to speak of the excellent quality of his political journalism, in which rising from his "Lounger's" attitude of elegant criticism and comment, at the beginning of the war, he has continued to treat all public questions with vigor and directness, looking at them from the most advanced point of view, and arguing them not merely as a Radical Republican, but as a Radical Christian, a Radical Gentleman. There is no noble purpose or project which has not had his voice, no baseness in or out of his party which he has hesitated to rebuke. A man does not thus habitually appeal to what is sincere and earnest in others, without ridding himself of his own affectations and caprices, and it is interesting in Mr. Curtis's political writing to note the change which has been wrought in his style. There is nothing in it that is not a result from tendencies perceptible in his earliest books, but all has passed out of it that could mark him as a sentimentalist, or a literary fine gentleman. It was morally impossible he should ever fall into that worst and commonest form of that sentimentality which is known as Buncombe; and it so happens that now no public man addresses the popular intelligence in more fit and unaffected terms than he who at first sought only the appreciation of the æsthetic few, and seemed to yield to every idle grace or wayward fancy that coquets with the diction of a young poet.

But while we cannot concede that Mr. Curtis has lost in nobility of purpose or work in turning to political life, (for we honor politics as one of the worthiest vocations in a republic, and think that the best cannot be better employed than in teaching men self-government,) we are very sensible how beneficial his active presence in letters has been. Each last new book throws all past new books into that abeyance which is the purgatory of accomplished works, and it is quite possible that not every one of Mr. Curtis's books will issue thence. Yet our literature has felt him as an admirable and original quality, as an influence and monition in the interest of literary grace, temperance and decency, whatever is to be the fate of his past performance, or whether or not he shall add to it hereafter. Again we decline the precarious honors of prophesy. To be sure, we feel that if he had undertaken a romance instead of a novel in his last work, that delicate fancy, humorous gayety and abundant sentiment of his had not been lost as it is in "Trumps," but we refrain from saying whether he shall ever give us that romance which he could have written so well. Doubtless it is a principle in a mind like his to attach itself more and more to reality, to the present, as we see in his turning from the pleasantest walks of belles-lettres to the stumps and platforms of politics. Having once and in earlier days expressed the flavor of his poetic nature in those unique books of travel, and in those delicious papers of "Prue and I," there must be a constantly increasing tendency with him to leave his realm of revery and reminiscence and to seek contact with the actual in our everyday world.

It is no purpose of ours to fix Mr. Curtis's rank in our literature, and we do not mean to measure his powers or his performance in classing him with Irving and Longfellow in literary refinement of tone, and a predominant grace of execution. He is bound to both by many ties of mental sympathy, though not right New Englander nor right New-Yorker, he has the spirit of either civilization in him, like his native city of Providence. He has for the old world the new-world love of both Irving and Longfellow, but he enjoys it more critically than either, and will commonly be found making a lesson of it, one way or other. He has not Irving's archaic spirit; and his writings, though they have dealt so much with the to-day which has now become yester-day, have a greater affinity with Longfellow's. In most things, however, and in essentials, he is alone; and he has so characteristic a vein that it could hardly ever be taken for another's, or not known for his. In all his books he is utterly free from provincialism and vulgarity of thought or feeling: he has neither American nor European narrowness. He has none of the frenzied or bad intention which is so common in our present literary art, and which comes chiefly from ignorance of life and the world. The effects he seeks are to be achieved only through his reader's refinement or innate fineness.

In the work he has accomplished he has given us studies of the East unique in their poetic sympathy and fidelity; a book of such original and freshly delightful romance, that it seems almost a new species in fiction, and occasional criticisms so sympathetically intelligent, and so subtile in their praise as sometimes to make praise appear the only virtue in criticism.

One does not, however, think of him exactly as a critic, nor without reserve speak of him as a traveller, satirist, or romancer, though he is, upon the face of things, all these. One equally shrinks from saying outright that he is a humorist or a poet, though he is undoubtedly humorous and poetical. Perhaps we must in any attempt at synthesis, return whither our analysis began, and speak of him as a moralist. There is a didacticism in all his work, very fine and courteous which is at the same time too marked not to be recognized, while in very much of that which he has done and is doing it is openly declared. As we have partly indicated before, it seems to us that this tendency has steadily taken him from those early dreams of this east in the Howadji novels to observation of fashionable life at American watering-places, in "Lotus-Eating," to study of New York society in "The Potiphar Papers" to the expression of pensive satire and regret in "Prue and I," to the effort of assembling the results of his knowledge and speculation upon our life in "Trumps," and so finally to politics. He lives in the world, and since he is not content to take it as it is and use it merely for artistic purposes, but will always be seeking immediately to persuade and better it, he is a moralist rather than a poet.

The only difficulty we find in accepting the conclusion at which we arrive is this: How can a moralist be so wholly charming? But this perplexed us in the beginning.

[*North American Review*, July 1868]

23

The New Taste in Theatricals.

THERE is this satisfaction in living, namely, that whatever we do will one day wear an air of picturesqueness and romance, and will win the fancy of people coming after us. This stupid and commonplace present shall yet appear the fascinating past; and is it not a pleasure to think how our rogues of descendants—who are to enjoy us æsthetically—will be taken in with us, when they read, in the files of old newspapers, of the quantity of entertainment offered us at the theatres during the season just ending, and judge us by it? I imagine them two hundred years hence looking back at us, and sighing, "Ah! there was a touch of the old Greek life in those Athenians! How they loved the drama in the jolly Boston of that day! That was the golden age of the theatre: in the winter of 1868–69, they had dramatic performances in seven places, of every degree of excellence, and the managers coined money." As we always figure our ancestors going to and from church, they will probably figure us thronging the doors of theatres, and no doubt there will be some historical gossiper among them to sketch a Boston audience in 1869, with all our famous poets and politicians grouped together in the orchestra seats, and several now dead introduced with the pleasant inaccuracy and uncertainty of historical gossipers. "On this night, when the beautiful Tostée reappeared, the whole house rose to greet her. If Mr. Alcott was on one of his winter visits to Boston, no doubt he stepped in from the Marlborough House,—it was a famous temperance hotel, then in the height of its repute,—not only to welcome back the great actress, but to enjoy a chat between the acts with his many friends. Here, doubtless, was seen the broad forehead of Webster; there the courtly Everett, conversing in studied tones with the gifted so and so. Did not the lovely such a one grace the evening with her presence? The brilliant and versatile Edmund Kirke was dead; but the humorous Artemas Ward and his friend Nasby may have attracted many eyes, having come hither at the close of their lectures, to testify their love of the beautiful in nature and art; while, perhaps, Mr. Sumner, in the intervals of state cares, relaxed into the enjoyment," etc. "Vous voyez bien le tableau!"

That far-off posterity, learning that all our theatres are filled every night, will never understand but we are a theatre-going people in the sense that it is the highest fashion to be seen at the play; and yet we are sensible that it is not so, and that the Boston which makes itself known in civilization—letters, politics, reform—goes as little to the theatre as fashionable Boston.

The stage is not an Institution with us, we should say; yet it affords recreation to a very large and increasing number of persons, and while it would be easy to over-estimate its influence for good or evil even with these, there is no doubt that the stage, if not the drama, is popular. Fortunately an inquiry like this into the present taste in theatricals concerns the fact rather than the effect of the taste; otherwise the task might become indefinitely hard alike for writer and for reader. No one can lay his hand on his heart, and declare that he is the worse for having seen *La Belle Hélène*, for example, or say more than that it is a thing which ought not to be seen by any one else; yet I suppose there is no one ready to deny that *La Belle Hélène* was the motive of those performances that most pleased the most people during the past winter. The season gave us nearly every kind of theatrical. In the legitimate drama we had such starry splendors as Booth, Hackett, and Forrest; and we had many new plays of the modern sort, given very effectively and successfully at the different theatres. We had, moreover, the grand opera, and not in a poverty-stricken way, as they have it in the native land of the opera, where one piece is repeated for a fortnight or a month, but superabundantly, as Americans have everything, except quality; twenty nights of opera, and a new piece, Italian, French, or German, nearly every night. Those who went said it was not very good, and I believe that the houses were no better than the performance. There was English opera, also; but best of all, and far more to our minds than her serious sisters, was the *opéra bouffe*, of which we had nearly a month, with Tostée, Irma, and Aujac. We greeted these artists with overflowing theatres; and the reception of the first, after a year's absence, was a real ovation, of which the historical gossiper will not afford posterity an idea too extravagant, however mistaken. There was something fascinating in the circumstances and auspices under which the united Irma and Tostée troupes appeared—*opéra bouffe* led gayly forward by *finance bouffe*, and suggesting Erie shares by its watered music and morals; but there is no doubt that Tostée's grand reception was owing mainly to the personal favor which she enjoys here, and which we do not vouchsafe to every one. Ristori did not win it; we did our duty by her, following her carefully with the libretto, and in her most intense effects turning the leaves of a thousand pamphlets with a rustle that must have shattered every delicate nerve in her; but we were always cold to her greatness. It was not for Tostée's singing, which was but a little thing in itself; it was not for her beauty, for that is now scarcely more than a reminiscence, if it was not always an illusion; was it because she rendered the spirit of M. Offenbach's operas so perfectly, that we liked her so much? "Ah, that movement!" cried an enthusiast, "that swing, that—that—wriggle!" She is undoubtedly a great actress, full of subtle surprises, and with an audacious appearance of unconsciousness in those exigencies where consciousness would summon the police—or ought to; she is so near, yet so far from, the worst that can be intended; in tones, in gestures, in attitudes, she is to the libretto just as the music is, now making it appear insolently and unjustly coarse, now feebly inadequate in its explicit immodesty.

To see this famous lady in *La Grande Duchesse* or *La Belle Hélène* is an experience never to be forgotten, and certainly not to be described. The former opera has undoubtedly its proper and blameless charm. There is something pretty and arch in the notion of the Duchess's falling in love with the impregnably faithful and innocent Fritz; and the extravagance of the whole, with the satire upon the typical little German court, is delightful. But *La Belle Hélène* is a wittier play than *La Grande Duchesse*, and it is the vividest expression of the spirit of *opéra bouffe*. It is full of such lively mockeries as that of Helen when she gazes upon the picture of Leda and the Swan: " 'aime à me recueiller devant ce tableau de famille! Mon père, ma mère, les voici tous les deux! O mon père, tourne vers ton enfant un bec favorable!''— or of Paris when he represses the zeal of Calchas, who desires to present him at once to Helen: "Soit! mais sans lui dire qui je suis;—je désire garder le plus strict incognito, jusq'au moment où la situation sera favorable à un coup de théâtre." But it must be owned that our audiences seemed not to take much pleasure in these and other witticisms, though they obliged Mademoiselle Tostée to sing *Un Mari sage* three times, with all those actions and postures which seem incredible the moment they have ceased. They possibly understood this song no better than the strokes of wit, and encored it merely for the music's sake. The effect was, nevertheless, unfortunate, and calculated to give those French ladies but a bad opinion of our understanding and morals. How could they comprehend that the new taste is, like themselves, imported, and that its indulgence here does not characterize us? It was only in appearance that, while we did not enjoy the wit, we delighted in the coarseness. And how coarse this travesty of the old fable mainly is! That priest Calchas, with his unspeakable snicker, his avarice, his infidelity, his hypocrisy, is alone infamy enough to provoke the destruction of a city. Then that scene interrupted by Menelaus! It is indisputably witty, and since all those people are so purely creatures of fable, and dwell so entirely in an unmoral atmosphere, it appears as absurd to blame it, as the murders in a pantomime. To be sure, there is something about murder—some inherent grace or refinement perhaps—that makes its actual representation upon the stage more tolerable than the most diffident suggestion of adultery. Not that *La Belle Hélène* is open to the reproach of over-delicacy in this scene, or any other, for the matter of that; though there is a strain of real poetry in the conception of this whole episode, of Helen's intention to pass all Paris's love-making off upon herself for a dream,—poetry such as might have been inspired by a muse that had taken too much nectar. There is excellent character, also, as well as caricature, in the drama; not alone Calchas is admirably done, but Agamemnon, and Achilles, and Helen, and Menelaus,—"pas un mari ordinaire . . . . un mari épique"—and the burlesque is good of its kind. It is artistic, as it seems French dramatic effort must almost necessarily be.

It can scarcely be called the fault of the *opéra bouffe* that the English burlesque should have come of its success; nor can the public blame it for the great favor the burlesque won last winter, if indeed the public wishes to bestow blame for this. No one, however, could see one of these curious travesties without being reminded, in an awkward way, of the *morale* of the *opéra bouffe*, and of the *personnel*—as we may say—of "The Black Crook," "The White Fawn," and the "Devil's Auction." There was the same intention of merriment at the cost of what may be called the marital prejudices, though it cannot be claimed that the wit was the same as in *La Belle Hélène*; there was the same physical unreserve as in the ballets of a former season; while in its dramatic form, the burlesque discovered very marked parental traits.

This English burlesque, this child of M. Offenbach's genius, and the now somewhat faded spectacular muse, flourished the past winter in three of our seven theatres for months,—five, from the highest to the lowest, being in turn open to it,—and had begun, in a tentative way, to invade the deserted stage even so long ago as last summer; and I have sometimes flattered myself that it was my fortune to witness the first exhibition of its most characteristic feature in a theatre into which I wandered, one sultry night, because it was the nearest theatre. They were giving a play called "The Three Fast Men," which had a moral of such powerful virtue that it ought to have reformed everybody in the neighborhood. Three ladies being in love with the three fast men, and resolved to win them back to regular hours and the paths of sobriety by every device of the female heart, dress themselves in men's clothes,—such is the subtlety of the female heart in the bosoms of modern young ladies of fashion,—and follow their lovers about from one haunt of dissipation to another, and become themselves exemplarily vicious,—drunkards, gamblers, and the like. The first lady, who was a star in her lowly orbit, was very great in all her different *rôles*, appearing now as a sailor, with the hornpipe of his calling, now as an organ-grinder, and now as a dissolute young gentleman,—whatever was the exigency of good morals. The dramatist seemed to have had an eye to her peculiar capabilities, and to have expressly invented edifying characters and situations that her talents might enforce them. The second young lady had also a personal didactic gift, rivalling, and even surpassing in some respects, that of the star; and was very rowdy indeed. In due time the devoted conduct of the young ladies has its just effect: the three fast men begin to reflect upon the folly of their wild courses; and at this point the dramatist delivers his great stroke. The first lady gives a *soirée dansante et chantante*, and the three fast men have invitations. The guests seat themselves—as at a fashionable party—in a semicircle, and the gayety of the evening begins with conundrums and playing upon the banjo; the gentlemen are in their morning-coats, and the ladies in a display of hosiery, which is now no longer surprising, and which need not have been mentioned at all except for the fact that, in the case of the first lady, it seemed not to have been freshly put on for that party. I hope the reader here recognizes preparation for something like that great final scene which distinguishes his favorite burlesque—is it "Ixion" or "Orpheus" or "Lucrezia Borgia?"—they all have it.

In this instance an element comical beyond intention was present, in three young gentlemen, an amateur musical trio, who had kindly consented to sing their favorite song of "The Rolling Zuyder Zee," as they now kindly did, with flushed faces, unmanageable hands, and much repetition of

> The ro-o-o-o—
> The ro-o-o-o—
> The ro-o-o-o-ll—
> Ing Zuyder Zee,
> Zuyder Zee,
> Zuyder Zee-e-e!

Then the turn of the three guardian angels of the fast men being come again, they get up and dance each one a breakdown, which seems to establish their lovers (now at last in the secret of the generous ruse played upon them) firmly in their resolution to lead a better life. They are in nowise shaken from it by the displeasure which soon shows itself in the manner of the first and second ladies. The former is greatest in the so-called Protean parts of the play, and is obscured somewhat by the dancing of the latter; but she has a daughter, who now comes on and sings a song. The pensive occasion, the favorable mood of the audience, the sympathetic attitude of the players, invite her to sing "The Maiden's Prayer," and so we have "The Maiden's Prayer." We may be a low set, and the song may be affected and insipid enough, but the purity of its intention touches, and the little girl is vehemently applauded. She is such a pretty child, with her innocent face, and her artless white dress, and blue ribbons to her waist and hair, that we will have her back again; whereupon she runs out upon the stage, strikes up a rowdy, rowdy air, dances a shocking little dance, and vanishes from the dismayed vision, leaving us a considerably lower set than we were at first, and glad of our lowness. This is the second lady's own ground, however, and now she comes out—in a way that banishes far from our fickle minds all thoughts of the first lady and her mistaken child—with a medley of singing and dancing, a bit of breakdown, of cancan, of jig, a bit of *Le Sabre de mon Père*, and of all memorable slang songs, given with the most grotesque and clownish spirit that ever inspired a woman. Each member of the company follows in his or her *pas seul*, and then they all dance together, to the plain confusion of the amateur trio, whose eyes roll like so many Zuyder Zees, as they sit lonely and motionless in the midst. All stiffness and formality are overcome. The evening party in fact disappears entirely, and we are suffered to see the artists in their moments of social relaxation, sitting as it were around the theatrical fireside. They appear to forget us altogether; they exchange winks and nods, and jests of quite personal application; they call each other by name, by their Christian names, their nicknames. It is not an evening party, it is a family party, and the suggestion of home enjoyment completes the reformation of the three fast men. We see them marry the three fast women before we leave the house.

On another occasion, two friends of the drama beheld a more explicit precursor of the coming burlesque at one of the minor theatres last summer. The great actress whom they had come to see on another scene was ill, and in their disappointment they embraced the hope of entertainment offered them at the smaller play-house. The drama itself was neither here nor there as to intent, but the public appetite or the manager's conception of it—for I am by no means sure that this whole business is not a misunderstanding—had exacted that the actresses should appear in so much stocking, and so little else, that it was a horror to look upon them. There was no such exigency of dialogue, situation, or character as asked the indecorum, and the effect upon the unprepared spectator was all the more stupefying from the fact that most of the ladies were not dancers, and had not countenances that consorted with impropriety. Their faces had merely the conventional Yankee sharpness and wanness of feature, and such difference of air and character as should say for one and another, shop-girl, shoe-binder, seamstress; and it seemed an absurdity and an injustice to refer to them in any way the disclosures of the ruthlessly scant drapery. A grotesque fancy would sport with their identity: "Did not this or that one write poetry for her local newspaper?" so much she looked the average culture and crudeness; and when such a one, coldly yielding to the manager's ideas of the public taste, stretched herself on a green baize bank with her feet towards us, or did a similar grossness, it was hard to keep from crying aloud in protest, that she need not do it; that nobody really expected or wanted it of her. Nobody? Alas! there were people there—poor souls who had the appearance of coming every night—who plainly did expect it, and who were loud in their applauses of the chief actress. This was a young person of a powerful physical expression, quite unlike the rest,—who were dyspeptic and consumptive in the range of their charms,—and she triumphed and wantoned through the scenes with a fierce excess of animal vigor. She was all stocking, as one may say, being habited to represent a prince; she had a raucous voice, an insolent twist of the mouth, and a terrible trick of defying her enemies by standing erect, chin up, hand on hip, and right foot advanced, patting the floor. It was impossible, even in the orchestra seats, to look at her in this attitude and not shrink before her; and on the stage she visibly tyrannized over the invalid sisterhood with her full-blown fascinations. These unhappy girls personated, with a pathetic effect not to be described, such arch and fantastic creations of the poet's mind as Bewitchingcreature and Exquisitelittlepet, and the play was a kind of fairy burlesque in rhyme, of the most melancholy stupidity that ever was. Yet there was something very comical in the conditions of its performance, and in the possibility that public and manager were playing at cross-purposes. There we were in the pit, an assemblage of hard-working Yankees of decently moral lives and simple traditions, country-bred many of us and of plebeian stock and training, vulgar enough perhaps, but probably not depraved, and excepting the first lady's friends certainly not educated to the critical enjoyment of such spectacles; and there on the stage were those mistaken women, in such sad variety of boniness and flabbiness as I have tried to hint, addressing their pitiable exposure to a supposed vileness in us, and wrenching from all original intent the innocent dulness of the drama, which for the most part could have been as well played in walking-dresses, to say the least.

The scene was not less amusing, as regarded the audiences, in the winter, when the English burlesque troupes which London sent us, arrived; but it was not quite so pathetic as regarded the performers. Of their beauty and their *abandon*, the historical gossiper, whom I descry far down the future, waiting to refer to me as "A scandalous writer of the period," shall learn very little to his purpose of warming his sketch with a color from mine. But I hope I may describe these ladies as very pretty, very blond, and very unscrupulously clever, and still disappoint the historical gossiper. They seemed in all cases to be English; no Yankee faces, voices, or accents were to be detected among them. Where they were associated with people of another race, as happened with one troupe, the advantage of beauty was upon the Anglo-Saxon side, while that of some small shreds of propriety was with the Latins. These appeared at times almost modest, perhaps because they were the conventional *ballerine*, and wore the old-fashioned ballet-skirt with its volumed gauze,—a coyness which the Englishry had greatly modified, through an exigency of the burlesque,—perhaps because indecorum seems, like blasphemy and untruth, somehow more graceful and becoming in southern than in northern races.

As for the burlesques themselves, they were nothing, the performers personally everything. M. Offenbach had opened Lemprière's Dictionary to the authors with *La Belle Hélène*, and there was commonly a flimsy ravelling of parodied myth, that held together the different dances and songs, though sometimes it was a novel or an opera burlesqued; but there was always a song and always a dance for each lady, song and dance being equally slangy, and depending for their effect mainly upon the natural or simulated charms of the performer.

It was also an indispensable condition of the burlesque's success, that the characters should be reversed in their representation,—that the men's *rôles* should be played by women, and that at least one female part should be done by a man. It must be owned that the fun all came from this character, the ladies being too much occupied with the more serious business of bewitching us with their pretty figures to be very amusing; whereas this wholesome man and brother, with his blond wig, his *panier*, his dainty feminine simperings and languishings, his falsetto tones, and his general air of extreme fashion, was always exceedingly droll. He was the saving grace of these stupid plays; and I cannot help thinking that the *cancan*, as danced, in "Ivanhoe," by Isaac of York and the masculine Rebecca, was a moral spectacle; it was the *cancan* made forever absurd and harmless. But otherwise, the burlesques were as little cheerful as profitable. The playwrights who had adapted them to the

American stage—for they are all of English authorship—had been good
enough to throw in some political allusions which were supposed to be effective with us, but which it was sad to see received with apathy. It was conceivable from a certain air with which the actors delivered these, that they were
in the habit of stirring London audiences greatly with like strokes of satire;
but except where Rebecca offered a bottle of Medford rum to Cedric the
Saxon, who appeared in the figure of ex-President Johnson, they had no
effect upon us. We were cold, very cold to all suggestions of Mr. Reverdy
Johnson's speech-making and dining; General Butler's spoons moved us just
a little; at the name of Grant, we roared and stamped, of course, though in a
perfectly mechanical fashion, and without thought of any meaning offered
us; those lovely women might have coupled our hero's name with whatever
insult they chose, and still his name would have made us cheer them. We
seemed not to care for points that were intended to flatter us nationally. I am
not aware that anybody signified consciousness when the burlesque sup-
ported our side of the Alabama controversy, or acknowledged the self-devotion with which a threat that England should be *made* to pay was delivered by
these English performers. With an equal impassiveness we greeted allusions
to Erie shares, and to Mr. Fiske, and to Mr. Samuel Bowles.

The burlesque chiefly betrayed its descent from the spectacular ballet in
its undressing; but that ballet, while it demanded personal exposure, had
something very observable in its scenic splendors, and all that marching and
processioning in it was rather pretty; while in the burlesque there seemed
nothing of innocent intent. No matter what the plot, it led always to a final
great scene of breakdown,—which was doubtless most impressive in that
particular burlesque where this scene represented the infernal world, and
the ladies gave the dances of the country with a happy conception of the
deportment of lost souls. There, after some vague and inconsequent dialogue, the wit springing from a perennial source of humor (not to specify the
violation of the seventh commandment), the dancing commenced, each performer beginning with the Walk-round of the negro minstrels, rendering its
grotesqueness with a wonderful frankness of movement, and then plunging
into the mysteries of her dance with a kind of infuriate grace and a fierce
delight very curious to look upon. It was perfect of its kind, that dancing, but
some things one witnesses at the theatre nowadays had better be treated as a
kind of confidence. I am aware of the historical gossiper still on the alert for
me, and I dare not say how sketchily these ladies were dressed, or indeed,
more than that they were dressed to resemble circus-riders of the other sex,
but as to their own deceived nobody,—possibly did not intend deceit. One of
them was so good a player that it seemed needless for her to go so far as she
did in the dance; but she spared herself nothing, and it remained for her
merely stalwart friends to surpass her, if possible. This inspired each who
succeeded her to wantoner excesses, to wilder insolences of hose, to fiercer
bravadoes of corsage; while those not dancing responded to the sentiment of
the music by singing shrill glees in tune with it, clapping their hands, and

patting Juba, as the act is called,—a peculiarly graceful and modest thing in woman. The frenzy grew with every moment, and, as in another Vision of Sin,—

> "Then they started from their places,
> Moved with violence, changed in hue,
> Caught each other with wild grimaces,
> Half-invisible to the view,
> Wheeling with precipitate paces
> To the melody, till they flew,
> Hair, and eyes, and limbs, and faces
> Twisted hard in fierce embraces,
> Like to Furies, like to Graces,"—

with an occasional exchange of cuffs and kicks perfectly human. The spectator found now himself and now the scene incredible, and indeed they were hardly conceivable in relation to each other. A melancholy sense of the absurdity, of the incongruity, of the whole absorbed at last even a sense of the indecency. The audience was much the same in appearance as other audiences, witnessing like displays at the other theatres, and did not differ greatly from the usual theatrical house. Not so much fashion smiled upon the efforts of these young ladies, as upon the *cancan* of the Signorina Morlacchi a winter earlier; but there was a most fair appearance of honest-looking, handsomely dressed men and women; and you could pick out, all over the parquet, faces, evidently of but one descent from the deaconship, which you wondered were not afraid to behold one another there. The truth is, we spectators, like the performers themselves, lacked that tradition of error, of transgression, which casts its romance about the people of a lighter race. We have not yet set off one corner of the Common for a Jardin Mabille; we have not even the concert-cellars of the gay and elegant New-Yorker; and nothing, really, has happened in Boston to educate us to the new taste in theatricals, since the fair Quakers felt moved to testify in the streets and churches against our spiritual nakedness. Yet it was to be noted with regret that our innocence, our respectability, had no restraining influence upon the performance; and the fatuity of the hope cherished by some courageous people, that the presence of virtuous persons would reform the stage, was but too painfully evident. The doubt whether they were not nearer right who have denounced the theatre as essentially and incorrigibly bad would force itself upon the mind, though there was a little comfort in the thought that, if virtue had been actually allowed to frown upon these burlesques, the burlesques might have been abashed into propriety. The caressing arm of the law was cast very tenderly about the performers, and in the only case where a spectator presumed to hiss,—it was at a *pas seul* of the indescribable,—a policeman descended upon him, and with the succor of two friends of the free ballet, rent him from his place, and triumphed forth with him. Here was an end of ungenial criticism; we all applauded zealously after that.

The peculiar character of the drama to which they devoted themselves had produced, in these ladies, some effects doubtless more interesting than profitable to observe. One of them, whose unhappiness it was to take the part of *soubrette* in the Laughable Commedietta preceding the burlesque, was so ill at ease in drapery, so full of awkward jerks and twitches, that she seemed quite another being when she came on later as a radiant young gentleman in pink silk hose, and nothing of feminine modesty in her dress excepting the very low corsage. A strange and compassionable satisfaction beamed from her face; it was evident that this sad business was the poor thing's *forte*. In another company was a lady who had conquered all the easy attitudes of young men of the second or third fashion, and who must have been at something of a loss to identify herself when personating a woman off the stage. But Nature asserted herself in a way that gave a curious and scarcely explicable shock in the case of that dancer whose impudent song required the action of fondling a child, and who rendered the passage with an instinctive tenderness and grace, all the more pathetic for the profaning boldness of her super-masculine dress or undress. Commonly, however, the members of these burlesque troupes, though they were not like men, were in most things as unlike women, and seemed creatures of a kind of alien sex, parodying both. It was certainly a shocking thing to look at them with their horrible prettiness, their archness in which was no charm, their grace which put to shame. Yet whoever beheld these burlesque sisters, must have fallen into perplexing question in his own mind as to whose was the wrong involved. It was not the fault of the public —all of us felt that: was it the fault of the hard-working sisterhood, bred to this as to any other business, and not necessarily conscious of the indecorum which pains my reader,—obliged to please somehow, and aiming, doubtless, at nothing but applause? *La Belle Hélène* suggests the only reasonable explanation of the new taste in theatricals: "C'est la fatalité."

The new taste, as has been said before, is not our taste. It came to us like any other mode from abroad, but, unlike the fashions in dress, received no modification or impression from our life; so that, though curiosity led thousands, not in Boston alone, but in all our great cities, to look at these lewd traversties, it could not be said that we naturalized among us a form of entertainment involving fable that we could not generally understand, satire that we cared nothing about, lascivious dancing, singing that expressed only a depraved cockneyism. It is with these spectacles, as with all other dramatic amusements, now so popular, and growing year by year in favor. They draw no life from our soil; they do not flower and fruit again in our air. For good or for evil, Puritanism has had its will. The theatre has never been opened since the Commonwealth, in our civilization. At this moment, comedy is almost as foreign here as the Italian opera, and the same anomaly is presented in the favor which either enjoys. The modern dramas deserve to be liked by playgoers, and I think they have been affectedly and unjustly scorned by criticism. I, for one, am not above being delighted by Mr. Charles

Reade when he dramatizes one of his novels; and I am in the belief that one should look a long while in the classic British Drama for a play so entirely charming as "Dora." They have given it in Boston in a manner which left nothing to be desired,—certainly not a comedy of Goldsmith's or Sheridan's in place of it. We all knew the story as it was outlined in the poem, and the playwright had kept in spirit very close to the poet; there was genuine sentiment in the piece, passion enough, wit enough, character enough; and it lost nothing in the acting, or in any theatrical accessory; so that it was a refined and unalloyed pleasure to witness its production. One must have been very stupid or very brilliant indeed not to enjoy Mr. Robertson's comedy of "School," though of course it was of flimsier and cheaper texture than "Dora." It was full of admirable situations; and if the hits were a little too palpable, they were still genuine strokes of nature, while the action and the *mise en scène* were nearly as perfect as in the better play. The same author's equally popular, but less artistic play of "My Lady Clara" merits all its success. It deals with several fresh persons and situations, and freshly with the old ones; it is in great degree impossible, of course, but its sketches of character are as lifelike as they are delightful. Even the sensation drama is founded for the most part upon the principle of fidelity to contemporary life. "Foul Play," at the Boston Theatre, was justly interesting; one need not have been any more ashamed to be thrilled by it, than by the marvellous and fascinating novel from which the drama springs; and if you come to such plays as "After Dark," and the "Lancashire Lass," with their steam-power effects and their somewhat wandering and incoherent plots, there is no denying but they make an evening pass quickly and pleasantly,—how much more quickly and pleasantly than the most brilliant party of the season!

But after we have praised these modern plays to their full desert, we must again recur to their foreign character. They have no relation to our life as a people; we can only appreciate them through our knowledge of English life derived from novel reading. Their interest all depends upon the conditions of English society; their characters are English; their scenes are English. Does some one tell me that the locomotive, which so nearly runs over the hero in "After Dark," has an American cow-catcher? I reply that, in the "Lancashire Lass," it is into a purely English dock that the "Party of the name of Johnson" is pitched; and that, at any rate, these tricks of the property-maker do not affect the central fact. Even the actors who present these English plays so charmingly are, except the subordinates, nearly all English and of English training; and it is undeniable that, while the theatre has been growing more artistic and popular among us, it has been growing less and less American. It was not in nature that the old Yankee farce should keep the stage; still less that some pre-historic American like Metamora should continue to interest forever; even the noble art of negro minstrelsy is expiring among us, and we have nothing to offer in competition with the English plays. The fact is not stated to raise regret, but merely to show that the comedy is, like the opera, alien. This does not interfere with the enjoyment of either as it appears; and as long as we are free to believe that their success here is due to our cosmopolitan spirit in receiving and making experiment of every sort of pleasure, we may feel rather proud of it than otherwise. Whether for the same reason we might take the same satisfaction in the success of the English burlesques, is a question which I shall not try to decide, chiefly because it is no longer "a live issue," as the politicians say.

It is very probable that we shall not see the burlesques again next winter, and that what has been here called the new taste in theatricals will then be an old-fashioned folly, generally ignored because it is old-fashioned, if not because it is folly. This belief is grounded, not so much upon faith in the power of the stage to reform itself, or the existence of a principle in the theatre-going public calculated to rebuke the stage's wantonness, as upon the fact that matters have already reached a point beyond which they cannot go. In the direction of burlesque, no novelty now remains which is not forbidden by statute.

[*Atlantic Monthly*, May 1869]

24

[Mark Twain's Innocents Abroad]

The Innocents Abroad, or the New Pilgrim's Progress.
Being some Account of the Steamship Quaker City's
Pleasure-Excursion to Europe and the Holy Land, with
Descriptions of Countries, Nations, Incidents, and
Adventures as they appeared to the Author; with two
hundred and thirty-four Illustrations. By Mark Twain
(Samuel S. Clements). [Issued by Subscription only.]
Hartford, Conn.: American Publishing Company.

THE character of American humor, and its want of resemblance to the
humor of Kamtschatka and Patagonia,—will the reader forgive us if we fail
to set down here the thoughts suggested by these fresh and apposite topics?
Will he credit us with a self-denial proportioned to the vastness of Mr.
Clements's very amusing book, if we spare to state why he is so droll, or—
which is as much to the purpose—why we do not know? This reticence will
leave us very little to say by way of analysis; and, indeed, there is very little to
say of "The Innocents Abroad" which is not of the most obvious and easy
description. The idea of a steamer-load of Americans going on a prolonged
picnic to Europe and the Holy Land is itself almost sufficiently delightful,
and it is perhaps praise enough for the author to add that it suffers nothing
from his handling. If one considers the fun of making a volume of six
hundred octavo pages upon this subject, in compliance with one of the main
conditions of a subscription book's success, bigness namely, one has a
tolerably fair piece of humor, without troubling Mr. Clements further. It is
out of the bounty and abundance of his own nature that he is as amusing in
the execution as in the conception of his work. And it is always good-
humored humor, too, that he lavishes on his reader, and even in its
impudence it is charming; we do not remember where it is indulged at the
cost of the weak or helpless side, or where it is insolent, with all its sauciness
and irreverence. The standard shams of travel which everybody sees through
suffer possibly more than they ought, but not so much as they might; and one
readily forgives the harsh treatment of them in consideration of the novel
piece of justice done on such a traveller as suffers under the pseudonyme of
Grimes. It is impossible also that the quality of humor should not sometimes
be strained in the course of so long a narrative; but the wonder is rather in
the fact that it is strained so seldom.

Mr. Clements gets a good deal of his fun out of his fellow-passengers,
whom he makes us know pretty well, whether he presents them somewhat
caricatured, as in the case of the "Oracle" of the ship, or carefully and
exactly done, as in the case of such a shrewd, droll, business-like, sensible,
kindly type of the American young man as "Dan." We must say also that the
artist who has so copiously illustrated the volume has nearly always helped

the author in the portraiture of his fellow-passengers, instead of hurting him, which is saying a good deal for an artist; in fact, we may go further and apply the commendation to all the illustrations; and this in spite of the variety of figures in which the same persons are represented, and the artist's tendency to show the characters on mules where the author says they rode horseback.

Of course the instructive portions of Mr. Clements's book are of a general rather than particular character, and the reader gets as travel very little besides series of personal adventures and impressions; he is taught next to nothing about the population of the cities and the character of the rocks in the different localities. Yet the man who can be honest enough to let himself see the realities of human life everywhere, or who has only seen Americans as they are abroad, has not travelled in vain and is far from a useless guide. The very young American who told the English officers that a couple of our gunboats could come and knock Gibraltar into the Mediterranean Sea; the American who at a French restaurant "talked very loudly and coarsely, and laughed boisterously, where all others were so quiet and well behaved," and who ordered "wine, sir!" adding, to raise admiration in a country where wine is as much a matter of course as soup, "I never dine without wine, sir"; the American who had to be addressed several times as Gordon, being so accustomed to hear the name pronounced Gorrdong, and who had forgotten most English words during a three months' sojourn in Paris; the Americans who pitilessly made a three days' journey in Palestine within two days, cruelly overworking the poor beasts they rode, and overtaxing the strength of their comrades, in order not to break the Sabbath; the American Pilgrims who travelled half round the world to be able to take a sail on the Sea of Galilee, and then missed their sole opportunity because they required the boatman to take them for one napoleon when he wanted two;—these are all Americans who are painted to peculiar advantage by Mr. Clements, and who will be easily recognized by such as have had the good fortune to meet them abroad.

The didactic, however, is not Mr. Clements's prevailing mood, nor his best, by any means. The greater part of his book is in the vein of irony, which, with a delicious impudence, he attributes to Saint Luke, declaring that Luke, in speaking of the winding "street, called Straight" in Damascus, "is careful not to commit himself; he does not say it is the street which *is* straight, but the 'street which is *called* Straight.' It is a fine piece of irony; it is the only facetious remark in the Bible, I believe." At Tiberias our author saw the women who wear their dowry in their head-dresses of coins. "Most of these maidens were not wealthy, but some few have been kindly dealt with by fortune. I saw heiresses there, worth, in their own right,—worth, well, I suppose I might venture to say as much as nine dollars and a half. But such cases are rare. When you come across one of these, she naturally puts on airs." He thinks the owner of the horse "Jericho," on which he travelled towards Jerusalem, "had a wrong opinion about him. He had an idea that he was one of those fiery, untamed steeds, but he is not of that character. I know the Arab had this idea, because when he brought the horse out for inspection in Beirout, he kept jerking at the bridle and shouting in Arabic, 'Ho! will you? Do you want to run away, you ferocious beast, and break your neck?' when all the time the horse was not doing anything in the world, and only looked like he wanted to lean up against something and think. Whenever he is not shying at things or reaching after a fly, he wants to do that yet. How it would surprise his owner to know this!" In this vein of ironical drollery is that now celebrated passage in which Mr. Clements states that he was affected to tears on coming, a stranger in a strange land, upon the grave of a blood-relation,—the tomb of Adam; but that passage is somewhat more studied in tone than most parts of the book, which are written with a very successful approach in style to colloquial drolling. As Mr. Clements writes of his experiences, we imagine he would talk of them; and very amusing talk it would be: often not at all fine in matter or manner, but full of touches of humor,—which if not delicate are nearly always easy,—and having a base of excellent sense and good feeling. There is an amount of pure human nature in the book, that rarely gets into literature; the depths of our poor unregeneracy—dubious even of the blissfulness of bliss—are sounded by such a simple confession as Mr. Clements makes in telling of his visit to the Emperor of Russia: "I would as soon have thought of being cheerful in Abraham's bosom as in the palace of an Emperor." Almost any topic, and any event of the author's past life, he finds pertinent to the story of European and Oriental travel, and if the reader finds it impertinent, he does not find it the less amusing. The effect is dependent in so great degree upon this continuous incoherence, that no chosen passage can illustrate the spirit of the whole, while the passage itself loses half in separation from the context. Nevertheless, here is part of the account given by Mr. Clements of the Pilgrims' excursion to the river Jordan, over roads supposed to be infested by Bedouins; and the reader who does not think it droll as it stands can go to our author for the rest.

"I think we must all have determined upon the same line of tactics, for it did seem as if we never would get to Jericho. I had a notoriously slow horse; but somehow I could not keep him in the rear to save my neck. He was forever turning up in the lead. In such cases I trembled a little, and got down to fix my saddle. But it was not of any use. The others all got down to fix their saddles, too. I never saw such a time with saddles. It was the first time any of them had got out of order in three weeks, and now they had all broken down at once. I tried walking for exercise,—I had not had enough in Jerusalem, searching for holy places. But it was a failure. The whole mob were suffering for exercise, and it was not fifteen minutes till they were all on foot, and I had the lead again. . . . . We were moping along down through this dreadful place, every man in the rear. Our guards, two gorgeous young Arab sheiks, with cargoes of swords, guns, pistols, and daggers on board, were loafing ahead. 'Bedouins!' Every man shrunk up and disappeared in his clothes like a mud-turtle. My first impulse was to dash forward and destroy the Bedouins. My second was to dash to the rear to see if there were any coming in that direction. I acted on the latter impulse. So did all the others. If any Bedouins had approached us then from that point of the compass, they would have paid dearly for their rashness."

Under his *nom de plume* of Mark Twain, Mr. Clements is well known to the very large world of newspaper-readers; and this book ought to secure him something better than the uncertain standing of a popular favorite. It is no business of ours to fix his rank among the humorists California has given us, but we think he is, in an entirely different way from all the others, quite worthy of the company of the best.

[*Atlantic Monthly*, December 1869]

25

Mr. Lowell's New Poem.

The Cathedral. By James Russell Lowell. Boston: Fields, Osgood & Co. 1870.

WE should like this poem to be at least two hundred years old, in order to be able to say all we feel in praise of it; for the effort to establish the greatness of any new poem seems, next to the prophet's, the most dangerous and the most thankless office. But as it is not only not two hundred years old, but is one of the most recent things in literature—is yet, in fact, to be given to the public in *The Atlantic Monthly* for January, and thereafter in the pretty book-form in which we have it here—we must content ourselves with averring that it is the noblest poem which Mr. Lowell has yet written. And this perhaps, after all, is saying enough to commend it to the best taste and appreciation.

Mr. Lowell, who is not less than the greatest of living poets in his mental reach, has had the secret vouchsafed to so few of knowing how always to keep his heart warm and his head cool. And he has never been more exquisitely and delicately sympathetic, and at the same time more entirely master of himself and his subject than in this poem, where it seems as if he had meant to assemble all the forces of pathos, humor, wit, humanity—or something we must call by that name, wanting a good one for it—and a peculiarly sunny and consoling philosophy, by which he has hitherto touched, or amused, or won us, and to show that he had still to be in some easier and supremer way, all that he had yet been. Through the whole, which is as full of unexpected lights and surprises of color and design as a painted window, plays a fine unity of meaning, and there is everywhere such security of touch that the slightest pulse of feeling, the most subtile ray of thought is not lost between poet and reader.

The idea is very simple. The poet is one day at Chartres, in France, and seeing there the famous old Cathedral, the type of a religious sentiment which has passed away—

> "By suffrage universal it was built,
> As practiced then; for all the country came
> From far as Rouen, to give votes for God,
> Each vote a block of stone securely laid
> Obedient to the master's deep-mused plan;
> . . . . the windows, pride of France,
> Each the bright gift of some mechanic guild

> Who loved their city and thought gold well spent
> To make her beautiful with piety—"

he falls to thinking of the cathedral as it is and as it always has been in humanity. He is moved by all losses of the beautiful through the processes of change. He confesses himself

> "The born disciple of an elder time,
> To me sufficient, friendlier than the new."

Yet he has perfect faith in the future, and he sees in the very anarchy of the religious world, and the apparent overthrow of all religious order, the promise of a more generous and more courageous faith than that of the past. The latest and grandest of the Christian is to be the so-called, not yet understood, democracy; and the poem closes in a strain of aspiration, which is as unlike technically devotional poetry, as the rest is unlike technically didactic, descriptive and humorous poetry.

The work, which has a manifold beauty, draws its health and sweetness from whatever there is of hope or memory in the poet's own life, and it opens with a note almost as rich and tender as that unmatchable prelude to the "Vision of Sir Launfal."

> "Far through the memory shines a happy day,
> Cloudless of care, down-shod to every sense,
> And simply perfect from its own resource,
> As to the bee the new campanula's
> Illuminate seclusion swung in air.
> Such days are not the prey of setting suns,
> Nor ever blurred with mist of afterthought;
> Like words made magical by poets dead,
> Wherein the music of all meaning is
> The sense hath garnered or the soul divined,
> They mingle with our life's ethereal part,
> Sweetening and gathering sweetness evermore,
> By beauty's franchise disenthralled of time."

Then the poet recalls with a felicity of description, in which the memories of inner and outer things are blent in one exquisite effect:

> "Days that seem farther off than Homer's now
> Ere yet the child had loudened to the boy.
> .   .   .   .
> One spring I knew as never any since:
> All night the surges of the warm southwest
> Boomed intermittent through the shuddering elms,
> And brought a morning from the Gulf adrift,
> Omnipotent with sunshine, whose quick charm
> Startled with crocuses the sullen turf

And wiled the bluebird to his whiff of song:
One summer hour abides, what time I perched,
Dappled with noonday, under simmering leaves,
And pulled the pulpy oxhearts, while aloof
An oriole clattered and the robins shrilled,
Denouncing me an alien and a thief:
One morn of autumn lords it o'er the rest,
When in the lane I watched the ash-leaves fall,
Balancing softly earthward without wind,
Or twirling with directer impulse down
On those fallen yesterday, now barbed with frost,
While I grew pensive with the pensive year:
And once I learned how marvelous Winter was,
When past the fence-rails, downy-gray with rime,
I creaked adventurous o'er the spangled crust
That made familiar fields seem far and strange
As those stark wastes that whiten endlessly
In ghastly solitude about the pole
And gleam relentless to the unsetting sun."

Any one whom we should have to ask if all this were not wonderfully good we fear could not be made to feel its beauty, its intimate and affectionate knowledge of nature, and its subtle perception of her relation to us, as she

—"safe in uncontaminate resource,
Lets us mistake our longing for her love,
And mocks with various echo of herself."

But we may safely leave such poetry to commend itself. From these memories of his earliest days the poet passes to the recollection of his day at Chartres.

"In that Old World so strangely beautiful
To us the disinherited of eld—
A day at Chartres, with no soul beside
To roil with pedant prate my joy serene
And make the minster shy of confidence."

Though before bringing us into the presence of the Cathedral, he sketches with delightful humor some figures, upon the truth of which the traveler can best pronounce, but which none can fail fully to enjoy. At the "pea-green inn," he met two Englishmen—

"Who made me feel, in their engaging way,
I was a poacher on their self-preserve,
Intent constructively on lese anglicism.
To them (in those old razor-ridden days)
My beard translated me to hostile French;

> So they, desiring guidance in the town,
> Half condescended to my baser sphere,
> And, clubbing in one mess their lack of phrase,
> Set their best man to grapple with the Gaul.
> 'Esker vous ate a nabitang?' he asked;
> 'I never ate one; are they good?' asked I;
> Whereat they stared, then laughed,—and we were friends.
> The seas, the wars, the centuries interposed,
> Abolished in the truce of common speech
> And mutual comfort of the mother-tongue.
> Like escaped convicts of Propriety,
> They furtively partook the joys of men,
> Glancing behind when buzzed some louder fly."

Then, as he says,

> "Eluding these, I loitered through the town,
> With hope to take my minster unawares
> In its grave solitude of memory.
> Chance led me to a public pleasure-ground,
> Where I grew kindly with the merry groups,
> And blessed the Frenchman for his simple art
> Of being domestic in the light of day.
> His language has no word, we growl, for Home;
> But he can find a fireside in the sun,
> Play with his child, make love, and shriek his mind,
> By throngs of strangers undisprivacied.
> He makes his life a public gallery,
> Nor feels himself till what he feels comes back
> In manifold reflection from without;
> While we, each pore alert with consciousness,
> Hide our best selves as we had stolen them,
> And each bystander a detective were,
> Keen-eyed for every chink of undisguise."

Following some fine instinct in his feet, the saunterer looks up at last and suddenly finds himself

> "Confronted with the minster's vast repose,
> Silent and gray as forest-leaguered cliff
> Left inland by the ocean's slow retreat,
> That hears afar the breeze-borne rote, and longs,
> Remembering shocks of surf that clomb and fell,
> Spume-sliding down the baffled decuman,
> It rose before me, patiently remote
> From the great tides of life it breasted once,
> Hearing the noise of men as in a dream.
> I stood before the triple northern port,
> Where dedicated shapes of saints and kings,

Stern faces bleared with immemorial watch,
Looked down benignly grave and seemed to say,
Ye come and go incessant; we remain
Safe in the hallowed quiets of the past;
Be reverent, ye who flit and are forgot,
Of faith so nobly realized as this."

And so thinking and feeling for his sport more than for himself, the poet enters the Cathedral, and speaks for all of us people of to-day in the presence of other ages, past and to come—utters our regrets, and tenderness for those, our hope and belief in these:

"—Here was sense of undefined regret,
Irreparable loss, uncertain what:
Was all this grandeur but anachronism,—
A shell divorced of its informing life,
Where the priest housed him like a hermit-crab,
An alien to that faith of elder days
That gathered round it this fair shape of stone?
Is old Religion but a spectre now,
Haunting the solitude of darkened minds,
Mocked out of memory by the skeptic day?
Nay, did Faith build this worder? or did Fear,
That makes a fetish and misnames it God
(Blockish or metaphysic, matters not),
Contrive this coop to shut its tyrant in,
Appeased with playthings, that he might not harm?
I turned and saw a beldame on her knees;
With eyes astray, she told mechanic beads
Before some shrine of saintly womanhood,
Bribed intercessor with the far-off judge,—
Such my first thought, by kindlier soon rebuked,
Pleading for whatsoever touches life
With upward impulse: be He nowhere else,
God is in all that liberates and lifts;
In all that humbles, sweetens, and consoles.

.   .   .   .   .

'Tis irrecoverable, that ancient faith,
Homely and wholesome, suited to the time,
With rod or candy for child-minded men:
No theologic tube, with lens on lens
Of syllogism transparent, brings it near,—
At best resolving some new nebula,
And blurring some fixed-star of hope to mist.
Science was Faith once; Faith were Science now,
Would she but lay her bow and arrows by
And arm her with the weapons of the time.
Nothing that keeps thought out is safe from thought,
For there's no virgin-fort but self-respect,

And Truth defensive hath lost hold on God.
Shall we treat Him as if He were a child
That knew not His own purpose? nor dare trust
The Rock of Ages to their chemic tests,
Lest some day the all-sustaining base divine
Should fail from under us, dissolved in gas?

. . . .

Idle who hopes with prophets to be snatched
By virtue in their mantles left below;
Shall the soul live on other men's report,
Herself a pleasing fable of herself?
Man cannot be God's outlaw if he would.
This life were brutish did we not sometimes
Have intimation clear of wider scope,
Hints of occasion infinite, to keep
The soul alert with noble discontent
And upward yearnings of unstilled desire:
Fruitless, except we now and then divined
A mystery of Purpose, gleaming through
The secular confusions of the world,
Whose will we darkly accomplish, doing ours.
No man can think nor in himself perceive,
Sometimes at waking, in the street sometimes,
Or on the hill-side, always unforewarned,
A grace of being, finer than himself,
That beckons and is gone, a larger life.

. . . . . .

Who that hath known these visitations fleet
Would strive to make them trite and ritual?
I, that still pray at morning and at eve,
Loving those roots that feed us from the past,
And prizing more than Plato things I learned
At that best academe, a mother's knee,
Thrice in my life perhaps have truly prayed,
Thrice, stirred below my conscious self, have felt
That perfect disenthralment which is God;
Nor know I which to hold worst enemy—
Him who on speculation's windy waste
Would turn me loose, stript of the raiment warm
By Faith contrived against our nakedness,
Or him who, cruel-kind, would fain obscure,
With painted saints and paraphrase of God,
The soul's east-window of Divine surprise,
Where others worship, I but look and long;
For, though not recreant to my fathers' faith,
Its forms to me are weariness, and most
That drony vacuum of compulsory prayer,
Still pumping phrases for the ineffable,
Though all the valves of memory gasp and wheeze.

Words that have drawn transcendent meanings up
From the best passion of all bygone time,
Steeped through with tears of triumph and remorse,
Sweet with all sainthood, cleansed in martyr-fires,
Can they, so consecrate and so inspired,
By repetition wane to vexing wind?
Alas! we cannot draw habitual breath
In the thin air of life's supremer hights,
We cannot make each meal a sacrament,
Nor with our tailors be immortal souls,
We men, too conscious of earth's comedy,
Who see two sides, with our posed selves debate,
And only on great days can be sublime!
Let us be thankful when, as I do here,
We can read Bethel on a pile of stones,
And, seeing where God has been, trust in Him."

Turning now from the past to the future, the poet beholds the advent

"Of Earth's anarchic children latest born,
Democracy, a Titan who hath learned
To laugh at Jove's old-fashioned thunderbolts.—"

And at the touch of whose "solvents merciless,"

"The calm Olympian hight
Of ancient order feels its bases yield,
And pale gods glance for help to gods as pale.
. . This Western giant coarse,
Scorning refinements which he lacks himself,
Loves not nor heeds the ancestral hierarchies,
Each rank dependent on the next above
In orderly gradation fixed as fate,
King by mere manhood, nor allowing aught
Of holier unction than the sweat of toil;

.   .   .   .

How make him reverent of a King of kings?
Or Judge self-made, executor of laws
By him not first discussed and voted on?

.   .   .   .

Doubtless his church will be no hospital
For superannuate forms and mumping shams,
No parlor where men issue policies
Of life-assurance on the Eternal Mind,
Nor his religion but an ambulance
To fetch life's wounded and malingerers in,
Scorned by the strong; yet he, unconscious heir
To the influence sweet of Athens and of Rome,
And old Judæa's gift of secret fire,

Spite of himself shall surely learn to know
And worship some ideal of himself,
Some divine thing, large-hearted, brotherly,
Not nice in trifles, a soft creditor,
Pleased with his world, and hating only cant
And, if his Church be doubtful, it is sure
That, in a world, made for whatever else,
Not made for mere enjoyment, in a world
Of toil but half-requited, or, at best,
Paid in some futile currency of breath,
A world of incompleteness, sorrow swift
And consolation laggard, whatsoe'er
The form of building or the creed professed.
The Cross, bold type of shame to homage turned,
Of an unfinished life that sways the world,
Shall tower as sovereign emblem over all.

In attempting, as we have done, to condense the argument of a poem which was already so compact and terse of expression that the loss of every word involved the loss of a thought, we have done it an injustice which the reader will easily detect and repair when he takes it up as a whole. All those passages in which Mr. Lowell celebrates his coming man—or coming mankind—reflect his most characteristic moods, and are singularly true to his many-sided genius in their varying irony and earnestness, their grotesqueness and beauty, their intellectual acuteness and cordial tenderness, and in a certain robust enjoyment of the dismay of the feeble-hearted and weak-minded at the promise, or threat, of the future. In artistic spirit the poem is like the gothic structure that suggested it, and is not only very grand and noble in its proportions, but is richly and exquisitely wrought. It is full, too, of subtle analogies, of which it hardly seems possible that poet himself could have been conscious till the whole was done. Here, for example, is praise of gothic art, which is not only very beautiful as poetry and fine as thought, but which sympathetically unites the æsthetic and the spiritual motives of the poem, and in many respects might stand for the best expression of its own character and significance:

"The Grecian gluts me with its perfectness,
Unanswerable as Euclid, self-contained,
The one thing finished in this hasty world,
Forever finished, though the barbarous pit,
Fanatical on hearsay, stamp and shout
As if a miracle could be encored.
But ah! this other, this that never ends,
Still climbing, luring fancy still to climb,
As full of morals half-divined as life,
Graceful, grotesque, with ever new surprise
Of hazardous caprices sure to please,

Heavy as nightmare, airy-light as fern,
Imagination's very self in stone!
With one long sigh of infinite release
From pedantries past, present, or to come,
I looked, and owned myself a happy Goth.
And they could build, if not the columned fane
That from the hight gleamed seaward many-hued,
Something more friendly with their ruder skies:
The gray spire, molten now in driving mist,
Now lulled with the incommunicable blue;
The carvings touched to meanings new with snow,
Or commented with fleeting grace of shade;
The statues, motley as man's memory,
Partial as that; so mixed of true and false,
History and legend meeting with a kiss
Across this bound-mark where their realms confine;
The painted windows, frecking gloom with glow,
Dusking the sunshine which they seem to cheer,
Meet symbol of the senses and the soul;
And the whole pile, grim with the Northman's thought,
Of life and death, and doom, life's equal fee,—
These were before me."

We cannot reproduce any more than we give the ease and lightness of the
poem, the felicities of thought and phrase in which it abounds; but a few of
its memorable lines and passages we must allow ourselves the pleasure of
quoting, in however disconnected and desultory fashion:

"Second-thoughts are prose;
For beauty's acme hath a term as brief
As the wave's poise before it break in pearl.
Our own breath dims the mirror of the sense,
Looking too long and closely; at a flash
We snatch the essential grace of meaning out,
And that first passion beggars all behind,
Heirs of a tamer transport prepossessed."

"I blame not in the soul this daintiness,
Rasher of surfeit than a humming-bird,
In things indifferent purveyed by sense;
It argues her an immortality
And dateless incomes of experience,—
This unthrift housekeeping that will not brook
A dish warmed-over at the feast of life,
And finds Twice stale, served with whatever sauce."

"Change is the mask that all Continuance wears
To keep us youngsters harmlessly amused;

Meanwhile some ailing or more watchful child,
Sitting apart, sees the old eyes gleam out,
Stern, and yet soft with humorous pity too."

"Whilere, men burnt men for a doubtful point,
As if the mind were quenchable with fire,
And Faith danced round them with her war-paint on,
Devoutly savage as an Iroquois;
Now Calvin and Servetus at one board
Snuff in grave sympathy a milder roast,
And o'er their claret settle Comte unread."

"The bird I hear sings not from yonder elm;
But the flown ecstasy my childhood heard
Is vocal in my mind, renewed by him,
Haply made sweeter by the accumulate thrill
That threads my undivided life and steals
A pathos from the years and graves between."

"Fagot and stake were desperately sincere:
Our cooler martyrdoms are done in types;
And flames that shine in controversial eyes
Burn out no brains but his who kindles them.
This is no age to get cathedrals built:
Did God, then, wait for one in Bethlehem?"

　　　　　　　　　　　"I gazed abashed,
Child of an age that lectures, not creates,
Plastering our swallow-nests on the awful Past,
And twittering round the work of larger men,
As we had builded what we but deface."

"Thou beautiful Old Time　　.　　.　　.　　.
.　　.　　.　　.　　perchance less fair
To who possessed thee, as a mountain seems
To dwellers round its bases but a heap
Of barren obstacle that lairs the storm
And the avalanche's silent bolt holds back
Leashed with a hair—meanwhile some far-off clown,
Hereditary delver of the plain,
Sees it an unmoved vision of repose,
Nest of the morning, and conjectures there
The dance of streams to idle shepherds' pipes,
And fairer habitations softly hung
On breezy slopes, or hid in valleys cool,
For happier men.

I fear not Thy withdrawal; more I fear,
Seeing, to know Thee not; hoodwinked with thought
Of signs and wonders, while, unnoticed, Thou,
Walking Thy garden still, commun'st with men,
Missed in the commonplace of miracle.''

As the reader will have perceived, Mr. Lowell has here written not a love poem for the young ladies—though that is an affair not to be despised—but something for men and women who have lived, and doubted, and aspired, pondering the riddle of life here and the mystery of life in the world to come. Yet the work is as far as possible from being a sermon or an essay; for, however great in its spiritual meaning and intellectual power, it is above all things a poem, and has its chief and final excellence in beauty. Among the minor poets, we have our little likes and dislikes, as among our friends, without the strictest regard to their merits; some quite vague and undefined quality draws us to them or repulses us, and we like now one and now another, without being able to give any very good reason for being off with the old love and on with the new. But this is never the case with poets of Mr. Lowell's rank, and with regard to "The Cathedral," we may hazard so much prophecy as to say that whoever discerns its scope and perceives its meaning, will be sensible that the powerful and positive qualities of the greatest and noblest poetry have won his admiration. It gives at once the impression of grandeur about which there can be no question, and the reader feels that the lapse of time cannot make it more classic than it is now. It does not seem, like most new poetry, subject to the mood in which it is approached, and though perhaps on the whole it is, more than any other poem, expressive of modern thought and aspiration, there is nothing of literary fashion in it—the thing which is so apt to charm and then so apt to weary us.

[New York *Tribune*, 16 December 1869]

26

[T. B. Aldrich's Bad Boy]

The Story of a Bad Boy. By Thomas Bailey Aldrich. With
Illustrations. Boston: Fields, Osgood, & Co.

MR. Aldrich has done a new thing in—we use the phrase with some gasps of
reluctance, it is so threadbare and so near meaning nothing—American
literature. We might go much farther without overpraising his pleasant book,
and call it an absolute novelty, on the whole. No one else seems to have
thought of telling the story of a boy's life, with so great desire to show what a
boy's life is, and so little purpose of teaching what it should be; certainly no
one else has thought of doing this for the life of an American boy. The
conception of such a performance is altogether his in this case; but with
regard to more full-grown figures of fiction, it is that of the best and oldest
masters of the art of story-telling; and it is one that will at last give us, we
believe, the work which has so long hovered in the mental atmosphere a
pathetic ante-natal phantom, pleading to be born into the world,—the
American novel, namely.

Autobiography has a charm which passes that of all other kinds of reading; it has almost the relish of the gossip we talk about our friends; and
whoever chooses its form for his inventions is sure to prepossess us; and if
then he can give his incidents and characters the simple order and air of
actual occurrences and people, it does not matter much what they are,—his
success is assured. We think this is the open secret of the pleasure which
"The Story of a Bad Boy" has afforded to the boys themselves, and to every
man that happens to have been a boy. There must be a great deal of fact
mixed up with the feigning, but the author has the art which imbues all with
the same quality, and will not let us tell one from the other. He asks us to
know a boy coming from his father's house in New Orleans, where he has
almost become a high-toned Southerner, to be educated under his grandfather's care in a little New England seaport. His ideas, impulses, and adventures here are those of the great average of boys, and the effect of a boy's
small interests, ignorant ambition, and narrow horizon is admirably produced and sustained. His year is half made up of Fourth-of-Julys and Thanks-
givings; he has so little vantage-ground of experience that life blackens
before him when he is left to pay for twelve ice-creams out of an empty
pocket; he has that sense of isolation and of immeasurable remoteness from
the sphere of men, which causes half the pleasure and half the pain of childhood; and his character and surroundings are all so well managed, that this

propriety is rarely violated. Now and then, however, the author mars the good result by an after-thought that seems almost an alien stroke, affecting one as if some other brain had "edited" the original inspiration. We should say, for example, that in all that account of the boy-theatricals it is the author who speaks, till after Pepper Whitcomb, standing for Tell's son, receives the erring bolt in his mouth, when, emulous of the natural touches, the editor appears and adds: "The place was closed; not, however, without a farewell speech from me, in which I said that this would have been the proudest moment of my life if I had n't hit Pepper Whitcomb in the mouth. Where-upon the audience (assisted, I am glad to state, by Pepper) cried, 'Hear! hear!' I then attributed the accident to Pepper himself, whose mouth, being open at the instant I fired, acted upon the arrow much after the fashion of a whirlpool, and drew in the fatal shaft. I was about to explain how a compara-tively small maelstrom could suck in the largest ship, when the curtain fell of its own accord, amid the shouts of the audience."

Most of the characters of the book are as good as the incidents and the principal idea. Captain Nutter, the grandfather, and Miss Abigail, the maiden aunt, are true New England types, the very truth of which makes them seem at first glance wanting in novelty; but they develop their originality gradually, as New England acquaintance should, until we feel for them the tenderness and appreciation with which they are studied. The Captain is the better of the two; he is such a grandfather as any boy might be glad to have, and is well done as a personage and as a sketch of hearty and kindly old age,—outwardly a little austere, but full of an ill-hidden tolerance and secret sympathies with the wildness of boyhood. Others among the townspeople, merely sketched, or seen falsely with a boy's vision, are no less living to us; the pony becomes a valued acquaintance; nay, the old Nutter house itself, and the sleepy old town, have a personal fascination. Of Kitty, the Irish servant, and of her sea-faring husband, we are not so sure,—at least we are not so sure of the latter, who seems too much like the sailors we have met in the forecastles of novels and theatres, though for all we know he may be a veritable person. We like much better some of the merely indicated figures, like that mistaken genius who bought up all the old cannon from the privateer at the close of the war of 1812, in the persuasion that hostilities must soon break out again; and that shrewd Yankee who looked on from his hiding-place while the boys stole his worn-out stage-coach for a bonfire, and then exacted a fabulous price from their families for a property that had proved itself otherwise unsalable. The boys also are all true boys, and none is truer than the most difficult character to treat,—Binny Wallace, whose gentleness and sweetness are never suffered to appear what boys call "softness"; and on the whole we think the chapter which tells of his loss is the best in the book; it is the simplest and directest piece of narration, and is singularly touching, with such breadth and depth of impression that when you look at it a second time, you are suprised to find the account so brief and slight. Mr. Aldrich has the same good fortune wherever he means to be pathetic. The touches with

which he indicates his hero's homesickness when he is first left at Rivermouth
are delicate and sufficient; so are those making known the sorrow that befalls
him in the death of his father. In these passages, and in some description of
his lovesickness, he does not push his effects too far, as he is tempted to do
where he would be most amusing. "Pepper," he says the hero said to his
friend who found him prowling about an old graveyard after his great disappointment, "don't ask me. All is not well here,"—touching his breast myste-
riously. "Earthly happiness is a delusion and a snare,"—all which fails to
strike us as an original or probable statement of the case; while this little
picture of a boy's forlorn attempt to make love to a young lady seems as
natural as it is charming:—

> "Here the conversation died a natural death. Nelly sank into a sort of dream,
> and I meditated. Fearing every moment to be interrupted by some member of
> the family, I nerved myself to make a bold dash:—
> " 'Nelly.'
> " 'Well.'
> " 'Do you—' I hesitated.
> " 'Do I what?'
> " 'Love any one very much?'
> " 'Why, of course I do,' said Nelly, scattering her revery with a merry laugh.
> 'I love Uncle Nutter, and Aunt Nutter, and you,—and Towser.'
> "Towser, our new dog! I could n't stand that. I pushed back the stool impa-
> tiently and stood in front of her.
> " 'That's not what I mean,' I said angrily.
> " 'Well, what do you mean?'
> " 'Do you love any one to marry him?'
> " 'The idea of it!' cried Nelly, laughing.
> " 'But you must tell me.'
> " 'Must, Tom?'
> " 'Indeed you must, Nelly.'
> "She had arisen from the chair with an amused, perplexed look in her eyes. I
> held her an instant by the dress.
> " 'Please tell me.'
> " 'O you silly boy!' cried Nelly. Then she rumpled my hair all over my fore-
> head and ran laughing out of the room."

Mr. Aldrich is a capital *conteur*; the narrative is invariably good, neither
hurried nor spun out, but easily discursive, and tolerant of a greal deal of
anecdote that goes finally to complete the charm of a life-like and delightful
little story, while the moralizing is always as brief as it is pointed and generous. When he comes to tell a tale for older heads,—as we hope he some day
will,—we shall not ask him to do it better than this in essentials, and in less
important particulars shall only pray him to be always himself down to the
very last word and smallest turn of expression. We think him good enough.

[*Atlantic Monthly*, January 1870]

27

[William Makepeace Thackeray]

Miscellanies. [Five Volumes.] By W. M. Thackeray. Household Edition. Boston: Fields, Osgood, & Co.

Catherine; A Story. By Ikey Solomons, Esq., Junior. [W. M. Thackeray.] Boston: Fields, Osgood, & Co.

WHETHER Thackeray's novels or his shorter stories and sketches are better is a question each reader will settle in favor of whichever he happens to be reading. We, for example, do not think he wrote anything more perfect than "The Luck of Barry Lyndon"; but then we have just been reading that over again, and it is some time since we looked at "Henry Esmond." We will only be certain that nearly all he did was masterly, and is inestimably precious now that he can do no more. They may say that his later gifts were somewhat poor and stale in quality; but we would rather have the rinsings—if "Philip" is to be so called—of that magical flask out which he poured such wonderful and various liquors, than the fulness and prime spirit of many a famous tap we could name. We will own even that he had not a good knack at invention: what need had he of it who could give us real men and women, and could portray life so truly that we scarcely thought of asking about a plot? We almost think that if he who rarely struck the wrong note in character had often been out of time and tune there, there would have been enough delight in his style to have atoned for all,—so much it seems compact of what is vigorous in men's daily speech and what is simple and elegant in literary art.

This style was never better than in the different tales and studies which are known as Thackeray's Miscellanies, and which are here produced anew with various papers not previously collected. Here is its earlier brilliancy and its later mellowness; and in these stories and essays is also to be noted that gradual change of Thackeray's humor, from what he called the "bumptiousness" of the period in which he laughed poor Bulwer to scorn, and fiercely attacked social shams in the "Book of Snobs" and other places, to the relenting or the indifference of the time in which he wrote the "Roundabout Papers" and "Philip." But what a marvellous savor in all! The first line is an appetizer that carries you hungry through the feast, whatever it is, and makes you wish for the time being there were no other dish but that in the world. Over "Barry Lyndon," or "Major Gahagan," or "Dennis Haggarty," you lament that he ever wrote anything but stories of Irish character (what lamentable comedy, what tragical mirth, are in the first and the last!); and, delaying yourself as much as you can in "The Four Georges," you feel that a man who could revive the past in that way ought to have written only social history. In the riot of his burlesques, and the caricatured Fitz-Boodle papers, he is not seen at his best, but his second-rate is much better than the first-rate of any one else in the same way. He has set up many smaller wits in that sort of humor which he may be said to have invented; and we cannot in our weariness of them do him complete justice; but this is not his fate in the quieter essays and sketches where no one could follow him. "From Cornhill to Cairo," "Coxe's Diary," the "Little Travels," "The Irish Sketches," "The Paris Sketch-Book," "Sketches and Travels in London," are still sole of their kind; and as for "The Great Hoggarty Diamond," some people think that not only stands alone, but is unsurpassed among its author's works. These may be people who have just been reading it, or who like the company of rather a greater number of kind-hearted and sensible women than Thackeray commonly allows us to know; but certainly he has not portrayed a finer and truer fellow than Samuel Titmarsh, and we do not dispute any one's good opinion of the book, while we do not relinquish our own concerning different ones.

Not that we are inclined to a great affection for the story of "Catherine," though this is very different from the tale last named. There is not a lovable person, high or low, in it,—not a soul to respect or even pity; and such purpose as Thackeray had in rebuking the romantic use of rascality in fiction, by depicting rogues and their female friends in their true characters, would seem to have been sufficiently served by it. We are far enough now from the days of "Eugene Aram" and the novels with murderers for heroes, but we have by no means got rid of immoral heroines, and the unvarnished adventures of "Catherine" may still be read with profit. She is in brief a bad young person, pretty, vain, and heartless, who becomes the mistress of a nobleman, and who, when deserted by him, marries an old rustic lover, and survives to meet her paramour many years after. In hopes of becoming his wife, she murders her husband with the help of her natural son, in whose company she is hanged. It is a horrible story from first to last; so horrible that there seems no sufficient reason for suppressing (as has been done by Thackeray's English publishers, whom Messrs. Fields, Osgood, & Co. have naturally followed) the account of the murder and execution, which Thackeray copied from newspapers describing actual occurrences, and the effect of which the reader misses. In this dreadful history, the author tears from the essential ugliness of sin and crime the veil of romance, and shows them for what they are; but while there is not the least glamour of sentiment in the book, it is full of the fascination of his wonderful art. The scene is laid in that eighteenth century which he loved to paint, and he has hardly ever caused certain phases of its life to be better acted or costumed. The Count Galgenstein, Catherine's lover, the handsome, stupid profligate, with all the vices of the English and German blood that mingled in his veins, who lapses at last into a garrulous, sickly, tedious, elegant old reprobate; Catherine, with no more morality or conscience than an animal,—pretty, ambitious, scheming, thrifty, and fond of her brutal son, who grows to manhood with whatever is bad from either parent become worse in him; Brock, Galgenstein's corporal and her Majesty's recruiting-sergeant, subsequently convict, and highwayman, and finally accomplice in the murder of Catherine's husband; this husband himself, with his avarice and cunning and cowardice,—are persons whose character and accessories are powerfully painted, and about whom are grouped many others more sketchily drawn, but still completely suggested. The book is one that will not let the reader go, horrible as it is, and little as it is to be liked for anything but its morality. This is admirable, to our thinking; it is very simple and obvious, as the morality is in all Thackeray's books; whence those who think that there is some mighty subtle difference between right and wrong have begun to say he is a shallow moralist.

Among the books satirized in "Catherine" is "Oliver Twist," and Nancy is laughed at as an impossibility. The reader will remember how a sort of reparation is afterwards made in "The Newcomes," where this novel is praised. We believe Thackeray felt no compunctions concerning Bulwer's romances, which here come in for a far larger share of his scorn.

[*Atlantic Monthly*, February 1870]

28

[Björnson's Fiction]

Arne: a Sketch of Norwegian Country Life. By Björnstjerne Björnson. Translated from the Norwegian by Augusta Plesner and S. Rugeley Powers. Cambridge and Boston: Sever, Francis, & Co.

The Happy Boy; a Tale of Norwegian Peasant Life. By Björnstjerne Björnson. Translated from the Norwegian, by H. R. G. Cambridge and Boston: Sever, Francis, & Co.

The Fisher-Maiden; A Norwegian Tale. By Björnstjerne Björnson. From the Author's German Edition, by M. E. Niles. New York: Leypoldt and Holt.

THE author of that unique essay, "The Glut of the Fiction Market," who had the good fortune to put more truth about novels into wittier phrase than any other essayist of this time, held that having exhausted all the types and situations and catastrophes of English fiction, we must give it up as a source of literary amusement; and, indeed, there are very few critics who do not now, in their heart of hearts (if they have any), secretly look forward to a time when people shall read nothing but book-notices.

Whilst this millennial period is still somewhat distant, their weariness of our own novelists is attested by nothing so vividly as the extraordinary welcome which has of late been given to translations of the novels of all other races; for, generally speaking, these invaders of our realm of fiction are not better than the novelists they have displaced, but only different. Miss Mühlbach, the author of a vast, and, we believe, increasing horde of blond romances, is the most formidable foe that our sorrier sort of fictionists have had to contend with, and in her train have followed unnumbered others, though none so popular and so poor. Amongst these, indeed, have appeared several of striking merit, and conspicuously Björnstjerne Björnson, the Norwegian, whose beautiful romances we wish all our readers to like with us. Concerning the man himself, we know little more than that he is the son of a country clergyman, and that, after a rather unpromising career in school and college, he has risen to the first place in the literature of the North, and has almost invented a new pleasure in the fresh and wonderful tales he writes about Norwegian life. He has been the manager of a theatre, and he has written many plays, but we believe he is known in English only by the three books of which we have given the titles below, and which form an addition to literature of as great and certain value as any which has been otherwise made during the last two years.

There is in the way the tales are told a singular simplicity, or a reticence and self-control that pass for this virtue, and that take the æsthetic sense as winningly as their sentiment touches the heart. The author has entire confidence in his reader's intelligence. He believes, it seems, that we can be fully satisfied with a few distinct touches in representing a situation or a character; he is the reverse, in a word, of all that is Trollopian in literary art. He does not concern himself with detail, nor with general statement, but he makes some one expressive particular serve for all introduction and explanation of a fact. The life he portrays is that, for the most part, of humble but decent folk; and this choice of subject is also novel and refreshing in contrast with the subjects of our own fictions, in which there seems to be no middle ground between magnificent drawing-rooms and the most unpleasant back-alleys, or between very refined and well-born company and the worst reprobates of either sex. How much of our sense of his naturalness would survive further acquaintance with Björnson we cannot venture to say; the conventionalities of a literature are but too perilously apt to be praised as *naïveté* by foreign criticism, and we have only the internal evidence that peasant-boys like Arne, and fisher-maidens like Petra, are not as common and tiresome in Norwegian fiction as we find certain figures in our own novels. We would willingly celebrate them, therefore, with a wise reserve, and season our delight with doubt, as a critic should; though we are not at all sure that we can do this.

Arne is the son of Margit Kampen and Nils the tailor, who is the finest dancer and the gallantest man in all the country-side; and it is with subtlety and feeling that the author hints the error by which Arne came to be:—

"The next time there was a dance in the parish Margit was there. She sat listening to the music, and cared little for the dancing that night; and she was glad that somebody else, too, cared no more for it than she did. But when it grew later, the fidler, Nils the tailor, rose and wished to dance. He went straight over and took out Margit, and before she well knew what she was doing she danced with him. . . .

"Soon the weather turned warmer, and there was no more dancing. That spring Margit took so much care of a little sick lamb, that her mother thought her quite foolish. 'It's only a lamb, after all,' said the mother. 'Yes; but it's sick,' answered Margit.

"It was a long time since Margit had been to church; somebody must stay at home, she used to say, and she would rather let the mother go. One Sunday, however, later in the summer, the weather seemed so fine that the hay might very well be left over that day and night, the mother said, and she thought both of them might go. Margit had nothing to say against it, and she went to dress herself. But when they had gone far enough to hear the church-bells, she suddenly burst into tears. The mother grew deadly pale; yet they went on to church, heard the sermon and prayers, sang all the hymns, and let the last sound of the bells die away before they left. But when they were seated at home again, the mother took Margit's face between her hands, and said, 'Keep back nothing from me, my child!' "

But Nils is in love with Birgit Böen, who loves him again, and is richer and handsomer than Margit. They torment each other, lover's fashion, Birgit being proud, and Nils capricious and dissipated, until one night at a dance he runs wilfully against Birgit and another lover of hers (who afterwards marries her), and knocks them over. Then this lover strikes Nils, who falls against the sharp edge of the fireplace, upon his spine. So Margit comes to claim him, and takes him home, and they are married; but as Nils grows better in health he grows a worse man, gives himself constantly to drink, and beats Margit cruelly. At last it comes to this awful scene, which is portrayed with peculiar force and boldness, and which is a good illustration of a manner so unaffected that manner hardly seems the word for it. Nils comes home after one of his drinking-bouts at a wedding-party, and finds Arne reading and Margit in bed.

"Arne was startled by the sound of a heavy fall in the passage, and of something hard pushing against the door. It was the father, just coming home.

" 'Is it you, my clever boy?' he muttered; 'come and help your father to get up.' Arne helped him up, and brought him to the bench; then carried in the violin-case after him and shut the door. 'Well, look at me, you clever boy; I don't look very handsome, now; Nils the tailor's no longer the man he used to be. One thing, I—tell—you—you shall never drink spirits; they're—the devil, the world, and the flesh. . . . . "God resisteth the proud, but giveth grace to the humble.". . . . O dear! O dear! How far gone I am!'

"He sat silent for a while, and then sang in a tearful voice,—

> 'Merciful Lord, I come to Thee;
> Help, if there can be help for me;
> Though by the mire of sin defiled,
> I'm still Thine own dear ransomed child.'

" ' "Lord, I am not worthy that Thou shouldest come under my roof; but speak the word only . . . ." ' He threw himself forward, hid his face in his hands, and sobbed violently. . . .

"Then he was silent, and his weeping became subdued and calm.

"The mother had been long awake, without looking up; but now when she heard him weeping thus like one who is saved, she raised herself on her elbows, and gazed earnestly at him.

"But scarcely did Nils perceive her before he called out, 'Are you looking up, you ugly vixen! I suppose you would like to see what a state you have brought me to. Well, so I look, just so!'. . . . He rose; and she hid herself under the fur coverlet. 'Nay, don't hide, I'm sure to find you,' he said, stretching out his right hand and fumbling with his forefinger on the bedclothes, 'Tickle, tickle,' he said, turning aside the fur coverlet, and putting his forefinger on her throat.

" 'Father!' cried Arne.

" 'How shrivelled and thin you've become already, there's no depth of flesh here!' She writhed beneath his touch, and seized his hand with both hers, but could not free herself.

" 'Father!' repeated Arne.

" 'Well, at last you're roused. How she wriggles, the ugly thing! Can't you scream to make believe I am beating you? Tickle, tickle! I only want to take away your breath.'

" 'Father!' Arne said once more, running to the corner of the room, and snatching up an axe which stood there.

" 'Is it only out of perverseness you don't scream? you had better beware; for I've taken such a strange fancy into my head. Tickle, tickle! Now, I think I shall soon get rid of that screaming of yours.'

" 'Father!' Arne shouted, rushing towards him with the axe uplifted.

"But before Arne could reach him, he started up with a piercing cry, laid his hand upon his heart, and fell heavily down. 'Jesus Christ!' he muttered, and then lay quite still.

"Arne stood as if rooted in the ground, and gradually lowered the axe. He grew dizzy and bewildered, and scarcely knew where he was. Then the mother began to move to and fro in the bed, and to breathe heavily, as if oppressed by some great weight lying upon her. Arne saw that she needed help; but yet he felt unable to render it. At last she raised herself a little, and saw the father lying stretched on the floor, and Arne standing beside him with the axe.

" 'Merciful Lord, what have you done?' she cried, springing out of the bed, putting on her skirt and coming nearer.

" 'He fell down himself,' said Arne, at last regaining power to speak.

" 'Arne, Arne, I don't believe you,' said the mother, in a stern reproachful voice: 'now Jesus help you!' And she threw herself upon the dead man with loud wailing.

"But the boy awoke from his stupor, dropped the axe and fell down on his knees: 'As true as I hope for mercy from God, I've not done it. I almost thought of doing it; I was so bewildered; but then he fell down himself; and here I've been standing ever since.'

"The mother looked at him, and believed him. 'Then our Lord has been here Himself,' she said, quietly, sitting down on the floor and gazing before her."

The terror and shadow of what he might have done hung long about Arne, making lonelier and sadder the life that was already melancholy and secluded. He has many dreams of going abroad, and escaping from the gloomy associations of his home and his past life; and, indulging these and other dreams, he begins to make songs and to sing them. All the processes of his thought are clearly suggested, and then almost as much is left to the reader's fancy as in any poem that stands so professed in rhyme. People are shown without effort to account for their presence further than it is explained in their actions, so that all has the charm of fact, about which there ever hangs a certain fascinating mystery; and the pictures of scenery are made with a confidence that they will please because they are beautiful. In these, natural aspects are represented as affecting the beholder in certain ways, and nature does not, as in our false sentimentilization, take on the complexion of his thoughts and reflect his mood.

By and by Arne is drawn somewhat away from the lonely life he has been leading, and upon a certain occasion he is persuaded to go nutting with a party of young girls; and here the author sketches with all his winning lightness and confidence the young-girl character he wishes us to see:—

> "So Arne came to the party, and was nearly the only young man among the many girls. Such fun as was there Arne had never seen before in all his life; and one thing which especially astonished him was, that the girls laughed for nothing at all: if three laughed, then five would laugh just because those three laughed. Altogether, they behaved as if they had lived with each other all their lives; and yet there were several of them who had never met before that very day. When they caught the bough which they jumped after, they laughed, and when they did not catch it they laughed also; when they did not find any nuts, they laughed because they found none; and when they did find some, they also laughed. They fought for the nutting-hook: those who got it laughed, and those who did not get it laughed also. Godfather limped after them, trying to beat them with his stick, and making all the mischief he was good for; those he hit laughed because he hit them, and those he missed laughed because he missed them. But the whole lot laughed at Arne because he was so grave; and when at last he could not help laughing, they all laughed again because he laughed."

This is the way in which all young girls appear to all boys, confounding them with emotions and caprices which they do not themselves understand; it is the history of a whole epoch of life; yet with how few words it is told! Think how one of our own story-tellers,—even a very clever one,—with the heavy and awkward traditions of the craft would have gone about it, if he or she had had the grace to conceive of anything so pretty and natural, and how it would have been explained and circumstantiated, and analyzed, and made detestable with the intrusion of the author's reflections and comments!

There is not much plot in "Arne." The task which the author seems chiefly to have proposed himself is the working out, by incident and encounter, of a few characters. In the person of Arne as in Petra, the fisher-maiden, he attempts a most difficult work; though Arne as a genius is far inferior to Petra. Still, there is in both the waywardness and strangeness produced by peculiar gifts, and both characters have to be handled with great delicacy to preserve the truth which is so often unlike truth, and the naturalness which is so uncommon as to appear unnatural. One of the maidens in the nutting-party is Eli Böen, the daughter of Birgit and Baard, the man who struck Arne's father that dreadful blow; and Arne, with as little consciousness as possible, and while still planning to go abroad, falls in love with her. It all ends, of course, with some delaying occurrence in their marriage, and in the heartfelt union of Eli's parents, who during twenty years have been secretly held apart by Birgit's old love for Nils, and by the memory of Baard's share in his ruin. This last effect, which is an incident of the main story, is inseparable from it, but is not hinted till far toward the end, and is then produced with that trusting and unhasty art which, together with the brevity of every scene and incident, makes the romance so enjoyable. There is something also very wise and fine in the management of the character of Margit, Arne's mother, who, in spite of the double tragedy of her life, is seen to be a passive and simple heart, to whom things merely happen, and who throughout merely loves, now her bad husband and now her affectionate yet unintelligible son, whom she singly desires to keep with her always. She is the type of maternity as nearly as it can exist unrelated to other phases and conditions; and when she hears that Arne is in love with Eli, she has no other thought than to rejoice that this is a tie which will bind him to home. Meeting Eli one evening in the road, she lures her to walk toward Kampen that she may praise Arne to her; then comes some dialogue which is contrived to show the artless artifices by which these two women strive to turn the talk to and from the object of their different love; and after that there are most enchanting little scenes in the home at Kampen, when the women find Arne's treasury of wedding-gear, and at the end some of the prettiest love-making when Arne himself comes home.

With people in another rank, Charles Reade would have managed this as charmingly, though he would have thrown into it somewhat too much of the brilliancy of the footlights; and Auerbach would have done it with equal naturalness; but neither could have cast about it that poetic atmosphere which is so peculiarly the gift of Björnson and of the Northern mind, and which is felt in its creations, as if the glamour of the long summer days of the North had got into literature. It is very noticeable throughout "Arne." The facts are stated with perfect ruggedness and downrightness when necessary, but some dreamy haze seems still to cling about them, subduing their hard outlines and features like the tender light of the slanting Norwegian sun on the craggy Norwegian headlands. The romance is interspersed with little lyrics, pretty and graceful in their form, but of just the quality to show that Björnson is wise to have chosen prose for the expression of his finer and stronger thoughts.

In that region of novel characters, wholesome sympathies, and simple interests to which he transports us, we have not only a blissful sense of escape from the jejune inventions and stock repetitions of what really seems a failing art with us, but are aware of our contact with an excellent and enviable civilization. Of course the reader sees the Norwegians and their surroundings through Björnson's poetic eyes, and is aware that he is reading romance; yet he feels that there must be truth to the real as well as the ideal in these stories.

"Arne" is the most poetical of the three, and the action is principally in a world where the troubles are from within, and inherent in human nature, rather than from any artificial causes, though the idyllic sweetness is chiefly owing to the circumstances of the characters as peasant-folk in a "North countree." In "The Happy Boy" the world of conventions and distinctions is more involved by the fortunes of the lovers; for the happy boy Oeyvind is made wretched enough in the good old way by finding out that there is a difference between riches and poverty in the eyes of grandparents, at least, and he is tormented in his love of Marit by his jealousy of a wealthier rival. It is Marit's worldly and ambitious grandfather who forbids their love, and will have only unpleasant things to say to Oeyvind, until the latter comes back from the Agricultural College, and establishes himself in his old home with the repute of the best farmer in the neighborhood. Meantime unremitted love-making goes on between Marit and Oeyvind, abetted by Oeyvind's schoolmaster, through whom indeed all their correspondence was conducted while Oeyvind was away at school. At last the affair is happily concluded when Ole Nordistuen, the grandfather, finds that his farm is going to ruin, and nothing can save it but the skill of Oeyvind.

In this story the peasant life is painted in a more naturalistic spirit, and its customs are more fully described, though here as always in Björnson's work the people are primarily studied as men and women, and secondarily as peasants and citizens; and the descriptions are brief, incidental, and strictly subordinate to the story. We imagine in this an exercise of self-denial, for Björnson must be in love with all that belongs to his characters or surrounds them, to the degree of desiring to dwell longer than he ever does upon their portrayal. His fashion in dealing with scenery and character both is well shown in this account of Marit's party, to which Oeyvind was invited, and at which he ceases with his experience of the world to be the entirely happy boy of the past:—

"It was a half clear, mild evening; no stars were to be seen; the next day it could not help raining. A sleepy kind of wind blew over the snow, which was swept away here and there on the white Heide fields; in other spots it had drifted. Along the side of the road, where there lay but little snow, there was ice which stretched along blue-black between the snow and the bare field, and peeped out in patches as far as one could see. Along the mountains there had been avalanches; in their track it was dark and bare, but on both sides bright and covered with snow, except where the birch-trees were packed together in black masses. There was no water to be seen, but half-naked marshes and morasses lay under the deeply fissured, melancholy looking mountain. The farms lay in thick clusters in the middle of the plain; in the darkness of the winter evening they looked like black lamps, from which light shot over the fields, now from one window, now from another; to judge by the lights, it seemed as if they were busy inside.

"Children, grown up and half grown up, were flocking together from all directions: the smaller number walked along the road; but they, too, left it when they came near the farms; and there stole along one under the shadow of the stable, a couple near the granary; some ran for a long time behind the barn, screaming like foxes, others answered far away like cats, one stood behind the wash-house, and barked like a cross old crack-voiced dog, until there became a general hunt. The girls came along in great flocks, and had some boys, mostly little boys, with them, who gathered around them along the road to seem like young men. When such a swarm of girls arrived at the farm, and one or a couple of the grown-up boys saw them, the girls separated, flew into the passages between the buildings or down in the garden, and had to be dragged into the house one by one. Some were so bashful that Marit had to be sent for, and compel them to come in. Sometimes, too, there came one who had not originally been invited, and whose intention was not at all to go in, but only to look on, until it turned out that she would just take one little dance. Those whom Marit liked much she invited into a little room where the old people themselves were, the old man sitting smoking and grandmamma walking about. There they got something to drink, and were kindly spoken to. Oeyvind was not among them, and that struck him as rather strange.''

When the dancing began, he scarcely dared to ask Marit to dance with him, and at last, when he did so, a tall, dark-complexioned fellow with thick hair threw himself in front of him. "Back, youngster!" he shouted, pushing Oeyvind so that the latter nearly fell backward over Marit.

"Nothing like this had ever happened to him before; never had any one been otherwise than kind to him, never had he been called 'Youngster,' when he wished to join in; he blushed scarlet, but said nothing, and drew back to where the new fiddler, who had just arrived, had sat down, and was busy tuning up his fiddle. . . . .

"He looked longer and longer at her; but, in whatever way he looked, it seemed to him as if Marit were quite grown up; 'it cannot be so, he thought, for she still coasts down hill with us.' But grown up she was, nevertheless; and the thick-haired man pulled her, after the dance was over, down on to his lap; she glided off, still remaining, however, sitting by his side.

So Oeyvind discovered that this young man was handsome, and that he was himself very shabbily dressed. He could bear his novel and inexplicable anguish no longer, and went out and sat upon the porch alone with his gloomy thoughts, till Marit, who loved him, missed him and came to seek him.

" 'You went away so soon,' she said to Oeyvind. He did not know what he should answer to this; thereupon, she also grew confused, and they were all three silent. But Hans stole away little by little. The two remained, not looking at each other, nor stirring. Then she said in a whisper: 'I have gone the whole evening with some Christmas goodies in my pocket for you, Oeyvind; but I have not had any chance to give them to you before.' She pulled out a few apples, a slice of a cake from town, and a little half-pint bottle, which she thrust over towards him, and said he could keep. Oeyvind took them. 'Thank you,' said he, and stretched out his hand; hers was warm; he dropped it immediately, as if he had burnt himself. 'You have danced a good deal this evening?' 'Yes, I have,' she answered; 'but you have not danced much,' she added. 'No, I have not.' 'Why not?' 'O—' 'Oeyvind.' 'What?' 'Why did you sit and look so at me?' 'O,—Marit!' 'Yes?' 'Why did n't you like to have me look at you?' 'There were so many people.' 'You danced a good deal with John Hatlen this evening.' 'O, yes!' 'He dances well.' 'Do you think so?' 'O, yes! I do not know how it is, but this evening I cannot bear to have you dance with him, Marit.' He turned away; it had cost him an effort to say it. 'I do not understand you, Oeyvind.' 'Nor do I understand it myself; it is so stupid of me. Farewell, Marit; I am going now.' He took a step without looking round. Then she called after him: 'It is a mistake what you thought you saw, Oeyvind.' He stopped. 'That you are already a grown-up girl is not a mistake.' He did not say what she had expected, and so she was silent."

This Marit's character is beautifully drawn, as it rises out of maiden coyness to meet the exigency of her lover's sensitive passion, and is so frank at once and so capricious in the sort of advances she is obliged to make to him. The correspondence carried on between the two while Oeyvind is in the Agricultural College is delightful with its mixture of prodigious formality and jealous tenderness on the hero's part, and mixture of jesting coquetry and fond consenting on Marit's side. A lover cannot take a joke from his mistress, and of course Marit shows superior to Oeyvind at this and some other times, but she is always patient and firm in her love for him.

The religious feeling which is a passive quality in "Arne" is a positive and controlling influence in "The Happy Boy," where it is chiefly exerted by the old schoolmaster. To him a long and bitter quarrel with an only brother, now dead, has taught lifelong meekness and dread of pride; and he affectingly rebukes Oeyvind's ambition to be first among the candidates for confirmation, in order that he may eclipse all others in Marit's eyes. But Björnson's religious feeling is not pietistic; on the contrary, it teaches, as in "The Fisher-Maiden," that a cheerful life of active goodness is the best interpretation of liberal and hopeful faith, and it becomes at no time a theological abstraction. It is always more or less blended with love of home, and a sense of the sweetness and beauty of natural affections. It is a strengthening property in the tenderness of a sentiment which seems almost distinctively his, or which at least is very clearly distinguished from German sentiment, and in which we Anglo-Saxon readers may indulge our hearts without that recoil of shame which otherwise attends the like surrender. Indeed, we feel a sort of inherent sympathy with most of Björnson's people on this and other accounts, as if we were in spirit, at least, Scandinavians with them, and the Viking blood had not yet died out of us. Some of the traits that he sketches are those now of New England fishermen and farmers and of Western pioneers,—that is, the pioneers of the time before Pacific Railroads. A conscientiousness also exists in them which is like our own,—for we have really a popular conscientiousness, in spite of many shocking appearances to the contrary,—though there seems to be practically more forgivenesses in their morality than in ours, especially towards such errors as those by which Arne and Petra came to be. But their incentives and expectations are all as different from ours as their customs are, and in these romances the reader is always sensible of beholding the life of a vigorous and healthful yet innumerous people, restricted by an unfriendly climate and variable seasons, and gaining a hard subsistence from the treacherous sea and grudging soil. Sometimes the sense of nature's reluctant or cruel attitude toward man finds open expression, as in "The Fisher-Maiden," where the pastor says to the "village saints": "Your homes are far up among the mountains, where your grain is cut down more frequently by the frost than by the scythe. Such barren fields and deserted spots should never have been built upon; they might well be given over to pasturage and the spooks. Spiritual life thrives but poorly in your mountain home, and partakes of the gloom of the surrounding vegetation. Prejudice, like the cliffs themselves, overhangs your life and casts a shadow upon it." Commonly, however, the pathos of this unfriendliness between the elements and man is not sharply uttered, but remains a subtile presence qualifying all impressions of Norwegian life. Perhaps it is this which gives their singular beauty to Björnson's pictures of the scenery amidst which the action of his stories takes place,—pictures notably of Nature in her kindlier moods, as if she were not otherwise to be endured by the imagination.

In "The Fisher-Maiden," which is less perfect as a romance than "Arne," Björnson has given us in Petra his most perfect and surprising creation. The story is not so dreamy, and it has not so much poetic intimacy with external things as "Arne," while it is less naturalistic than "The Happy Boy," and interests us in characters more independently of circumstance. It is, however, very real, and Petra is a study as successful as daring. To work out the character of a man of genius is a task of sufficient delicacy, but the difficulty is indefinitely enhanced where it is a woman of genius whose character is to be painted in the various phases of childhood and girlhood, and this is the labor Björnson undertakes in Petra. She is a girl of the lowest origin, and has had, like Arne, no legal authority for coming into the world; but like him she has a wonderful gift, though it is different from his. Looking back over her career from the close of the book, one sees plainly enough that she was born for the stage; but it is then only that the author's admirable art is apparent, and that we are reconciled to what seemed extravagances and inconsistencies, and are even consoled for the disappointment of our foolish novel-reading desire for the heroine's marriage. Petra does not marry any of the numerous lovers whom she has won in her unconscious effort to surround herself with the semblances that charm her imagination but never touch her heart; she is wedded to dramatic art alone, and the author, with a wisdom and modesty almost rare enough to be called singular, will not let us see whether the union is happy or not, but closes his book as the curtain rises upon Petra's first appearance. In fact, his business with her was there ended, as the romancer's used to be with the nuptials of his young people; what followed could only have been commonplace in contrast with what went before. The story is exquisitely pleasing; the incidents are quickly successive; the facts are in great part cheerful and amusing, and even where they are disastrous there is not a hopeless or unrelieved pathos in them; the situations are vivid and picturesque, and the people most refreshingly original and new, down to the most slightly seen and least important personage. There is also unusual range and variety in the characters; we have no longer to do with the peasants, but behold Norwegian nature as it is affected by life in towns, refined by education and thought, and sophisticated by wealth and unwise experience of the world. The figures are drawn with a strength and fineness that coexist more in this author than in any other we know, and that strike us peculiarly in the characters of Petra's mother, Gunlaug, who lets her own compassionate heart deceive her with regard to that pitiful Pedro Ohlsen, and thereafter lives a life of stormy contempt towards her seducer, forgiving him at last in a tacit sort of way sufficiently to encourage the feeble-souled creature to leave Petra his money; of Gunnar, the young sailor, who being made love to by Petra because she wants the figure of a lover for her reveries, furiously beats Ingve Vold because he has stolen Petra's airy affections from him; of Ingve Vold, the Spanish-travelled, dandified, handsome young rich man, who, after capturing Petra's fancy with stories of Spain, in turn lets his love get the better of his wickeder designs, and is ready to do anything in order to call Petra his wife; of the pastor's son, Oedegaard, who has educated Petra and has then fallen in love with her, and been accepted by her after that imaginative person has promised herself to Gunnar and Ingve; of the country pastor in whose house Petra finds refuge (after her mother's house has been mobbed because of her breaking so many hearts, and she has been driven out of her native village), and in despite of whom she dreams and thinks of nothing but the stage, till finally he blesses her aspiration.

Two scenes in the story appear to us the most interesting; and of course the chief of these is Petra seeing a play for the first time at the theatre in Bergen, which stands quite alone as a sympathetic picture of the amaze and exaltation of genius in the art destined henceforth to express it and to explain it to itself. It is long after this before Petra comes fully to understand her past life from her present consuming desire, and perhaps she never does it so fully as another does,—as Oedegaard, or the reader; but that experience at once gives shape and direction to her future, and it is so recorded as to be nearly as much a rapture to us as to her.

After this the most admirable episode is that scene in which the "village saints" come to expostulate with the pastor against countenancing music and dancing and other wicked cheerfulnesses, and in which the unanswerable arguments of the pastor in self-defence are made subtly to undermine the grounds of his own opposition to Petra's longing for the theatre. In this scene the religious and earnest element of Björnson's genius appears with great effect. The bigoted sincerity of the saints is treated with beautiful tenderness, while their errors are forcibly discovered to them. In a little space these people's characters are shown in all their individual quaintness, their narrow life is hinted in its gloom and loneliness, and the reader is made to feel at once respect and compassion for them.

There is no room left here to quote from "The Fisher-Maiden"; but the reader has already been given some idea of Björnson's manner in the passages from "Arne" and "The Happy Boy." This manner is always the same in its freedom from what makes the manner of most of our own stories tedious and abominable: it is always direct, unaffected, and dignified, expressing nothing of the author's personality, while fully interpreting his genius, and supplying no intellectual hollowness and poverty with tricks and caprices of phrase.

We hope that his publishers will find it profitable to give us translations of all his works. From him we can learn that fulness exists in brevity rather more than in prolixity; that the finest poetry is not ashamed of the plainest fact; that the lives of men and women, if they be honestly studied, can, without surprising incident or advantageous circumstance, be made as interesting in literature as are the smallest private affairs of the men and women in one's own neighborhood; that telling a thing is enough, and explaining it too much; and that the first condition of pleasing is a generous faith in the reader's capacity to be pleased by natural and simple beauty.

[*Atlantic Monthly*, April 1870]

29

[Bret Harte's Fiction]

The Luck of Roaring Camp, and other Stories. By Fr. Bret
Harte. Boston: Fields, Osgood, & Co.

THE most surprising things in that very surprising publication, "The
Overland Monthly," have been the stories or studies of early California life,
in which Mr. Harte carried us back to the remote epochs of 1849 and 1850,
and made us behold men and manners now passing or wholly passed away, as
he tells us. Readers who were amazed by the excellent quality of the whole
magazine were tempted to cry out most of all over "The Luck of Roaring
Camp," and the subsequent papers by the same hand, and to triumph in a
man who gave them something new in fiction. We had reason indeed to be
glad that one capable of seeing the grotesqueness of that strange life, and
also of appreciating its finer and softer aspects, had his lot cast in it by the
benign destiny that used to make great rivers run by large towns, and that
now sends lines of railway upon the same service. But we incline to think that
nothing worth keeping is lost, and that the flower born to blush unseen is
pretty sure to be botanized from a bud up by zealous observers. These
blossoms of the revolver-echoing cañon, the embattled diggings, the lawless
flat, and the immoral bar might well have been believed secure from notice,
and were perhaps the last things we should have expected to unfold
themselves under such eyes as Mr. Harte's. Yet this happened, and here we
have them in literature not overpainted, but given with all their natural
colors and textures, and all their wildness and strangeness of place.

The finest thing that could be said of an author in times past was that he
dealt simply, directly, and briefly with his reader, and we cannot say anything
different about Mr. Harte, though we are sensible that he is very different
from others, and at his best is quite a unique figure in American authorship,
not only that he writes of unhackneyed things, but that he looks at the life he
treats in uncommon lights. What strikes us most is the entirely masculine
temper of his mind, or rather a habit of concerning himself with things that
please only men. We suppose women generally would not find his stories
amusing or touching, though perhaps some woman with an unusual sense of
humor would feel the tenderness, the delicacy, and the wit that so win the
hearts of his own sex. This is not because he deals often with various unpre-
sentable people, for the ladies themselves, when they write novels, make us
acquainted with persons of very shocking characters and pursuits, but because he does not touch any of the phases of vice or virtue that seem to take

the fancy of women. We think it probable that none but a man would care for the portrait of such a gambler as Mr. John Oakhurst, or would discern the cunning touches with which it is done, in its blended shades of good and evil; and a man only could relish the rude pathos of Tennessee's partner, or of those poor, bewildered, sinful souls, The Duchess and Mother Shipton. To the masculine sense also must chiefly commend itself the ferocious drollery of the local nomenclature, the humor with which the most awful episodes of diggings life are invested by the character of the actors, and the robust vigor and racy savor of the miners' vernacular; not that these are very prominent in the stories, but that they are a certain and always noticeable quality in them. Mr. Harte could probably write well about any life he saw; but having happened to see the early Californian life, he gives it with its proper costume and accent. Of course, he does this artistically, as we have hinted, and gets on without a great use of those interconsonantal dashes which take the sinfulness out of printed profanity. You are made somehow to understand that the company swear a good deal, both men and women, and are not examples to their sex in any way; yet they are not offensive, as they might very well be in other hands, and it is the life beneath their uncouth exteriors that mainly interests. Out of this Mr. Harte has been able to make four or five little romances, which we should call idyls if we did not like them better than most recent poetry, and which please us more and more the oftener we read them. We do not know that they are very strong in plot; perhaps they are rather weak in that direction; but the world has outlived the childish age in fiction, and will not value these exquisite pieces the less because they do not deal with the Thrilling and the Hair's-breadth. People are growing, we hope,— and if they are not, so much the worse for people,—to prefer character to situations, and to enjoy the author's revelations of the former rather than his invention of the latter. At any rate, this is what is to be liked in Mr. Harte, who has an acuteness and a tenderness in dealing with human nature which are quite his own, and such a firm and clear way of handling his materials as to give a very complete effect to each of his performances.

Amongst these we think "The Outcasts of Poker Flat" is the best, for the range of character is greater, and the contrasts are all stronger than in the others; and, in spite of some sentimentalized traits, Mr. John Oakhurst, gambler, is the best figure Mr. Harte has created, if, indeed, he did not copy him from life. The whole conception of the story is excellent;—the banishment of Oakhurst, Uncle Billy, The Duchess, and Mother Shipton from Poker Flat, their sojourn in the cañon, where they are joined by the innocent Tommy Simson, eloping with his innocent betrothed; Uncle Billy's treacherous defection with the mule; the gathering snows, the long days spent round the camp-fire listening to Tommy's version of Pope's Homer; the approaches of famine, and the self-sacrifice of those three wicked ones for the hapless creatures whose lot has been cast with theirs. As regards their effort to adapt their conduct to Tommy's and Piney's misconception of their characters and relations, the story is a masterpiece of delicate handling, and affecting as it is humorous. Mr. Harte does not attempt to cope with the difficulties of bringing those curiously assorted friends again into contact with the world; and there is no lesson taught, save a little mercifulness of judgment, and a kindly doubt of total depravity. Perhaps Oakhurst would not, in actual life, have shot himself to save provisions for a starving boy and girl; and perhaps that poor ruined Mother Shipton was not really equal to the act ascribed to her: but Mr. Harte contrives to have it touch one like the truth, and that is all we can ask of him. "It became more and more difficult to replenish their fires, even from the fallen trees beside them, now half hidden in the drifts. And yet no one complained. The lovers turned from the dreary prospect and looked into each other's eyes, and were happy. Mr. Oakhurst settled himself coolly to the losing game before him. The Duchess, more cheerful than she had been, assumed the care of Piney. Only Mother Shipton—once the strongest of the party—seemed to sicken and fade. At midnight on the tenth day she called Oakhurst to her side. 'I'm going,' she said, in a voice of querulous weakness, 'but don't say anything about it. Don't waken the kids. Take the bundle from under my head and open it.' Mr. Oakhurst did so. It contained Mother Shipton's rations for the last week, untouched. 'Give 'em to the child,' she said, pointing to the sleeping Piney. 'You've starved yourself,' said the gambler. 'That's what they call it,' said the woman, querulously, as she lay down again, and, turning her face to the wall, passed quietly away."

Even in "Miggles," which seems to us the least laudable of these stories, the author, in painting a life of unselfish devotion, succeeds in keeping the reader's patience and sympathy by the heroine's unconsciousness of her heroism, and the simple way in which she speaks of it. She has abandoned her old way of life to take care of Jim, a paralytic, who in happier days "spent all his money on her," and she is partially hedged in by a pet grizzly bear which goes about the neighborhood of her wild mountain home with her. If you can suppose the situation, the woman's character is very well done. When the "judge" asks her why she does not marry the man to whom she has devoted her youthful life, "Well, you see," says Miggles, "it would be playing it rather low down on Jim to take advantage of his being so helpless. And then, too, if we were man and wife now, we'd both know that I was bound to do what I now do of my own accord." Of course all the people are well sketched; in fact, as to manners, Mr. Harte's touch is quite unfailing. The humor, too, is good, as it is in all these pieces. Miggles's house is papered with newspapers, and she says of herself and Jim: "When we are sitting alone, I read him these things on the wall. Why, Lord," says Miggles, with her frank laugh, "I've read him that whole side of the house this winter."

The Idyl of Red Gulch suffers from some of the causes that affect the sketch of Miggles unpleasantly, but it is more natural and probable, and the interview between Miss Mary and Tommy's mother is a skilful little piece of work. But we believe that, after "The Outcasts of Poker Flat," we have the greatest satisfaction in "Tennessee's Partner," though even in this we would fain have stopped short of having the partners meet in Heaven. Tennessee is a gambler, who is also suspected of theft. He has run away with his partner's wife, and has got himself into trouble by robbing a stranger near the immaculate borders of Red Dog. The citizens rise to take him, and in his flight he is stopped by a small man on a gray horse.

> "The men looked at each other a moment in silence. Both were fearless, both self-possessed and independent; and both types of a civilization that in the seventeenth century would have been called heroic, but, in the nineteenth, simply 'reckless.' 'What have you got there? I call,' said Tennessee, quietly. 'Two bowers and an ace,' said the stranger, as quietly, showing two revolvers and a bowie-knife. 'That takes me,' returned Tennessee; and, with this gamblers' epigram, he threw away his useless pistol, and rode back with his captor."

Tennessee refuses to make any defence on his trial before Judge Lynch. "I don't take any hand in this yer game," he says, and his partner appears in court to buy him off, to the great indignation of the tribunal, which sentences Tennessee at once. "This yer is a lone hand played alone, without my pardner," remarks the unsuccessful advocate, turning to go, when the judge reminds him that if he has anything to say to Tennessee he had better say it now. "Tennessee smiled, showed his white teeth, and saying, 'Euchred, old man!' held out his hand. Tennessee's partner took it in his own, and saying, 'I just dropped in as I was passing to see how things was getting on,' let the hand passively fall, and adding that it was 'a warm night,' again mopped his face with his handkerchief, and without another word withdrew." So Tennessee was hanged, and his body was given to his partner, who invited the citizens of Red Dog to attend the funeral. The body was borne to the grave in a coffin made of a section of sluicing and placed on a cart drawn by Jinny, the partner's donkey; and at the grave this pathetic speech was made:—

> " 'When a man,' began Tennessee's partner, slowly, 'has been running free all day, what's the natural thing for him to do? Why, to come home. And if he ain't in a condition to go home, what can his best friend do? Why, bring him home! And here's Tennessee has been running free, and we brings him home from his wandering.' He paused, and picked up a fragment of quartz, rubbed it thoughtfully on his sleeve, and went on: 'It ain't the first time that I've packed him on my back, as you see'd me now. It ain't the first time that I brought him to this yer cabin when he could n't help himself; it ain't the first time that I and "Jinny" have waited for him on yon hill, and picked him up, and so fetched him home, when he could n't speak, and did n't know me. And now that it's the last time, why—' he paused, and rubbed the quartz gently on his sleeve—'you see it's sort of rough on his pardner. And now, gentlemen,' he added, abruptly, picking up his long-handled shovel, 'the fun'l 's over; and my thanks, and Tennessee's thanks, to you for your trouble.' "

As to the "Luck of Roaring Camp," which was the first and is the best known of these sketches, it is, like "Tennessee's Partner," full of the true color of life in the diggings, but strikes us as less perfect and consistent, though the conception is more daring, and effects are achieved beyond the limited reach of the latter. As in "Miggles," the strength and freshness are in the manners and character, and the weakness is in the sentimentality which, it must be said in Mr. Harte's favor, does not seem to be quite his own. His real feeling is always as good as his humor is fresh.

We want to speak also of the author's sentiment for nature, which is shown in sparing touches, but which is very fine and genuine. Such a picture as this: "A hare surprised into helpless inactivity sat upright and *pulsating* in the ferns by the roadside, as the *cortège* went by,"—is worth, in its wildness and freshness, some acres of word-painting. The same love of nature gives life and interest to "High-Water Mark," "A Lonely Ride," "Mliss," and some other pieces (evidently written earlier than those we have just been speaking of), with which Mr. Harte has filled out his book. These pieces, too, have the author's characteristic cleverness; and the people in "Notes by Flood and Field" are almost as lifelike as any in his recent work. The dog "Boonder" is a figure entirely worthy to appear in the most select circles of Red Dog or Poker Flat.

[*Atlantic Monthly*, May 1870]

30

[Rossetti's Poetry]

Poems by Dante Gabriel Rossetti. Boston: Roberts Brothers.

IT will always be a question, we think, whether Mr. Rossetti had not better have painted his poems and written his pictures; there is so much that is purely sensuous in the former, and so much that is intellectual in the latter. But we do not suppose that those who like his work will let the question mar their enjoyment of either, though they will probably enjoy both in the same kind and degree. It seems a pity, however, for the sake of readers who do not know any of his pictures, that these poems should not have been illustrated by the author's hand. We should then have had in his volume a proof of the curious fusion of the literary and artistic nature in him. But as it is, though one cannot here see the poetry in the painting, the painting in the poetry is plain enough.

On the whole, except the sonnets, the best poem is "The Blessed Damozel," and in this the author's characteristics are very marked. The picture with which it opens is exactly in the spirit of a Pre-Raphaelite painting, with its broad and effective contrasts of color,—yellow, blue, and white.

> "The blessed damozel leaned out
>   From the gold bar of Heaven;
> Her eyes were deeper than the depth
>   Of waters stilled at even;
> She had three lilies in her hand,
>   And the stars in her hair were seven.

> "Her robe, ungirt from clasp to hem
>   No wrought flowers did adorn,
> But a white rose of Mary's gift,
>   For service meetly worn;
> Her hair that lay along her back
>   Was yellow like ripe corn."

This is the new Pre-Raphaelite, and here, following, in the lines we have italicized, is the old, as one sees it very often in the fading frescos of mediæval churches. Of course it is very beautifully and very vividly expressed; and the whole picture is a lovely one.

"She ceased.
The light thrilled towards her, filled
With angels in strong level flight.
Her eyes prayed, and she smiled.

"(I saw her smile.) But soon their path
Was vague in distant spheres:
And then she cast her arms along
The golden barriers,
And laid her face between her hands,
And wept. (I heard her tears.)"

In this poem Mr. Rossetti strives for that heart of pure and tender rapture which, it seems to mediæval-minded poets, must have beat in the centre of the Romish mystery, and he is more successful in his effort than Mr. Tennyson in his later yearnings, but not so much so as the latter was when he wrote Sir Galahad. We are conscious, however, of attributing too explicit a feeling to Mr. Rossetti's poem, which is really a series of mystic and devotional pictures, and scarcely more exegetic than if they had actually been painted. Here are three of the pictures, which are very charming, and take you again and again with ravishing suggestions of the old religious art, but which have no great intellectual merit, and scarcely any independent merit at all, except a luxury of words, that most well-read people can nowadays command:—

"And still she bowed herself and stooped
Out of the circling charm;
Until her bosom must have made
The bar she leaned on warm,
And the lilies lay as if asleep
Along her bended arm.
· · · · ·
" 'Circlewise sit they, with bound locks
And foreheads garlanded;
Into the fine cloth white like flame
Weaving the golden thread,
To fashion the birth-robes for them
Who are just born, being dead.
· · · · ·
" 'Herself shall bring us, hand in hand,
To Him round whom all souls
Kneel, the clear-ranged unnumbered heads
Bowed with their aureoles:
And angels meeting us shall sing
To their citherns and citoles.' "

For reasons already sufficiently expressed, we think that, after "The Blessed Damozel," and two or three other strictly pictorial poems, the "Son-

nets for Pictures" are the best of Mr. Rossetti's things, though these again
are not to be perfectly enjoyed in themselves. Nevertheless, for a July day, we
shall never ask a distincter pleasure than we get from this sonnet on Giorgione's *Festa Campestre*, that delicious fable, wherein a Venetian lady and
cavalier sit amidst a pastoral landscape, and pause from their own music, to
hear the piping of the enigmatical person,—perhaps their embodied love
and happiness,—who sits confronting them, clothed in nothing but her own
white loveliness. The sonnet is this:—

"A VENETIAN PASTORAL.

By Giorgiona.
(*In the Louvre.*)
"Water, for anguish of the solstice:—nay,
  But dip the vessel slowly,—nay, but lean
  And hark how at its verge the wave sighs in
Reluctant. Hush! Beyond all depth away
The heat lies silent at the brink of day:
  Now the hand trails upon the viol-string
  That sobs, and the brown faces cease to sing,
Sad with the whole of pleasure. Whither stray
Her eyes now, from whose mouth the slim pipes creep
  And leave it pouting, while the shadowed grass
    Is cool against her naked side? Let it be;—
Say nothing now unto her lest she weep,
  Nor name this ever. Be it as it was,—
    Life touching lips with Immortality."

It is easy to choose an exquisite picture from these poems at random, like
this from the "Dante at Verona":—

"Through leaves and trellis-work the sun
  Left the wine cool within the glass,—
  They feasting where no sun could pass:
And when the women, all as one,
  Rose up with brightened cheeks to go,
  It was a comely thing, we know."

Or this, from "A Last Confession," more perfect, more delicate even, and
liker an old painting:—

"I know last night
I dreamed I saw into the garden of God,
Where women walked whose painted images
I have seen with candles round them in the church.
They bent this way and that, one to another,
Playing: and over the long golden hair
Of each there floated like a ring of fire

Which when she stooped stooped with her, and when she rose
Rose with her. Then a breeze flew in among them,
As if a window had been opened in heaven
For God to give his blessing from, before
This world of ours should set: (for in my dream
I thought our world was setting, and the sun
Flared, a spent taper;) and beneath that gust
The rings of light quivered like forest-leaves.
Then all the blessed maidens who were there
Stood up together, as it were a voice
That called them; and they threw their tresses back,
And smote their palms, and all laughed up at once,
For the strong heavenly joy they had in them
To hear God bless the world."

Or this, from the sonnets:—

"BEAUTY AND THE BIRD.

"She fluted with her mouth as when one sips,
   And gently waved her golden head, inclined
   Outside his cage close to the window-blind;
Till her fond bird, with little turns and dips,
Piped low to her of sweet companionships.
   And when he made an end, some seed took she
   And fed him from her tongue, which rosily
Peeped as a piercing bud between her lips.

"And like the child in Chaucer, on whose tongue
   The Blessed Mary laid, when he was dead,
A grain,—who straightway praised her name in song:
   Even so, when she, a little lightly red,
Now turned on me and laughed, I heard the throng
   Of inner voices praise her golden head."

Dramatic power is so closely allied to that of the painter, that one naturally expects it in this charming colorist,—though as to color, the reader will notice that he gets his delight only from the positive richness and splendor of each hue, not at all from the subjection of one color to another, or their harmony.

In the poems where the color does not predominate, we see Mr. Rossetti's weaknesses more plainly. He has numbers of affectations, and they are not all his own. Some of Mr. Browning's, for example, are pretty clear in "A Last Confession," and those of the imitation-old-ballads are the property of the trade. Of course these ballads are the poorest of Mr. Rossetti's poems, and they are not fairly characteristic of him. Some of them are very poor indeed, and others are quite idle.

It is a curious thing in a poet whose purity of mind and heart makes such a very strong impression, that his imagination should be so often dominated by character and fact which are quite other than pure. We think there has been more than enough of the Fallen Woman in literature; we wish that if she cannot be reformed, she might be at least policed out of sight; and we have a fancy (perhaps an erroneous, perhaps a guilty fancy) that some things, even in "The House of Life," however right they are, had best be kept out of speech. Otherwise, unless on account of the climate, it appears that clothes and houses are a waste of substance. We do not intend to give an unjustly broad impression of what is only a trait of Mr. Rossetti's poetry, after all, and we note it quite as much because it is phenomenal and not quite accountable as because it is objectionable. He has a painter's joy in beauty, and an indifference to what beauty, or whose, it is; and his celebration of love is chiefly sensuous, but beauty and love are both most highly honored at their highest by him. Yet here and there, as in the sonnet "Nuptial Sleep," we feel that we are too few removes from Mr. Whitman's alarming frankness, and that it is but a step or two from "turning aside and living with the cattle."

In most of Mr. Rossetti's sonnets one is reminded of the best Italian sonneteers, and of our English poets when the Italians were their masters. They are more mystical, however, and more abundant in conceits, than almost any other English sonnets, and recall, most vividly of all, the sonnets of Dante's Vita Nuova. The fact is particularly felt in such a one as this.

"LOVE'S BAWBLES.

"I stood where Love in brimming armfuls bore
    Slight wanton flowers and foolish toys of fruit:
    And round him ladies thronged in warm pursuit,
Fingered and lipped and proffered the strange store:
And from one hand the petal and the core
    Savored of sleep; and cluster and curled shoot
    Seemed from another hand like shame's salute,—
Gifts that I felt my cheek was blushing for.

"At last Love bade my Lady give the same:
    And as I looked, the dew was light thereon;
    And as I took them, at her touch they shone
With inmost heaven-hue of the heart of flame.
    And then Love said: 'Lo! when the hand is hers,
    Follies of love are love's true ministers.' "

But the meaning is not often so plain as it is here, and there is a vexing obscurity in the greater part of Mr. Rossetti's poems, which some other peculiarities of his make us doubt whether it is quite worth while to explore. We find in him a love for rank, lush, palpitating, bleeding, and dripping words, which we think does not mark the finest sense of expression; and yet, when he has himself well under control, no one can say a thing more subtly, as this little poem may witness.

"THE WOODSPURGE.

"The wind flapped loose, the wind was still,
Shaken out dead from tree and hill:
I had walked on at the wind's will,—
I sat now, for the wind was still.

"Between my knees my forehead was,—
My lips, drawn in, said not Alas!
My hair was over in the grass,
My naked ears heard the day pass.

"My eyes, wide open, had the run
Of some ten weeds to fix upon;
Among those few, out of the sun,
The woodspurge flowered, three cups in one.

"From perfect grief there need not be
Wisdom or even memory:
One thing then learnt remains to me,—
The woodspurge has a cup of three."

Here, also, is an idea, now rather common in literature, finely suggested:—

"SUDDEN LIGHT.

"I have been here before,
But when or how I cannot tell:
I know the grass beyond the door,
The sweet keen smell,
The sighing sound, the lights around the shore.

"You have been mine before,—
How long ago I may not know:
But just when at that swallow's soar
Your neck turned so,
Some veil did fall,—I knew it all of yore."

And here is this poetry of the nerves still more skilfully caught:—

"This is her picture as she was:
It seems a thing to wonder on,
As though mine image in the glass
Should tarry when myself am gone.
. . . . .

"In painting her I shrined her face
   Mid mystic trees, where light falls in
Hardly at all; a covert place
   Where you might think to find a din
Of doubtful talk, and a live flame
Wandering, and many a shape whose name
   Not itself knoweth, and old dew,
   And your own footsteps meeting you,
And all things going as they came."

But then you see he is always better as a painter:—

"Watch we his steps. He comes upon
   The women at their palm-playing.
   The conduits round the gardens sing
And meet in scoops of milk-white stone,
   Where wearied damsels rest and hold
   Their hands in the wet spurt of gold."

Of the longer poems in the volume, after "The Blessed Damozel," comes, we suppose in point of merit, the by-no-means-blessed damozel "Jenny," though we praise it reluctantly. "Dante at Verona" makes no very impressive figure, and "The Burden of Nineveh" rests heavily upon the reader.

Have we been saying, on the whole, that we think Mr. Rossetti no great poet? Let us say, then, that we think him, on the whole, a very pleasing one to read once at least:—whether twice, or thrice, or indefinitely, we do not know, for we write from the first impression, and not without our modest misgivings both of the praise and blame we have bestowed. The book is a very characteristic one,—we are not sure that it is very genuine. Yet it has many charms, and at eighteen, if you are of one sex, or at twenty-two if of the other, you might wish to be parted from it only in death. The trouble is, you cannot always be eighteen or twenty-two.

In some respects, the comparison is a strained and unfair one, but we feel that Mr. Rossetti the poet is to such a poet as Keats what Mr. Rossetti the painter is to such a painter as Giorgione.

[*Atlantic Monthly*, July 1870]

31

[Ralph Keeler's Adventures]

Vagabond Adventures. By Ralph Keeler. Boston: Fields, Osgood, & Co.

IT is given to so few people to have run away from home in very early life, to have adopted the profession of negro-minstrelsy in fulfilment of the ambition of every boy for some sort of histrionic eminence, to have abandoned this art for the purpose of going through college, and then, after much travel in Europe and a course of study at Heidelberg University upon less money than most of us would like to starve upon at home, to have settled quietly down to writing for the magazines, that Mr. Keeler has at least one reason for making this curious and entertaining little book. The story was worth telling, even if he could have imparted to it no charm of narration and suggested no pleasant or useful reflections to his reader. But he has made it lively and agreeable in style, and he has addressed himself so skilfully to the reader's good sense as well as interest, that we believe the public will find it, as we do, a novelty in literature, and something very much better than a novelty. There is the flavor in it of the picaresque novel, without the final unpleasant tang of that species of fiction; and the author has so objectively studied his hero, that even where the latter falls into unpoetizable squalor, and has things happen him that you wish had not happened, you do not refer your repugnance to the historian, who, you feel, sees these things in the same light you do. On reflection, too, you are glad that he treats his subject so unsparingly, for a book has no business to be merely literature; and such a book as this especially ought to teach something,—ought to disenchant youth with adventure, and show Poverty in her true colors, that people may use every honest effort to avoid her. That lean nymph is so apt in literature to take the imagination of the young, that it is well for once to see her as she is in real life: Mr. Keeler, who has walked up and down with her, like Constance with grief, and has the same reason to be fond of her, paints anything but a seducing picture of her. He keeps a surprising cheerfulness of temper throughout, but he does not pretend that his intimacy with poverty is ever enviable; and indeed there never was but one man had the heart voluntarily to perpetuate such a thing, and he was a saint, and not a literary man.

There is something quite touching in the first of these vagabond adventures, that is to say, in the account of the boy who ran away from home; but the author does not directly appeal to sympathy for him. So strange facts have rarely been so simply told, and with such strict regard to the truth of local color and the integrity of the hero's character, who never thinks or does anything beyond his years. Those of our readers who remember Mr. Keeler's Atlantic papers, "Three Years as a Negro Minstrel" and "The Tour of Europe for $181 in Currency," are as well qualified as ourselves to pronounce them very interesting in substance and agreeable in manner: he has somewhat enlarged them, as they now stand, and they will bear a second reading singularly well. We think that the first two parts of the book are better in every way than the last: they are better in style, and in fact they are more curious; for the poverty-stricken traveller and student is not so novel in literature, whilst the runaway boy and negro-minstrel, surviving to write of himself, is absolutely new. The minstrelsy paper is peculiarly entertaining to us people of the audience, who are always longing to know what the actors are like behind the scenes, and who have here the chance to see our delightful old friends with their burnt-cork off. It is immensely gratifying to find so much human nature in them,—yes, so much more human nature than falls to the lot of most other men; and we ought all to be obliged to Mr. Keeler for the sincerity and good taste in which he has presented them. That company on the Floating Palace is one that it is charming to know through him; and the whole paper has now an historical value, for negro-minstrelsy, that sole growth of drama from American life, is now almost wholly passed away, and was waning even before slavery perished. Something else pleased us in this paper: perhaps it may be roughly described as confirmation of our belief that the truly American novel, when it comes to be written, will be a story of personal adventure after the fashion of Gil Blas, and many of the earlier English fictions.

No one should be a prophet who can possibly avoid it, and so far we have kept ourselves pretty free from prediction. It is well for Mr. Keeler to have here grouped together these singular facts of his life, but it will be no surprising fortune if he shall come after a while to regard his work as crude in some ways: at least, he has given such evidence of growth since his first book as to make us hope this. But with these haunting reminiscences once fairly uttered, and, as far as he is concerned, dismissed to the limbo of all known facts and accomplished purposes, he can turn to more imaginative tasks with an expectation of success which will be fulfilled in proportion as he remembers (what he ought to know better than any one) that, truth is stranger than fiction, and not only this, but is better even in the airiest regions of the ideal, and that the only condition of making life like ours tolerable in literature is to paint it exactly as it is.

[*Atlantic Monthly*, December 1870]

32

[Sylvester Judd's New England Romance]

Margaret. A Tale of the Real and Ideal, of Blight and Bloom. By Sylvester Judd. Boston: Roberts Brothers.

THE sense of novelty and freshness which this beautiful old romance gives the reader is a most useful witness of the fact that, to be always modern and always new, it is only necessary to be of no fashion,—neither the fashion of one's own day nor the fashion of a former day. This, to be sure, is nearly as difficult as simplicity, of which perhaps it is a phase. Here and there, in all the history of the world, but few men have achieved so great an end in literature: the author of "Margaret" is of these few.

We, who read the romance for the first time in this latest edition of it, must feel how vastly better it is, how much more recent it is, than the best new novel of our generation, and must peruse it with something of the contented wonder with which we should linger over "Wilhelm Meister" or a play of Shakespeare if they were as strange to us. The comparison is of kind, not of degree; but if "Margaret" were compared with any other romance of its own time, excepting the romances of Hawthorne, we should feel that there was no comparison for it save with the masterpieces. Like these it is epoch and fashion and method to itself. It is not nature, but the love of nature; it is not reality, but truth. It is very far indeed from artistic perfection; you may overfeast yourself in it, but you cannot famish.

Without more space than we can now give, any criticism of ours must fail to discover what the essence of such a book as "Margaret" is. It is easy enough to say that the scene is laid in a backwoods settlement of New England, in the time just after the Revolution; that the life and manners of the place and period are painted very effectively, with a strong dash of caricature, and that there is such sympathy with the inarticulate life of nature that the reader cannot help sharing the author's rapture; that Margaret and nearly all the other personages are fantastic; that the fascination of the book is not in the plot. But all this is a dim and distorted reflex of the romance, and might be quite as true of a work done in a wholly different spirit and manner; the very heart of the matter is left untouched, and is scarcely approached. It does not help much to add that the romance is largely religious, and that where the religious purpose prevails over the artistic feeling the work suffers; or that the story seems always to run along the edge of a precipice, and you are liable to be dropped into limitless depths of airiness at any moment, though the author's poise is kept, and the reader carried safely to the end,—it must be owned he is considerably dizzied towards the last.

It is curious to find in English a romance that confides so much in the reader's sympathy: here we have long pauses for discussion and reflection as in German romances, yet the book is not otherwise German, but singularly American, with inexhaustible sweetness, quaintness, and tenderness, and most American in its fantasticality. It is marvellously, almost matchlessly frank in dealing with the rude life in which its scenes are laid, and no more moralizes that life or is ashamed of it than the sunshine would have been. It is with the reform of what civilization he finds that the author is concerned; and this is not the only point on which he shows himself generous and wise, and one of the truest and foremost of his nation.

[*Atlantic Monthly*, January 1871]

33

[John Woolman's Journal]

The Journal of John Woolman. With an Introduction by
John G. Whittier. Boston: James R. Osgood & Co.

IN John Woolman the great antislavery movement may be said to have
actively begun. He was born early in the last century, at Mount Holly, New
Jersey, and in due time became a tailor by trade; but he early relinquished his
calling, and spent his time chiefly in going to and fro among the Quakers, to
whose society he belonged, and animating them to a consciousness of the
iniquity of holding slaves; and he was mainly instrumental in their ceasing to
do so. He was also "under a concern" to press forward in many other good
works, some of which have since been taken up as reforms, and others
remanded among the impossibilities. He was one of the first teetotalers, but
the most rigorous water-drinker of our day would hardly be willing to follow
John Woolman in retrenching and finally destroying a very modest business,
because it led him into a vain and superfluous manner of living; or in
refusing coffee and sugar because they were the products of slave labor; or in
wearing undyed garments because dyes were used in cloth to conceal dirt,
"and hiding that which is not clean by coloring our garments seems contrary
to the sweetness of sincerity"; or in refusing to send letters by post, lest he
should share in the guilt attaching to the cruel overworking of horses and
post-boys in making the rapid trips of the stage-coaches. John Woolman was
something more than incarnate conscience, he was incarnate scruple; in his
endeavor to make his life Christ-like and blameless he went, like other
ascetics, further than Christ himself taught by example. But he was a saintly
soul, however painful. At the bottom even of his absurdities there was a grain
of sense, and in all he did his motive was truly loving and good.

His intuitions in regard to slavery were vivid and unerring. Long before
Jefferson had phrased it he had said "that liberty was the right of all men
equally"; and no observer of Southern society since has had a keener eye for
the bad effects of slavery upon the general character. In that day even
Quakers dealt in slaves, and Woolman writes: "I saw in these Southern Prov-
inces so many vices and corruptions increased by this trade and way of life,
that it appeared to me as a dark gloominess hanging over the land; and," he
adds with prophetic forecast of evils that have since befallen, "though now
many willingly run into it, yet in future the consequences will be grievous to
posterity."

John Woolman's Journal, beyond most books, may be read with edification and pleasure. It is good to be in the intimacy of so singularly pure, truthful, and serviceable a soul, and it is amusing to find such intense scrupulosity set forth in terms so quaint and sincere. The Journal is a well of the best English, and in reading it one feels all Henry Crabb Robinson's amazement: "An illiterate tailor, he writes in a style of the most exquisite purity and grace. His moral qualities are transferred to his writings." There is in the whole, also, a flavor that makes it inexpressibly fascinating. Thinking of marriage, he says: "My heart was turned to the Lord with desires that he would give me wisdom to proceed therein agreeably to his will, and he was pleased to give me a well-inclined damsel," to whom he was married. He was sorely tried about wearing dyed raiment of any kind, but he says: "I felt easy to wear my garments heretofore made, and continued to do so for about nine months, ... when, being deeply bowed in spirit before the Lord, I was made willing to submit to what I apprehended was required of me, and when I returned home got a hat of the natural color of the fur." When about to sail for England, he "feels a draught in his mind towards the steerage of the ship"; and being pressed for his reasons against going in the cabin, he answered that he had observed "on the outside of that part of the ship where the cabin was sundry sorts of carved work and imagery," and in the cabin "some superfluity of workmanship of several sorts"; and as these things enhanced the cost of passage, "he felt a scruple with regard to paying money to be applied to such purposes." In this way, without intending it, John Woolman is a humorist of the rarest quality; and we cannot help suspecting that the love borne him by Charles Lamb, who said, "Get the writings of John Woolman by heart," was quite as much for the devoted reformer's unintended humorousness as because of gifts in exhortation, though of course he must have loved a soul so lowly, so simple, and so brave, and must have enjoyed the beauty of his religious thought.

The Introduction to this edition, by Mr. Whittier, is written with a tender appreciation of Woolman's character and writings, and is a satisfactory study of his circumstances as well as of his work. In a word, Mr. Whittier speaks of him with the reverence which you expect from one of the truest Friends of our day for one of the best of any day; with the grateful honor due from an Abolitionist to the first of the Abolitionists. When you read "John Woolman's Journal," you think that it needs no comment; when you read Mr. Whittier's Introduction, you feel that it needed just that.

[*Atlantic Monthly*, August 1871]

34

[Joaquin Miller's Verses]

Songs of the Sierras. By Joaquin Miller. Boston: Roberts Brothers.

MR. Miller's poetry, which has been called a new creation,—the phrase is novel and happy,—has not quite freed itself of all the traits of the parent chaos; and vast tracts of water and very dry land are still wrapped in the dimness of more or less forgotten intention, though here and there a lonely height or favored valley is touched with the light of

"The consecration and the poet's dream."

One poem he has written, as we must believe in spite of the foolish praises lavished upon all his work,—an imperfect and now and then ludicrously faulty poem, but still a poem. This is the "Arizonian," a moving story, vividly told, with passages of peculiar beauty and force. The passage following the quarrel of the Arizonian and his brown Indian love is one of these:—

> " 'She turn'd from the door and down to the river,
> And mirror'd her face in the whimsical tide;
> Then threw back her hair, as if throwing a quiver,
> As an Indian throws it back far from his side
> And free from his hands, swinging fast to the shoulder,
> When rushing to battle; and, rising, she sigh'd
> And shook, and shiver'd as aspens shiver.
> Then a great green snake slid into the river,
> Glistening, green, and with eyes of fire;
> Quick, double-handed she seized a boulder,
> And cast it with all the fury of passion,
> As with lifted head it went curving across,
> Swift darting its tongue like a fierce desire,
> Curving and curving, lifting higher and higher,
> Bent and beautiful as a river moss;
> Then, smitten, it turn'd, bent, broken, and doubled,
> And lick'd, red-tongued, like a forkéd fire,
> And sank, and the troubled waters bubbled,
> And then swept on in their old swift fashion.' "

A sudden Arizonian tempest destroys her, and the miner goes home to find the fair early love, some reminiscence of whom had roused the jealous fury of the Indian; but he finds instead her daughter, woman grown. The scene where he comes into the village "in the fringe of the night" (we object to the phrase), and mistakes the daughter for the mother, is well painted; and the poem is often excellently dramatic, told as it is by the Arizonian himself, with his half-crazed sense of his own blame, and his half-conscious struggle to justify his part, and his groping sorrow and trouble in it all. But the rude strength of his figure is sadly marred by the scraps of Old-World tinsel with which he is decorated. It is so difficult, in speaking of Mr. Miller's verse, not to take cognizance of the clamor about him, that we may forgive ourselves for suggesting that these ornaments seem to have been lent him by his English friends for the embellishment of his hero. When we find, for example, in the possession of the Arizonian, such phraseology as this,

"As the wave sang strophes in the broken reeds,"

we suspect an ill-timed generosity on the part of the classic Mr. Swinburne; and when the much-untravelled miner speaks of

"That beautiful bronze with its soul of fire,"

are we not to imagine a like error of the head, but not of the heart, in the mediæval Mr. Rossetti?

We are trying to say, in an ungracious fashion, that it is rather a ruinous thing to be a phenomenon anywhere, and that Mr. Miller is the worse poet for his English triumph; but our consolation is that he will never believe us. In "With Walker in Nicaragua" he shows a deepening consciousness, and a high resolution to be surprisingly untamed, unkempt, top-booted and long-spurred, and lariated and serapéd. "He was a brick," he says of Walker at the outset,

"And brave as Yuba's grizzlies are,
Yet gentle as a panther is,
Mouthing her young in her first fierce kiss,"

in which figurative beast of prey we fear that we detect again the taint of a decrepit civilization; she is a heroine of modern cockney mediæval and classical poetry, who is always fierce in her affections, and kisses in just that way. When Mr. Miller will consent to forget himself and admirers, he can paint a striking picture; and in this poem are several very striking ones. Here is a glimpse of a march through a tropic wood, which is very brilliant in color; how true we do not know:—

"And snakes, long, lithe, and beautiful
As green and graceful-bough'd bamboo,
Did twist and twine them through and through
The boughs that hung red-fruited full.
One, monster-sized, above me hung,

Close eyed me with his bright pink eyes,
Then raised his folds, and sway'd and swung,
And lick'd like lightning his red tongue,
Then oped his wide mouth with surprise;
He writhed and curved, and raised and lower'd
His folds like liftings of the tide,
And sank so low I touched his side,
As I rode by, with my broad sword.

"The trees shook hands high overhead,
And bow'd and intertwined across
The narrow way, while leaves and moss
And luscious fruit, gold-hued and red,
Through all the canopy of green,
Let not one sunshaft shoot between.

"Birds hung and swung, green-robed and red,
Or droop'd in curved lines dreamily,
Rainbows reversed, from tree to tree,
Or sang low-hanging overhead,—
Sang low, as if they sang and slept,
Sang faint, like some far waterfall,
And took no note of us at all,
Though nuts that in the way were spread
Did crush and crackle as we stept."

The reader perceives the tawdriness of such lines as

"The trees shook hands high overhead";

and these are too many to be specified, though we must say that we particularly object to

"With wild soul plashing to the sky,"

and

"The warm sea laid his dimpled face
With every white hair smoothed in place."

We wish also to express our doubts if the cockatoos do not sing too much in Mr. Miller's tropic; though in that zone, of course, he has most of his critics at a disadvantage.

The "Kit Carson's Ride" is so outrageously bad as a poem that it need not be discussed. But its injustice to a man of simply heroic life, and, by all accounts, of generous deeds and instincts, is something that the badness of the poetry cannot repair, and ought not to pass without protest. Kit Carson is a figure of rough sublimity in the annals of the Far West; and an author who has the ear of the world—it is not so fine as it is long—has no right to give his name to a selfish, theatrical knave, fit only to ride over a green-baize prairie before a painted fire into a canvas river.

The best poem in the book, after "Arizonian," is "The Tale of the Tall Alcalde," though this, like some of the worst, has the misery of a dreary unreality upon it all,

> "An agony
> Of lamentation like a wind that shrills
> All night in a waste land where no one comes,
> Or hath come since the making of the world,"

and leaves the reader unwholesomely doubtful of the existence of the Pacific slope, its Indian tribes, its borderers and renegades. Yet this poem too has noble effects, and here is a picture of an after-battle scene that has the repose and high beauty of the best art:—

> "The calm, that cometh after all,
> Look'd sweetly down at shut of day,
> Where friend and foe commingled lay
> Like leaves of forest as they fall.
> Afar the sombre mountains frown'd,
> *Here tall pines wheel'd their shadows round*
> *Like long, slim fingers of a hand*
> *That sadly pointed out the dead.*
> Like some broad shield high overhead
> The great white moon led on and on,
> As leading to the better land.
> You might have heard the cricket's trill,
> Or night-birds calling from the hill,
> The place was so profoundly still."

But on the other hand the poem abounds in such insanities as this:—

> "And through the leaves the silver moon
> Fell *sifting* down in silver *bars*
> And play'd upon her raven hair,
> And darted through like *dimpled* stars
> That dance through all the night's sweet noon
> To echoes of an unseen choir."

And you come to the good things only after hope deferred has made the heart sick.

We will not speak of the remaining poems in Mr. Miller's volume, for they have the same characteristics with those we have mentioned, and afford no ground for farther comment. He is a poet whom we cannot at all accept at the valuation of his panegyrists, but in whom we are glad to recognize a true dramatic and descriptive faculty amidst a dreadful prolixity and chasmal vacancies. As yet, he cannot be said to have secured any place in literature. But he has the hearing of the world and a grand opportunity.

[*Atlantic Monthly*, December 1871]

35

[Taine and the Science of Art-History][1]

A humorist like Dickens, whose celebrity amongst us came from our love of humor, could declare that we had no sense of it; and he was a man of our own race, religion, and domestic, if not social and political traditions. Such a misconception goes near to make one sad, and one has no heart for his revenge when he takes up the all-too-vivid Monsieur Taine's History of English Literature, and reads there the sparkling errors of that ingenious gentleman about Dickens and Thackeray and the society that produced them. No doubt troubles M. Taine, who flashes his jack-a-lantern over the boggy ups and downs of English life, and upon the pages of the great romancer and the great satirist, with a lively belief in its solar power. We speak slightly now of only a small part of a large work, which may have more value than we have been led to hope by what we have read in it. If the suspicion which our partial acquaintance has cast upon the whole proves unjust, we shall be prepared to make full amends hereafter; but in the mean time we own our misgiving. In treating of the remoter literary epochs, M. Taine has us more on his own ground, for our ancestors are a kind of foreigners to us; yet if we may guess from his criticism on Dryden, which we have read, we must still prefer a critic who has not had to judge his author with all his finest and his sweetest left out. It is not so much that he is mainly mistaken; Dryden is rather too plain a case; but if any one will read Mr. Lowell's essay on Dryden after M. Taine's, he will have our meaning, and will perceive the difference between interpreting a poet by every delicate faculty, and feeling for him with the thumb. Still, one has to admire M. Taine's zeal and industry, and the strictly historical portions of his work. He succeeds better, we think, in relating the history of a foreign people to its art, as in his "Art in Greece," than to its literature; but his success there may be chiefly in our necessary modern ignorance of antiquity, and, if they could, those poor ancients might cry out in indignant protest. It is certain that it is safer to infer Greek art from Greek life, as M. Taine does, than to infer Greek character from Greek art, as Mr. Ruskin would prefer to do. His method of

[1] *History of English Literature*. By H. Taine. Translated by H. Van Laun. With a Preface prepared expressly for this Translation by the Author. 2 vols. New York: Holt and Williams. 1871.
Art in Greece. By H. Taine. Translated by John Durand. New York: Holt and Williams. 1871.

189

showing the influences of daily life upon art is admirably brilliant and effective, but the reader will do well to guard himself against the author's too inflexible and exclusive application of his theory. Stated in rather an extreme form, it is this: given the time and climate of a people, their art can be accurately deduced therefrom, without reference to their artistic productions,—just as Agassiz can sketch you off a portrait of our affectionate forefathers the ichthyosaurus or the pterodactyl, after glancing at their fossilized foot-tracks. M. Taine's method does not take into sufficient account the element of individuality in the artist. Rigorously applied, it would make us expect to find all the artists of a given people at a given time cast in one mould, good or bad as the case might be. In the history of art it should be borne in mind that, beside the study of works of art proper, not only the general circumstances of the time and people are to be considered, but the personal circumstances of each great artist,—his obstacles and aids, his failures and triumphs, which modify the character of his works. Each study should supplement the other two. By following these three paths *seriatim*, among every people in every period, and comparing the results, we arrive at a comprehensive knowledge of the world's art. In respect to Greece, the study of biography and of art-products is, of course, mainly out of the question, from the absence of material. But in the study of modern art, it should always be remembered that M. Taine's method is only one side of a complete view. Much gratitude, however, is due him for his valuable contributions to one portion of the science of art-history.

[*Atlantic Monthly*, February 1872]

36

[Three Recent American Works of Fiction][1]

In three works of fiction lately published we have some very faithful studies of American life in the principal phases which it once showed, and which the events of not many years have put quite out of sight if not out of being. In the Oldtown stories the Yankee world of tradition is revived; in Mr. DeForest's "Kate Beaumont" the high-tone Southern society of the times before the war, as it was with slavery and chivalry, with hard drinking and easy shooting, appears again; and in Mr. Eggleston's "Hoosier Schoolmaster" we are made acquainted with the rudeness and ugliness of the intermediate West, after the days of pioneering, and before the days of civilization,—the West of horse-thief gangs and of mobs, of protracted meetings and of extended sprees, of ignorance drawn slowly through religious fervors towards the desire of knowledge and decency in this world. The scene of the story is in Hoopole County, Indiana, a locality which we hope the traveller would now have some difficulty in finding, and in a neighborhood settled, apparently, by poor whites from Virginia and Kentucky, sordid Pennsylvania Dutchmen, and a sprinkling of 'cute dishonest Yankees. The plot is very simple and of easy prevision from the first, being the struggles of Ralph Hartsook with the young idea in the district school on Flat Creek, where the twig was early bent to thrash the schoolmaster. He boards round among the farmers, starting with "old Jack Means," the school trustee, whose son Bud, the most formidable bully among his pupils, he wins over to his own side, and whose daughter, with her mother's connivance, falls in love with him and resolves to marry him. But the schoolmaster loves their bound girl Hannah, and makes enemies of the mother and daughter; and they are not slow to aid in the persecution which rises against him, and ends in his arrest for a burglary committed by the gang of the neighborhood, including some of the principal citizens of Flat Creek. Of course it comes out all right, though the reader is none the less eager because he foresees the fortunate end. The story is very well told in a plain

---

[1] *The Hoosier Schoolmaster.* A Novel. By Edward Eggleston. With Twenty-nine Illustrations. New York: Orange Judd & Co. 1872.

Kate Beaumont. By J. W. DeForest. Boston: J. R. Osgood & Co. 1872.

Oldtown Fireside Stories. By Harriet Beecher Stowe. With Illustrations. Boston: J. R. Osgood & Co. 1872.

fashion, without finely studied points. It is chiefly noticeable, however, as a picture of manners hitherto strange to literature, and the characters are interesting as part of the picture of manners, rather than as persons whose fate greatly concerns us; yet they all have a movement of their own, too, and are easily known from each other,—which is much for characters. One of the best is old Mrs. Means, who is also one of the worst in another sense. Her talk is the talk of all Flat Creek; and we cannot suggest the dialect in which the conversation of the story is chiefly written better than by giving a speech of hers:—

> "Here Mrs. Means stopped to rake a live coal out of the fire with her skinny finger, and then to carry it in her skinny palm to the bowl—or to the *hole*—of her cob-pipe. When she got the smoke agoing she proceeded:
> " 'You see this ere bottom land was all Congress land in them there days, and it sold for a dollar and a quarter, and I says to my ole man, "Jack," says I, "Jack, do you git a plenty while you 're a gittin'. Git a plenty while you 're a gittin'," says I, "fer 't won't never be no cheaper'n 'tis now," and it ha' n't been, I knowed 't would n't,' and Mrs. Means took the pipe from her mouth to indulge in a good chuckle at the thought of her financial shrewdness. ' "Git a plenty while you 're a gittin'," says I. I could see, you know, they was a powerful sight of money in Congress land. That 's what made me say, "Git a plenty while you 're a gittin'." And Jack, he 's wuth lots and gobs of money, all made out of Congress land. Jack did n't git rich by hard work. Bless you, no! Not him. That a'n't his way. Hard work a'n't, you know. 'T was that air six hundred dollars he got along of me, all salted down into Flat Crick bottoms at a dollar and a quarter a acre, and 't was my sayin', "Git a plenty while you 're a gittin'," as done it.' And here the old ogre laughed, or grinned horribly, at Ralph, showing her few straggling, discolored teeth.
> "Then she got up and knocked the ashes out of her pipe, and laid the pipe away and walked round in front of Ralph. After adjusting the 'chunks' so that the fire would burn, she turned her yellow face toward Ralph, and scanning him closely came out with the climax of her speech in the remark, 'You see as how, Mr. Hartsook, the man what gits my Mirandy 'll do well. Flat Crick land 's worth nigh upon a hundred a acre.' "

We should say the weak side of Mr. Eggleston's story was the pathos that gets into it through some of Little Shocky's talk, and the piety that gets into it through Bud Means; and we mean merely that these are not so well managed as the unregeneracy, and not at all that they are not good things to have in a story. The facts about Shocky are touching enough, and the facts about Bud most respectable.

Mr. Eggleston is the first to touch in fiction the kind of life he has represented, and we imagine that future observers will hardly touch it in more points. Its traits seem to be all here, both the good and the bad; but that it is a past or passing state of things is sufficiently testified by the fact, to which Mr. Eggleston alludes in his Preface, that the story, as it appeared serially, was nowhere more popular than in Southern Indiana. Flat Creek, Hoopole

County, would not, we imagine, have been so well pleased thirty years ago with a portrait which, at any rate, is not flattered.

Some of the worst characteristics of the West have been inherited from the slaveholding South,—from Virginia and North Carolina and Maryland,—out of which the poor whites emigrated with their vicious squalor to the new Territories; and there is no very great difference between some of the persons depicted in "The Hoosier Schoolmaster," and low-down people who figure in some chapters of "Kate Beaumont," except that the Western type, escaped from the social domination of the great planters, is full of a rude independence lacking in its ancestry. The Flat-Creekers of Hoopole County, Indiana, are of the same race and lineage as the poor whites of Saxonburg, South Carolina, and the same system is responsible for both. But in spite of their bad instincts and their inherited vices, the Flat-Creekers take to the protracted meeting and the spelling-school for amusement, and the Saxonburgers to the fierce carouse which Mr. DeForest has so strongly painted; after fifty years Saxonburg shall perhaps attain the level which Flat Creek reached twenty-five years ago. There is at least now an opportunity of change for the better in that which could hardly have changed for the worse, the conditions on which Mr. DeForest founds his story having vanished with slavery.

Those who followed the fortunes of Kate Beaumont from month to month in these pages will agree with us that the author did not present Southern people in an entirely odious light, whatever may have been his treatment of Southern life. On the contrary, there are few of his persons who have not some fascination that makes us almost forget their frailties, from Colonel Kershaw to General Johnson. Hitherto Southern character has been treated almost always in direct reference to slavery, and Mr. DeForest gains an immense advantage in refusing to deal with slavery except as a social fact. In this way we are brought nearer to his Southerners as men and women, and enabled to like or dislike them for purely personal reasons; though any one who supposed him indifferent to the question in abeyance would singularly mistake him, and would lose half his meaning. The whole effect of his story is so lifelike, that we are persuaded to believe it the first full and perfect picture of Southern society of the times before the war; certainly it is the most satisfactory; and if the duels and informal combats and debauches and difficulties of all kinds seem too frequent for the truth, we must not forget that our author is working artistically, with a right to assemble the dramatic points of his material, and we must remember also what the truth was about that bygone state of things. As we read Mr. DeForest we might fancy ourselves in the midst of such genteel Irish life as Thackeray touches in "The Luck of Barry Lyndon," or among Florentine or Veronese gentlemen of the Middle Ages. The structure of that old South Carolinian society is none the less feudal because the supremacy of its aristocrats is a matter of personal quality and of sentiment rather than of legal force; and one of the nicest and most amusing points of Mr. DeForest's study is that the young Beaumonts, educated in Paris and Berlin, come back to their native barbarism with an almost unshaken devotion. Frank McAlister, to be sure, returns from Europe with a profound contempt for this barbarism, and a particular scorn for the family feud of the Beaumonts and McAlisters: he means to develop the mineral resources of South Carolina and civilize her; but even he loves her above all other lands, and once happily married to Kate Beaumont he can do nothing but acquiesce in the local conditions, and become a model country gentleman after the best Carolinian fashion. The other McAlisters, with all their seriousness and coolness, are as ready for the duel and the rencounter as the Beaumonts, and in none of the many particulars touched do the proprieties of South Carolina seem to be violated. The elders—passionate, homicidal, affectionate old Peyton Beaumont, and his lifelong enemy Judge McAlister, urbane and canny and cold—are equally stiff-necked and besotted in their contempt of all the world outside of their native State, and in their love of her political and social traits.

The personage who rises above all in a peculiar beauty and nobility of character is old Colonel Kershaw, whose virtues are presented to us with a clearness and force worthy of them. It is so like a study from some actual character known to Mr. DeForest, that we hesitate to credit him with its invention. Serene, brave, peaceful, that good old man, the type of such Southern manhood as flowered into the tranquil and simple greatness of Washington, is one of most realistic figures in a novel abounding in diversely marked characters.

As we said in speaking of "Overland," Mr. DeForest has an uncommon success in the presentation of his personages. There is not one in this book that is feebly treated, and the range is great. Vincent Beaumont, somewhat cynical, Parisianized, quick-tempered, yet not bad-hearted; Poinsett, fat, easy, *persifleur*, yet a Beaumont through and through when it comes to the family honor; Tom, the young drunkard, with his blackguard self-respect, and his boyish desire to excel in devotion to the family feud;—how distinctly they are set before us in contrast to the McAlisters! Among these, Bruce appears only subordinately, yet we know almost as from our own senses his tall, consumptive person, his winning manner, his husky voice; as we do Bent Armitage with his game foot and his slangy talk. Those two ancients, Colonel Lawson and General Johnson, so opposite in their flatteries and their purposes, with a broad likeness in their eloquent habits, good as they are, are no better drawn than all the loafers and politicians of Hartland, or the wild low-downers of Saxonburg. Of the women, Nelly Armitage, as a character, is the best, and her courageous patience with her drunken husband is one of the best passages in the book; it is quite conceivable of her that she should first favor Frank McAlister's love for Kate, then want him killed because he tied her brother Tom, and then again espouse his cause because he is so magnanimous and so miserable. It is not, we suppose, one of the least truthful strokes in the general portrayal of South Carolinianism, that both the Beaumonts and McAlisters are agreed that Frank might have killed Tom without giving just cause of complaint, but having tied him he has afforded him ground for a challenge.

Kate and Frank are interesting as the centre around which the rapid events move; and for lovers they are very well indeed: she lovable and worshipful, he loving and worshipping her with a large, ceaseless, desperate, unquenchable devotion that is itself full of character. Yet we doubt if the old coquette, Mrs. Chester, and the drunken Randolph Armitage, are not more entertaining to middle-life. Mrs. Chester is made too much of, however, for a woman so simply selfish and disagreeable.

We say nothing of the plot of this excellent novel, for all our readers know it, and we feel that we have but scantly indicated its merits, which besides those of character-painting are humor, dramatic faculty, and a vigorous and agreeable style. With "Miss Ravenel's Conversion" and "Overland," "Kate Beaumont" forms, to our mind, strong proof that we are not so much lacking in an American novelist as in a public to recognize him.

A curious contrast to the kind of talk we have quoted from Mr. Eggleston's story might be found on almost any page of "Oldtown Fireside Stories." Uncouth as the Yankee talk is, it is always glib and easy, and suggests the life of an old provincialized community, with its settled order and its intimacy and familiarity: it suggests the occupation of a new country by large companies of men of the same stock, creed, and education; while the Hoosier talk, loath, languid, awkward, with its want of fixed character, hints a people of various origin, silenced, each man, by his solitary battle with the wilderness, and carrying his aguish stiff-jointedness into a dialect which shows upon a ground of Southern phrase the rusticities of nearly every part of the country. In everything the life of one book is a contrast to that of the other, though in both it is rural life. Sam Lawson, who tells these stories, is doubtless the most worthless person in Oldtown; but compare his amusing streaks of God-fearing piety, his reverence for magistracies and dignities, his law-abidingness, his shrewdness, his readiness, with the stolid wickedness, the indifference and contempt of those backwoods ruffians for every one else, and you will have some conception of the variety of the brood that the bird of freedom has gathered under her wings. To be sure, the backwoods have long been turned into railroad-ties and cord-wood, and Oldtown is no more, but this only adds to the interest and value of true pictures of them. Mrs. Stowe, we think, has hardly done better work than in these tales, which have lured us to read them again and again by their racy quaintness and the charm of the shiftless Lawson's character and manner. The material is slight and common enough, ghosts, Indians, British, and ministers lending their threadbare interest to most of them; but round these familiar protagonists moves a whole Yankee village-world, the least important figure of which savors of the soil and "breathes full East." The virtues of fifty years and more ago, the little local narrowness and intolerance, the lurking pathos, the hidden tenderness of a rapidly obsolescent life, are all here, with the charm of romance in their transitory aspects,—which, we wonder, will the Hibernian Massachusetts of future times appreciate? At least this American generation can, keenly, profoundly, and for ourselves, we have a pleasure in the mere talk of Sam Lawson which can only come from the naturalness of first-rate art.

[*Atlantic Monthly*, March 1872]

37

[Hawthorne's French and Italian Notebooks][1]

It would be hard to say what chiefly delights the reader of Hawthorne's Italian Note-Books, unless it is the simple charm of good writing. There is very little of that wonderful suggestiveness which the American Note-Books had, with their revelations of the inventive resource and the habitual operation of the romancer's genius, and rarely that sympathy with which the descriptions in the English journals were filled. To the last, Hawthorne confessedly remained an alien in Italy, afflicted throughout by her squalor, her shameless beggary, her climate, her early art, her grimy picture-frames, and the disheartening absence of varnish in her galleries. We suppose that his doubt whether he was not bamboozling himself when he admired an old master, is one which has occurred, more or less remotely, to most honest men under like conditions; but it is odd that his humor did not help him to be more amused by the droll rascality and mendicancy with which a foreigner's life in Italy is enveloped. His nature, however, was peculiarly New-Englandish; the moral disrepair, like the physical decay, continually offended him beyond retrieval by his sense of its absurdity. He abhorred an intrusive beggar as he did a Giotto or a Cimabue, and a vile street was as bad to him as a fresco of the thirteenth century. But even the limitations of such a man are infinitely interesting, and, as one reads, one thanks him from the bottom of his soul for his frankness. Most of us are, by the will of heaven, utterly ignorant of art, and it is vastly wholesome to have this exquisite genius proclaim his identity with us, and in our presence to look with simple liking or dislike upon the works he sees, untouched by the traditional admiration of all ages and nations. The affectation of sympathy or knowledge is far more natural to our fallen humanity, and the old masters send back to us every year hordes of tiresome hypocrites, to whom we recommend Hawthorne's healing sincerity. It is not that we think him right in all his judgments, or many of them; but that if any one finds in the varnish and bright frames of the English galleries greater pleasure than in the sacredly dingy pictures of Italian churches and palaces, or thinks Mr. Brown finer than Claude, his

---

[1] *Passages from the French and Italian Note-Books of Nathaniel Hawthorne.* Boston: J. R. Osgood & Co.

truth in saying so is of as good quality as in his declaration that he loves
Gothic better than classic architecture.

At times Hawthorne's feeling about art seems capable of education, but
he appears himself to remain nearly always in doubt about it, and to find this
misgiving a kind of refuge. It is true that in regard to sculpture he has not so
much hesitation as he has about different paintings. The belief that it is an
obsolete art, hinted in "The Marble Faun," is several times advanced in these
journals, and he affirms again and again his horror of nudity in modern
sculpture,—a matter in which, we think, he has the better of the sculptors,
though it is not easy to see how the representation of the nude is to be forbid
without abolishing the whole art. It is a fact, which tells in favor of such
critics as believe sculpture to be properly an accessory of architecture and
nothing more, that though Hawthorne's sympathies with other forms of art
were slight and uncertain, he instinctively delighted in good and noble architecture. This is probably the case also with most other refined people who
have no artistic training, and it is doubtful if either painting or sculpture can
have any success among us except in union with architecture,—the first of
the arts in appealing to the natural sense of beauty.

The reader of these Notes will not learn more of Italian life than of
Italian art; it is Hawthorne's life in Italy, and often without contact with Italy,
that is here painted. But it is not his most intimate life; it is his life as an
author, his intellectual life; and one often fancies that the record must have
been kept with a belief that it would some day be published; for with respect
to his literary self, Hawthorne was always on confidential terms with the
world, as his frank prefaces show. It has nothing of carelessness, though
nothing of constraint in the mental attitude, while in the midst of its grace
and delightfulness there is frequent self-criticism. He says after a somewhat
florid passage, "I hate what I have written," and he considers and reconsid-
ers his ideas throughout, like a man conscious of daily growth. Sometimes,
but quite rarely, there is a glance of *personal* self-examination, as where, with
a half-humorous air, he gives his impression that Miss Bremer thinks him
unamiable: "I am sorry if it be so, because such a good, kindly, clear-sighted,
and delicate person is very apt to have reason at the bottom of her harsh
thoughts when, in rare cases, she allows them to harbor with her."

An amusing trait of the literary consciousness with which the journal is
written is the author's habit of introducing his quaint or subtle reflections
with that unnatural, characteristic "methinks" of his, which, like Mr. Emerson's prose "'t is," is almost a bit of personal property. But if Hawthorne
tells little of himself, he atones for it as far as may be by so sketching ever so
many other interesting people, and the queer at-odds life foreigners lead in
Italy. There is a precious little picture of a tea-drinking with Miss Bremer in
her lodging near the Tarpeian Rock, which precedes the passage we have just
quoted, and the account of a ride with Mrs. Jameson, which we would fain
transfer hither, but must leave where they are. Story, Browning, Mrs. Browning, Powers, and a host of minor celebrities are all painted with that firm,

delicate touch, and that certain parsimony of color which impart their pale charm to the people of Hawthorne's romances. Most prominent is the sculptor Powers, for whom the author conceived a strong personal liking, and by whose universal inventiveness and practical many-mindedness his imagination was greatly impressed. He listened with so much respect and conviction to all the sculptor's opinions upon art, that the dismay into which he falls when Mr. Powers picks the Venus de' Medici to pieces, just after Hawthorne has taught himself to adore her, is little less than tragical, and there is something pathetically amusing in his subsequent efforts to rehabilitate her perfection. At the same time the reader's sense of Hawthorne's own modesty and sincerity is indefinitely deepened. In the whole range of art he is confident of but one or two things,—that modern nude sculptures are foolish and repulsive, and that the works of Giotto and Cimabue are hideous, and had better be burnt. Yet we think that his journals might be read with greater instruction upon art than many critical works.

The life at Florence, with its poetical and artistic neighborhood, its local delightfulness, its ease, its cheapness, is temptingly sketched; but perhaps the reader of "The Marble Faun" will not be quite content to find Donatello's Tower in the Villa Montauto on Bello-Sguardo. Not that the place is not beautiful enough for any romance, but that most will have conceived of a wilder and remoter Monte Beni. It is interesting, by the way, to note that it is not till Hawthorne's fourth or fifth visit to the Capitol that he seems to have observed the statue which suggested his romance. Then at last he says: "I looked at the Faun of Praxiteles, and was sensible of a peculiar charm in it; a sylvan beauty and homeliness, friendly and wild at once. The lengthened, but not preposterous ears, and the little tail, which we infer, have an exquisite effect. . . . . A story, with all sorts of fun and pathos in it, might be contrived on the idea of one of their species having become intermingled with the human race. . . . . The tail might have disappeared by dint of constant intermarriages with ordinary mortals; but the pretty hairy ears should occasionally reappear, ... and the moral and intellectual characteristics of the faun might be most picturesquely brought out, without detriment to the human interest of the story. Fancy," he concludes, "this combination in the person of a young lady!" Here it is evident that he thinks merely of a short story, with no shadow of tragedy in it. Afterwards how the idea expanded and deepened and darkened! And is it not curious to reflect that Donatello *might* have been a girl?

At times, in reading these journals, the romance seems the essence not only of what was profound in Hawthorne's observation in Italy, but also his notice of external matters, such as the envy and mutual criticism of artists; all the roots of the book are here, and the contrast of them with their growth there above ground is a valuable instruction.

It belongs to criticism of "The Marble Faun," rather than these Note-Books, to remark how the strictly Italian material of Hawthorne's experience scarcely sufficed for the purposes of the romancer; but it is true that he remained Gothic and Northern to the last moment in the classicistic South, even to the misspelling of nearly all Italian words. We believe, however, that he describes not only himself in Italy when he says: "I soon grew so weary of admirable things that I could neither enjoy nor understand them. My receptive faculty is very limited; and when the utmost of its small capacity is full, I become perfectly miserable, and the more so the better worth seeing are the objects I am forced to see." This is the picture of our whole race in that land.

[*Atlantic Monthly*, May 1872]

38

[Mark Twain's Roughing It]¹

WE can fancy the reader of Mr. Clemens's book finding at the end of it (and its six hundred pages of fun are none too many) that, while he has been merely enjoying himself, as he supposes, he has been surreptitiously acquiring a better idea of the flush times in Nevada, and of the adventurous life generally of the recent West, than he could possibly have got elsewhere. The grotesque exaggeration and broad irony with which the life is described are conjecturably the truest colors that could have been used, for all existence there must have looked like an extravagant joke, the humor of which was only deepened by its nether-side of tragedy. The plan of the book is very simple indeed, for it is merely the personal history of Mr. Clemens during a certain number of years, in which he crossed the Plains in the overland stage to Carson City, to be private secretary to the Secretary of Nevada; took the silver-mining fever, and with a friend struck "a blind lead" worth millions; lost it by failing to comply with the mining laws; became local reporter to a Virginia City newspaper; went to San Francisco and suffered extreme poverty in the cause of abstract literature and elegant leisure; was sent to the Sandwich Islands as newspaper correspondent; returned to California, and began lecturing and that career of humorist, which we should all be sorry to have ended. The "moral" which the author draws from the whole is: "If you are of any account, stay at home and make your way by faithful diligence; but if you are of 'no account,' go away from home, and then you will *have* to work, whether you want to or not."

A thousand anecdotes, relevant and irrelevant, embroider the work; excursions and digressions of all kinds are the very woof of it, as it were; everything far-fetched or near at hand is interwoven, and yet the complex is a sort of "harmony of colors" which is not less than triumphant. The stage-drivers and desperadoes of the Plains; the Mormons and their city; the capital of Nevada, and its government and people; the mines and miners; the social, speculative, and financial life of Virginia City; the climate and characteristics of San Francisco; the amusing and startling traits of Sandwich Island civilization,—appear in kaleidoscopic succession. Probably an encyclopædia

---

¹*Roughing It.* By Mark Twain. (Samuel T. Clemens.) Fully illustrated by eminent artists. [Published by Subscription.] Hartford, Conn.: American Publishing Company. 1872.

could not be constructed from the book; the work of a human being, it is not unbrokenly nor infallibly funny; nor is it to be always praised for all the literary virtues; but it is singularly entertaining, and its humor is always amiable, manly, and generous.

[*Atlantic Monthly*, June 1872]

39

[Forster's Biography of Dickens][1]

THE second volume of Mr. Forster's Life of Dickens is not so interesting as the first. It does not reach the period of Dickens's separation from his wife, and it gives no facts of his *vie intime* to compare in effect with those already related of his childhood. On the other hand, it has all the disagreeable qualities of the first volume: it is even more bragging in tone, feeble and wandering in analysis, and comical in criticism. It tells the story of Dickens's life from 1842 to 1852,—a period of great literary activity and of varied experiences; for during these years the American Notes, Martin Chuzzlewit, The Christmas Carol, The Chimes, Pictures from Italy, Dombey and Son, and David Copperfield were written, and the author spent much time abroad, residing at Genoa for a year, then for a long time in Switzerland, and then at Paris.

In 1842 he had just returned from America, and was busy with those Notes in which he stated as mildly as he could his displeasure with this Republic, but which our exacting population of that day refused to find lenient. It seems all a very droll business to us, who are so much wiser than our fathers, but perhaps we should not have liked it ourselves. We do not like the patronizing letter which he writes to Mr. Forster in 1868 from America: "I see *great changes* for the better socially. Politically, no. England governed by the Marylebone vestry, and England as she would be after years of such governing, is what I make of *that*." We do not like it, but we do not care much about it, and our predecessors cared a great deal. That is the difference. Still, great as was the clamor the ill-advised Americans of that day made over the Notes, Dickens amusingly exaggerated it; he really thought that the whole course of business and pleasure upon this continent was suspended in order to let the public rage about his book. But it is plain that he always felt himself an object of universal and unceasing interest: he wrote his books as we celebrate our Fourths, with the eyes of the world upon him. As to us poor Americans, he never changed his mind about us; he never liked us; and it is a pity that we cannot get over that vice of wanting other people to like us. There are some forty millions of us now; is it not enough if we like each

---

[1] *The Life of Charles Dickens.* By John Forster. Volume II. Philadelphia: J. B. Lippincott & Co. 1873.

other? It is impossible that a man should like any nation besides his own; the best he can do is to like here and there a person in it. Dickens did this, and so does his biographer after him. Mr. Forster thinks there is no higher type than the accomplished and genial American, just as we think there is nobody so charming as the thoroughly agreeable Englishman, though even he has his little foible: for example, he does not exist. But it was not merely his dislike that the Americans of old complained of in Charles Dickens; it was his unfairness, his giving only the truth that told against them, and his downright misrepresentations. Who shall say if they were right? Some things in this book support their side. Dickens pretends that he met five Americans on a Genoese steamer, and one of them called out, "Why, I'm blarmed if it ain't Dickens!" and having introduced the others all round, added, "Personally, you and my fellow-countrymen can fix it pleasant, I do expectuate." Honest Mr. Forster sets down this frantic rubbish, and seems to believe that it reports the parlance of the American people. We can well imagine, however, that Dickens found the Italians much smoother and more agreeable than he found us, and that he felt it the greatest injustice to call the Swiss "the Americans of the Continent," for they saluted people whom they met very politely. It must be owned that in point of manners we are perhaps the least successful people on earth, and to be ranked with none but the English.

Beyond the superficial observations of Italian life which afterwards took more perfect form in Pictures from Italy, Dickens's letters from Genoa contain little but the usual extravagant statements of his own conditions of mind, his achievements, and his purposes. Something prodigious, or horrible, or enormous, or petrifying, or terrible, or magnificent, or astounding in a superlative degree happens to him so often, that at last it becomes fatiguing. The letters throughout the book are nearly always to Mr. Forster; as if Mr. Forster did not like to connect any other name with Dickens's. It is true that he quotes some passages of the letters to President Felton from Mr. Fields's Yesterdays with Authors, and these are so much better than any written to himself that one wishes his biographer had cast about him a little to see if he could not discover some other correspondent of Dickens. Though the letters given are not easy reading, though their fun seems often pitilessly forced, and their seriousness of the blackest midnight hue, and their fervor of the very red hottest, they are extremely useful in possessing us fully with an idea of the pressure under which Dickens felt, joked, wept, wrote, lived. His whole existence was a prolonged storm and stress, and the wonder is, not that he died so young, but that he lived to be so old. This pressure told upon his quality. A man of unquestionable genius, his material, at its finest, was never of the finest. The melodramatic was his notion of the dramatic, the eloquent was his idea of the poetic; his humor was burlesque; his pathos was never too deep for tears. It seems that he could not like anything better, if we are to judge from his estimate of Hawthorne's matchless romance: "I finished the Scarlet Letter yesterday. It falls off sadly, after that fine opening scene. The psychological part of the story is very much overdone, and not truly done, I think. Their suddenness of meeting and agreeing to go away together, after all those years, is very poor. Mr. Chillingworth ditto. The child out of nature altogether. And Mr. Dimmesdale never could have begotten her." This failure to understand the subtle perfection of art so far above his is all the more sadly amusing when one thinks, in connection with it, of the shapelessness of his own plots, the unnaturalness of his situations, the crudity of his treatment of characters similar to those he censures. Indeed, when you go back to the most popular of the Dickens romances, you marvel at the effect the earlier books had upon the generation in which they were written, and question whether there is not some witchery in the mere warmth and novelty of a young author's book that makes it captivating to his contemporaries. In this biography you read with amazement the letters of Lord Jeffrey, in which the old reviewer bewails himself over little Nell and Paul Dombey. Does any peer of the realm now shed tears for their fate? Dickens, full of his Chimes, came all the way from Italy in midwinter to read it to Carlyle, Forster, Jerrold, and other intimate friends, and made them cry; but he could hardly do that with any literary company now if he came back from the dead. And is it then all a fashion only?

The tireless industry of Dickens continued throughout the years recorded in this volume, but he performed no such feat as the simultaneous production of Pickwick, Nickleby, and Oliver Twist. Yet he wrote always with the printer at his heels, and in one of his letters he tells how it startled him to hear, in a stationer's shop, a lady inquire for a certain number of David Copperfield when he had just bought the paper to write it. His literary history is very fully given, and amidst much that is not important there is a great deal that is very interesting. His method of publication was adverse to any exactness of plot; and as he wrote from month to month his romances took shape from the suggestions and exigencies of the passing time. It is easy to see how he padded when he could not otherwise fill out the due number of pages; in some of his books, as The Old Curiosity Shop, he wholly changed his plan, and in Our Mutual Friend it is hard to believe that he had any plan. For this reason we are not persuaded, in the matter of Mr. Cruikshank's claim to have suggested the idea of Oliver Twist, that Mr. Forster has all the truth upon his side. Doubtless the artist claims too much in saying that he furnished the principal characters and scenes, and implying that the letterpress merely illustrated his pictures; but it is not at all improbable that Dickens, who was then writing Pickwick and Nicholas Nickleby, as well as Oliver Twist, may really have changed his plot after poring over a series of sketches in the artist's portfolio. The letter of Dickens, which Mr. Forster prints with so much emphasis, he merely declares at the time of writing that he had just seen "a *majority* of the plates for the first time." Nobody will ever believe that Mr. Cruikshank originated Oliver Twist; but Dr. Mackenzie's statement of the matter was so far within the range of possibility, that, after all but calling him a liar, it seems a grudging reparation for Mr. Forster to say that he is not guilty of "the worst part of the fable." But, then, graciousness is not a characteristic of this odd biography, in which the unamiable traits of the biographer combine with the unamiable traits of his subject to give the book as disagreeable a tone as a book ever had. We behold in one case a high-pressure egotist, living a world pervaded by himself, eager for gain, and dismayed by smaller profits than he expected, suspicious of those whom he dealt with in business, relentless in his own interests, a dreadful machine capable of walking ten miles every day and writing a chapter of fiction, quoting himself continually, and behaving himself generally in a manner to be wearisome to the flesh and spirit of all other men; and, on the other hand, we have a jealous and greedy intimate of his who insists upon representing him solely from his own personal and epistolary knowledge. But we feel sure that this is a false view of Charles Dickens. The letters to Mr. Forster are of less value than his other letters, because they have the stamp of an exaggerated and exacting friendship on them; they are all of the operatic pitch; and latterly they appear to have been written with a consciousness that they were some day to be used as literary material. It is not credible that these letters alone were accessible to the biographer, and it is strange that he seldom or never gives any reminiscences of Dickens besides his own. The closest friend cannot see the whole character of any man; but this biography seems to be written upon the contrary theory, and it renders another life of Dickens necessary. It must always remain as a most entertaining mass of material, but there could be no greater misfortune to Charles Dickens's memory than that it should be permanently accepted as his history.

[*Atlantic Monthly*, February 1873]

40

[Turgenev's Novel of Russian Life][1]

THE reader who is curious to note the difference between a tragedy written by a man of great talent and one by a man of great genius should compare Joseph Noirel's Revenge (which we noticed last month) and the Liza of Turgénieff. The first is a book of singular power and of fascinating interest: it thrills you by its masterly management of the strangest facts and situations, its audacious subjection, not merely of improbabilities, but impossibilities to its effects. The other is—life; nothing more, nothing less; and though life altogether foreign to our own, yet unmistakably real. Everything is unaffected and unstrained. Here is not so much of the artificer as even his style: this author never calls on you to admire how well he does a thing; he only makes you wonder at the truth and value of the thing when it is done. He seems the most self-forgetful of the story-telling tribe, and he is no more enamored of his creations than of himself; he pets none of them; he upbraids none; you like them or hate them for what they are; it does not seem to be his affair. It is hard to reconcile the sense of this artistic impartiality with one's sense of the deep moral earnestness of the author's books: he is profoundly serious in behalf of what is just and good, even when he appears most impassive in respect to his characters; one feels the presence, not only of a great genius, but a clear conscience in his work. His earnestness scarcely permits him the play of humor; his wit is pitiless irony or cutting sarcasm.

Liza is the story of Fedor Ivanovich Lavretsky, whose handsome wife is, after his discovery of her unfaithfulness, left to lead the life that pleases her at Paris, at Baden, and elsewhere, while he goes back to Russia. He has had a strange and unnaturally secluded childhood; his wife was the first woman of his own rank that he had met, and he loved her; now that is past; but though he is a man who has suffered greatly, it is not a ruined life that he brings home, for he is a man of sense as well as strong affections. Lizaveta Mikhailovna is his distant relation, a young girl of nineteen when he comes to live on his estate near the town where her family resides. She is of a pure, high, religious nature, sensitively conscientious, and of a reserved and thoughtful temperament. Before either is aware they are in love. A paper

---

[1] Liza. A Russian Novel. By Ivan S. Turgénieff. Translated by W. R. S. Ralston. New York: Holt and Williams. 1872.

comes to Lavretsky with the announcement of his wife's death; and he shows it to Liza. That night they meet by accident in her mother's garden, and are surprised into the acknowledgment of their love. It is a moment of rapture to him and of doubt and trouble to her; and the next night Lavretsky's wife, who is not dead, returns. Then all is over; he rids himself of her, but Liza goes into a convent; old friends die, children grow up into men and women; Lavretsky's wife leads her old life in Paris; Lavretsky becomes forty-five; Liza remains in her convent and that is the way the story ends.

The action scarcely begins till the story is two thirds told; all that precedes is devoted to the work of accounting for the characters and placing them and their ancestors and kindred, by a series of scenes, anecdotes, and descriptions, fully before you. In the mean time you come to know also a great deal of Russian life in general, though apparently no study of it has been made for your instruction: you Russianize, as you read, till you wish to address your acquaintances by their Christian names and patronymics. But suddenly, at a certain point, the threads which seemed to lie so loose in the author's hand are drawn closer and closer, till the interest is of the most intense degree. Everything that went before, tells: the effect of character, passion, situation, deepens and deepens; as the climax approaches, the light touches with which the tragedy is darkened are added one after one, till it appears impossible that you should bear more; then the whole work stands complete before you in its transcendent, hopeless pathos. It is sorrow that commands your reverence as well as your pity; Liza is so good, Lavretsky so worthy of happiness, that you can make their grief your own without losing your self-respect.

It is hard to say which of the numerous personages is best painted, and fortunately it is not necessary; it is enough that they are all done with consummate art, consummate naturalness. The same is to be said of the different scenes, unless, indeed, we single out the evening at the house of Liza's mother, when Lavretsky's wife has returned to be pardoned, as she calls it, and flatters the selfish sentimental old woman into a belief in her repentance, and flirts with Liza's rejected lover Panshine, and makes fun of all of them without their knowing it, and so rides home with the old gossiping Gedeonovsky.

> "Panshine bowed gravely to all the party; afterwards, as he stood on the steps after seeing Varvara into her carriage, he gave her hand a gentle pressure, and exclaimed, as she drove away, '*Au revoir!*' Gedeonovsky sat by her side in the carriage, and all the way home she amused herself by putting the tip of her little foot, as if by accident, on his foot. He felt abashed and tried to make her complimentary speeches. She tittered and made eyes at him when the light from the street-lamps shone into the carriage. The waltz she had played rang in her ears and excited her. Wherever she might be she had only to imagine a ball-room and a blaze of light, and swift circling round to the sound of music, and her heart would burn within her, her eyes would glow with a strange lustre, a smile would wander around her lips, a kind of bacchanalian grace would seem to diffuse itself over her whole body. When they arrived at her house, Varvara

lightly bounded from the carriage, as only a *lionne* could bound, turned towards Gedeonovsky, and suddenly burst out laughing in his face. 'A charming creature,' thought the councillor of state, as he made his way home to his lodgings, where his servant was waiting for him with a bottle of opodeldoc. 'It's as well that I'm a steady man—But why did she laugh?' "

This scene is perfect in its way, and yet we are not sure that it is finer than some closing passages of the drama, wherein Lavretsky, long years after the ruin of his hopes, returns to the house of Liza's mother, and finds it full of gay young people, the friends and relations of her younger brother and sister, who have grown up and married. All the old people are dead.

" 'Won't you go into the garden?' said Kalitine, addressing Lavretsky. 'It is very pleasant now, although we have neglected it a little.'

"Lavretsky went into the garden, and the first thing he saw there was that very bench on which he and Liza had once passed a few happy moments,— moments that never repeated themselves. It had grown black and warped, but still he recognized it, and that feeling took possession of his heart which is unequalled as well for sweetness as for bitterness,—the feeling of lively regret for vanished youth, for once familiar happiness.

"He walked by the side of the young people along the alleys. The lime-trees looked older than before, having grown a little taller during the last eight years and casting a denser shade. All the underwood, also, had grown higher, and the raspberry-bushes had spread vigorously, and the hazel copse was thickly tangled. From every side exhaled a fresh odor from the forest and the wood, from the grass and the lilacs.

" 'What a capital place for a game at Puss in the Corner!' suddenly cried Lenochka, as they entered upon a small grassy lawn surrounded by lime-trees. 'There are just five of us.'

" 'But have you forgotten Fedor Ivanovich?' asked her brother; 'or is it yourself you have not counted?'

"Lenochka blushed a little. . . . .

"But Lavretsky returned to the house, went into the dining-room, approached the piano, and touched one of the notes. It responded with a faint but clear sound, and a shudder thrilled his heart within him. With that note began the inspired melody, by means of which, on that most happy night long ago, Lemm, the dead Lemm, had thrown him into such raptures. Then Lavretsky passed into the drawing-room, and did not leave it for a long time.

"In that room, in which he had seen Liza so often, her image floated more distinctly before him; the traces of her presence seemed to make themselves felt around him there. But his sorrow of her loss became painful and crushing; it bore with it none of the tranquillity which death inspires. Liza was still living somewhere, far away and lost to sight. He thought of her as he had known her in actual life; he could not recognize the girl he used to love in that pale, dim, ghostly form, half-hidden in a nun's dark robe and surrounded by waving clouds of incense.

"Nor would Lavretsky have been able to recognize himself, if he could have looked at himself as he in fancy was looking at Liza. In the course of those eight years his life had attained its final crisis,—that crisis which many people never experience, but without which no man can be sure of maintaining his principles firm to the last. He had really given up thinking about his own happiness, about what would conduce to his own interests. He had become calm, and—why should we conceal the truth?—he had aged; and that not in face alone or frame, but he had aged in mind; for, indeed, not only is it difficult, but it is even hazardous to do what some people speak of,—to preserve the heart young in bodily old age."

Is not this exquisitely, penetratingly sad in its simple truthfulness?

[*Atlantic Monthly*, February 1873]

41

[Robert Browning's Antic Night-Cap Poem][1]

THE Red Cotton Night-Cap Country is the antic name of that strange last performance of Mr. Browning's, to which, for reasons of his own, he has given the outward form and typographical mask of poetry; but why he should have called it Red Cotton Night-Cap Country, sooner than The Man in the Moon, or Ding-Dong Bell, does not finally appear to the distracted reader of the work. The story is, if we do not misstate the parenthetical nightmare, founded on the case of a certain Monsieur Léonce Miranda, son of a rich jeweller of Paris, who lives out of wedlock with a Madame Clara Muhlhausen, a lady accustomed to a variety of protection, till his mother suddenly dies, when, being at heart ascetic as well as sensual, he is stricken with such terrible remorse that he renounces his mistress, appoints a time to meet his relations and pass over his father's now-inherited business to them, and is discovered, through the key-hole, reading his love-letters, which he finally puts into a chest and holds in the fire till it is consumed and his guilty hands with it. He fights with the burning stumps the cousins who rush in to save him from himself; he lies weeks in a mad joy at his sacrifice, and with the first return of health drives straight to his mistress, and resumes his old relations with her. He sells out the jewelry business at an extremely good price to his kinsfolk, and retires with his leman to his country-place in Normandy, where they become the devoutest benefactors of a particular Madonna in a certain church; he gives jewels, and madame bestows laces; and at last one fine morning, after twenty years of adultery winked at by the Church, the devout Miranda leaps from the top of his château, in the persuasion that the Virgin of La Ravissante will bear him safely up and set him safely down in front of her shrine. This of course does not happen. M. Miranda is killed, his cousins come to break the will and turn out Madame Muhlhausen; but that notable woman had previously caused Miranda to leave his substance to the church of La Ravissante, and to give herself only a life-use of the estate. The church sustains her, and so does the court, deciding that as the cousins have done business with Miranda all these years, they can now allege no proof of his insanity; and there Madame Muhlhausen still lives till the church inherits her.

---

[1] *Red Cotton Night-Cap Country; or, Turf and Towers.* By Robert Browning. Boston: J. R. Osgood & Co. 1873.

Such is the story, not otherwise than horrible and revolting in itself; and it is so told as to bring out its worst with a far-reaching insinuation, and an occasional frantic rush at expression of its unseemliness for which the manure-heap affords the proper imagery of "dung," and "devil's dung." We suppose we shall be told of power in the story; and power there undeniably is, else no one could be dragged through the book by it. The obscurity of three fourths of it—of nearly all, one might say, except the merely narrative passages—becomes almost amusing. It seems as if Mr. Browning lay in wait, and, lest any small twinkling or glimmer of meaning should reach his reader, sprang out and popped a fresh parenthesis on the offending chink that let it through. Fifty-six mortal pages explain why the story is called Red Cotton Night-Cap Country, but without making the reader understand why, and he is left dancing upon nothing for many pages more, till his aching foot is glad to rest even on the uncleanly history of M. Miranda's intrigue and lunacy. The poem—if it is a poem—is as unhandsome as it is unwholesome; it is both bad art and bad taste, and is to be defended, it seems to us, neither as a lesson from a miserable fact, nor as a successful bit of literary realism.

[*Atlantic Monthly*, July 1873]

42

[Heine's Fantastic Attitudes][1]

THE Scintillations from Heine's prose works which Mr. Stern gives us are passages from essays and letters not before translated, and that weird, romantic monologue called Florentine Nights, in which a man tells in part the story of his life to a dying girl, and beguiles her last moments with the wildest inventions and caprices. It is incoherent, changeful, lawless, natural, and enchanting as a dream, full of the tenderness and insult of Heine's passion, with enough of his fine and coarse suggestion; the slight thread of narrative is dropped whenever the author likes, and his fancy ranges satirically to anything else in the world,—art, politics, religion, and the odiousness of England and the English people, the delightfulness of Paris and the Parisians, the violin playing of Paganini, and the apparition of Paganini's agent, "the dramatist and anecdotist Harris of Hanover," whose form Satan has borrowed, while "along with other trash the poor soul of that poor creature remains locked up in a chest in Hanover, until the Devil returns his carnal envelope; when, in the nobler disguise of a black poodle, he will accompany his master Paganini through the world."

Heine can never be read aright save in the pale moonshine of the German tongue; dragged into the daylight of our speech, he loses that softness of outline, that play of light and shadow, which characterize him; he becomes harsh, sharp, sometimes shabby, and you see how, occasionally, he forces his fantastic attitudes. Perhaps also he is best read by very young men not past the age of liking even the faults of genius; he wearies middle life a little, though he remains wonderful. However, there are passages of the Florentine Nights which do not suffer mortally from translation and the years of discretion, and one of these is that very Heinesque bit where Max tells of his passion for the beautiful statue which he found when a boy in the neglected garden of his mother's château:—

> "The wrath of time and of man had spared but one statue, and even that had been thrown from its pedestal and was lying in the high grass. It lay there, uninjured,—a marble goddess, with pure, lovely features, and noble, finely chis-

[1] *Scintillations from the Prose Works of Heinrich Heine.* Translated from the German by Simon Adler Stern. New York: Holt and Williams. 1873.

Monographs, Personal and Social. By Lord Houghton. New York: Holt and Williams. 1873.

elled bosom, shining forth from the high grass like a Grecian revelation. I was almost frightened when I first beheld it; the sight filled me with a strange feeling of oppression and fear, while awkward bashfulness prevented me from spending much time in looking at the beautiful object. . . . . What with the strange couch and the excitement, I could not sleep. The moonlight streamed in through the broken panes, as if to entice me out into the clear summer evening. I tossed from right to left, closed my eyes and opened them again without being able to banish the thought of the beautiful statue out in the grass. I could not account for the bashfulness that overpowered me when I beheld it, and felt vexed because of my childishness. 'To-morrow,' I muttered, 'I will kiss thee, thou beauteous face of marble! on the corner of thy beautiful mouth, where the lips, joining, lose themselves in the lovely dimple.' Wondrous impatience consumed me, and at last, losing all control over the strange desire, I sprang from my couch, exclaiming, 'What odds, lovely creature! I shall kiss thee this very night!' . . . . All lay quiet and solemn, bathed in the gentle moonlight. The shadows of the trees looked as if they were nailed to the ground. When I approached the lovely goddess lying motionless in the grass, I almost feared that by the slightest sound I might awaken her. Her beautiful limbs seemed locked in deep slumber, rather than chained by some marble deity. I bent over her in order to admire her perfect features; shuddering fear held me back, while boyish desire impelled me towards her; my heart beat as if I were about to commit a murder; and at last I kissed the lovely goddess! Since that time I have never kissed with such ardor, such tenderness, or such wild despair. Nor have I ever forgotten the sweet, shuddering sensation that flowed through my soul while my lips pressed the cold lips of marble. And let me tell you, Maria: while I stood there looking at you, I was reminded of the white statue in the green grass. . . . . We left on the following day. I never saw the beautiful statue again, but it filled my heart for nearly four years, and awakened a strange passion for statuary, that has clung to me ever since. It was only this morning that I again felt its strength. After leaving the Laurentian library, I found myself, scarce knowing how I got there, in the chapel where Italy's noblest race peacefully rests on the bed of jewels it prepared for its couch. For full an hour I remained lost in contemplation of a female statue, whose powerful physique revealed the force and boldness of Michael Angelo, while the whole figure seemed enveloped in an atmosphere of ethereal sweetness, rarely looked for in the works of that master. It seemed as if the spirit of dreamland, with all its serene blissfulness, lay buried in that marble form; as if graceful repose dwelt in its beautifully proportioned limbs, and gentle moonlight flowed through its veins. It was NIGHT—By Michael Angelo Buonarotti. Ah! how gladly would I sleep the sleep eternal in the arms of such a night!''

All expressions of Heine's mind were tinged or interspersed with the same sort of passionate sentimentalism,—his criticism, satire, politics, religion, even his contempt. There was always something creative, too, in his writing; the poet in him constantly strove to give objective shape to what he felt or thought, and the process was the same, whether he was allegorizing his youthful love of beauty or recording his youthful detestation of England. No extract, however, can give a general idea of Florentine Nights; in fact, the tale is a wandering and wilful expression of Heine's mind upon anything that comes into it; and there is no unity in it save that of charm. We need not say, we suppose, that something of it is not for reading aloud to young ladies.

The other scintillations are as satisfactory as such selections can very well be; but probably each lover of Heine will find fault with them, as not the best, and, in his turn, would doubtless choose passages which Mr. Stern might condemn for the same good reason. The book is prefaced by a very sensibly written sketch of Heine's life, with some study of his genius; and this also will not meet with much favor from his habitual readers. Indeed, he lends himself as little as any author that ever lived to the purposes of the biographer or critic, perhaps because he has himself so thoroughly done the work of autobiography and self-criticism that nothing really remains for others. He eludes even so subtle and delicate a touch as that of Mr. Matthew Arnold, whose essay on Heine is so inadequate; and even for the *reminiscencer* there was very little of him.

—This unmanageableness of Heine's character is also felt in the paper devoted to him among Lord Houghton's Monographs. The old ground is gone over again: Heine was born a Jew, with strong sympathies for romantic art, and an equally strong regret for the beauty of Greek paganism, and so he held a very perplexing relation to modern Lutheran, Philistine Germany, which was not simplified by his turning Christian, after a fashion; he was so much a democrat in principle as to be obliged to exile himself from Prussia, and he loathed the commonness of his fellow-revolutionists with such contemptuous frankness that they hated him; he adored the grandeur of the religions, Christian and Hebrew, which he scoffingly denied; he endured a martyrdom such as few men suffer with a patience which was not resignation, and a courage which was founded on no faith, or a faith that he laughed at and clung to by turns. These facts have been stated many times, but they always fail to explain Heine. He was a poetic humorist, and there is an end of the chapter; comment can only add obscurity. His character, perhaps because it is so hard to fathom or explain, remains perpetually fascinating; and the lover of his work is always so eager to learn more of his life that he will be thankful for some memories of Heine's last days, which Lord Houghton gives from the letter of an English lady. He had petted her and played with her when she was a child, and in Paris she went to see him when he lay stretched upon his ten years' bed of death,

"his body so wasted that it seemed no bigger than a child under the sheet which covered him; the eyes closed; and the face altogether like the most painful and wasted 'Ecce Homo' ever painted by some old German painter. His voice was very weak, and I was astonished at the animation with which he talked. Evidently his mind had wholly survived his body. He raised his powerless eyelids with his thin white fingers. . . . . When I kissed him, his beard felt like swandown or baby's hair, so weak had it grown, and his face seemed to me to have gained a certain beauty from pain and suffering. . . . . On the whole, I never saw a man bear such horrible pain and misery in so perfectly unaffected a manner. He complained of his sufferings, and was pleased to see tears in my eyes, and then at once set to work to make me laugh heartily, which pleased him just as much. He neither paraded his anguish nor tried to conceal it, or to put on any stoical airs."

This lady's reminiscences are given with a feeling that quite imparts the fantastic pathos of Heine's humorous personality in its most tragical attitude; but after all, the sketch is a very slight one, and for something fuller the reader must go to Alfred Meissner's *Erinnerungen*, which form in some sort a history of Heine's last years.

[*Atlantic Monthly*, August 1873]

43

[Turgenev's Study of Character][1]

DIMITRI Roudine, which Messrs. Holt and Williams have reprinted from the excellent version published in Every Saturday, is mainly the study of one man's character, but a character so complex that there is little to ask of the author in the way of a story. In fact Dimitri Roudine is himself sufficient plot; and the reader is occupied from the moment of his introduction with the skilful development of his various traits, to the exclusion of the other incidents and interests. The other persons of the fiction are of a kind which the reader of Turgénieff's stories may begin to classify in some degree, or at least find in a certain measure familiar. The women are, as usual, very well portrayed, especially the young girl Natalie, whose ignorant trust, courage, love, and adoration for Roudine, changing to doubt and scorn,—whose whole maidenly being,—are expressed in a few scenes and phrases. Her mother, Daria Michaëlovna, is also exceedingly well done. She is of an entirely different type, a woman of mind, as she supposes, with advanced ideas, but really full of the pride of caste, worldly, and slight of intellect, though not wanting in selfish shrewdness or a strong will. The reader ought to note with what delicacy, and yet with what force, Turgénieff indicates, in Alexandra Paulovna, a sweet, placid, self-contained maturity, alike different from the wild fragrance of Natalie's young girlhood and the artificial perfume of Daria's well-preserved middle life; though he could hardly fail to do this, for nothing is more observable in Turgénieff than his success in characterizing the different epochs of womanhood. Volinzoff's conscious intellectual inferiority to Natalie, and his simple, manly love for her are nearly all there is of him; Pigasoff, who peculated in office when younger and who in provincial retirement is a brutal censor of the follies of human nature, is rather a study than an actor in the drama which develops Roudine; and Leschnieff, who promises something in himself, and does really prove of firm and generous stuff, is after all hardly more than a relief and explanation of the principal person. It is he who expresses the first doubt of Roudine after that philosopher has made his appearance at Daria Michaëlovna's, crushing Pigasoff, bewildering and charming Natalie, mystifying Alexandra, and provoking Volinzoff. Leschnieff knew him in his student days, when filial

---

[1] *Dimitri Roudine.* A Novel. By Ivan Turgénieff. New York: Holt and Williams. 1873.

love, friendship, and all real things were lost in his habit of eloquent phrasing; when Roudine was cruelly ungrateful and mean in fact, that he might be magnanimous in the abstract; and the shadow of this dark recollection Leschnieff casts upon Roudine's new friends. He does not wish him to marry Natalie, who, he sees, is fascinated with him; but after Roudine's miserable weakness ends their love and all the others despise him, then Leschnieff does justice to his elevation of ideas and purposes.

"He may have genius; I won't deny it; but the trouble is he has no character. . . . . He is full of enthusiasm; and you can believe a phlegmatic man like me when I say that it is a most precious quality, especially in a time like the present. We are unendurably cold-blooded, indifferent, and apathetic. . . . . Once when I was talking of Roudine I accused him of coldness. I was both just and unjust. His coldness is in his blood,—he 's not to blame for it,—not in his head. I was wrong in calling him an actor; he is no swindle, no cheat; he does not live on other people like a parasite, but like a child. Yes, he may die in loneliness and misery, but shall we throw stones at him on that account? He will never accomplish anything because he lacks energy and a strong will; but who can say that he has never done, or never will do, any good? That his words have never sown good seed in some young heart, to which nature has not denied the force to carry out what it has conceived?"

It is touchingly related in an epilogue how, after several years, Roudine and Leschnieff came together by chance in the same inn. Leschnieff asks his old comrade to dine with him, and the two elderly men thee and thou each other in the student fashion. Roudine tells of his successive failures since they last met:—

" 'Yes, brother,' he began, 'I can now cry with Kolzoff, "Where hast thou brought me, my youth? I have no longer where to lay my head!"'. . . . And was I really good for nothing, and was there nothing for me to do in this world? I have often asked myself this question, and, in spite of all my attempts to set myself lower in my own esteem, I can't help feeling that I have certain abilities which don't fall to the lot of every one. Why must this force remain powerless? Then, too, dost thou remember when we travelled abroad together, how self-confident and blind I was? . . . . . It is true, I did n't know definitely what I wanted, I revelled in the sound of my own voice, I chased vain phantoms. But now, on the contrary, I can say aloud to the whole world what it is I want; I have nothing to hide; I am, in the fullest sense of the word, a well-meaning man; I have become humble, I am willing to adapt myself to circumstances, I have limited my wishes, I don't strive for any remote object, I confine myself to doing even the slightest service; and yet I do not succeed in anything. What is the reason of this persistent failure? Why can't I live and work like others? I no sooner get a definite position, I no sooner establish myself somewhere, than fate casts me pitilessly out again. . . . . I begin to fear my fate. . . . . Why is this? Explain this puzzle!'

" 'Puzzle!' repeated Leschnieff. 'It is true, thou hast always been a puzzle to me. Even in our youth, when I saw thee acting ill and speaking well in turn, and that time after time, even then I could not understand thee clearly; that was the

reason I ceased to love thee. . . . . Thou hast so much fire, so earnest a longing
for the ideal.' . . . .

" 'Words, nothing but words. Where are the deeds?' interrupted Roudine.

" 'Yes; but a good word is a deed too.'

"Roudine looked at Leschnieff without speaking, and shook his head."

We almost forget, in following this tender yet keen analysis of a pathetic
character, that there is really something of a story in the book. Roudine
imagines that he loves Natalie, and he wins her brave, inexperienced heart;
but when their love is prematurely discovered to her mother, and Natalie
comes to him ready to fly with him, to be his at any cost, he is paralyzed at the
thought of Daria's opposition. "We must submit," he says. The scene that
follows, with Natalie's amazement, wounded faith, and rising contempt, and
Roudine's shame and anguish, is terrible,—the one intensely dramatic passage in the book, and a masterpiece of literary art which we commend to all
students and lovers of that art.

We are not quite sure whether we like or dislike the carefulness with
which Roudine's whole character is kept from us, so that we pass from admiration to despite before we come finally to half-respectful compassion; and
yet is this not the way it would be in life? Perhaps, also, if we fully understood
him at first, his relations to the others would not so much interest us. But do
we wholly understand him at last? This may be doubted, though in the mean
time we are taught a merciful distrust of our own judgments, and we take
Leschnieff's forgiving and remorseful attitude towards him. It may be safely
surmised that this was the chief effect that Turgénieff desired to produce in
us; certainly he treats the story involved in the portrayal of Roudine's character with almost contemptuous indifference, letting three epilogues limp in
after the first rambling narrative has spent itself, and seeming to care for
these only as they further reveal the hero's traits. But for all this looseness of
construction, it is a very great novel,—as much greater than the novel of
incident as Hamlet is greater than Richard III. It is of the kind of novel
which can alone keep the art of fiction from being the weariness and derision
of mature readers; and if it is most deeply melancholy, it is also as lenient and
thoughtful as a just man's experience of men.

[*Atlantic Monthly*, September 1873]

44

[Bryant's Orations and Addresses][1]

MR. Bryant's Orations and Addresses were delivered on a variety of occasions, such as commemorative observances in honor of eminent authors and artists, the dedications of statues and institutions, and the celebration of great public interests, like the electric telegraph, Italian unity, and the reform of city government. But the greater part of the volume into which they are now collected is filled by the orations on Cole the painter, on Cooper, Irving, Halleck, and Verplanck; and it need not disparage the rest to say that these are altogether the best. They are longer and more complete, and they form the most intelligent and intelligible sketch we have of the main intellectual and social features of our first great literary epoch. Mr. Bryant, of course, must speak of those times with something of a contemporary's slight of detail; but on the whole the reader of his criticisms (for such in a high and generous sense they are) cannot very well fail of a true conception of the period which we have called a great one. Our literature has since vastly increased in variety, and it has no doubt gained in depth and subtilety; but the men who first made it known—the Knickerbocker School, as it has been called—were masters in their art, and in their several ways remain unsurpassed. Irving is still the first of American writers in ease and grace, and if we could but lift the veil of the large popular world, which is so remote from the critic, we suspect that we should still find him first in the general favor and admiration. The publishers multiply editions of Cooper, and the translations of his works continue to introduce the American name to readers who know nothing and care nothing for our later literature. That school underwent and overcame more than any since, and gave us fame abroad when English criticism was as maliciously inimical as it is now mischievously fond. Indeed, it is doubtful if even Mrs. Stowe's great novel has made us more widely known than Cooper's romances; and it is a satisfaction to have the work he accomplished so heartily recognized by a contemporary who was himself a great part of the literary epoch of which he speaks. Mr. Bryant does not stint his praise; neither does he fail to trace the limitations, or to point out the faults of the author he praises; and whatever may be thought of his estimate of them, it must be allowed that his analyses

[1] *Orations and Addresses.* By William Cullen Bryant. New York: G. P. Putnam's Sons. 1873.

are models of criticism, in temperance, discrimination, and liberality. The discourse on Cooper is particularly interesting, because of the approval given by a life-long journalist to Cooper in his contests with the newspapers. The press had aspersed his motives in attacking his works, and Cooper sued his unfair critics in the courts. Mr. Bryant doubted the policy, not the justice of the proceeding. "I said to myself,

'Alas! Leviathan is not so tamed!'

As he proceeded, however, I saw that he understood the matter better than I. He put a hook into the nose of this huge monster, wallowing in his inky pool, and bespattering the passers-by; he dragged him to the land and made him tractable. One suit followed another; one editor was sued, I think, half a dozen times; some of them found themselves under a second indictment before the first was tried," and he beat every one who did not retract his libels. "The occasion of these suits was far from honorable to those who provoked them, but the result was, as I had almost said, creditable to all parties: to him as the courageous prosecutor, to the administration of justice in this country, and to the docility of the newspaper press, which he had disciplined into good manners."

The orations on Irving and Halleck are of the same general character as that on Cooper, and unite biographical notices with a sketch of their times and an examination of their work. Irving's world has been kept present with us by the vitality of his writings; but Halleck's world, and that of Verplanck, are curiously lost and forgotten. One splendid dramatic lyric and one exquisite elegy are nearly all that remain of a poet who wrote satires, and laughed at fashions, and mocked magistrates, and made the town talk of him. Of Verplanck—the eminent citizen, the friend of letters, the conscientious politician—there is even less left; but if it is mournfully instructive to recall the faded glories of the poet, it is also useful to consider, in Mr. Bryant's tribute to his friend, how very little time it is since public men in New York had liberal culture, and combined social worth with popular influence. He does full justice to the valuable qualities of such a man, and he gathers with a generous tenderness the remnants of Halleck's fame around an amiable figure; but it seems to us that Irving is more affectionately touched than either of the others. One of the closing passages of the discourse on him embodies so much that is characteristic of Mr. Bryant's warmer strain in these commemorations of his old friends, and so much that is true concerning the endurance of all good literature, and its elevating and consoling influence, that we cannot render his admirable volume a less service than to quote it:—

"Since he began to write, empires have risen and passed away; mighty captains have appeared on the stage of the world, performed their part, and been called to their account; wars have been fought and ended which have changed the destinies of the human race. New arts have been invented and adopted, and have pushed the old out of use; the household economy of half mankind has undergone a revolution. Science has learned a new dialect and forgotten the old; the chemist of 1807 would be a vain babbler among his brethren of the present day, and would in turn become bewildered in the attempt to understand them. Nation utters speech to nation in words that pass from realm to realm with the speed of light. Distant countries have been made neighbors; the Atlantic Ocean has become a narrow frith, and the Old World and the New shake hands across it; the East and the West look in at each other's windows. The new inventions bring new calamities, and men perish in crowds by the recoil of their own devices. War has learned more frightful modes of havoc, and armed himself with deadlier weapons; armies are borne to the battle-field on the wings of the wind, and dashed against each other and destroyed with infinite bloodshed. We grow giddy with this perpetual whirl of strange events, these rapid and ceaseless mutations; the earth seems to reel under our feet, and we turn to those who write like Irving, for some assurance that we are still in the same world into which we were born; we read and are quieted and consoled. In his pages we see that the language of the heart never becomes absolete; that Truth and Good and Beauty, the offspring of God, are not subject to the changes which beset the inventions of men."

[*Atlantic Monthly*, October, 1873]

45

[The Perfection of Longfellow's Poetry][1]

EVERY poet creates a type of himself, by which all that he does afterwards is felt as his, and variance from which is not easily forgiven. He becomes his own rival, as has often been said; yet even in his self-rivalry it is not his likeness but his unlikeness to himself that displeases; and whilst we protest against any criticism that presumes to limit a poet to any vein, or to dictate how and what he shall write, as vulgar and impudent, we confess a sympathy with the popular expectation that each poet shall be in manner what he has been, as nearly as he can. In the love we bear a man's poetry there is something analogous to the repetition-asking principle in music; some recurrence of accustomed mental attitudes we all desire. It was the absence of these in Mr. Longfellow's New England Tragedies and Divine Tragedy which disappointed a generation unable to read as impartially as the future, and unwilling to accept their severe outlines in place of the pictures and opulent reliefs they were used to being pleased with in him. The next generation will do what we hardly can: read the Christus with a due sense of it as a whole. For us, with whom The Golden Legend was long ago accepted as a complete poem, and to whom The New England Tragedies and The Divine Tragedy came afterwards without warrant of their relationship till the last, they must always remain disunited in our thought, whatever they are in fact. The two latter parts, indeed, are the fruit of artistic moods quite different from that which produced the first. Something of the self-denying strictness with which the Dante was translated seems to have forbidden them the richness and the quaint detail of the earlier drama. But in the three books of Mr. Longfellow's Tales of the Wayside Inn, the last of which is now closed in the volume called Aftermath, the dominant mood is always the same, so that the three series are as intimately related in manner as are the different Idyls of the King.

Moreover, in Aftermath, the poet appears willing to recall to the lovers of his poetry all their favorites among his works. It is a pensive, delicious refrain, the melodious reverberation, in delicately subdued effects, of the old colors, tones, feelings; and the art is mellowed to that last flavor of perfection which in Tennyson's Gareth and Lynette is almost enough of itself to consti-

[1] *Aftermath.* By H. W. Longfellow. Boston: J. R. Osgood & Co. 1873.

tute a poem. Those who have loved a poet long and constantly feel the charm of this with a keenness unknown to the fickle and impatient; but there is certainly in the ripe performance of every great master of style a delight which no intelligent reader can miss. By exercise and study of his art all its highest effects come easily to him; he has but to wave his hand, as it appears, and they are there; sometimes it even appears as if they came unbidden. Besides, in Aftermath, we have somehow a better sense than before of the tranquil breadth of our poet's genius. The perfect serenity of his mental atmosphere widens those clear horizons along which lurks a melancholy light, and lets us perceive how great his range has been, and in what an ample spirit he has touched his many themes. These poems, as effortless, as uncompelled, as the color and sweet of Nature, affect us as if they came from a store as rich as hers, and suggest her largeness as well as her fertility.

We suppose this sense of their spontaneity is heightened by their freedom from the didactic tendency which characterized some of Mr. Longfellow's shorter poems, at an earlier period. The tales are simply stories, teaching by incident and character, and often not teaching at all; and the poems that follow them, brief and few in number, are almost pure expressions of feeling; or are expressions of feeling tacitly directed towards a lesson, not bearing it as a burden. And on the whole we believe we are ready to set some of these poems before any in the language of a similar kind,—of quite the same kind there are none. Take, for example, this called

CHANGED.

From the outskirts of the town,
    Where of old the mile-stone stood,
Now a stranger, looking down
I behold the shadowy crown
    Of the dark and haunted wood.

Is it changed, or am I changed?
    Ah! the oaks are fresh and green,
But the friends with whom I ranged
Through their thickets are estranged
    By the years that intervene.

Bright as ever flows the sea,
    Bright as ever shines the sun,
But alas! they seem to me
Not the sun that used to be,
    Not the tides that used to run.

This is full of the feeling to be conveyed; but it is not surcharged by the slightest touch, it is exquisitely balanced; and this which follows is such a pleasure in its artistic loveliness and completeness as a whole literature can but twice or thrice afford:—

AFTERMATH.

When the Summer fields are mown,
When the birds are fledged and flown,
    And the dry leaves strew the path;
With the falling of the snow,
With the cawing of the crow,
Once again the fields we mow
    And gather in the aftermath.

Not the sweet, new grass with flowers
Is this harvesting of ours;
    Not the upland clover bloom;
But the rowen mixed with weeds,
Tangled tufts from marsh and meads,
Where the poppy drops its seeds
    In the silence and the gloom.

Fata Morgana is almost as good as these two poems, but is perhaps not so marvellously poised, not so wholly freed from all process of art; and then we have The Haunted Chamber, The Meeting, and The Challenge, that suggest in mood and movement the best of Mr. Longfellow's earlier short poems, and are worthy a place in our memories with The Beleaguered City, The Footsteps of Angels, and other kindred pieces, which they equal in richness and tenderness of sentiment and surpass in the evidence of poetic mastery.

Of the Tales of a Wayside Inn, our readers already know Scanderbeg, and have, we hope,

"liked the canter or the rhymes
That had a hoof-beat in their sound,"

and the midnight solemnity of the atmosphere thrown about the wild, fierce tragedy; and they have also enjoyed the peculiarly Longfellowish humor of The Rhyme of Sir Christopher. All the other tales, and of course the interludes and preludes, are here printed for the first time. It is the Spanish Jew who tells the story of Scanderbeg, and he tells also the first story in the series, that of Azrael and Solomon, and the Rajah who flies from the death-angel only to meet him at his own door. The Poet's tale of Charlemagne, which follows next, is a rather singular achievement in literature. Its climax is simply the terror of the Lombard King Desiderio at the sight of Charlemagne; it is a scene, a spectacle, rather than a story, and affects the reader as a painting of the same subject might; it is dramatic in the last degree, and the critical reader will notice with what consummate skill, with what fulness and yet with what wise reticence, he is possessed of the situation. The Student's tale is that old and pretty story of the king's daughter who carried her lover from her bower lest his footsteps in the snow should betray them both; and we need not say how sweetly it is told, and how it turns as innocent in the poet's verse as the Theologian's tale of the fair Quakeress Elizabeth Haddon, who as she rode through the woods to meeting, with her guest John Estaugh, lingered behind the others a little, and whispered:—

> " 'Tarry awhile behind, for I have something to tell thee,
> Not to be spoken lightly, nor in the presence of others;
> Them it concerneth not, only thee and me it concerneth.'
> And they rode slowly along through the woods conversing
>   together.
> It was a pleasure to breathe the fragrant air of the forest;
> It was a pleasure to live on that bright and happy May morning!
>
> "Then Elizabeth said, though still with a certain reluctance,
> As if impelled to reveal a secret she fain would have guarded:
> 'I will no longer conceal what is laid upon me to tell thee;
> I have received from the Lord a charge to love thee, John
>   Estaugh.'
>
> "And John Estaugh made answer, surprised by the words she had
>   spoken,
> 'Pleasant to me are thy converse, thy ways, thy meekness of
>   spirit;
> Pleasant thy frankness of speech, and thy soul's immaculate
>   whiteness,
> Love without dissimulation, a holy and inward adorning.
> But I have yet no light to lead me, no voice to direct me.
> When the Lord's work is done, and the toil and the labor
>   completed
> He hath appointed to me, I will gather into the stillness
> Of my own heart awhile, and listen and wait for his guidance.'
>
> "Then Elizabeth said, not troubled nor wounded in spirit,
> 'So is it best, John Estaugh. We will not speak of it further.
> It hath been laid upon me to tell thee this, for to-morrow
> Thou art going away, across the sea, and I know not
> When I shall see thee more; but if the Lord hath decreed it,
> Thou wilt return again to seek me here and to find me.'
> And they rode onward in silence, and entered the town with the
>   others."

This purely Quaker love-story, in which of course John Estaugh finally "has freedom" to accept the love of Elizabeth, is perhaps the best in the book. The quaint and homely material is wrought into a texture marvellously delicate; and its colorless fineness clothes a beauty as chaste and soft as the neutral-tinted garments of the fair, meekly bold Quaker maiden. The English hexameter which Mr. Longfellow has so intimately associated with his name, he has never more successfully handled, we think, than in this poem, which recalls Evangeline and The Courtship of Miles Standish at their best, and yet has a humor and sweetness quite its own, and unmistakably knowable for Longfellow's. But the humor is his quietest, naturally. That gayety, that *esprit* which among modern poets is almost peculiar to him, finds its broadest expression in the Sicilian's tale of the Monk of Casal-Maggiore, who pretended that he had been changed into an ass for the sin of gluttony. It is as the poet says of it,

> "A tale that cannot boast forsooth,
> A single rag or shred of truth;
> That does not leave the mind in doubt
> As to the with it or without;
> A naked falsehood and absurd
> As mortal ever told or heard."

And it is as merry as a tale of Chaucer's and told with a relish for all its comic points and extravagances which the reader cannot refuse to share. All the character-painting is in the mellowest tones,—the wily, worthless, jovial monk, the simple peasant, the hospitable housewife, the old grandsire with his memories of the French and Milanese wars. How good is this picture of the rogue of a friar, supping at the peasant's board:—

> "It was a pleasure but to see him eat,
>   His white teeth flashing through his russet beard,
> His face aglow and flushed with wine and meat,
>   His roguish eyes that rolled and laughed and leered!
> Lord! how he drank the blood-red country wine
> As if the village vintage were divine!

> "And all the while he talked without surcease,
>   And told his merry tales with jovial glee
> That never flagged, but rather did increase,
>   And laughed aloud as if insane were he,
> And wagged his red beard, matted like a fleece."

When Brother Timothy returns to his convent, the prior sends to market the ass which the guilty monk had persuaded Farmer Gilbert to believe his penitential shape.

> "Gilbert was at the Fair; and heard a bray,
>   And nearer came, and saw that it was he,
> And whispered in his ear, 'Ah, lackaday!
>   Good father, the rebellious flesh, I see,
> Has changed you back into an ass again,
> And all my admonitions were in vain.'

"The ass, who felt this breathing in his ear,
        Did not turn round to look, but shook his head,
As if he were not pleased these words to hear,
        And contradicted all that had been said.
And this made Gilbert cry in voice more clear,
        'I know you well; your hair is russet-red;
Do not deny it; for you are the same
Franciscan friar, and Timothy by name.'

"The ass, though now the secret had come out,
        Was obstinate, and shook his head again;
Until a crowd was gathered round about
        To hear this dialogue between the twain;

        .   .   .   .   .

" 'If this be Brother Timothy,' they cried,
        'Buy him, and feed him on the tenderest grass;
Thou canst not do too much for one so tried
        As to be twice transformed into an ass.'
So simple Gilbert bought him, and untied
        His halter, and o'er mountain and morass
He led him homeward, talking as he went
Of good behavior and a mind content.

"The children saw them coming, and advanced,
        Shouting with joy, and hung about his neck,—
Not Gilbert's, but the ass's,—round him danced,
        And wove green garlands wherewithal to deck
His sacred person; for again it chanced
        Their childish feelings, without rein or check,
Could not discriminate in any way
A donkey from a friar of Orders Gray.

" 'O brother Timothy,' the children said,
        'You have come back to us just as before;
We were afraid, and thought that you were dead,
        And we should never see you any more.'
And then they kissed the white star on his head,
        That like a birth-mark or a badge he wore,
And patted him upon the neck and face,
And said a thousand things with childish grace."

This, which is so charmingly said, has all the elder story-teller's amiable pleasure in the truth of such simple details as the children's fond and credulous rapture, and the donkey's gravity of behavior. The ass, in fact,

        "Lazily winking his large, limpid eyes,"

or, as he stands

"Twirling his ears about,"

is studied with the same humorous observance and appreciation of brute-character as Chaucer brings to the portrayal of Chanticleer and Dame Part-let,—a whimsical playfulness akin to that with which our poet indicates the kind of animal with whom Sir Christopher Gardiner found refuge from the justice of Massachusetts Bay:—

> —"the noble savage who took delight
> In his feathered hat and his velvet vest,
> His gun and his rapier, and the rest,
> But as soon as the noble savage heard
> That a bounty was offered for this gay bird,
> He wanted to slay him out of hand,
> And bring in his beautiful scalp for a show,
> Like the glossy head of a kite or a crow."

The Musician's tale is a version of the affecting Norse ballad of The Mother's Ghost; but we care less for it than for the others. The whole book, however, seems to us the best that we could ask of the poet whom it suggests, if it does not reveal, in his whole range; and who has given more pleasure of a high and refined sort to more people than any other poet of our time.

[*Atlantic Monthly*, November 1873]

46

[Landor's Poetic Conceits][1]

WE asked a friend, out of that constant doubt we have of the taste of any one generation, whether the poem, Rose Aylmer (in those Cameos which Messrs. Stedman and Aldrich have selected with so much judgment from the works of Landor), did not probably affect Charles Lamb through his own or his contemporaries' mood, and perhaps by some charm of melody or movement, rather than by the appeal of any veritable poetic substance in it; for otherwise we did not understand his extravagant admiration of it. When our friend answered, No, he did not think so,—he but confirmed our first impression and quite undermined our good opinion of him. It is with the belief that no reader of ours will deal himself a like fatal blow, that we give the poem here.

ROSE AYLMER.

Ah, what avails the sceptred race!
Ah, what the form divine!
What every virtue, every grace!
Rose Aylmer, all were thine.

Rose Aylmer, whom these wakeful eyes
May weep, but never see,
A night of memories and of sighs
I consecrate to thee.

Pretty, very; very delicate, very graceful, very sweet; but upon the stainless conscience of a book-noticer, nothing more. Yet on this slender diet the good Lamb professes (to be sure, in a letter to the author) to have lived for days; and an emulous American essayist of like stomach declares to the editors of the Cameos that he did exactly the same thing. In these cases, however, as in those anomalous instances of people subsisting for a long time upon nothing at all, we should like to make sure that some sort of nourishment was not covertly taken; say that this American essayist had

[1] *Cameos: selected from the Works of Walter Savage Landor.* By E. C. Stedman and T. B. Aldrich. With an Introduction. Boston: J. R. Osgood & Co. 1874.

not sustained fainting nature with secret draughts from the Helicon of Percival or of George P. Morris. For in this poem of Rose Aylmer, we do not find even the attenuated nutriment of suggestion; but for the fact given by Landor's biographer that it refers to a lady of Lord Aylmer's family, whom he regarded with a very tender sentiment, and who died very young, how could this melodious trifle move one? There are many other fancies in the present book, quite as slight, which have the real poetic life and root; this seems at best but a tuberose blossom skillfully wired for a bouquet. Compare it, coinciding reader, with certain bits of Tennyson or Emerson; or with such expressions of pure feeling as Longfellow's After-math, and Changed; and its lack appears. Here, we foresee that the lovers of Rose Aylmer, who have been waiting to disable us, will come out with "Obtuse!" and "Dull-witted!" Whereupon we retort that the danger of liking a poet not generally liked is that you fall into willfulness and affecta-tion, and like everything he has done, simply because other people do not. The world, after all, is a wise old head, and does not overlook its good things. It knows which are its most interesting cities and finest mountains; its noblest statues, churches; its most beautiful pictures; it also knows which are its truest and greatest poets. Possibly, then, if Landor has been the least enjoyed of his contemporaries, he is really the least of them in genius, and the present fashion of crying out, "Oh, Landor,—yes, in-deed!" is only a fashion, after all.

We should say of the present collection, so full of exquisite colors and precious forms, that the value was never so much in the quality of the thought, as in the skill with which it is wrought; and we doubt if any reader coming newly to these gems here, without prejudice in favor of their author, will receive a lasting impression from them. A vague pleasure will remain in his mind, a memory of intellectual delight, a sense of grace-ful attitudes and gleams of color; but his heart will not have been deeply stirred or often touched, though his fancy will have been constantly charmed, not his imagination,—these little, lovely things are always, we believe, fanciful, and never quite imaginative. The limpid rill of rhyme runs on and presently sparkles into a bewitching conceit, or glows with some brilliant image; but it does not diffuse any strong influence, or haunt the mind afterward with any very fertile thought. One might say indeed that these Cameos were mostly only a more exquisite kind of *vers de société*; some of them hardly rise above the ordinary *vers de société*; but it must be understood that such verses are of the most difficult to write well. Take this, for example:—

IN NO HASTE.

Nay, thank me not again for those
Camellias, that untimely rose;
But if, whence you might please the more,

And win the few unwon before,
I sought the flowers you loved to wear,
O'erjoyed to see them in your hair,
Upon my grave, I pray you, set
One primrose or one violet. . . . .
Stay . . . I can wait a little yet.

This is deliciously playful and freakish, but it is not more; and Under the Lindens, which every one knows and loves, is scarcely more. Here is another trifle, elegant, perfect, so finely cut and subtly tinted that it seems the farthest art can go in its way,—which is the way of nearly all the others:—

DEFIANCE.

Catch her and hold her if you can. . . .
See, she defies you with her fan,
Shuts, opens, and then holds it spread
In threatening guise above your head.
Ah! why did you not start before
She reached the porch and closed the door?
Simpleton! will you never learn
That girls and time will not return?
Of each you should have made the most;
Once gone, they are forever lost.
In vain your knuckles knock your brow,
In vain will you remember how
Like a slim brook the gamesome maid
Sparkled, and ran into the shade.

The opening picture in this is heavenly fair; the closing image is happy enough for a while to lure back one's youth; but the whole thing is merely a graceful fancy, and all these Cameos—with the exception of some such fine painting as An Evening Picture, and some personal tributes, to Browning, to Julius Hare, to Lamb and others—are conceits, neither more nor less. This gives a certain monotony to the collection, which is relieved by the variety of mood expressed in them, though the mood is hardly ever entirely serious. It is most serious, we should say, in this, which is perhaps less than any other a conceit:—

ON MUSIC.

Many love music but for music's sake;
Many because her touches can awake
Thoughts that repose within the breast half dead,
And rise to follow where she loves to lead.
What various feelings come from days gone by!

What tears from far-off sources dim the eye!
Few, when light fingers with sweet voices play,
And melodies swell, pause, and melt away,
Mind how at every touch, at every tone,
A spark of life hath glistened and hath gone.

It is most winningly tender in this hinted drama of passion in a young girl's heart:—

MARGARET.

Mother, I cannot mind my wheel;
  My fingers ache, my lips are dry;
Oh if you feel the pain I feel!
  But who could ever feel as I!
No longer could I doubt him true,
  All other men may use deceit;
He always said my eyes were blue,
  And often swore my lips were sweet.

But an arch gayety is the temper in which most of the pieces are conceived, and with that their touches of melancholy and regret do not discord, of course.

"It seems to us," say the editors, "that precisely the amount of benefit which a familarity with the antique models can render to a modern poet is discernible in the greater portion of our selections. Their clearness and terseness are of the classic mold, but the language, thought, emotion, are Landorian and English." This is reasonable, and we think all refined readers will be glad of the proof of it in this very fortunate little selection. But a poet, sick and poor, comparatively little learned, and dying very young, could be more Greek in what is worth having, as well as more English, than the rich, well-born, erudite student who died rather obscure at eighty years of age: nearly every line that Keats wrote has affected English poetry since, and we are anxious not to lose a word of his; Landor may be said not to have affected it at all, and we gladly forget whole epics that he wrote. Such trifles as these Cameos will perhaps constitute hereafter Landor's chief claim to remembrance amongst English poets. He had a real poetic genius, no doubt, but his temperament undid him; he could not or would not see himself in his real relation to things.

Turguénieff wisely says that nothing great is accomplished outside of nationality, that one is great only as one is of one's own country; and he might have gone further and said that a man achieves little who refuses to be his own contemporary. Landor was not content to be an English poet of the nineteenth century; he was a dreamer, as great poets never are; he would be a Greek of the polite time of Aspasia and Pericles; consequently he has not yet found a secure place in the English heart, and the Athenians, besides not knowing English, have been dead so long that they cannot conveniently receive him into theirs.

[*Atlantic Monthly*, March 1874]

47

[Eggleston's Story of Backwoods Ohio][1]

No American story-teller has of late years had greater success, of a good kind, than Mr. Eggleston, who in four years has given us consecutively, The Hoosier Schoolmaster, The End of the World, The Mystery of Metropolisville, and now The Circuit Rider. His books have been read by the hundred thousands; they have been respectfully considered by the most difficult criticism amongst us, they have been translated, we believe, and misunderstood in the *Revue de Deux Mondes*, they have enjoyed the immortality of English republication. They merited as much. They were exceedingly well theorized. Mr. Eggleston considered the vast fields of fiction lying untouched in the region of his birth and the home of his early manhood, and for his plots, scenes, and characters, he acted on Mr. Greeley's famous advice, and went West. It must have been that he truthfully painted the conditions and people whom he aimed to portray, for it was in the West that his popularity began, and it is there doubtless that it is now the greatest. He does not deal with the contemporary West, by with the West of forty or fifty years ago; and except in The Mystery of Metropolisville he does not leave the familiar ground of the Ohio Valley. The scene of his first two stories is in Southern Indiana, that of the last is in Southern Ohio. On this ground he was at home, yet he was able to view all the people and situations from the outside, and in the light of subsequent life in the East. Some disadvantages came from this advantage. He was too conscious of the oddity of his material, and he placed an inartistic stress upon unimportant details of dialect, customs, and character. Even in The Circuit Rider, he stops from time to time, in the description of some rude or grotesque scene, to make the reader an ironical or defiant apology for treating of such unrefined matters; or, if he has some wild incident or trait to handle, pauses to expatiate upon it and caress its singularity. This is bad art, as Mr. Eggleston must himself feel, and he ought not to indulge it. The novelist's business is to paint such facts of character and custom as he finds so strongly that their relative value in his picture will be at once apparent to the reader without a word of comment: otherwise his historical picture falls to the level of the panorama with a

---

[1] *The Circuit Rider: A Tale of the Heroic Age*. By Edward Eggleston. Illustrated. New York: J. B. Ford & Co. 1874.

showman lecturing upon the striking points and picking them out for observance with a long stick. It is not in this way that the masters of the art which Mr. Eggleston reveres accomplish their results. Björnson does not add a word to impress on our imaginations the Norwegian incidents and characters he sets before us in *Arne*; and Turgénieff, in such a Russian tale as The Lear of the Steppes, leaves all comment to the reader. Everything necessary to the reader's intelligence should be quietly and artfully supplied, and nothing else should be added.

We speak the more frankly of this blemish in Mr. Eggleston's last work because we find The Circuit Rider such a vast advance upon his former stories. The Mystery of Metropolisville was disappointing; for though it showed a good sense of character and the story was interesting, it was not so fresh as The Hoosier Schoolmaster, and it had not such poetic elements as The End of the World. It was not an advance; it was something of a retrogression. But in our pleasure with The Circuit Rider we have been willing to forget this, and we are glad to recognize the author in his most fortunate effort. The story is of backwoods life in Ohio at the time when the Methodists began to establish the foundations of their church in the new land, among the children of the Indian-fighters and pioneers, and the hero of the story is one of those ardent young preachers who throughout the Southwest were known as circuit riders. They were each given a certain field of labor by the Conference, and they traveled on horseback from point to point in this field, preaching, praying, and turning sinners to repentance, and at due seasons assembling their forces in mighty camp-meetings, and gathering whole neighborhoods into the capacious bosom of their church at once. No history is more picturesque or dramatic than theirs, and Mr. Eggleston has well called their time the heroic age.

The tale is a very simple love-story, in which Morton Goodwin, amidst the lawless impulses of his first youth, is converted to Methodism, and becomes the Circuit Rider, and Patty Lumsden, the prettiest and richest and proudest girl of the region, who, preserving in the backwoods the tradition of the Old Virginia Anglicanism of her mother's family, resents his conversion, and ends by becoming herself a Methodist, and in due course the Circuit Rider's wife. Abundant incident of many sorts promotes and delays this conclusion, and all the persons of an early Western neighborhood figure before us. The civilizing forces of Methodism in conflict with the native tendencies to horse-stealing, counterfeiting, bloodshed, drunkenness, gaming, and dancing are very well and very distinctly studied. The coarseness, touched here and there with inborn delicacy and fineness; the sordid rapacity of some and the barbaric generosity of most; the despotism of public opinion; the elevation and purifying of popular feeling by the strong religious fervors of Methodism, are facts of the time and place very forcibly seized. The heroine is a real girl, as Mr. Eggleston's heroines are apt to be, and the hero is a heartily conceived ideal of young manhood submitting itself to duty, and turning its wild tendencies to account in battling with sin and in personal encounter with unrepentant sinners; for Morton Goodwin's spiritual progress is from the point where he helps to break up a Methodist meeting, to the point where he leads the sheriff's posse in thrashing and dispersing the interlopers at a camp-meeting in which he is himself an exhorter. Yet we confess that the glimpse we have of the fair, the wily, and (as it is hinted) the many-experienced Sister Meachem, provokes a greater interest in us than Miss Patty's fortunes awaken and we fancy that in the adventurous career of the former the social life of the time could have been more vividly painted. We forgive ourselves for liking this sinner because we have so high an estimate of the most sublime character of the book, Kike Lumsden, who is also, to our thinking, the most powerfully presented. He is the cousin of Patty, and her father is about to cheat him out of his property when the story begins. He is "sixteen; one of those sallow-skinned boys with straight black hair, that one often sees in southern latitudes," and he is of the homicidal southwestern temperament. He defies his uncle and it is in his heart to kill him, when suddenly the circuit rider Magruder appears in the neighborhood, and preaches of each man's sins, as well as of the common wickedness, to him.

> "When at last he came to speak of revenge, Kike, who had listened intently from the first, found himself breathing hard. The preacher showed how the revengeful man was 'as much a murderer as if he had already killed his enemy, and hid his mangled body in the woods, where none but the wolf could ever find him.' At these words, he turned to the part of the room where Kike sat, white with feeling. Magruder, looking always for the effect of his arrows, noted Kike's emotion, and paused. The house was utterly still, save now and then a sob from some anguish-smitten soul. The people were sitting as if waiting their doom. Kike already saw the mutilated form of his uncle Enoch hidden in the leaves, and scented by the hungry wolves. He waited to hear his own sentence. Hitherto the preacher had spoken with vehemence. Now he stopped, and began again with tears and a voice broken with emotion, looking in a general way toward where Kike sat: 'O young man, there are stains of blood on your hands! How dare you hold them up before the Judge of all? You are another Cain, and God sends his messenger to you to-day to inquire after him whom you have already killed in your heart. *You are a murderer!* Nothing but God's mercy can snatch you from hell!' . . . Kike's . . . frail form shook with fear and penitence, as it had before shaken with wrath. 'O God, what a wretch I am!' cried he, hiding his face in his hands."

Kike becomes himself a preacher at once. He meets his uncle shortly after-wards, the old man taunts him with his conversion, and strikes him in the face; the young apostle, in heroic obedience to Scripture, has the force literally to "offer him the other cheek also."

He is a sickly, slender boy, and under the hardships of his vocation he breaks down at a camp-meeting, and is carried to the house of the nearest doctor, whose young daughter nurses him through his sickness. They love, and a great struggle takes place in Kike's heart between this passion and his sense of responsibility in his calling; if he marries he must cease to be a circuit rider, the vineyard must lose a laborer. He leaves his love unspoken, and, rising from his bed, goes forth again upon his mission. In a few years he wears out; he is brought back to the good doctor's house to die, and on his death-bed he weds with his love. It is a noble tragedy, finely set forth. It is worthy to have formed in itself the substance of a romance. Of all the figures in Mr. Eggleston's book, Kike stands first in our imagination.

[*Atlantic Monthly*, June 1874]

48

[Aldrich's New England Romance][1]

NOTHING could be *handier* to say than that Mr. Aldrich's strength is in writing short stories: that follows with such fascinating obviousness from the fact that he has written them successfully! But this convenient criticism is not the whole truth, for in Prudence Palfrey he has shown the same skill in maneuvering his figures on the ample field of a novel that entertained us in such miniature romances as Marjorie Daw and Mademoiselle Zabriski. Indeed, if the public,—which does not like to have an author do two things well, and is fond of saying that one had better stick to his verse or his prose, or his essays or his sketches, or his short stories or his long stories, when he tries to please in a new way,—if the public would reflect (it is asking a good deal), we think it must own that Mr. Aldrich has fairly earned the right hereafter to please it as he pleases. Perhaps the public has read his new romance with too great expectation of being duped, at the end, and has done him the injustice of looking for a lighter effect than he intended; something of the sort was inevitable from its past experience of him; but we believe he would rather value himself upon the success with which he consistently works out the character of Dillingham, than on surprising the reader finally with the fact that Dillingham and Nevins are the same. Call that rogue by either name, he is the finest and firmest figure in the story; and we think he is better as Nevins than as Dillingham. The glimpses we get of him in the mining camp suggest a personage that we should like to know better in his proper quality of rascal; and those scenes in the far West seem fresher than the passages of life at Rivermouth: it may be that in the atmosphere of clerical delinquency we do not get quite away from the stories of Dr. Holmes, which deal with like sinners. Mr. Aldrich is apt, if anything, to be over-literary, to see life through a well-selected library window; but he has broken a whole sash in getting a look into the western mountains, and has made so strong a sketch of the place and people that we wish in his next story he would step quite out of doors.

Very likely it is because New England village-life has been so often and so minutely painted that we find the people of Rivermouth somewhat conventional. At any rate they give us little surprise, in the way they are many of

---

[1] *Prudence Palfrey*. A Novel. By T. B. Aldrich. Boston: J. R. Osgood & Co. 1874.

them presented, causually, slightly, more for the purpose of moving the story forward and of working the machinery, so to speak, than that of interesting us in them severally. This stricture will not apply to the more deliberately studied persons. Of Parson Hawkins, though he is slightly caricatured, like most of the village people, is an excellent portrait in the first and second chapters; and the scene of the two deacons remorsefully coming to tell him of his dismissal is affectingly and humorously done. There are also flashes of witty observation that light up a whole condition of things in the good-naturedly, impudently curious village world, as when Mr. Stebbins says, "I see Capen Chris Bell at Seth Wiggins's this mornin'; he bought that great turkey of Seth's, and six pounds of steak right off the tender-loin. Guess he expects his brother-in-law's family down from Boston." Another condition of things, as amusing, is as wittily suggested in the comments of Sam Knubley on the village aristocrats who are "eternally shinning up the family tree. There's old Blydenburgh, who's always perching himself on the upper branches, and hurling down the cocoa-nuts of his ancestors at common folks."

We hardly know whether the pretty Miss Prue herself shares the defect which we have perhaps only imagined in some other Rivermouth people. After a certain time of life the reader feels towards the heroine of a romance as calmly as the upright man feels towards his neighbor's handsome wife; he is willing the hero should have her; and it is the rarest thing for him to be moved to impassioned covetousness about her. Miss Prudence has traits of a veritable girlhood; it is but too sadly natural that her heart should waver in its true allegiance, when she finds Dillingham at first indifferent and then devoted, and, above all, wanted by all the other girls! She gives you the sense of a pretty, sufficiently willful, sufficiently obedient, natural, good-hearted girl, and that is as much as one ought to ask of any heroine. John Dent is not always perfectly accounted for in his movements and delays and long silences; but he escapes conventionality of character; he has a substance and being of his own; and he comes out freshly in the last scenes. His uncle, however, is too much like the unreally actuated uncle of comedy. Here, indeed, in the absence of due motive on the part of the elder Dent, is the weak point of the plot, and not in the imposture of Dillingham. The newspapers and records of the law are too full of histories of successful imposture for us to say that a wolf in shepherd's clothing might not occupy the pulpit of a New England country town half a year without being found out. Besides, certain premises must be granted the story-teller; and after all, the reader will do well to remember that a novel is not a true narrative. It is testimony in favor of the general life-like character of Mr. Aldrich's fiction that there have been bitter complaints against him on this point. "Dear friends," he might make answer, "no such thing happened, but it was necessary to my scheme for your amusement that we should suppose it did. The ghost really did not walk, in Hamlet; there are no such things in nature as the three weird sisters; the two Dromios were not so like but you could tell them apart; but fiction is full of these suppositions; and if you want to pin me down to the facts, I must own that no part of my story happened: it is all make-believe from beginning to end." And for our part we contend that in this matter he has preserved the internal harmony and proportion of his own invention: the only sort of consistency that can be fairly exacted of a romancer.

We say romancer, because in spite of the title-page, and of many aspects of a novel in setting and local circumstance, Prudence Palfrey is hardly a novel. It is told in that semi-idyllic key, into which people writing stories of New England life fall so inevitably that we sometimes think a New England *novel* is not possible; that our sectional civilization is too narrow, too shy, too lacking in high and strong contrasts, to afford material for the dramatic realism of that kind of fiction. Hawthorne renounced and denounced the idea of such a thing; we all know how Mr. Hale in his bright sketches immaterializes his good, honest, every-day facts; Dr. Holmes's fictions are rather psychological studies than novels: in fact, the New England novel does not exist. Mr. Aldrich is nearer giving it in Prudence Palfrey than anybody else, but he does not give it.

In execution his methods are still largely those of an essayist, if we may distinguish execution from construction. This was true always of Thackeray; it may be said to be true of the whole English school of fiction, in which the author of the scene permits himself to come forward and comment on the action and on things in general, and subordinate the drama to himself. Whether this is the best art or not, we must confess that its results are delightful when the author happens to be a man of singular wittiness, as Mr. Aldrich is. He is always the most charming personality in the book; we would rather hear him speak than anybody else. "The Bannock tribe had an ugly fashion of waylaying the mail, and decorating their persons with canceled postage-stamps. . . . If Dillingham had been a centipede he could not have worn out the slippers (bestowed by the young ladies of his church); if he had been a hydra, he could not have made head against the study caps. . . . Miss Veronica Blydenburgh, who had flirted in a high-spirited way with various religious professions. . . . I have encountered two or three young gentlemen in the capital of the Commonwealth of Massachusetts who seemed to have the idea that *they* were killed at the battle of Bunker Hill. . . . A No kept on ice for a twelvemonth could not have been colder. . . . Exit Larkin, lined with profanity,"—the book abounds in strokes of a humorous and witty fancy. Indeed, we think nothing wittier, using the word in a strict sense, has been written in this country, if we except three books of Dr. Holmes's.

[*Atlantic Monthly*, August 1874]

49

[J. W. De Forest: The Only American Novelist]¹

MR. Aldrich is an essayist of the finest New England type in his regard for
literary form; he means that every point of his work shall shine; he is a poet,
writing prose with the minute carefulness of verse, and often producing the
true lyrical effects in his romance. Mr. DeForest, who has recently given us
The Wetherel Affair, is more in earnest about making a novel, and so far he is
really the only American novelist. We have before this discussed his merits,
and we shall not enlarge upon them now. His field is wide, and it is not
preferably New England, though great part of the action of The Wetherel
Affair takes place in the New Yorkized section of New England, and one of
the characters—the rich old Wetherel whom the young adventurer, the
Polish count, murders for his money—is a true Puritan type. This old man is
the finest conception of all; he is imagined with the seriousness that gave us
Colonel Kershaw in Kate Beaumont, and that goes far to neutralize a certain
harsh, rank flavor to be tasted in the DeForest novels. His coldness, his sort
of stony stillness of surface with the attenuated tenderness underneath, his
bleak religiosity and his fine, solemn, scripturalized phraseology; his uncouth
ways,—skipping the bits of chicken off his fork on to the plates of his
guests,—his unlovely excellence of character, are extremely well caught, and
the portrait is full of artistic repose and mellowness. The missionary's
daughter, Nestoria, whom old Wetherel's spendthrift, disinherited nephew
falls in love with, is sweetly indicated, but she is not sufficiently *motivée* in her
career after her lover is suspected of the murder she sees done by the count.
Alice and her mother are vastly better: in fact we find them altogether
admirable and true. The mother is that reserve of sense and heart still
preserving American society, and the daughter is the dashing, bright,
reckless, New Yorky girl whom serious-minded Americans deplore—and
marry, when they can. She is a fool by her social education, but a person of
the hardest common-sense by nature; and she is charming. She will have the
count, though all her friends unite in proving him a swindler; when his bills
come to her mother by mistake before the marriage, she raves, she storms in
a good, honest, vulgar fashion, but she has character enough to tear the love
out of her heart at one wrench—and she wants the count thrashed. The

---

¹ *The Wetherel Affair.* By J. W. DeForest. New York: Sheldon & Co. 1874.

count is well drawn and not overdrawn; so is young Wetherel, who comes to the honest Puritan stuff in himself when he falls in love on his last dollar;— the dandification of himself and Wolverton is one of the casual bits of painting that please us in the book. Some minor persons are so good that we are sorry to have them slightly treated—Lehming, Bowder, and Miss Jones, who is quite inexcusably caricatured. In fact The Wetherel Affair, as compared with Miss Ravenel's Conversion, and Kate Beaumont, is nothing but a superb sketch. It reads easily, however, and the interest mounts to intensity before the end, which one foresees, and it is full enough of strong, manly talent to make the fortunes of a dozen ordinary story-writers.

[*Atlantic Monthly*, August 1874]

50

[The Abounding Charm of Bret Harte's Poetry][1]

THERE is something in Mr. Bret Harte's poetical work which goes over or under, or at least past, the critical sense, and reaches the humanity of his reader by direct course; and the oddest part of this is that the reader who most keenly feels the good in his performance is most annoyed by the bad in it. Since he began to be widely known, we should say that Mr. Harte's workmanship—we will not call it his art, for it must be that his art is still good—has grown worse. His verse is more slovenly and seems more wantonly careless, slighting the niceties of rhyme and accent, and as to the matter of it, we have again and again the same great-hearted blackguards and heroic topers; the same old mine keeps caving in and crushing its habitual victim; here is that unhappy lady in men's clothes for the third or fourth time; here are the dying agonies of persons who have loved and lost, or played and lost, in Mr. Harte's poetry any time this last five years. They talk that cockneyfied Yankee Pike of which he seems to have the patent, with a lift now and then into a literary strain worthy of the poet's corner; and when they do not perish untimely by violence or unaccountable sickness, they leave the poems in which they are celebrated so subtle of sense that one gives it up in despair after a certain number of guesses;—or perhaps this ought to be said rather of those difficult Spaniards of either sex who masquerade in Mr. Harte's verse. Here also as in former books are frank copies or flying suggestions of divers modern poets, including Mr. Harte himself, whom one beholds travestied, as it were, in some of the pieces, after a fashion peculiarly bewildering.

What remains? Simply that Mr. Harte's work still abounds in that something which may be called charm, for want of another word; without which the virtues are dead, but having which other matters are trifles in the way of your pleasure. There is a certain warmth, a nameless stir and pulse, in it all, before which you cannot continue unmoved. Somehow you are coaxed into enjoyment against which your criterions and principles severally and collectively protest; and while you lament that this genius should not be better ruled, you feel that it *is* genius, and yield yourself to it. It may not be of equal force for another generation; we think it will not; but it is potent now; and we

---

[1] *Echoes of the Foot-Hills*. By Bret Harte. Boston: J. R. Osgood & Co. 1875.

own that with all his lapses and trespasses, each new book of his is a new pleasure for us. We make sure of much real humor along with the false; there is wit nearly always; if we are shy of the pathos, we are still often touched by it; in the very heart of the theatricality are springs of genuine drama. We amuse ourselves moreover with the notion that Mr. Harte knows that now and then a poem in this volume, like Truthful James to the Editor, or The Ghost that Jim Saw, or Guild's Signal, is pure self-parody, or open commonplace, or solicited emotion, as well as we know it; and that when he tries to give an air of familiar ease to the situation by speaking of

"Old commuters along the road,"

he understands better than any one can tell him the worth of his attempt. Apparently, he chooses to chance it with the republication of these things; or he may be yielding to the necessity of making out a certain number of pages, a case which shall be sacred from our reproach.

There are several poems in this last book which merit no reproach. Grandmother Tenterden would be one of these, but for the too great vagueness of the close, in which the reader is vexed with diverse conjecture whether it was the living or the dead son come back to upbraid the mother, or whether living or dead he meant to upbraid her; and we have nothing but liking for the truly fine poem with which the book opens. The reader of The Atlantic will recall the beautiful story of Concepcion de Arguello, and how tenderly Mr. Harte has told it. There was matter in it for a much longer poem, which we should be disposed to quarrel with him for not making, if we were not so well content with the touching ballad as it is. The story is that of the daughter of the Spanish Comandante at San Francisco and of the Russian count who once came to look at California with a view to buying it for his master the Czar. The young people promise themselves to each other, and the count, going to get his master's approval, never returns, while his faithful, despairing Concepcion passes out of the world into a convent, and is an old woman when one day she learns that her lover was killed by falling from his horse on his way to St. Petersburg. We believe the tale is true; if it is not a fact, still Mr. Harte has made it true in telling it. The most poetic part of the poem is that descriptive passage by help of which the sense of Concepcion's long waiting is conveyed:—

"Day by day on wall and bastion beat the hollow empty breeze,—
Day by day the sunlight glittered on the vacant, smiling seas;

"*Week by week the near hills whitened in their dusty leather cloaks,—*
Week by week the far hills darkened from the fringing plain of oaks;

"Till the rains came, and far-breaking, on the fierce southwester tost,
Dashed the whole long coast with color, and then vanished and were lost.

"So each year the seasons shifted: wet and warm and drear and dry;
Half a year of clouds and flowers,—half a year of dust and sky.

"Still it brought no ship nor message,—brought no tidings ill nor meet
For the statesmanlike Commander, for the daughter fair and sweet.

"Yet she heard the varying message, voiceless to all ears beside:
'He will come,' the flowers whispered; 'Come no more,' the dry hills
    sighed.

"Still she found him with the waters lifted by the morning breeze,—
Still she lost him with the folding of the great white-tented seas;

"Until hollows chased the dimples from her cheeks of olive brown,
And at times a swift, shy moisture dragged the long sweet lashes down."

The unchangingness of the scenes here described embodies all the monotony of longing, hopeless waiting, as nothing else could. There is a mighty
fine Spanish feeling in that line which portrays the hills "that whitened in
their dusty leathern cloaks," and so makes old Castilians of them; and the
winterless California year was never, and can never be more perfectly said
than it is in the verse,—

"Half a year of clouds and flowers,—half a year of dust and
    sky."

In fact, this line is the highest point of achievement in the poem. What
follows next is also as good as need be of its kind: nothing could be
sweeter, or more paternally helpless in the case than the Comandante's efforts, when he

"Comforted the maid with proverbs,—wisdom gathered from afar;

"Bits of ancient observation by his fathers garnered, each
    As a pebble worn and polished in the current of his speech."

And the sympathetic reader will find the effect only the more touching from
the charming irrelevance of several of the consoling adages. All this part of
the poem is very tenderly and delicately managed; and in continuing the
same strain of narration there is another descriptive passage almost as fine as
that we have quoted, in which the old, dull, dead Spanish California lives
again:—

"Yearly, down the hill-side sweeping, came the stately cavalcade,
    Bringing revel to vaquero, joy and comfort to each maid;

"Bringing days of formal visit, social feast and rustic sport;
    Of bull-baiting on the plaza, of love-making in the court.

"Vainly then at Concha's lattice,—vainly as the idle wind
  Rose the thin high Spanish tenor that bespoke the youth too kind;

"Vainly, leaning from their saddles, caballeros, bold and fleet,
  Plucked for her the buried chicken from beneath their mustang's
    feet;

"So in vain the barren hill-sides with their gay serapes blazed,
  Blazed and vanished in the dust-cloud that their flying hoofs had
    raised."

    The climax of the poem is good, though a trifle too expected, perhaps;
but it seems as if Mr. Harte might have given us lines less commonplace than

"All to honor Sir George Simpson, famous traveler and guest,"
"And exchanged congratulation with the English baronet."

This is a really small matter, however, and they were doubtless meant to be
just as prosaic as they are upon some theory.

    The best parts of For the King are the opening stanzas giving the interior
of the New Mexican church, with some graphic strokes that our readers
cannot have forgotten. It is interesting throughout, and must be numbered
among the most successful of Mr. Harte's non-dialect poems. Of the dialect
pieces in this volume, Luke is easily first. In argument it is as thoroughly
unreal as Tasso's Aminta, or any dream of the *bell' età de l'oro*; but the character is forcibly realized, and much of the humor is exquisite. You say, If it
were possible that such a delicate, refined girl should have been smitten with
that great, burly, ignorant fellow, Luke, it would be a pretty thing to consider; and before the end—such is the authority that anything excellently
done carries with it—you find yourself inclining to believe that it might have
happened, or to wish that it had, for the charm's sake.

[*Atlantic Monthly*, February 1875]

51

[Henry James's Marvelous First Book][1]

Mr. Henry James, Jr., has so long been a writer of magazine stories, that most readers will realize with surprise the fact that he now presents them for the first time in book form. He has already made his public. Since his earliest appearance in The Atlantic people have strongly liked and disliked his writing; but those who know his stories, whether they like them or not, have constantly increased in number, and it has therefore been a winning game with him. He has not had to struggle with indifference, that subtlest enemy of literary reputations. The strongly characteristic qualities of his work, and its instantly recognizable traits, made it at once a question for every one whether it was an offense or a pleasure. To ourselves it has been a very great pleasure, the highest pleasure that a new, decided, and earnest talent can give; and we have no complaint against this collection of stories graver than that it does not offer the author's whole range. We have read them all again and again, and they remain to us a marvel of delightful workmanship. In richness of expression and splendor of literary performance, we may compare him with the greatest, and find none greater than he; as a piece of mere diction, for example, The Romance of Certain Old Clothes in this volume is unsurpassed. No writer has a style more distinctly his own than Mr. James, and few have the abundance and felicity of his vocabulary; the precision with which he fits the word to the thought is exquisite; his phrase is generous and ample. Something of an old-time stateliness distinguishes his style, and in a certain weight of manner he is like the writers of an age when literature was a far politer thing than it is now. In a reverent ideal of work, too, he is to be rated with the first. His aim is high; he respects his material; he is full of his theme; the latter-day sins of flippancy, slovenliness, and insincerity are immeasurably far from him.

In the present volume we have one class of his romances or novelettes: those in which American character is modified or interpreted by the conditions of European life, and the contact with European personages. Not all the stories of this sort that Mr. James has written are included in this book, and one of the stories admitted—The Romance of Certain Old Clothes— belongs rather to another group, to the more strictly romantic tales, of which

[1] *The Passionate Pilgrim and other Tales.* By Henry James, Jr. Boston: J. R. Osgood & Co. 1875.

the author has printed several in these pages; the scene is in America, and in this also it differs from its present neighbors. There is otherwise uncommon unity in the volume, though it has at first glance that desultory air which no collection of short stories can escape. The same purpose of contrast and suggestion runs through A Passionate Pilgrim, Eugene Pickering, The Madonna of the Future, and Madame de Mauves, and they have all the same point of view. The American who has known Europe much can never again see his country with the single eye of his old ante-European days. For good or for evil, the light of the Old World is always on her face; and his fellow-countrymen have their shadows cast by it. This is inevitable; there may be an advantage in it, but if there is none, it is still inevitable. It may make a man think better or worse of America; it may be refinement or it may be anxiety; there may be no compensation in it for the loss of that tranquil indifference to Europe which untraveled Americans feel, or it may be the very mood in which an American may best understand his fellow-Americans. More and more, in any case, it pervades our literature, and it seems to us the mood in which Mr. James's work, more than that of any other American, is done. His attitude is not that of a mere admirer of Europe and contemner of America—our best suffers no disparagement in his stories; you perceive simply that he is most contented when he is able to confront his people with situations impossible here, and you fancy in him a mistrust of such mechanism as the cis-Atlantic world can offer the romancer.

However this may be, his book is well worth the carefullest study any of our critics can give it. The tales are all freshly and vigorously conceived, and each is very striking in a very different way, while undoubtedly A Passionate Pilgrim is the best of all. In this Mr. James has seized upon what seems a very common motive, in a hero with a claim to an English estate, but the character of the hero idealizes the situation: the sordid illusion of the ordinary American heir to English property becomes in him a poetic passion, and we are made to feel an instant tenderness for the gentle visionary who fancies himself to have been misborn in our hurried, eager world, but who owes to his American birth the very rapture he feels in gray England. The character is painted with the finest sense of its charm and its deficiency, and the story that grows out of it is very touching. Our readers will remember how, in the company of the supposed narrator, Clement Searle goes down from London to the lovely old country-place to which he has relinquished all notion of pretending, but which he fondly longs to see; and they will never have forgotten the tragedy of his reception and expulsion by his English cousin. The proprietary Searle stands for that intense English sense of property which the mere dream of the American has unpardonably outraged, and which in his case wreaks itself in an atrocious piece of savagery. He is imagined with an extraordinary sort of vividness which leaves the redness of his complexion like a stain on the memory; and yet we believe we realize better the dullish kindness, the timid sweetness of the not-at-once handsome sister who falls in love with the poor American cousin. The atmosphere of the story, which is at first that of a novel, changes to the finer air of romance during the scenes at Lockley Park, and you gladly accede to all the romantic conditions, for the sake of otherwise unattainable effects. It is good and true that Searle should not be shocked out of his unrequited affection for England by his cousin's brutality, but should die at Oxford, as he does, in ardent loyalty to his ideal; and it is one of the fortunate inspirations of the tale to confront him there with that decayed and reprobate Englishman in whom abides a longing for the New World as hopeless and unfounded as his own passion for the Old. The character of Miss Searle is drawn with peculiar sweetness and firmness; there is a strange charm in the generous devotion masked by her trepidations and proprieties, and the desired poignant touch is given when at the end she comes only in time to stand by Searle's death-bed. Throughout the story there are great breadths of deliciously sympathetic description. At Oxford the author lights his page with all the rich and mellow picturesqueness of the ancient university town, but we do not know that he is happier there than in his sketches of Lockley Park and Hampton Court, or his study of the old London inn. Everywhere he conveys to you the rapture of his own seeing; one reads such a passage as this with the keen transport that the author felt in looking on the scene itself:—

"The little village of Hampton Court stands clustered about the broad entrance of Bushey Park. After we had dined we lounged along into the hazy vista of the great avenue of horse-chestnuts. There is a rare emotion, familiar to every intelligent traveler, in which the mind, with a great, passionate throb, achieves a magical synthesis of its impressions. You feel England; you feel Italy. The reflection for the moment has an extraordinary poignancy. I had known it from time to time in Italy, and had opened my soul to it as to the spirit of the Lord. Since my arrival in England I had been waiting for it to come. A bottle of excellent Burgundy at dinner had perhaps unlocked to it the gates of sense; it came now with a conquering tread. Just the scene around me was the England of my visions. Over against us, amid the deep-hued bloom of its ordered gardens, the dark red palace, with its formal copings and its vacant windows, seemed to tell of a proud and splendid past; the little village nestling between park and palace, around a patch of turfy common, with its tavern of gentility, its ivy-towered church, its parsonage, retained to my modernized fancy the lurking semblance of a feudal hamlet. It was in this dark, composite light that I had read all English prose; it was this mild, moist air that had blown from the verses of English poets; beneath these broad acres of rain-deepened greenness a thousand honored dead lay buried."

A strain of humor which so pleasantly characterizes the descriptions of the London inn, tinges more sarcastically the admirable portrait of the shabby Rawson at Oxford, and also colors this likeness of a tramp—a fellow-man who has not had his picture better done:—

"As we sat, there came trudging along the road an individual whom from afar I recognized as a member of the genus 'tramp.' I had read of the British tramp, but I had never yet encountered him, and I brought my historic consciousness to bear upon the present specimen. As he approached us he slackened pace and finally halted, touching his cap. He was a man of middle age, clad in a greasy bonnet, with greasy ear-locks depending from its sides. Round his neck was a grimy red scarf, tucked into his waistcoat; his coat and trousers had a remote affinity with those of a reduced hostler. In one hand he had a stick; on his arm he bore a tattered basket, with a handful of withered green stuff in the bottom. His face was pale, haggard, and degraded beyond description,—a singular mixture of brutality and finesse. He had a history. From what height had he fallen, from what depth had he risen? Never was a form of rascally beggarhood more complete. There was a merciless fixedness of outline about him, which filled me with a kind of awe. I felt as if I were in the presence of a personage—an artist in vagrancy.

" 'For God's sake, gentlemen,' he said, in that raucous tone of weather-beaten poverty suggestive of chronic sore-throat exacerbated by perpetual gin,—'for God's sake, gentlemen, have pity on a poor fern-collector!'—turning up his stale dandelions. 'Food has n't passed my lips, gentlemen, in the last three days.'

"We gaped responsive, in the precious pity of guileless Yankeeism. 'I wonder,' thought I, 'if half a crown would be enough?' And our fasting botanist went limping away through the park with a mystery of satirical gratitude superadded to his general mystery."

Mr. James does not often suffer his sense of the ludicrous to relax the sometimes over-serious industry of his analyses, and when he has once done so, he seems to repent it. Yet we are sure that the poetic value of A Passionate Pilgrim is enhanced by the unwonted interfusion of humor, albeit the humor is apt to be a little too scornful. The tale is in high degree imaginative, and its fascination grows upon you in the reading and the retrospect, exquisitely contenting you with it as a new, fine, and beautiful invention.

In imaginative strength it surpasses the other principal story of the book. In Madame de Mauves the spring of the whole action is the idea of an American girl who will have none but a French nobleman for her husband. It is not a vulgar adoration of rank in her, but a young girl's belief that ancient lineage, circumstances of the highest civilization, and opportunities of the greatest refinement, must result in the noblest type of character. Grant the premises, and the effect of her emergence into the cruel daylight of facts is unquestionably tremendous: M. le Baron de Mauves is frankly unfaithful to his American wife, and, finding her too dismal in her despair, advises her to take a lover. A difficulty with so French a situation is that only a French writer can carry due conviction of it to the reader. M. de Mauves, indeed, justifies himself to the reader's sense of likelihood with great consistency, and he is an extremely suggestive conjecture. Of course, he utterly misconceives his wife's character and that of all her race, and perceives little and understands nothing not of his own tradition:—

"They talked for a while about various things, and M. de Mauves gave a humorous account of his visit to America. His tone was not soothing to Longmore's excited sensibilities. He seemed to consider the country a gigantic joke, and his urbanity only went so far as to admit that it was not a bad one. Longmore was not, by habit, an aggressive apologist for our institutions; but the baron's narrative confirmed his worst impressions of French superficiality. He had understood nothing, he had felt nothing, he had learned nothing; and our hero, glancing askance at his aristocratic profile, declared that if the chief merit of a long pedigree was to leave one so vaingloriously stupid, he thanked his stars that the Longmores had emerged from obscurity in the present century, in the person of an enterprising lumber merchant. M. de Mauves dwelt of course on that prime oddity of ours, the liberty allowed to young girls; and related the history of his researches into the 'opportunities' it presented to French noblemen,—researches in which, during a fortnight's stay, he seemed to have spent many agreeable hours. 'I am bound to admit,' he said, 'that in every case I was disarmed by the extreme candor of the young lady, and that they took care of themselves to better purpose than I have seen some mammas in France take care of them.' Longmore greeted this handsome concession with the grimmest of smiles, and damned his impertinent patronage."

This is all very good character, and here is something from the baron that is delicious:—

"I remember that, not long after our marriage, Madame de Mauves undertook to read me one day a certain Wordsworth,—a poet highly esteemed, it appears, *chez vous*. It seemed to me that she took me by the nape of the neck and forced my head for half an hour over a basin of *soupe aux choux*, and that one ought to ventilate the drawing-room before any one called."

The baron's sister, in her candid promotion of an intrigue between Madame de Mauves and Longmore, we cannot quite account for even by the fact that she hated them both. But Madame de Mauves is the strength of the story, and if Mr. James has not always painted the kind of women that women like to meet in fiction, he has richly atoned in her lovely nature for all default. She is the finally successful expression of an ideal of woman which has always been a homage, perhaps not to all kinds of women, but certainly to the sex. We are thinking of the heroine of Poor Richard, of Miss Guest in Guest's Confession, of Gabrielle de Bergerac in the story of that name, and other gravely sweet girls of this author's imagining. Madame de Mauves is of the same race, and she is the finest,—as truly American as she is womanly; and in a peculiar fragrance of character, in her purity, her courage, her inflexible high-mindedness, wholly of our civilization and almost of our climate, so different are her virtues from the virtues of the women of any other nation.

The Madonna of the Future is almost as perfect a piece of work, in its way, as A Passionate Pilgrim. It is a more romantic conception than Madame de Mauves, and yet more real. Like A Passionate Pilgrim, it distinguishes itself among Mr. James's stories as something that not only arrests the curiosity, stirs the fancy, and interests the artistic sense, but deeply touches the heart. It is more than usually relieved, too, by the author's humorous recognition of the pathetic absurdity of poor Theobald, and there is something unusually good in the patience with which the handsome, common-minded Italian woman of his twenty years' adoration is set before us. Our pity that his life should have slipped away from him in devout study of this vulgar beauty, and that she should grow old and he should die before he has made a line to celebrate her perfection or seize his ideal, is vastly heightened by the author's rigid justice to her; she is not caricatured by a light or a shadow, and her dim sense of Theobald's goodness and purity is even flattered into prominence. In all essentials one has from this story the solid satisfaction given by work in which the conception is fine, and the expression nowhere falls below it—if we except one point that seems to us rather essential, in a thing so carefully tempered and closely wrought. The reiteration of the Italian figure-maker's philosophy, "Cats and monkeys, monkeys and cats; all human life is there," is apparently of but wandering purport, and to end the pensive strain of the romance with it is to strike a jarring note that leaves the reader's mind out of tune. Sometimes even the ladies and gentlemen of Mr. James's stories are allowed a certain excess or violence in which the end to be achieved is not distinctly discernible, or the effect so reluctantly responds to the intention as to leave merely the sense of the excess.

Eugene Pickering is, like Madame de Mauves, one of those realistic subjects which we find less real than the author's romantic inspirations. There is no fault with the treatment; that is thoroughly admirable, full of spirit, wit, and strength; but there is a fancifulness in the outlines of Pickering's history and the fact of his strange betrothal which seems to belong to an old-fashioned stage-play method of fiction rather than to such a modern affair as that between the unsophisticated American and Madame Blumenthal; it did not need that machinery to produce this effect, thanks to common conditions of ours that often enough keep young men as guileless as Pickering, and as fit for sacrifice at such shrines as hers. However, something must always be granted to the story-teller by way of premises; if we exacted from Mr. James only that he should make his premises fascinating, we should have nothing to ask here. His start, in fact, is always superb; he possesses himself of your interest at once, and he never relinquishes it till the end; though there he may sometimes leave your curiosity not quite satisfied on points such as a story-teller assumes to make clear. What, for example, were exactly the tortuous workings of Madame Blumenthal's mind in her self-contradictory behavior towards Pickering? These things must be at least unmistakably suggested.

Since Hawthorne's Donatello, any attempt to touch what seems to be the remaining paganism in Italian character must accuse itself a little, but The Last of the Valerii is a study of this sort that need really have nothing on its conscience. It is an eminently poetic conceit, though it appeals to a lighter sort of emotions than any other story in Mr. James's book; it is an airy fabric woven from those bewitching glimpses of the impossible which life in Italy affords, and which those who have enjoyed them are perfectly right to over-value. It has just the right tint of ideal trouble in it which no living writer could have imparted more skillfully than it is here done. If the story is of slighter material than the others, the subtlety of its texture gives it a surpass-ing charm, and makes it worthy to be named along with the only other purely romantic tale in the book.

To our thinking, Mr. James has been conspicuously fortunate in placing his Romance of Certain Old Clothes in that eighteenth-century New England when the country, still colonial, was no longer rigidly puritanic, and when a love of splendor and accumulating wealth had created social conditions very different from those conventionally attributed to New England. It is among such bravely dressing provincials as Copley used to paint, and as dwelt in fine town mansions in Boston, or the handsome country-places which still remem-ber their faded grandeur along Brattle Street in Cambridge, that Mr. James finds the circumstance and material of his personages; and we greatly enjoy the novelty of this conception of what not only might, but must have existed hereabouts in times which we are too prone to fancy all close-cropped and sad-colored. The tale is written with heat, and rapidly advances from point to point, with a constantly mounting interest. The sisterly rivalry is shown with due boldness, but without excess, and the character of Viola is sketched with a vigor that conveys a full sense of her selfish, luxurious beauty. The scene between her and Perdita when the engagement of the latter is betrayed, the scene in which she unrolls the stuff of the wedding-dress and confronts her-self in the glass with it falling from her shoulder, and that in which she hastily tries the garment on after her sister's marriage, are pictures as full of charac-ter as they are of color. The most is made of Perdita where she lies dying, and bids her husband keep her fine clothes for her little girl; it is very affecting indeed, and all the more so for the explicit human-nature of the dying wife's foreboding. In the whole course of the story nothing is urged, nothing is dwelt upon; and all our story-tellers, including Mr. James himself, could profitably take a lesson from it in this respect. At other times he has a ten-dency to expatiate upon his characters too much, and not to trust his reader's perception enough. For the sake of a more dramatic presentation of his persons, he has told most of the stories in this book as things falling within the notice of the assumed narrator; an excellent device; though it would be better if the assumed narrator were able to keep himself from seeming to patronize the simpler-hearted heroes, and from openly rising above them in a worldly way.

But this is a very little matter, and none of our discontents with Mr. James bear any comparison to the pleasure we have had in here renewing our acquaintance with stories as distinctly characteristic as anything in literature. It is indeed a marvelous first book in which the author can invite his critic to the same sort of reflection that criticism bestows upon the claims of the great reputations; but one cannot dismiss this volume with less and not slight it.

Like it or not, you must own that here is something positive, original, individual, the result of long and studious effort in a well-considered line, and mounting in its own way to great achievement. We have a reproachful sense of leaving the immense suggestiveness of the book scarcely touched, and we must ask the reader to supply our default from the stories themselves. He may be assured that nothing more novel in our literature has yet fallen in his way; and we are certain that he will not close the book without a lively sense of its force. We can promise him, also, his own perplexities about it, among which may be a whimsical doubt whether Mr. James has not too habitually addressed himself less to men and women in their mere humanity, than to a certain kind of cultivated people, who, well as they are in some ways, and indispensable as their appreciation is, are often a little narrow in their sympathies and poverty-stricken in the simple emotions; who are so, or try to be so, which is quite as bad, or worse.

[*Atlantic Monthly*, April 1875]

52

[Miss Woolson's Lake-Country Sketches][1]

THE Lake-Country which Miss Woolson sketches is the region of the great inland seas, Superior, Huron, Erie, and the rest, and the term is allowably stretched to include that part of Northern Ohio in which the community of the Zoar Separatists prosperously doze their lives away. The ground is new, and Miss Woolson gathers from it a harvest out of which the grain had not been threshed long ago. Our readers already know three of her stories, Solomon, The Lady of Little Fishing, and Wilhelmina, which are the best in this book, and fairly suggest its range, for it is now poetically realistic in circumstance like the first and last, and now poetically fanciful like the second. Both kinds rest upon the same solid basis—truth to human nature; and because Miss Woolson has distinctly felt the value of this basis, we are the more surprised at her projecting such an air-founded fabric as Castle Nowhere. In this we are asked to suppose a wretch who beacons lake schooners to shipwreck on the rocks, and plunders them that he may keep in luxury the young girl whom he has adopted for his daughter, and who lives in an inaccessible tower on a secret isle of the lake. A subtle confusion of all the conceptions of right and wrong is wrought by this old reprobate's devotion to the child, and his inability to feel that any means to her pleasure and comfort can be bad; but we doubt whether this is an intended effect, and if it is, we think it not worth the writer's or reader's pains. Castle Nowhere is the least satisfactory of the stories; one is harassed from beginning to end by a disagreeable fantasticality.

The notion, in Peter the Parson, of the poor little ritualist who lives a missionary among the ruffians of the Northwestern lumbering town, and daily reads the service to himself in his empty chapel, is altogether better, though we wish the matter were less sketchily treated. Miss Woolson had something in Rose's unrequited love for the parson, and the tragic end it brings him to, worthy her most patient and careful art. The Old Agency is another good sketch, or study, tasting racily of the strange time and place. It is the ancient government agency building at Mackinac, about which linger the memories of the Jesuit missions, and in which, after its desertion, an old

---

[1] *Castle Nowhere: Lake-Country Sketches*. By Constance Fenimore Woolson. Boston: J. R. Osgood & Co. 1875.

soldier of Napoleon comes to spend his last days: the story gains color from its supposed narration by the Jesuit father Piret; for the French have had the complaisance to touch our continent with romance wherever they have touched it at all as soldiers, priests, exiles, or mere adventurers. St. Clair Flats is apparently a transcript from the fact, and with its portraits of the strange prophet, Waiting Samuel, and his wife, it is a not at all discouraging example of what our strangely varied American real life can do in the way of romance; it seems only to need the long-denied opportunity in fiction which some of our later writers have afforded it—none with greater promise of a successful interpretation in certain ways than Miss Woolson herself. Her story of Solomon is really a triumph of its kind—a novel kind, as simple as it is fresh. The Zoar Community, with its manners and customs, and that quaint mingling of earthy good-feeding and mild, coarse kindliness with forms of austere religious and social discipline, which seems to characterize all the peculiar German sectarians, has had the fortune to find an artist in the first who introduces us to its life. Solomon's character is studied with a delicate and courageous sympathy, which spares us nothing of his grotesqueness, and yet keenly touches us with his pathetic history. An even greater success of literary art is his poor, complaining wife, the faded parody of the idol of his young love, still beautiful in his eyes, and the inspiration of all his blind, unguided efforts in painting. His death, after the first instruction has revealed his powers to himself, is affectingly portrayed, without a touch of sentimentalistic insistence. It is a very complete and beautiful story. Wilhelmina, of which the scene is also at Zoar, is not quite so good; and yet it is very well done, too. Perhaps the reader's lurking sense of its protractedness dulls his pleasure in it. But it is well imagined, of new material, and skillfully wrought. The Lady of Little Fishing is as fine, in its different way, as Solomon. That is a very striking and picturesque conceit, of the beautiful religious enthusiast who becomes a sort of divinity to the wild, fierce fur-hunters among whom she pitches her tent, and who loses her divine honors by falling in love with one of them; and all the processes of this romance and its catastrophe are revealed with dramatic skill and force. It argues a greater richness in our fictitious literature than we have been able to flatter ourselves upon, or a torpidity in our criticism which we fear we must acknowledge, that such a story should not have made a vivid impression. It has that internal harmony which is the only allegiance to probability we can exact from romance, and it has a high truth to human nature never once weakened by any vagueness of the moral ideal in the author,—as happens with Mr. Harte's sketches, the only sketches with which we should care to compare it.

[*Atlantic Monthly*, June 1875]

53

[The Quaintness of William Morris's Poems]

Mr. William Morris's poetry has always, we will confess it, been a somewhat perplexing affair to us, and this new reprint of some old poems of his only increases our besetting doubt whether it is quite worth while to do the things he does so well. From first to last in him there is a sort of prepense return to former mental conditions and feelings; and to read his poems is like looking through a modern house equipped with Eastlake furniture, adorned with tiles, and painted in the Pompeiian style, or hung with Mr. Morris's own admirable wall-papers: it is all very pretty indeed; charming; but it is consciously mediæval, consciously Greek, and it is so well aware of its quaintness, that on the whole one would rather not live in it. Then, is Mr. Morris's poetry a kind of decorative, household art? Not quite; but it suggests that. For example, the first four poems in this little book,[1] The Defence of Guenevere, King Arthur's Tomb, Sir Galahad, and The Chapel in Lyoness, are the sort of thing that one would like to have painted on large, movable screens. As it is, they are rather painted than written, and might perhaps serve the desired purpose of decoration if pasted on the screens. They are doubtless true enough to the fabulous Arthur-world which it is so pleasant to muse upon; but in Sir Harpdon's End we have a literary daylight that is more easy to be in, and a resemblance to mediæval feelings, ideas, and traits that once actually were. He is a French knight in the English service just after the time of the invading Edwards, and having cut off the ears of his cousin, he is taken by the French and hanged, and the squire of a French knight who tries to save him is sent to tell his lady; and then "one sings from the outside" something all in Italics. This Italic song had to come in, of course. The rest is very hardly realistic, and the situation is boldly painted, and the compliments that passed between the cousins are set down in good round, relishing terms. There is character in the piece; not much drama; and we take it there is truth. So there is in The Haystack in the Floods; which is a butcherly, dreadfully vivid episode, leaving the nerves on edge. But there seems to be less time lost, and fewer words wasted in expressing the mediæval "situation" in the short poem called Shameful Death. The good

---

[1] *The Defence of Guenevere, and other Poems.* By William Morris. (Reprinted without Alteration from the Edition of 1858.) London: Ellis and White. Boston: Roberts Brothers. 1875.

Lord Hugh is hung by Sir John of the Fen, who takes him by stealth and treachery. The brother of Lord Hugh, who cuts the cord from his neck, speaks:—

> "I am three score years and ten
> And my hair is all turned gray,
> But I met Sir John of the Fen,
> Long ago on a summer day,
> *And am glad to think of the moment when*
> *I took his life away.*"

No misgivings here; no twinges of remorse; no uncleanly scruples; in all the years that have passed, this good soul has been perfectly clear and happy about it! If this is modern, it seems still a wonderfully good conception of things and men as they were. So, too, even in the vagueness of the Arthurian poems, the poet now and then strikes a note that in its great simplicity rings out full and distinct from all the wandering music, as where Guenevere, speaking of her sin with Lancelot, says:—

> "Unless you pardon, what shall I do, Lord,
> But go to hell? and there see day by day
> Foul deed on deed, hear foulest word on word,
> Forever and ever such as on the way
>
> "To Camelot I heard once from a churl,
> *That curled me up upon my jennet's neck*
> *With bitter shame; how then, Lord, should I curl*
> *For ages and for ages?*"

It took courage to use the word *curl*, here; it is almost funny; it is also inexpressibly pathetic, and beyond all other possible phrases true to the sense of the shame lamented.

[*Atlantic Monthly*, August 1875]

54

[Mark Twain's Sketches, Old and New]

It is easy to say that these new and old sketches[1] by Mr. Clemens are of varying merit; but which, honest reader, would you leave out of the book? There is none but saves itself either by its humor or by the sound sense which it is based on, so that if one came to reject the flimsiest trifle, one would find it on consideration rather too good to throw away. In reading the book, you go through a critical process imaginably very like the author's in editing it; about certain things there can be no question from the first, and you end by accepting all, while you feel that any one else may have his proper doubts about some of the sketches.

The characteristic traits of our friend—he is the friend of mankind—are all here; here is the fine, forecasting humor, starting so far back from its effect that one, knowing some joke must be coming, feels that nothing less than a prophetic instinct can sustain the humorist in its development; here is the burlesque, that seems such plain and simple fun at first, doubling and turning upon itself till you wonder why Mr. Clemens has ever been left out of the list of our *subtile* humorists; here is that peculiar extravagance of statement which we share with all sufficiently elbow-roomed, unneighbored people, but which our English cousins are so good as to consider the distinguishing mark of American humor; here is the incorruptible right-mindedness that always warms the heart to this wit; here is the "dryness," the "breadth,"—all the things that so weary us in the praises of him and that so take us with delight in the reading of him. But there is another quality in this book which we fancy we shall hereafter associate more and more with our familiar impressions of him, and that is a growing seriousness of meaning in the apparently unmoralized drolling, which must result from the humorist's second thought of political and social absurdities. It came to Dickens, but the character of his genius was too intensely theatrical to let him make anything but rather poor melodrama of it; to Thackeray, whom our humorists at their best are all like, it came too, and would not suffer him to leave anything, however grotesque, merely laughed at. We shall be disappointed if in Mr. Clemens's case it finds only some desultory expression, like Lionizing Mur-

---

[1] *Mark Twain's Sketches*. New and Old. Now first published in Complete Form. Sold only by Subscription. The American Publishing Company. 1875.

derers and A New Crime, though there could not be more effective irony than these sketches so far as they go. The first is a very characteristic bit of the humorist's art; and the reader is not so much troubled to find where the laugh comes in as to find where it goes out—for ten to one he is in a sober mind when he is done. The other is more direct satire, but is quite as subtle in its way of presenting those cases in which murderers have been found opportunely insane and acquitted, and gravely sandwiching amongst them instances in which obviously mad people have been hanged by the same admirable system.

Nothing more final has been thought of on the subject of a great public, statutory wrong, than Mark Twain's petition to Congress asking that all property shall be held during the period of forty-two years, or for just so long as an author is permitted to claim copyright in his book. The whole sense and justice applicable to the matter are enforced in this ironical prayer, and there is no argument that could stand against it. If property in houses or lands—which a man may get by dishonest trickery, or usury, or hard rapacity—were in danger of ceasing after forty-two years, the whole virtuous community would rouse itself to perpetuate the author's right to the product of his brain, and no griping bidder at tax-sales but would demand the protection of literature by indefinite copyright. The difficulty is, to condition the safety of real estate in this way; but Mark Twain's petition is a move in the right direction.

We should be sorry to give our readers the impression that they are unconsciously to imbibe political and social wisdom from every page of Mr. Clemens's new book, when we merely wished to point out one of his tendencies. Though there is nearly always sense in his nonsense, yet he is master of the art of pure drolling. The grotesque cannot go further than in that Mediæval Romance of his, where he is obliged to abandon his hero or heroine at the most critical moment, simply because he can see no way to get him or her out of the difficulty; and there is a delicious novelty in that Ghost Story, where the unhappy spectre of the Cardiff giant is mortified to find that he has been haunting a plaster cast of himself in New York, while his stone original was lying in Albany. The Experiences of the McWilliamses with the Membranous Croup is a bit of *genre* romance, which must read like an abuse of confidence to every husband and father. These are amongst the new sketches, though none of them have staled by custom, and the old sketches are to be called so merely for contradistinction's sake. How I once edited an Agricultural Paper, About Barbers, Cannibalism in the Cars, The Undertaker's Chat, The Scriptural Panoramist, To raise Poultry, A Visit to Niagara, are all familiar favorites, which, when we have read them we wish merely to have the high privilege of immediately reading over again. We must not leave the famous Jumping Frog out of their honorable and pleasant company; it is here in a new effect, first as the Jumping Frog in Mark Twain's original English, then in the French of the Revue des deux Mondes, and then in his literal version of the French, which he gives that the reader may see how his frog has been made to appear "to the distorted French eye."

But by far the most perfect piece of work in the book is A True Story, which resulted, we remember, in some confusion of the average critical mind, when it was first published in these pages a little more than one year ago. It is simply the story an old black cook tells of how her children were all sold away from her, and how after twenty years she found her youngest boy again. The shyness of an enlightened and independent press respecting this history was something extremely amusing to see, and we could fancy it a spectacle of delightful interest to the author, if it had not had such disheartening features. Mostly the story was described in the notices of the magazine as a humorous sketch by Mark Twain; sometimes it was mentioned as a paper apparently out of the author's usual line; again it was handled noncommittally as one of Mark Twain's extravagances. Evidently the critical mind feared a lurking joke. Not above two or three notices out of hundreds recognized A True Story for what it was, namely, a study of character as true as life itself, strong, tender, and most movingly pathetic in its perfect fidelity to the tragic fact. We beg the reader to turn to it again in this book. We can assure him that he has a great surprise and a strong emotion in store for him. The rugged truth of the sketch leaves all other stories of slave life infinitely far behind, and reveals a gift in the author for the simple dramatic report of reality which we have seen equaled in no other American writer.

[*Atlantic Monthly*, December 1875]

55

[The Genius of Longfellow's Art]

IN the volume which Mr. Longfellow[1] has given us, the artistry becomes a positive delight. You rest upon it, and know in behalf of even your most morbid sensibility that it cannot betray your confidence by the smallest dereliction. Secrets of melody, surprises of harmony, float from the perfect instrument which responds to a touch that now cannot err; you are enriched by the results of care which has become a joy. Men of genius we do not lack and have not lacked, but as yet we have had but one other with patience to be such a perfect artist,—Hawthorne. One may say that this patience is the gift of temperament; but that is only giving greatness another name, not changing the fact.

Hawthorne is Hawthorne almost to the paper and print; and if you take Longfellow even in the attempts which are least responsive to his genius, you cannot read a single passage without knowing his hand and heart. Throughout is that simplicity which is the most satisfying thing in poetry; for when we read poetry, we wish to be spoken with face to face, to be amused, touched, uplifted by something elemental, by a power like that which charms children—the same power matured and, as it were, grown up. Art must be there; but conscious culture, the pride of intellect, can only offer impertinences.

Pleasure unmixed with the alloy of any base gratification, this is what our poet's verse has always given, but in his latest book it is a more pensive pleasure than he has given before. The Masque of Pandora is the only poem of the collection not more or less tinged with the vague regrets of accumulating years, which in some of the sonnets take the deeper color of a personal grief. Here is The Hanging of the Crane, a poem over which broods the sadness of life, increasing and decreasing; the beautiful Morituri Salutamus, which the poet last year addressed to his old college classmates; several reminiscences of places which his youth knew, and which are now consecrated by the loss of his youth; and then a book of sonnets, which we fancy will be read oftenest. Three of the sonnets are on friends of his who have joined the greater number, and in these he takes the world at its word, and speaks his sorrow to its sympathetic regard; nothing could be franker or more moving.

---

[1] *The Masque of Pandora, and other Poems.* By Henry Wadsworth Longfellow. Boston: J. R. Osgood & Co. 1875.

"In vain I stretch my hands to clasp their hands;
 I cannot find them,"

he laments; and he asks of Felton,—

"Oh what hadst thou to do with cruel Death,
 Who wast so full of life, or Death with thee,
 That thou shouldst die before thou hadst grown old?"

of Agassiz,

"When thou hadst read
Nature's mysterious manuscript, and then
 Wast ready to reveal the truth it bears,
 Why art thou silent? why shouldst thou be dead?"

And in that supreme sonnet he addresses Sumner,—

"Good night! good night! as we so oft have said
 Beneath this roof at midnight, in the days
 That are no more, and shall no more return.
Thou hast but taken thy lamp and gone to bed;
 I stay a little longer, as one stays
 To cover up the embers that still burn."

How beautiful they all are, those sonnets; how wise, how good, how simple! Look at the wording of them: it is of the plain, small pebbles of our Saxon speech that those exquisite mosaics are formed; but the effect, in this sonnet on Chaucer, is of a rich translucence, like that of precious stones.

CHAUCER.

An old man in a lodge within a park;
 The chamber walls depicted all around
 With portraitures of huntsman, hawk, and hound,
 And the hurt deer. He listeneth to the lark,
Whose song comes with the sunshine through the dark
 Of painted glass in leaden lattice bound;
 He listeneth and he laugheth at the sound,
 Then writeth in a book like any clerk.
He is the poet of the dawn, who wrote
 The Canterbury Tales, and his old age
 Made beautiful with song; and as I read
I hear the crowing cock, I hear the note
 Of lark and linnet, and from every page
 Rise odors of plowed field or flowery mead.

But there is something better still than this delightful art, namely, the fraternal heart to which the sacrifices of humanity have always been so dear and sacred.

A NAMELESS GRAVE.

"A soldier of the Union mustered out,"
    Is the inscription on an unknown grave
    At Newport News, beside the salt-sea wave,
    Nameless and dateless; sentinel or scout
Shot down in skirmish, or disastrous rout
    Of battle, when the loud artillery drave
    Its iron wedges through the ranks of brave
    And doomed battalions, storming the redoubt.
Thou unknown hero sleeping by the sea
    In thy forgotten grave! with secret shame
    I feel my pulses beat, my forehead burn,
When I remember thou hast given for me
    All that thou hadst, thy life, thy very name,
    And I can give thee nothing in return.

We have all felt this so often that it has seemed a part of our daily talk; it is so mere an utterance of the best in us that any one might believe himself to have said just these words; the poet has only divined what was in our hearts and on our tongues. But to surprise us with ourselves, this is the great miracle of which only the highest genius holds the secret.

The Masque of Pandora is the old story of our race's disaster, which myth and Scripture are agreed in attributing to the first woman; only here the old story is as fresh as if newly invented. Mr. Longfellow has never done anything more graceful, and if we always find choruses of voices the bearers of mystical messages not important in due proportion to their length, we have in this case the compensation of delicately felt character in the persons of the drama. The austere, inflexible grandeur of Prometheus, the poet-soul of his brother, the fascination of Pandora, even after her calamity-working, are lightly projected upon the fancy, which, in our own case, we find most pleased with the faintly cynical humorousness of Hermes in his relation to the affair.

The Morituri Salutamus must be thought one of the most beautiful things Mr. Longfellow has written, and the key in which it is pitched is that of nearly all the other pieces. A regret which will not lose heart, and forbids itself the vulgar luxury of despair, is the prevailing note, and it wins the reader to perfect accord with its mood. After fifty years the poet confronts those with whom he parted at the threshold of manhood; to those wrinkled brows and white heads he can only say, "We are old, but let us not be sad; our best is done, but let us still do our best." And what could be mournfuller than this? This is the burden of the Morituri Salutamus, which also is a poem perfumed with a delightful spirit of literature distilled from a long and loving acquaintance with books, and filling the soul like the breath of Nature herself. It is all very literary: the gladiators before Cæsar, Dante, Priam, Hector, the learned clerk of the mediæval legend, Cato, Sophocles, Goethe, Chaucer, these are the shapes that come and go upon the imagination, moving, warning, consoling, inciting; for there is this difference between Longfellow's learning and that of others, that it makes you feel constantly the intimate relation of literature and life; it is not a tribunal before which you tremble for your ignorance, not an order with which he decorates himself and humbles you, not the badge of his separation but of his union with you. In those poems of places which he calls Birds of Passage it is the same gracious companionship which charms. "You remember Cadenabbia," he seems to say; "you slept at Monte Cassino; you noticed that old monk at Amalfi?" and he makes us believe him. "Yes, yes," we are well ready to answer, "it was I, I was there; I am there now, for all I never was in Italy save in this verse of yours." Graciousness—that is the word for this book, in all its phases; perhaps it is the best word that one could find for the poet's spirit in all his work.

It is not his contemporaneity that makes one feel this; but how will it be hereafter about that keen pleasure we take in some turn of phrase, some image, some touch, some movement of his, simply because it is like him? Is this a thing that can last? Will his readers of another generation rejoice for our reasons in the pensive optimism of the sonnet called A Shadow, or the solemn march of the poem on Charles Sumner, or the figure—

> "The great design unfinished lies,
>   Our lives are incomplete.
>
> But in the dark unknown
> Perfect their circles seem,
> Even as a bridge's arch of stone
>   Is rounded in the stream"?

If not, then a joy dies with us, and we are in that degree sorry for the fine fellows to come after us.

[*Atlantic Monthly*, January 1876]

56

[Browning's Formless Melodrama]

It may not be Mr. Browning's intention that we should earn our poetry, like our bread, by the sweat of our brows, but there really seems to be some such curse denounced against his readers, which the lapse of time does not soften. We were about to say that Mr. Browning goes from bad to worse, but we remember how much harder to read some parts of the Ring and the Book were than The Inn Album;[1] we remember Fifine at the Fair, unreadable; we remember the Red Cotton Night-Cap Country and its outer darkness; and— no, we cannot say that Mr. Browning goes from bad to worse in want of intelligibility. You can get at the whole story of The Inn Album if you will try hard enough and long enough. As to special passages and expressions, that is another thing; and as to the whole, it is not at all certain that it is worth while. But this is a matter of opinion which we willingly leave to each reader to settle after he has taken breath from the violent gymnastics of its perusal. Doubtless there are those who will feel paid for their pains, and we would be far from infecting such satisfied souls with our discontent. But they will own, we think, that the story is exceedingly disagreeable, and that the poet finally shirks his responsibility to the reader, and leaves him with a series of inconclusive and clumsily contrived situations in his mind, rather than an effect of dramatic unity. We have, to begin with, those old acquaintance, the two men who game till dawn, and rise and let the morning light in upon the fact that one owes the other ten thousand pounds. The characters are rather interesting: one is a high-souled, rich, good young plebeian; the other is a middle-aged brilliant aristocrat, *roué* and gambler, whom the young fellow worships for his intellectual superiority, and whom he strives to make accept forgiveness of the ten thousand pounds which, contrary to all expectation, he has just won of him. They have come down together to the country inn where the album is,—it serves to give a title to the poem and is otherwise mechanically employed,—and the young man is to see that morning his cousin, to whom he has been languidly making love for some time, and get her final yes or no as to their marriage. While he walks with his friend to the station where the latter is to take the train, he asks him why his life, which might be so triumphant in Parliament and elsewhere, is so aimless, and learns

---

[1] *The Inn Album.* By Robert Browning. Boston: J. R. Osgood & Co. 1876.

from him, in much darkling parenthesis, that it is because some years before he betrayed a beautiful girl, who then refused what he supposed the reparation of a marriage, and went off and married a country curate—where, he does n't know; but some day, he feels sure, they shall meet, and in the mean time her hate blasts his life. Then the young man tells how he too met and loved a beautiful girl, who refused him in mysterious terms, and whose memory makes him quite indifferent whether his cousin shall say yes or no to him, presently. They loiter in their talk, and lose the train, and then the old adventurer must go back to the inn where the album is, and wait while the young man goes to see his cousin at her house near by. The young lady, however, has in the mean while gone to the inn to meet—whom but the curate's wife?—her very dear and adored friend, who has this once consented—for the convenience of Mr. Browning's poem—to leave the deep retirement in which she lives, and come to the inn to see her young friend and advise with her on the subject of her meditated marriage. They discuss the matter with Mr. Browning's well-known parsimony of the definite and indefinite article, but as luck will have it the young lady has run away to say yes to her lover just at the moment when the gambler-roué-aristocrat (nobody is named in the poem) arrives; and he meets face to face the woman whom he had injured past all matrimony. The scene that then ensues is very fine and strong; his remorse and self-abasement, and her implacable scorn, and then his real falseness and baseness appearing fully, are very powerfully expressed. They are expressed apparently in the speech of the different persons, but in fact it is always one person who speaks, namely, the poet. The women are in no wise distinguished from the men by anything feminine in their phrase in this story, as they are in real life and real drama, and no one is characterized by any mental or other peculiarity not plainly attributive; they are the creatures of Mr. Browning, who has not been able to deny himself the indulgence of making them act and speak from his occasions rather than theirs. While he is making these two talk at each other in the potent fashion he undoubtedly does, the young man returns, and, bursting in upon them, perceives in her no other than the woman whom he had loved in vain. He suspects a plot between them to hoodwink him, and not only get the lord free of his debt of ten thousand pounds, but make his creditor bleed further in the debtor's behalf, and he instantly declares his thought. But his error soon appears to him, and he sides with the woman in what follows. The inn album is lugged in from time to time, and one and another writes in it—unnecessarily, except that having got an inn and an album one must do something with them. It is practicable also in this curious transaction for the lord to get the lady to go out of the room on purpose to let him vilify her to the young man, but in turn he has already handsomely written something in the album that altogether damns himself. It all ends by the young man's shooting him dead in her behalf, and by her taking thereupon some "soon-spreading gear" of which she dies instantly. While the young man stands contemplating this *dénouement*, the voice of the young girl singing is heard, as she comes to rejoin her friend and find her cousin. But before she enters, the curtain falls—very luckily for the poet, who has things quite his own way throughout, and at the end, by this simple device of the descending curtain, is able to leave the reader with the distracted lovers on his hands, the dead to be somehow got rid of, and the young man to be tried and somehow acquitted for the homicide.

The story is not, of course, so hideous as that of the Red Cotton Night-Cap Country, but it is not far from as hideous, and one feels, in looking back over it, like asking for what reason the poet has subjected him to such an experience. There was a time when the answer, "For art's sake," would have sufficed, but this comprehensive reply is no longer sufficient, especially in a case where the art is not very good. It was certainly worth while to consider the mood and mind of a woman who, having given all to a man, finds him too false and too hateful even to be made that sort of pitiable refuge from society and himself which her seducer becomes by marriage with her. Such a marriage, which is supposed to "make her an honest woman," is really only an added desecration and infamy, and, if it were possible, society should honor her for refusing it. But that is not possible now, and probably never will be. The wronged woman must therefore hope to right herself only in her own eyes and in those of divine justice, and she must be a woman of extraordinary character and courage who will resolve to forego the defense of marriage even with a man who has proved himself unworthy of her. Such an heroic creature Mr. Browning supposes, and the strength, the whole essence, of his poem lies in confronting her, after years, with her betrayer, who has never, perhaps, been able to understand why she should have foregone the reparation offered her. In this encounter you have one of the most highly dramatic situations, and it is a thousand pities that Mr. Browning could not have contented himself with studying and portraying it, and left out all those cloudy impertinences that go before and after it in his poem. Almost nothing else is well done: though his work can never have a vulgar air, still it is not well done. The machinery is, as we have said, really clumsy, and the character and the expression of character, apart from this great encounter, are hardly worth considering. "This bard's a Browning; he neglects the form," he says somewhere in the course of the poem. Well, we think this a pity, whether it happens through willfulness or not, and we would earnestly urge that bard, whoever he is, to drop being a Browning, so far as neglect of the form goes. The form is helpless by itself, yet nothing but the void exists without it, and, highly scorn it as he will, Mr. Browning himself is never a poet save when he attends to it. Our own Mr. Walt Whitman is a poet who has carried neglect of the form to its logical conclusions, and has arrived at a sort of literary resemblance to all out-doors, and is much such a poet as a summer morning is, or an alarm of fire, or some unpleasant smell which he would personally prefer to prayer. Mr. Browning, in The Inn Album, has not well observed the limits which the narrative poem, the novel, and the drama give themselves, and has willfully striven to weave them all together, getting a texture, if any texture at all, which seems to combine the coarseness of all. Except in the conception of the main idea, the drama is too melodramatic; the action is all melodramatic. The prose novel in these days has been wrought by its masters to a fineness of characterization, method, and incident to which this story in verse can by no means pretend; and as a poem The Inn Album lacks the charm— the grace, the color, the music—which can alone justify the story-teller's departure from prose narration. It is, in short, a curiously willful piece of bad literary art, which its attempts to outlaw itself cannot render in any degree interesting, save for the first moment of surprise.

[*Atlantic Monthly*, March 1876]

57

[Mark Twain's Boys' Book]

Mr. Aldrich has studied the life of A Bad Boy as the pleasant reprobate led it in a quiet old New England town twenty-five or thirty years ago, where in spite of the natural outlawry of boyhood he was more or less part of a settled order of things, and was hemmed in, to some measure, by the traditions of an established civilization. Mr. Clemens, on the contrary, has taken the boy of the Southwest for the hero of his new book,[1] and has presented him with a fidelity to circumstance which loses no charm by being realistic in the highest degree, and which gives incomparably the best picture of life in that region as yet known to fiction. The town where Tom Sawyer was born and brought up is some such idle, shabby little Mississippi River town as Mr. Clemens has so well described in his piloting reminiscences, but Tom belongs to the better sort of people in it, and has been bred to fear God and dread the Sunday-school according to the strictest rite of the faiths that have characterized all the respectability of the West. His subjection in these respects does not so deeply affect his inherent tendencies but that he makes himself a beloved burden to the poor, tender-hearted old aunt who brings him up with his orphan brother and sister, and struggles vainly with his manifold sins, actual and imaginary. The limitations of his transgressions are nicely and artistically traced. He is mischievous, but not vicious; he is ready for almost any depredation that involves the danger and honor of adventure, but profanity he knows may provoke a thunderbolt upon the heart of the blasphemer, and he almost never swears; he resorts to any stratagem to keep out of school, but he is not a downright liar, except upon terms of after shame and remorse that make his falsehood bitter to him. He is cruel, as all children are, but chiefly because he is ignorant; he is not mean, but there are very definite bounds to his generosity; and his courage is the Indian sort, full of prudence and mindful of retreat as one of the conditions of prolonged hostilities. In a word, he is a boy, and merely and exactly an ordinary boy on the moral side. What makes him delightful to the reader is that on the imaginative side he is very much more, and though every boy has wild and fantastic dreams, this boy cannot rest till he has somehow realized them. Till he has actually run off with two other boys in the character of buccaneer, and lived for a week on an

---

[1] *The Adventures of Tom Sawyer*. By Mark Twain. Hartford: American Publishing Co. 1876.

island in the Mississippi, he has lived in vain; and this passage is but the prelude to more thrilling adventures, in which he finds hidden treasures, traces the bandits to their cave, and is himself lost in its recesses. The local material and the incidents with which his career is worked up are excellent, and throughout there is scrupulous regard for the boy's point of view in reference to his surroundings and himself, which shows how rapidly Mr. Clemens has grown as an artist. We do not remember anything in which this propriety is violated, and its preservation adds immensely to the grown-up reader's satisfaction in the amusing and exciting story. There is a boy's love-affair, but it is never treated otherwise than as a boy's love-affair. When the half-breed has murdered the young doctor, Tom and his friend, Huckleberry Finn, are really, in their boyish terror and superstition, going to let the poor old town-drunkard be hanged for the crime, till the terror of that becomes unendurable. The story is a wonderful study of the boy-mind, which inhabits a world quite distinct from that in which he is bodily present with his elders, and in this lies its great charm and its universality, for boy-nature, however human-nature varies, is the same everywhere.

The tale is very dramatically wrought, and the subordinate characters are treated with the same graphic force that sets Tom alive before us. The worth-less vagabond, Huck Finn, is entirely delightful throughout, and in his prom-ised reform his identity is respected: he will lead a decent life in order that he may one day be thought worthy to become a member of that gang of robbers which Tom is to organize. Tom's aunt is excellent, with her kind heart's sorrow and secret pride in Tom; and so is his sister Mary, one of those good girls who are born to usefulness and charity and forbearance and unvarying rectitude. Many village people and local notables are introduced in well-conceived character; the whole little town lives in the reader's sense, with its religiousness, its lawlessness, its droll social distinctions, its civilization quali-fied by its slave-holding, and its traditions of the wilder West which has passed away. The picture will be instructive to those who have fancied the whole Southwest a sort of vast Pike County, and have not conceived of a sober and serious and orderly contrast to the sort of life that has come to represent the Southwest in literature. Mr. William M. Baker gives a notion of this in his stories, and Mr. Clemens has again enforced the fact here, in a book full of entertaining character, and of the greatest artistic sincerity.

Tom Brown and Tom Bailey are, among boys in books, alone deserving to be named with Tom Sawyer.

[*Atlantic Monthly*, May 1876]

58

[Lowell's Complete Poetical Works]

WHOEVER has felt the stalwart strength, the broad movement, and the full, wholesome life of Mr. Lowell's poetry will receive a fresh and vigorous impression of these traits, as well as his more delicate qualities, from the volume in which his poems are now presented complete.[1] Such a reader will hardly fail, either, of making his reflections, as he meets the older and the newer friends in the book, upon the fact that here is a man who has himself been part of all that he has sung, not only in the sense in which all poets are so, but in the special way in which a robust, courageous, and positive personality identifies itself with the feelings and events of its time. Any political history of the years since the great moral revolt against slavery began to ennoble our politics would be incomplete without notice of the share taken by literature in the struggle, and we know not what author could so well stand for the self-righting national instinct in regard to it as Lowell. He is not one whom you class merely as antislavery; he is not partisan or sectarian; he is humane, and too full of the clear light of humor to be humanitarian. Not scorning the wrong too fiercely to remember that there are men in it, he has never, on the other hand, sentimentalized political sinners, and his blows were delivered from a hand that was kinder to the oppressed than to the oppressors. This volume witnesses how strong and many they were both when he spoke for himself and when he let the true New England heart speak in the homely New England tongue for him; and here, too, you see perhaps more clearly than before how in the thick of the strife he was inventing types of Cervantean character, adding to poetry a new strain, and creating in literature an American kind. As you go through the book, you perceive with an increasing sense how this poet has always been and is *ours*. When you come to the war-poems—that mighty group beginning with The Washers of the Shroud and ending with the Commemorative Ode and the last of the Biglow Papers—you see that they represent the literature of the war. Other things remain, too, beautiful, touching, and grand, but without these the war would have no literature which could stand monumentally distinct and solid. In the contemplative poems which he has

[1] *The Poetical Works of James Russell Lowell.* Household Edition. Boston: J. R. Osgood & Co. 1876.

printed since is almost the sole recognition which the misgivings of patriotism during the last six years have received in literature proper. We do not mean to go into any extended consideration of his poetry here; we have been noting a very obvious side of it, and as concerns art a superficial aspect. What treasures of sweetness, of tenderness, of wise humor and wise pathos underlie this, no one need be told. The characteristics of his poetry are now part of a cultivated American's literary consciousness. The wit that always championed the wronged weak—not the merely weak—against the strong, the sense of beauty so high and fine as scarcely to have left the verse sensuous enough, the keen passion for Nature and the intimate knowledge of all her moods, the music native and fresh as the rhythms of his own June, the imagery drawn fragrant and living from the familiar fields and skies, the clear and joyous inspirations,—one knows these as one knows the strong thought that drives dangerously near the borders of prose, the hard-packed metaphors pushed one upon another, the humor that sometimes escapes into fun, the lofty psalm that loses itself in the echoes of the sounding-board, the whole noble art which now and then too generously forgets that it is equally noble with truth and duty. The Biglow Papers, the poems of the war, the group of pieces represented by The Cathedral, the totally different group which we shall recall by Auf Wiedersehen, the still different strain of The Vision of Sir Launfal and its order, were sufficient witnesses of a many-sidedness in which the same genius was felt so potently that six lines of any one of the poems declared its authorship; yet the volume that sets them all compactly before us is rich in novel suggestion; and one somehow feels as never before how vast is the range of the poet's achievement, how great and many and various are the things he has done.

[*Atlantic Monthly*, January 1877]

59

[Sarah Orne Jewett's Sketches of Local Life]

THE gentle reader of this magazine cannot fail to have liked, for their very fresh and delicate quality, certain sketches of an old New England sea-port, which have from time to time appeared here during the last four years. The first was Shore House, and then there came Deephaven Cronies and Deephaven Excursions. These sketches, with many more studies of the same sort of life, as finely and faithfully done, are now collected into a pretty little book called Deephaven,[1] which must, we think, find favor with all who appreciate the simple treatment of the near-at-hand quaint and picturesque. No doubt some particular sea-port sat for Deephaven, but the picture is true to a whole class of old shore towns, in any one of which you might confidently look to find the Deephaven types. It is supposed that two young girls—whose young-girlhood charmingly perfumes the thought and observation of the whole book—are spending the summer at Deephaven, Miss Denis, the narrator, being the guest of her adored ideal, Miss Kate Lancaster, whose people have an ancestral house there; but their sojourn is only used as a background on which to paint the local life: the three or four aristocratic families, severally dwindled to three or four old maiden ladies; the numbers of ancient sea-captains cast ashore by the decaying traffic; the queer sailor and fisher folk; the widow and old-wife gossips of the place, and some of the people of the neighboring country. These are all touched with a hand that holds itself far from every trick of exaggeration, and that subtly delights in the very tint and form of reality; we could not express too strongly the sense of conscientious fidelity which the art of the book gives, while over the whole is cast a light of the sweetest and gentlest humor, and of a sympathy as tender as it is intelligent. Danny is one of the best of the sketches; and another is The Circus at Denby, which perhaps shows better than any other the play of the author's observation and fancy, with its glancing lights of fun and pathos. A sombre and touching study is that of the sad, simple life so compassionately depicted in In Shadow, after which the reader must turn to the brisk vigor and quaintness of Mrs. Bonny. Bits of New England landscape and characteristic marine effects scattered

---

[1] *Deephaven*. By Sarah O. Jewett. Boston: J. R. Osgood & Co. 1877.

throughout these studies of life vividly localize them, and the talk of the people is rendered with a delicious fidelity.

In fact, Miss Jewett here gives proof of such powers of observation and characterization as we hope will some day be turned to the advantage of all of us in fiction. Meanwhile we are very glad of these studies, so refined, so simple, so exquisitely imbued with a true feeling for the ideal within the real.

[*Atlantic Monthly*, June 1877]

60

[J. J. Piatt: A Poet of Genuine Promise]

In the two volumes, Western Windows and The Lost Farm,[1] Messrs. Osgood
& Co. present to the public all that is best in the work of a genuine and very
original poet; and we know of no two books of recent verse that we could
more heartily urge upon the buyers of holiday gifts. The quality and value of
Mr. Piatt's work have already been discussed in these pages, and we shall not
now enter upon any extended criticism. But we have to say that a fresh
examination of his poems in the present collection leaves us disposed to
reaffirm with increased emphasis all that we have ever said in their praise. He
is a poet whose charm is often too subtle for instant perception, and the very
simplicity of his expression sometimes bewilders the sophisticated literary
sense; but his poetry has that element of growth in it that is sure of a future.
In material and in form it is so distinctly individual that almost any stanza—
we were going to say any line—of his books will declare its authorship; no
poetry of our time has a more proper or more recognizable atmosphere.
Something very wild and sweet, like the scent of dusky woodland depths or
the breath of clover overrunning the site of fallen homes or the track of
deserted highways, is its perfume; its tender light is the clear, pensive
radiance of autumnal eves. So much of it deals with themes which are
Western in their physical aspects that a hasty criticism might content itself
with recognizing their local truth; but we are not disposed to resign Mr. Piatt
to the section with whose color and life he has done so wisely to tinge and
vitalize his rhyme. A man is cosmopolitan only by being first patriotic, and
Mr. Piatt is broadly American because he is so thoroughly Western; he is true
to human experience everywhere, because he is true to what he has himself
known and felt in the locality where he was born. It is the poet's duty and
privilege to divine the universal in the simple and common things; and the
soft pathos of these poems, which touch with transfiguring loveliness the past
of the Western pioneers and farmers, appeals to all hearts. The farm
devoured by the growing city; the old well, secret and clear beneath its curb
choked with stones and brambles; the chimney tottering, gaunt and lonely,
above the empty cellar of the vanished log-cabin; the deserted tavern beside

---

[1] *Western Windows, and other Poems. Landmarks: The Lost Farm and other Poems.* By J. J. Piatt.
Boston: J. R. Osgood & Co. 1877.

the forsaken highway,—these are symbols of the homely past which is dear to the whole human race, and which in various symbols stirs always the same fond and piercing regret. The West may well be proud of her poet's fealty, but he belongs to us all in moods which come to us all. Not that Mr. Piatt is merely the poet of these moods. His range is as great in feeling, if not in theme, as that of most of his contemporaries, and his work abounds in lines that reveal the thinker as well as the dreamer. But there is undeniably—and fortunately—the idyllic and dreamful tendency in him, and this makes him a poet. Examine certain of his airiest fancies,—butterflies that seemed to toss hither and thither in an air of intellectual caprice,—and you find them flowers of strong and fruitful stem, fast rooted in the soil of experience. His dreams, however mystical, have their meaning; they prophesy and warn and console. Wherever he touches matters of fact and knowledge, as in his poems about the war, it is with the transfiguring touch of the poet, but also the warm and vigorous grasp of a man. His pensiveness is not morbid; his regret is impersonal, universal in its sense, however intimate its source; and his sympathy with nature is often as joyous and sound as Wordsworth's. Here is a sonnet of his which we have always liked for its rich vitality and hearty pleasure in the wholesome gladness of the earth:—

SEPTEMBER.

All things are full of life this autumn morn;
The hills seem growing under silver cloud;
A fresher spirit in Nature's breast is born;
The woodlands are blowing lustily and loud;
The crows fly, cawing, among the flying leaves;
On sunward-lifted branches struts the jay;
The fluttering brooklet, quick and bright, receives
Bright frosty silverings slow from ledges gray
Of rock in buoyant sunshine glittering out;
Cold apples drop through orchards mellowing;
'Neath forest-eaves quick squirrels laugh and shout;
Farms answer farms as through bright morns of Spring,
And joy, with dancing pulses full and strong,
Joy, everywhere, goes Maying with a song!

This is like Wordsworth in the way in which one poet may be like another without ceasing to be entirely himself. In almost all respects we think Mr. Piatt shows less than any other poet of his generation the influence of his elders. His art, his technique is singularly his own.

We are tempted to quote another of Mr. Piatt's sonnets, which we have always admired:—

TRAVELERS.

We may not stand content: it is our part

To drag slow footsteps after the far sight,
The long endeavor following up the bright
Quick aspiration; there is ceaseless smart
Feeling but cold-hand surety for warm heart
Of all desire; no man may say at night
His goal is reach'd; the hunger for the light
Moves with the star; our thirst will not depart,
Howe'er we drink. 'T is what before us goes
Keeps us aweary, will not let us lay
Our heads in dreamland, though the enchanted palm
Rise from our desert, though the fountain grows
Up in our path, with slumber's flowering balm:
The soul is o'er the horizon far away.

In the lyrical pieces the reader who recurs to them again and again, as we do, will find a peculiar and alluring music; and in poems which have to do with character, he will feel not less the touch of genius. The Mower in Ohio and Riding to Vote are studies as diverse as they are strong and true. Few things are more affecting than the former, more delicately, more vividly suggestive. Mr. Piatt is no mere colorist; while his diction does not lack richness, it is rather refined than opulent; and of his art generally it may be said that you have the sense of something done rather than of something being done; he values your sympathy rather than your surprise. Pure in thought as in ideal, his verse has the charm of the best in its remoteness from all that may be indicated as Swinburnian; and we cannot but believe that a wider and wider appreciation awaits his work, which, not to our credit, has been more cordially praised by English than American criticism hitherto.

[*Atlantic Monthly*, January 1878]

61

[Henry James's Essays on French Authors]

IF novelists and poets are not the best critics of their art, they are often the most suggestive commentators upon it; and when they have the skill to formulate and weave together their opinions they give us something rather better than mere criticism. Readers of Mr. Henry James, Jr., were for some time, and a few of them may still be, in doubt whether he is more a novelist than critic; but we think his recent volume of essays[1] may go a good way towards fixing the opinion that his peculiar attractiveness in this line of writing is due in great measure to the fact that he is himself a creative artist. His reviews of other writers are not precisely criticism, but they possess a pleasant flavor of criticism, agreeably diffused through a mass of sympathetic and often keenly analytical impressions. It is saying a great deal when we admit that he reminds us more of Sainte-Beuve than any other English writer; but he is more a *causeur* than the author of the famous Causeries, and less a critic in the systematic sense. We hardly know how we can fully illustrate our meaning except by more references and quotations than it is convenient to make here. But let the reader turn to the splendid chapter on Balzac, who has never before received so abundant and interesting a showing, within similar compass, as at Mr. James's hands. In this there are to be found most of the interesting facts of Balzac's life grouped with good judgment, a sketchy view of the character of his works, and a great many vivid statements of the impressions produced by them. But we can imagine that to a person who had read nothing of Balzac the article would have an exasperating inconclusiveness. It is a mixture of the frankest admiration and (to use Mr. James's own word) of brutal snubbing, which continues to the very last page. The one unqualified statement—and that, by the way, is a real gain to one's stock of well-defined perceptions—is that Balzac's great characteristic was his "sense of this present terrestrial life, which has never been surpassed, and in which his genius overshadowed everything else." For the rest, we are given to understand that his greatest merits were his greatest faults; that his novels are ponderous and shapeless, yet have more composition and more grasp on the reader's attention than any others, etc. "He believed that he was about as creative as the Deity, and that if mankind

---

[1] *French Poets and Novelists.* By Henry James, Jr. London: Macmillan & Co. 1878.

and human history were swept away the Comédie Humaine would be a perfectly adequate substitute for them," is the writer's witty statement of the degree of his conceit; and he quotes Taine, approvingly, as saying that after Shakespeare Balzac is our great magazine of documents on human nature; yet this he partially retracts, again, by saying that when Shakespeare is suggested we feel rather Balzac's differences from him. The French novelist's atmosphere, we are told, is musty, limited, artificial. In the next sentence, however, Mr. James assures us that, notwithstanding this "artificial" atmosphere, Balzac is to be taken, like Shakespeare, as a final authority on human nature. Then again he lowers him a peg by saying that he lacked "that slight but needful thing,—charm." "But our last word about him is that he had incomparable power." The writer himself seems to feel, in this closing sentence, that he has given a somewhat too paradoxical summary. The same difficulty could be raised with all the other essays in this collection, excepting the one on Tourguéneff, which comes near being a masterpiece of criticism, and perhaps ought to be decidedly rated as such. In general, there is a want of some positive or negative result clearly enunciated; and the presence of such results is what, to our mind, distinguishes the systematic critic like Sainte-Beuve or Matthew Arnold from the highly suggestive, charming talker like Mr. James.

If we are speaking of criticism, the question is whether we are to approach as nearly as possible to an equation of conflicting views, or whether we are to work out a problem to some conclusion on one side or the other. As a matter of definition we are inclined to say that pure criticism has for its aim the latter task. In the case of Balzac, for example, there is a wonderful stimulus and surprise in the obvious inadequacy and disrelish with which Sainte-Beuve treats him. The very narrowness of his judgment has a value. Mr. James may say that he does not write either for readers who simply want information about French authors, or for those who prefer opinions that cut only one way; and that he cultivates breadth, of set purpose. It is not necessary, however, to be narrow in taking a side: there are critics who show the finest comprehension of all the aspects of a genius, yet on the whole advocate a certain view with satisfactory unity and consecutiveness. We find fault with Mr. James's attitude, judged as a critic, because it implies a certain nervousness that if he curtails his contradictory impressions he may not appear liberal enough. With less extreme expression and more art, liberality need not fear to be overlooked. A fault connected with this is the tone of patronage which the writer is led to take towards the larger minds among those which he discusses; and possibly attributable to the same source is a not altogether pleasant jocularity in the treatment of those dubious relations between men and women which the themes selected naturally involve.

But we have said that a creative artist discoursing on the works of other creators can be more entertaining than the mere critic; and Mr. James is irresistible in the ease and brilliancy of his style, and the felicity with which he calls our attention to the qualities most to be admired in his subjects and

traces some of the reasons why they are admirable. Next to the Tourguéneff
we like best the paper on De Musset, which differs from all the others in
having to some extent the tone of advocacy, and pushing its view of the poet
with a thoroughly enjoyable ardor. That on Mérimée's Letters is almost too
slight to keep company with the rest, and we do not know how to excuse, in
the essay on the Théatre Français, the haste with which Mlle. Sarah Bernhard
is passed by. Even with the style, too, one is occasionally dissatisfied, owing to
some obscurity which seems to be due to a disinclination to correct. It is
regrettable that we have not space to pay the homage of quotation to several
of the searching, the humorous, the sympathetic things which Mr. James
scatters copiously over his pages; and we cannot deny ourselves, in closing,
the privilege of reproducing here, if only in tribute to our own appreciative-
ness, these fragments from the shrewd and trenchant essay on Baudelaire.
"A good way to embrace Baudelaire at a glance is to say that he was in his
treatment of evil exactly what Hawthorne was not,—Hawthorne, who felt the
thing at its source, deep in the human consciousness. Baudelaire's infinitely
slighter genius apart, he was a sort of Hawthorne reversed." "The crudity of
sentiment of the advocates of 'art for art' is often a striking example of the
fact that a great deal of what is called culture may fail to dissipate a well-
seated provincialism of spirit. They talk of morality as Miss Edgeworth's in-
fantine heroes and heroines talk of 'physic' . . . It is in reality simply a part of
the essential richness of inspiration,—it has nothing to do with the artistic
process, and it has everything to do with the artistic effect." That is almost
the best thing in this superior book. The point has hardly been put with so
much grasp and cleverness before.

[*Atlantic Monthly*, July 1878]

62

[W. H. Bishop's Blending of Romance and Novel]

Mr. Bishop calls his artistic and pleasing story a romance;[1] and so it is as to motive, but the characters and the incidents—all except the shattering of the mirror in the Palazzo Grazzini—are the characters and the incidents of a novel. The story is, in fact, a rarely successful blending of the two kinds, and is itself of a kind of which there are few examples. We have always thought the motive uncommonly good, and we are glad to testify here to our sense of the poetic insight with which it is managed. Our readers ought all to remember it: that notion of two men plotting a crime for which one voluntarily suffers the whole legal penalty, and transmits to his son the shame and misery of his inexpiable wrong, while the other goes free. Nothing can be better than the study of Detmold's consciousness under the agony of his inherited disgrace, which he hides from every one in a distant city, and under which he is now abjectly hopeless of any good in life, and now recklessly defiant and resolute to seize love and happiness in spite of his unjust degradation. Nor is the father less strikingly portrayed. When he comes out of prison he lives down his crime in the very place where it was committed, and wins the respect, the affection, all but the silence, of his fellow-townsmen, who, after exhausting every other sensation possible from his history, continue to tell it to strangers for the sake of enjoying their surprise, and out of a sort of local pride in a man who could so survive his disastrous past. These are points, as the reader perceives, not only very subtle, but very strong. The situation is powerfully conceived, and it is pictured with a reserve, a cool mastery, that in the end is profoundly affecting. There can be no hope for Detmold except in the identification of Mr. Starfield's adoptive daughter with the daughter of his father's partner in guilt, which duly happens after he has followed her to Europe for love, and their friendship has deepened throughout those charming scenes in Verona. This conclusion is strictly and rightly in accordance with the romantic idea of the plot,—the romance being, like the poem, at once more elevated and a little more mechanical than the novel.

The story is well balanced, and is most conscientiously wrought out to the end with care that never falters and never visibly becomes anxiety. The inter-

---

[1] *Detmold: A Romance.* By W. H. Bishop. Boston: Houghton, Osgood & Co. 1879.

est culminates with the betrayal of Detmold's secret to Alice at the ball in
Verona. She does not know her own relation to it, but one feels in one's
heart that she is related to it, and that they will marry before the end of the
book. Yet if one did not read to the end, he would lose much of the best
work. There are everywhere very penetrating touches,—but few better than
the final allusions to Detmold's father, and the young man's remorse, when
his father is dead, that he should have striven so hard and so long to dissoci-
ate himself from a man whom Alice justly "looked upon as cast in a heroic
mold." If Mr. Bishop wishes a hint for another story, let him enlarge the
sketch of the elder Detmold to the dimensions of a romance. The character
here so firmly outlined would bear elaboration, and the story is a pathetic
and noble one.

Alice Starfield, the heroine of the present romance, has charm,—that
first essential of a heroine. The thought of her lingers in the mind like a
delicate perfume, and there is a distinct sense of her maidenliness which we
hardly know how the author has contrived to impart. The slow ripening of
her friendship for Detmold into love, her gentle reluctance to be other than
she is, her sort of bewilderment at his passion,—there is something exquisitely innocent and lovely in all this; and there is something fine in the instant
fusion of her regard into a warmer feeling when she believes Detmold slan-
dered. The love-making throughout the book is charming, and the talk between the lovers is real lovers' talk,—not an easy kind of talk to keep going.
Let the reader turn to that chapter where Detmold and Alice are sketching at
the Museo Civico; or to that extremely pretty episode called The Idyl of an
Italian Hillside. At the Museo the talk is light, gay, and on her side unconscious; on the hillside, where they lounge on the grass, it deepens to tenderness and trembles to confession. It is something uncommonly nice where
Detmold is suffered to engrave "an imaginary monogram with a pencil upon
the stone of a turquoise ring she wore," and there are constantly things to
commend them to the reader's recognition as veritable young people, who
are none the worse for being "silly sooth." At the Museo, "he placed himself
at a little distance, for her to make a rapid sketch of his head and shoulders
in a certain position. 'This is not to be regarded as a finished likeness, you
know,' said she, regarding him quizzically, as the work drew to a close. 'You
are not particular about having the nose in, are you?' 'Not at all,—don't
mention it. You might omit the eyes and mouth if it is any object.' 'I have
them in already. They are not so hard to do as noses!' Then she showed him a
remote resemblance to himself, much flattered." Somehow, this young lady's
presence is a tangible affair to the reader; she is not minutely painted, but
sketched with an occasional minuteness which is very effective. At other
times, Mr. Bishop knows how to employ this art, and, still better, how to
spare it. Pages of description could not say so much as the simple phrase,
"Detmold turned feebly to depart," in the tragic moment when Castelbarco
has betrayed his secret to Alice.

We must pay our tribute to the literary workmanship throughout the book. It is fine without being superfine, and it is delicate without weakness. The subordinate persons are exceedingly well done, especially Hyson; Mr. Starfield, intelligent American business man, is very good, and so is Signor Niccolo, the Italian farmer, whose farm is a hitherto unpainted bit of real value. But Castelbarco strikes us as rather conventional; he is the weakness of a book which has few weak points and many strong ones. We shall be disappointed if its excellent quality, its very distinct and characteristic flavor, is not generally appreciated. It has humor, too, of a fresh and original sort, which agreeably relieves the prevailingly sombre cast of the story. It is in fine a finished achievement of a high sort in fiction, and it gives us the right to expect other good things from Mr. Bishop.

[*Atlantic Monthly*, August 1879]

63

[Trollope's Lucubrations on Thackeray]

READING Mr. Anthony Trollope's essay on Thackeray,[1] one is at a loss to know just what portion of the British public is addressed in Mr. Morley's biographies of English Men of Letters. Is it young people, or persons of feeble mind? Or is the average reader in England to be amused or instructed by this sort of thing? With all one's American willingness to think ill of Englishmen, one hopes not. Apparently, however, there is a British public which may be expected to sympathize with Mr. Trollope's feeling that a man like Mr. Trollope may fitly talk down on a man like Thackeray. Or is this only appearance, and is Mr. Trollope singular in his impression? Or is it, after all, the inevitable attitude of a man who is in some sort alive toward a man who is in some sort dead? Whatever it is, the patronage begins almost at the beginning, and is shared pretty equally between the reader and the subject of what Mr. Trollope would call his lucubrations. But the introductory biographical sketch is not so offensive as the special criticism of Thackeray's work with which the book is filled out. Mr. Trollope has not yet struck his triumphant note. This is first heard toward the end of the chapter, where he palliates while he is obliged to condemn the spirit and the language in which Thackeray spoke of the Four Georges. "If we wish ourselves to be high," he says with perfect gravity, "we should treat that which is over us as high. And this should not depend altogether on personal character, though we know— as we have reason to know—how much may be added to the firmness of the feeling by personal merit." Is it possible? The same liberal casuist, however, condones the fault of a brother who happened to be made differently from himself. "Thackeray's loyalty was no doubt true enough, but was mixed with little of reverence. *He was one who revered modesty and innocence rather than power*, against which he had, in the bottom of his heart, something of republican tendency. His learning was no doubt of the more manly kind." After this, no one will be surprised to learn that Mr. Trollope believes Thackeray was morbidly sensitive to the existence of snobbishness, and that, in sum, snobbishness is not so bad. A curious proof of the thickness of the medium through which Mr. Trollope considers Thackeray is his entire

[1] *Thackeray*. By Anthony Trollope. [English Men of Letters. Edited by John Morley.] New York: Harper and Brothers. 1879.

confusion of mind upon this point. He finds, after going over the whole matter, that if you do not lie and steal you are not a snob; whereas it was the very essence of Thackeray's effort to show that you might have none of the vices and yet be a snob, if you had not social courage,—if you "meanly admired mean things," if, in other words, you "wished to be high by treating that which was over you as high." Mr. Trollope thinks the snob papers were carried too far, and that their author would better have divided snobs into fewer classes. This may be, but one wishes that he were yet alive to give us a subdivision devoted to the biographical snob.

Generally speaking, Mr. Trollope's discussion of Thackeray's work is as entirely idle and valueless a disquisition as any we know. It does not throw a ray of new light upon Thackeray's methods or motives; it does not analyze acutely; it is without insight. He has indeed the luck to say that Barry Lyndon is not surpassed "in imagination, language, construction, and general literary capacity," by anything else the author did; but he thinks it wonderful that the author should so tell the supposed autobiographer's story as to appear to be altogether on the hero's side. This Mr. Trollope cannot understand,—perhaps because it is a stroke of genius; but he is good enough to assure his readers that "no one will be tempted to undertake the life of a *chevalier d'industrie* by reading the book, or be made to think that cheating at cards is either an agreeable or a profitable profession." "Sir," asked his admirer of Mr. Wordsworth, "don't you think Milton was a great poet?" And Charles Lamb, whom Hunt was trying to suppress, called out from behind the door, "Let me feel his bumps! Let me feel his bumps!"

The commonness, the thumb-fingered awkwardness, of the criticism prevades the language and imagery of the book, and Mr. Trollope talks of "the literary pabulum given for our consumption;" of "the then and still owners of Punch;" of a "doctrine which will not hold water;" of Beatrix, who wished to rise in the world, and whose "beauty was the sword with which she must open her oyster." And Mr. Trollope keeps his family "skeleton," not in the closet, but "in the cupboard."

Mr. Trollope was simply unfit for the work to which he was appointed. When he does not speak of Thackeray he sometimes speaks very well, and there are certain passages referring to the office and responsibility of the modern novelist which we wish to quote for their truth and suggestiveness. They are not brilliant or graceful, but they are just, and they ought to be read:—

"I should be said to insist absurdly on the power of my own confraternity if I were to declare that the bulk of the young people in the upper and middle classes receive their moral teaching chiefly from the novels they read. Mothers would no doubt think of their own sweet teaching; fathers of the examples which they set; and schoolmasters of the excellence of their instructions. Happy is the country that has such mothers, fathers, and schoolmasters! But the novelist creeps in closer than the schoolmaster, closer than the father, closer almost than the mother. He is the chosen guide, the tutor whom the young pupil chooses for herself. . . . Shall he, then, to whom this close fellowship is allowed—this inner confidence—shall he not be careful what words he uses, and what thoughts he expresses, when he sits in council with his young friend? This, which it will certainly be his duty to consider with so much care, will be the matter of his work.''

[*Atlantic Monthly*, August 1879]

64

Dickens's Letters.

THE letters of Charles Dickens,[1] which Miss Hogarth and Miss Mary Dickens have lately given the public, are material which for one reason or another was not placed in the hands of the late Mr. John Forster for use in his biography of the novelist. Some of them are such as it is incredible a biographer should not have asked for,—even so autobiographical a biographer as Mr. Forster. They are what he would have wished to see, even if he did not wish to use them, but we are not at all sure that they would have lent much value to his work. They do not throw fresh light upon a character which we have learned to know in its energetic and egotistic hardness, upon a philosophy extraordinarily limited; upon the life so separately lived in its personal and its literary phases that the same man may be said to have carried on a double train of being. In most lives authorship reflects experience, or takes form and color from it; but Dickens's work after the wreck of his domestic happiness did not lose the charm that it had drawn from such happiness, and did not cease to portray it. His iron nerve was equal to this tremendous *tour de force*; but the sort of consciousness in which it resulted is matter for no analysis less subtle than George Eliot's or Hawthorne's, and is not pleasant to imagine. It seems to have resulted at least in an intensification of his disposition to centralize all things in himself. He was a man who did not arrive at a Copernican conception of the universe. The sun always rose on his right hand and set on his left, and for the rest employed its time in revolving about him. As he advanced in life his universe narrowed, till there was scarcely room in it for the sun to perform this necessary function without incommoding the central figure. His last letters from America are curious and pathetic witness of his self-absorption. No fable was too gross for his vanity. He wrote home to Miss Hogarth in the actual belief that people brought their beds and slept all night in the streets, that they might be up betimes to buy tickets to his readings, and he mistook the movement of newspaper gossip about him for an excitement stirring the country to its depths. Life in the United States appears from these letters to have been a struggle for three terrible months to see and hear Charles Dickens; and the

[1] *The Letters of Charles Dickens*. Edited by his Sister-in-Law and his eldest Daughter. In two volumes. New York: Charles Scribner's Sons. 1879.

sound of Mr. Dolby stamping thousands of tickets in the room above the
novelist's bed-chamber was a noise that rose above all public and private
clamor in a nation that was then settling the terms upon which a conquered
empire was to be readmitted to union and self-government. Twice he is sure
that half Boston will be out to see his agent walk a match; and he is
perpetually astonished that, though people turn and look after him, they do
not follow him up, or block his progress on the street. The letters are not
very discreetly edited, as regards America, and the boasted English
tenderness of the privacy of living persons has not been used. Those who had
the misfortune to be immediately connected with Dickens suffer most; they
are classed with his doorkeeper and his man-servant; but very few Americans
whom he mentions escape his patronage. He finds the country much
reformed, in respect to himself; and the nation at large seems to have made a
vast advance in not intruding upon him. But otherwise he did not find much
to surprise him. The tobacco-chewers and the newspapers keep it up as badly
as ever; and there are furnaces and stoves everywhere that discomfort him.
There is a disease, he tells us, known as the American catarrh; he has this
terribly, and he insists upon it a great deal.

But for observation of the country, or reflections upon it of the slightest
value, the reader will look in vain. Perhaps it was the professional habit of
exaggeration that had grown upon him; perhaps we did not deserve the exact
truth; but he puts even unimportant facts concerning us a little awry. Mr.
Staunton, as he calls the great secretary of war, he found remarkable as
knowing Dickens's novels better than Dickens himself; and he pronounces
upon the subtlety of his own insight by admiring the late President Johnson.
His letters from this country during his last visit are, in fine, chiefly a shout of
astonishment and exultation at the success of his readings. They are written
in the boisterously high spirits, tending to horseplay in the humorous passages, which characterize all the letters. He did not like us, and small blame
to him. We stood before him in the attitude of pirates offering a splendid
ovation to their victim, and he naturally found us ridiculous and contemptible. His purpose was to get all the money he could out of us; and, if we
would not legally grant him his rights in his property, and pay for the privilege of reading him, at least to make us pay for seeing and hearing him. He
did not have any hope of the international copyright, which we now fondly
trust is near; and he did not recognize the fact that all decent American
publishers now pay copyright to English authors, while American authors
seldom receive compensation from English publishers. He was not a philosopher, and it is probable that the loss of copyright colored his opinions of us
in all respects. He was not our friend during the war; and even after the war
he was sorry that England had not joined the "French usurper" in breaking
us up. A certain vulgarity of heart is shown in the terms in which he speaks of
the Eyre massacre of the blacks in Jamaica; but he shared this vulgarity with
another eminent paper-philanthropist, and it is probable that if they had

both lived he would have stood shoulder to shoulder with Canon Kingsley in the foremost ranks of the Jingoes.

The letters relating to his first visit to America are few and unimportant; but they are characterized by the same inability to philosophize,—by the same narrow horizon, shutting down ten feet away from an observer who saw superficial generalities with preternatural keenness within that limit; though even within that limit he did not see detail correctly, or was unable to report it correctly. His literary conscience was a matter of slow growth; the critical reader of his earlier books must see how willing he is to sacrifice truth to effect, and stage effect at that; but he cannot help seeing, too, that while Dickens clings, to the last, to certain conventionalities and mannerisms of his own, he grows more and more truly dramatic, and more and more true to life. In these letters, however, there is no growth, apparently, of judgment or feeling. They are a young man's letters in 1837, and a young man's letters in 1870; a young man always in high spirits, fluent, quick, restless, not deep nor wise. Considering that the half century of Dickens's literary life covered a period full of the most important events in the world's history; considering that he passed them in a great capital where he must daily have met famous and interesting people of every sort, it is prodigiously astonishing how devoid of generous interest they are. They relate almost wholly to himself, and not even to himself in an entertaining or significant way. They tell how he came and went, where he slept, and what he had for dinner. In the second volume they are intolerably full as to his readings and his amateur theatricals, and his audiences and his fellow performers. Unless his whole heart was in these things, they show very little of his intimate life. They are even more silent as to his literary art and method, and the reader of his books will get no light from his letters. A fair half of his work was such as the author of these letters might have produced, you say; but the other half seems beyond him. Perhaps no greater proof of his genius could be demanded than this fact, that his own work seems greater than he in any light which he or his friends have been able to throw upon him. Great genius he was and remains, and his genius will shine more and more as his personality becomes remote.

[*Atlantic Monthly*, February 1880]

65

James's Hawthorne.[1]

MR. James's book on Hawthorne, in Morley's English Men of Letters series, merits far closer examination and carefuller notice than we can give it here, alike for the interest of its subject, the peculiarity of its point of view, and the charm and distinction of its literature. An American author writing of an American author for an English public incurs risks with his fellow-countrymen which Mr. James must have faced, and is much more likely to possess the foreigner whom he addresses with a clear idea of our conditions than to please the civilization whose portrait is taken. Forty-six, fifty, sixty-four, are not dates so remote, nor are Salem and Concord societies so extinct, that the people of those periods and places can be safely described as provincial, not once, but a dozen times; and we foresee, without any very powerful prophetic lens, that Mr. James will be in some quarters promptly attainted of high treason. For ourselves, we will be content with saying that the provinciality strikes us as somewhat over-insisted upon, and that, speaking from the point of not being at all provincial ourselves, we think the epithet is sometimes mistaken. If it is not provincial for an Englishman to be English, or a Frenchman French, then it is not so for an American to be American; and if Hawthorne was "exquisitely provincial," one had better take one's chance of universality with him than with almost any Londoner or Parisian of his time. Provinciality, we understand it, is a thing of the mind or the soul; but if it is a thing of the experiences, then that is another matter, and there is no quarrel. Hawthorne undoubtedly saw less of the world in New England than one sees in Europe, but he was no cockney, as Europeans are apt to be.

At the same time we must not be thought to deny the value and delight-fulness of those chapters on Salem and Brook Farm and Concord. They are not very close in description, and the places seem deliciously divined rather than studied. But where they are used unjustly, there will doubtless be abundant defense; and if Salem or Brook Farm be mute, the welkin will probably respond to the cries of certain critics who lie in wait to make life sorrowful to any one dealing lightly with the memory of Thoreau or the presence of the

---

[1] *Hawthorne.* [Morley's English Men of Letters.] By Henry James, Jr. London: Macmillan & Co. New York: Harper and Brothers. 1880.

poet Channing. What will happen to a writer who says of the former that he was "worse than provincial, he was parochial," and of the latter that he resembled the former in "having produced literary compositions more esteemed by the few than by the many," we wait with the patience and security of a spectator at an *auto da fé*, to see. But even an unimbattled outsider may suggest that the essential large-mindedness of Concord, as expressed in literature, is not sufficiently recognized, although it is thoroughly felt. The treatment of the culture foible and of the colorless æsthetic joys, the attribution of "a great deal of Concord five and thirty years ago" to the remark of a visitor of Hawthorne that Margaret Fuller "had risen perceptibly into a higher state of being since their last meeting," are exquisite,—too exquisite, we fear, for the sense of most Englishmen, and not too fine only for the rarefied local consciousness which they may sting. Emerson is indeed devoutly and amply honored, and there is something particularly sweet and tender in the characterization of such surviving Brook Farmers as the author remembers to have met; but even in speaking of Emerson, Mr. James has the real misfortune to call his grand poem for the dedication of the monument to Concord Fight a "little hymn." It is little as Milton's sonnet on Shakespeare is little.

We think, too, that in his conscience against brag and *chauvinism* Mr. James puts too slight a value upon some of Hawthorne's work. It is not enough to say of a book so wholly unexampled and unrivaled as The Scarlet Letter that it was "the finest piece of imaginative writing put forth in" America; as if it had its parallel in any literature. When he comes to speak of the romances in detail, he repairs this defect of estimation in some degree; but here again his strictures seem somewhat mistaken. No one better than Mr. James knows the radical difference between a romance and a novel, but he speaks now of Hawthorne's novels, and now of his romances, throughout, as if the terms were convertible; whereas the romance and the novel are as distinct as the poem and the novel. Mr. James excepts to the people in The Scarlet Letter, because they are rather types than persons, rather conditions of the mind than characters; as if it were not almost precisely the business of the romance to deal with types and mental conditions. Hawthorne's fictions being always and essentially, in conception and performance, romances, and not novels, something of all Mr. James's special criticism is invalidated by the confusion which, for some reason not made clear, he permits himself. Nevertheless, his analysis of the several books and of the shorter tales is most interesting; and though we should ourselves place The Blithedale Romance before The House of the Seven Gables, and should rank it much higher than Mr. James seems to do, we find ourselves consenting oftener than dissenting as we read his judgments. An admirably clear and just piece of criticism, we think, is that in which he pronounces upon the slighter and cheaper *motif* of Septimius Felton. But here there are not grounds for final sentence; it is possible, if that book had received the author's last touches, it might have been, after all, a playful and gentle piece of irony rather than a tragedy.

What gives us entire satisfaction, however, is Mr. James's characterization, or illustration, of Hawthorne's own nature. He finds him an innocent, affectionate heart, extremely domestic, a life of definite, high purposes singularly unbaffled, and an "unperplexed intellect." The black problem of evil, with which his Puritan ancestors wrestled concretely, in groans and despair, and which darkens with its portentous shadow nearly everything that Hawthorne wrote, has become his literary material; or, in Mr. James's finer and more luminous phrase, he "transmutes this heavy moral burden into the very substance of the imagination." This strikes us as beautifully reasonable and true, and we will not cloud it with comment of ours. But satisfactorily as Mr. James declares Hawthorne's personality in large, we do not find him sufficient as to minor details and facts. His defect, or his error, appears oftenest in his discussion of the note-books, where he makes plain to himself the simple, domestic, democratic qualities in Hawthorne, and yet maintains that he sets down slight and little aspects of nature because his world is small and vacant. Hawthorne noted these because he loved them, and as a great painter, however full and vast his world is, continues to jot down whatever strikes him as picturesque and characteristic. The disposition to allege this inadequate reason comes partly from that confusion of the novelist's and the romancer's work of which we have spoken, and partly from a theory, boldly propounded, that it needs a long history and "a complex social machinery to set a writer in motion." Hawthorne himself shared, or seemed to share, this illusion, and wrote The Marble Faun, so inferior, with its foreign scene, to the New England romances, to prove the absurdity of it. As a romancer, the twelve years of boyhood which he spent in the wild solitudes of Maine were probably of greater advantage to him than if they had been passed at Eton and Oxford. At least, until some other civilization has produced a romantic genius at all comparable to his, we must believe this. After leaving out all those novelistic "properties," as sovereigns, courts, aristocracy, gentry, castles, cottages, cathedrals, abbeys, universities, museums, political class, Epsoms, and Ascots, by the absence of which Mr. James suggests our poverty to the English conception, we have the whole of human life remaining, and a social structure presenting the only fresh and novel opportunities left to fiction, opportunities manifold and inexhaustible. No man would have known less what to do with that dreary and worn-out paraphernalia than Hawthorne.

We can only speak of the excellent comment upon Hawthorne's Old Home, and the skillful and manly way in which Mr. James treats of that delicate subject to his English audience. Skillful and manly the whole book is,—a miracle of tact and of self-respect, which the author need not fear to trust to the best of either of his publics. There is nothing to regret in the attitude of the book; and its literature is always a high pleasure, scarcely marred by some evidences of hurry, and such *writerish* passages as that in which *sin* is spoken of as "this baleful substantive with its attendant adjective."

It is a delightful and excellent essay, refined and delicate in perception, generous in feeling, and a worthy study of the unique romancer whom its closing words present with justice so subtle and expression so rich:—

"He was a beautiful, natural, original genius, and his life had been singularly exempt from worldly preoccupations and vulgar efforts. It had been as pure, as simple, as unsophisticated, as his work. He had lived primarily in his domestic affections, which were of the tenderest kind; and then—without eagerness, without pretension, but with a great deal of quiet devotion—in his charming art. His work will remain; it is too original and exquisite to pass away; among the men of imagination he will always have his niche. No one has had just that vision of life, and no one has had a literary form that more successfully expressed his vision. He was not a moralist, and he was not simply a poet. The moralists are weightier, denser, richer, in a sense; the poets are more purely inconclusive and irresponsible. He combined in a singular degree the spontaneity of the imagination with a haunting care for moral problems. Man's conscience was his theme, but he saw it in the light of a creative fancy which added, out of its own substance, an interest, and, I may almost say, an importance."

[*Atlantic Monthly*, February 1880]

66

Mark Twain's New Book.[1]

IN the natural disgust of a creative mind for the following that vulgarizes and cheapens its work, Mr. Tennyson spoke in parable concerning his verse:

> "Most can raise the flower now,
>   For all have got the seed.
> And some are pretty enough,
>   And some are poor indeed;
> And now again the people
>   Call it but a weed."

But this bad effect is to the final loss of the rash critic rather than the poet, who necessarily survives imitation, and appeals to posterity as singly as if nobody had tried to ape him; while those who rejected him, along with his copyists, have meantime thrown away a great pleasure. Just at present some of us are in danger of doing ourselves a like damage. "Thieves from over the wall" have got the seed of a certain drollery, which sprouts and flourishes plentifully in every newspaper, until the thought of American Humor is becoming terrible; and sober-minded people are beginning to have serious question whether we are not in danger of degenerating into a nation of wits. But we ought to take courage from observing, as we may, that this plentiful crop of humor is not racy of the original soil; that in short the thieves from over the wall were not also able to steal Mr. Clemens's garden-plot. His humor springs from a certain intensity of common sense, a passionate love of justice, and a generous scorn of what is petty and mean; and it is these qualities which his "school" have not been able to convey. They have never been more conspicuous than in this last book of his, to which they may be said to give its sole coherence. It may be claiming more than a humorist could wish to assert that he is always in earnest; but this strikes us as the paradoxical charm of Mr. Clemens's best humor. Its wildest extravagance is the break and fling from a deep feeling, a wrath with some folly which disquiets him worse than other men, a personal hatred for some humbug or pretension that embitters him beyond anything but laughter. It must be because

---

[1] *A Tramp Abroad.* By Mark Twain (Samuel L. Clemens). Sold by subscription only. Hartford: American Publishing Company. 1880.

he is intolerably weary of the twaddle of pedestrianizing that he conceives the notion of a tramp through Europe, which he operates by means of express trains, steamboats, and private carriages, with the help of an agent and a courier; it is because he has a real loathing, otherwise inexpressible, for Alp-climbing, that he imagines an ascent of the Riffelberg, with "half a mile of men and mules" tied together by rope. One sees that affectations do not first strike him as ludicrous, merely, but as detestable. He laughs, certainly, at an abuse, at ill manners, at conceit, at cruelty, and you must laugh with him; but if you enter into the very spirit of his humor, you feel that if he could set these things right there would be very little laughing. At the bottom of his heart he has often the grimness of a reformer; his wit is turned by preference not upon human nature, not upon droll situations and things abstractly ludicrous, but upon matters that are out of joint, that are unfair or unnecessarily ignoble, and cry out to his love of justice for discipline. Much of the fun is at his own cost where he boldly attempts to grapple with some hoary abuse, and gets worsted by it, as in his verbal contest with the girl at the medicinal springs in Baden, who returns "that beggar's answer" of half Europe, "What you please," to his ten-times-repeated demand of "How much?" and gets the last word. But it is plain that if he had his way there would be a fixed price for those waters very suddenly, and without regard to the public amusement, or regret for lost opportunities of humorous writing.

It is not Mr. Clemens's business in Europe to find fault, or to contrast things there with things here, to the perpetual disadvantage of that continent; but sometimes he lets homesickness and his disillusion speak. This book has not the fresh frolicsomeness of the Innocents Abroad; it is Europe revisited, and seen through eyes saddened by much experience of *table d'hôte*, old masters, and traveling Americans,—whom, by the way, Mr. Clemens advises not to travel too long at a time in Europe, lest they lose national feeling and become traveled Americans. Nevertheless, if we have been saying anything about the book, or about the sources of Mr. Clemens's humor, to lead the reader to suppose that it is not immensely amusing, we have done it a great wrong. It is delicious, whether you open it at the sojourn in Heidelberg, or the voyage down the Neckar on a raft, or the mountaineering in Switzerland, or the excursion beyond Alps into Italy. The method is that discursive method which Mark Twain has led us to expect of him. The story of a man who had a claim against the United States government is not impertinent to the bridge across the river Reuss; the remembered tricks played upon a printer's devil in Missouri are the natural concomitants of a walk to Oppenau. The writer has always the unexpected at his command, in small things as well as great: the story of the raft journey on the Neckar is full of these surprises; it is wholly charming. If there is too much of anything, it is that ponderous and multitudinous ascent of the Riffelberg; there is probably too much of that, and we would rather have another appendix in its place. The appendices are all admirable; especially those on the German language and the German newspapers, which get no more sarcasm than they deserve.

One should not rely upon all statements of the narrative, but its spirit is the truth, and it honestly breathes American travel in Europe as a large minority of our forty millions know it. The material is inexhaustible in the mere Americans themselves, and they are rightful prey. Their effect upon Mr. Clemens has been to make him like them best at home; and no doubt most of them will agree with him that "to be condemned to live as the average European family lives would make life a pretty heavy burden to the average American family." This is the sober conclusion which he reaches at last, and it is unquestionable, like the vastly greater part of the conclusions at which he arrives throughout. His opinions are no longer the opinions of the Western American newly amused and disgusted at the European difference, but the Western American's impressions on being a second time confronted with things he has had time to think over. This is the serious undercurrent of the book, to which we find ourselves reverting from its obvious comicality. We have, indeed, so great an interest in Mr. Clemens's likes and dislikes, and so great respect for his preferences generally, that we are loath to let the book go to our readers without again wishing them to share these feelings. There is no danger that they will not laugh enough over it; that is an affair which will take care of itself; but there is a possibility that they may not think enough over it. Every account of European travel, or European life, by a writer who is worth reading for any reason, is something for our reflection and possible instruction; and in this delightful work of a man of most original and characteristic genius "the average American" will find much to enlighten as well as amuse him, much to comfort and stay him in such Americanism as is worth having, and nothing to flatter him in a mistaken national vanity or a stupid national prejudice.

[*Atlantic Monthly*, May 1880]

67

A New Observer.

It is hardly necessary to recall to the reader familiar with these pages that series of clear, penetrating studies of American life,[1] at once so dispassionate and so sympathetic, which began with the impressive paper giving its title to the articles in their collected form. Certain Dangerous Tendencies in American Life; The Nationals, their Origin and their Aim; Three Typical Workingmen; Workingmen's Wives; The Career of a Capitalist; Study of a New England Factory Town; Preaching; Sincere Demagogy,—no one can have forgotten their unsparing reality, their humane temper, and their fine and rare intellectual quality. Those interested in the growth of a literature which shall embody our national life must have felt that here was a man with the artist's eye for seeing as perhaps no other American had seen our conditions; and those who believe that life is above literature—is not to be treated as mere material from which characters and situations are to be quarried—must have been glad of the self-sacrifice which presented the rich results of the writer's observation uncolored and almost uncommented. Nothing is further from him than the novelist's purpose or the novelist's method of using the facts which he sees with all a novelist's keenness, and more than the keenness of any novelist who has yet looked at the same aspects of our civilization. Sometimes, almost against his will, as it seems, the matter takes a picturesque shape, as in certain descriptions of the New England Factory Town; but his sympathetic earnestness is felt through the things that make us smile, and we know that he wishes us to think rather than smile. Some of these passages are worthy the great masters who have set down simply the things they have seen; that account of the "first-class" entertainment, where the girl in spangled tights sang her comic song to an audience unalloyed by factory people, and that sketch of an evening in the musical beer-hall at Fall River, are worthy of Thackeray's "Spec." In all the papers the characters are studied to such strong and serious purpose that they need but a touch of drama to make them move in artistic sequence and effect.

It is best, however, to have them as they are. We would be apt to lose

---

[1] *Certain Dangerous Tendencies in American Life, and other Papers.* Boston: Houghton, Osgood & Co. 1880.

sense of their need of help in a fiction, or of our own relation to them; and this we are not likely to do here, except as we imagine their case already become historical. Events move so rapidly with us, and superficially conditions change so suddenly, that with the present return of prosperity we shall be in danger of regarding the tendencies and characteristics of American life which this writer deplores as merely traits of the long period of adversity which is passing away. But what this essayist strives to do throughout is to persuade his reader that the relief which may come from better times is temporary and delusive; that hard times will return in their course, and then all the dangerous tendencies of two years ago will beset us again. He does not feel himself to be dealing with casual errors, but faults of character and mind not radical but well-nigh inveterate, and his remedy for them is simpler and honester life, resulting from the diffusion of real intelligence concerning its problems, from habits of frugality in spending and closeness in thinking, from home-training in unselfishness and benevolence, from a better understanding between the different stations and conditions of society. We state in generals what he states in particulars; for he does not shrink from that hard part of his task which consists in specifying the means that people should take to help themselves. He differs from many other philosophers, who have taught us of late, in prescribing work, and a great deal of it, for all classes as the prime agent in the purification of public and private morals. He has very little to say about the amusement of the people, and much about their edification,—about giving them good reading and good preaching; no doubt he thinks they may be trusted to take all the play they need. He does nothing new, perhaps, in prescribing this regimen for the poor, but he is refreshing in suggesting it for the rich also: he would not have stupid and idle rich people any more than ignorant paupers, and would doubtless think the one class as mischievous as the other.

More than once during the magazine publication of these essays we found the charge of pessimism brought against their author. The phrase probably recommended itself to his critics by its cheapness; certainly nothing could be more inexact, unless pessimism consists in the recognition of needlessly deplorable conditions, and the expression of a belief that the sufferers have the cure in their own hands. If it is pessimism to show the rich what excellent types of character exist among workingmen and their wives, and to teach the poor how a capitalist may be necessarily their friend, by all means let us have nothing but pessimism hereafter. We shall come to a better conception of each other, and learn to bear and forbear through that desperate doctrine. The essays really most discouraging are those on The Nationals and Sincere Demagogy, from which it appears that those who do most of our voting are not ready to do our thinking to advantage. Yet they are not so much corrupted as stupefied by the leaders who repeat to their credulity the thrice-exploded delusions of the past concerning the inherent virtue and wisdom of the people, the injustice of society to the poor, and the tyranny of capital; who preach their rights and say nothing of their duties. These studies are discouraging, because they show us how low the capacity of the masses—the public-schooled masses—still is for right thinking. The writer does not deny their capacity, and perhaps even his distrust of their intelligence may seem refuted just now, when returning prosperity has put us all in good humor with one another, and every one has apparently come to a clearer perception of things. But very possibly he might insist that this was a transitory and illusory appearance; and that the supine acquiescence of those who confide in it was material for a still more discouraging paper than any he had yet written.

[*Atlantic Monthly*, June 1880]

68

Goldwin Smith's Cowper.[1]

No one, we think, is so much master of the art of giving the essence of things, without the tediousness of detail, as Mr. Goldwin Smith. His study of Irish History—the book by which most of us probably came to know him first—possessed the reader with a sense of the people and their story in a fashion which was and remains unique. The exquisitely clear style, the vigorous and positive thinking, the unsentimental sympathy, the distinct and unmistakable point of view, are all excellences which unite to one effect. There is no waste of words in his work, but no diction is farther from crabbedness. The sparing is from a full mind; the reticence is that of one who knows how to withhold useless knowledge. If the reader wishes for a recent instance of his peculiar force and directness in characterization, let him turn to the quite matchless portrait of Swift in the paper on Pessimism, lately printed here; or if he would have something almost as good, and indefinitely more pleasing, let him take this little book on Cowper. It is charming, but that does not begin to say all; for it will be one's own fault if one is not more than charmed. One ought to be put in thorough sympathy with a nature which, in spite of insanity and almost immeasurable weakness, became a great power in the world, to the glory, as Mr. Smith points out, of Christian civilization; and one may profitably turn from our time, when so much has been said and so much insinuated in favor of a scientific return to barbarism, and recur to the time when human brotherhood began to be asserted, and the virtue of might to be questioned. Cowper was the prophet of the new impulse, and he long dictated the morality of that simple and now rather old-fashioned world, in which it was conceded that the feeble and inferior had paramount claims, that it was wrong to give pain, and that selfishness was wicked. It would not be surprising if, in a revulsion from our present collective way of taking ourselves, and condoning injustice and aggression as a perhaps necessary part of the general design, he should regain something of his old popularity. He could never get it all back; the world can never again, we hope, be so didactic as his world, but we trust it can be as gentle, as domestic, as religious.

---

[1] *Cowper*. [Morley's English Men of Letters.] By Goldwin Smith. New York: Harper and Brothers. 1880.

His world was a world apart,—another world,—even in his own time; but it is historically important because the best modern feeling and morality had their spring in it. The sentiment of religious democracy, the abhorrence of slavery, the recognition of the brotherhood of men, we owe to that world, and Cowper was its poet. He was so much secluded from what seemed the prevailing influences of his time that it is hard to conceive of him as the contemporary of Johnson and Goldsmith, of Sterne and Fielding, of Garrick and Burke, and all that made London splendid and memorable; but, with the exception of Goldsmith, he has had a message for more human hearts than any or all of the others. He has been, like Milton, the poet whom militant devotion has spared, and he has kept the sense of beauty alive in thousands of righteous households where Shakespeare was held profane, and almost the whole body of English poetry was thought as ungodly as card-playing and horse-racing. Yet he was nearly his whole life a hypochondriac, and he had accesses of madness in which he more than once attempted suicide; so frail, so seemingly unfit, are the instruments through which Providence works its will upon the world.

Mr. Smith traces once more, with his graphic force, the outline of the story which is so well known,—the poet's sickly and solitary childhood, darkened by the loss of his mother, and imbittered by his sufferings at school from the brutality of his fellows and teachers; the brief glimpse of gayety and worldly happiness, when "his days were spent in 'giggling and making giggle' with his cousins Theodora and Harriet;" his moment of ambition, when he aspired to be clerk of the journals in the House of Lords, and recoiled from the possible opposition to his appointment in terror that drove him to his first attempt upon his own life; the transition from the mad-house to the household of the good clergyman Unwin, with whose wife he formed that singular friendship, not so much to be called Platonic as Evangelic, which lasted till her death; the residence of the pair with the austere and devout old ex-slaver, Newton; their removal from his too powerful theologic influence, and their episodic relations with the potentially romantic Lady Austen; the domestication of Lady Hesketh, Cowper's cousin, with them; and finally Mrs. Unwin's death, and Cowper's decline to a peaceful end. The biographer fills up this necessarily meagre sketch with special and general criticisms on Cowper's literary growth and performances, and no doubt there will be those to say that he quotes the best of his poetry. It is true that it has formed the pleasure mostly of those for whom a very little poetry in their prose is enough; but it is to be hoped that Mr. Smith's clear and just study will send his reader to it for the means of revising, or perhaps forming, his own opinion of its qualities. "Once for all," he tells us, the reader "must make up his mind to acquiesce in religious forms of expression. If he does not sympathize with them, he will recognize them as phenomena of opinion, and bear them like a philosopher. He can easily translate them into the language of psychology," or, he adds, with a touch of characteristic irony, "even of physiology, if he thinks fit."

Although Cowper was "the great poet of the religious revival which marked the latter part of the eighteenth century in England," we think that some of Mr. Smith's readers, even after their pleasure and profit in his admirable book, will doubt whether he was "the most important English poet of the period between Pope and the illustrious group headed by Wordsworth, Byron, and Shelley." Not especially to name Goldsmith, the supreme poet of the affections, whose influence remains almost undiminished, there are too many other names of that period to permit a ready assent to this sort of claim, which it does not seem to us is ever a useful one for the critic to make. Mr. Smith is on much safer ground in defining Cowper's importance to the religious and moral reform which he promoted; and nothing in his book is more interesting than his sketch of the prevalent irreligion and immorality which Methodism found in England.

He quotes from a letter of the Duchess of Buckingham to Lady Huntingdon, one of the first converts, a delicious passage which expresses the astonishment and indignation of the better classes at the impudence of the preachers, "whose doctrines are most repulsive, and strongly tinctured with disrespect towards their superiors. . . . It is monstrous to be told that you have a heart as sinful as the common wretches that crawl on the earth. This is highly insulting and offensive; and I cannot but wonder that your ladyship should relish any sentiment so much at variance with high rank and good breeding." Here the primal conception of Christianity was extinct, and it was to the redemption of society at its best so godless that Cowper was important. He might have been all in all to it without being the most important poet of that long period, for finally a poet's importance is through literature.

Without giving Cowper the place assigned him by Southey, as the best of English letter-writers, Mr. Smith is inclined to think it is shared with him by Byron alone; and he gives a delightful chapter to those letters in which Cowper unaffectedly paints his life, with its literary and religious interests, its simple pleasures and cares, and its small excitements, amidst the gentle and good women with whom his lot was cast. When he is not writing at their suggestion, or reading to them, he is amusing himself with his hares or his flowers, or he is holding thread for them to wind. It is not at all a heroic life; but it is an immediately harmless one, and ultimately most beneficent. This poor, sick soul, who dwells like a frail child in the shelter of feminine sympathy, and for whom beyond it there is no way but that towards madness, is inspired to be the voice and the courage of a sentiment which we in our own day have seen extinguish slavery on fields of blood, and which silently works and has worked to the amelioration of all the wrongs that humanity suffers. The means is so strange, so apparently inadequate, and so little proportioned to the end that we cannot consider it without awe, nor help recurring to the biographer's conviction that it "is a remarkable triumph of the influences which have given birth to Christian civilization." The sense of beauty is inherent in all races, times, and religions; the love of practical righteousness, the feeling for others' woe, the horror of cruelty and wrong, find through Christianity their laureate in the shrinking and self-accusing poet, whose singing-robe was sometimes a strait-jacket.

[*Atlantic Monthly*, September 1880]

69

Mr. Aldrich's Fiction.

MR. Aldrich's first essay in fiction, or the first that he has thought worth the remembrance of his readers, was strictly romantic in substance. It was that little story, which with difficulty keeps itself from rhyming, called Père Antoine's Date Palm, printed nearly twenty years ago in these pages. Hawthorne was then living, and he took the pains to find out the author, and then gave himself the pleasure of writing to the young poet in recognition of its charm. Its tragedy is of an airier sort than his own; it is rather allied to the pathos of Mr. Curtis in his Prue and I sketches; but the master of romance felt its exquisite art with sympathetic satisfaction. In fact, there are few passages in it which the critic now reperusing it would wish to change. Even these he might change for the worse.

When it appeared, Mr. Aldrich had already the reputation of a poet, whose verse was jeweled and tinted in the taste which we, who were younger then, all remember. A great many could do something like it; at its worst, it was very much like something better. But in due time it became evident that the substance which Mr. Aldrich was so painfully encrusting with colored pastes was real gold, of a fineness now incontestable; that he was himself better than what he had tried to do. His native grace, his feeling for form, his love of artistic purity, came to express themselves in a manner of his own, which characterizes certain lyrics destined to please while there is a responsive sense of these things.

His Père Antoine's Date Palm remained his sole attempt in fiction till he wrote, seven or eight years later, The Story of a Bad Boy. This again was an excursion in dreamland, for boyhood, realized with whatever conscientiousness, is in the region of romance. We do not suppose that Mr. Aldrich intended, even in the most autobiographical particulars, to study his own boyhood very minutely, and this left it everybody's boyhood. Even its extravagances and excesses added to its universal verisimilitude: we all fell into its humor, and knew that those were the things which we would have liked to have happen to us when we were boys.

In his unique romance of Marjorie Daw he invented a new pleasure: a surprise so fine that it must remain unmatched, and contrived with such consummate skill that every reader, upon discovering that there never was any Marjorie Daw, felt a pang which qualified his sense of being hoaxed with a soft personal regret for the charming creation thus resolved into nothingness. It is not easy to trace to its source the charm of any piece of art, and to say confidently that it lies here or there; but we suspect that the charm of Marjorie Daw is largely in the comedy-like frame-work, the letters and telegrams in which the story is told performing the effect of dialogue; in the realism of certain particular touches within the general unreality. From the first we lend ourselves to its influence as to that of a play; we delight even in little conventionalities; people do not throw books at servants' heads, nowadays, but we like to have John Flemming do it.

The reader need not be reminded of Miss Mehetabel's Son and Mademoiselle Olympe Zabriskie, as other essays in this sort. They preceded, with some sketches and studies, Mr. Aldrich's first novel, Prudence Palfrey, whose merits and defects were those easily predicable of a novel by the author of those admirable short stories; it excelled in particular passages, which were so good that the general plan suffered in contrast. It was the old-fashioned scheme of a novel,—the novel of incident, in which inferior writers seem to succeed best. As often as he has adopted this scheme it seems to us that Mr. Aldrich has made a mistake; it is for him to deal with motive and character, and it does not matter if these be a little or even quite fantastic. After Marjorie Daw he has drawn no other girlish figure so good as that of the heroine in The Queen of Sheba. That story is more poetically imagined than any other that he has done, and it is the most shapely and best wrought. Nothing that is not acceptably painful is felt in her temporary hallucination, and all that is bizarre and amusingly tricksy and whimsical in it is enjoyed. The elfishness which casts its spell upon the young man is made a fascination for the reader; but it is wisely managed that when the hero meets her again, and falls in love with her anew, there should be no trace of this wildness in her, but only a sweet and natural girlishness. Here, once more, is the poet's, the romancer's, effect, rather than the novelist's; it is produced from conscientiously ascertained fact, and is accompanied by studies of life full of humorous reality; but the lasting impression from the story is the poetic interest of a man's heart attaching itself to that from which a return of love is impossible, and the transformation of the alien creature to human consciousness. It is a conception which gains from the realistic setting, and from the humor that plays through it and naturalizes its fanciful spirit to our own world.

In The Stillwater Tragedy Mr. Aldrich writes a novel which is not at all a romance. It is the story of a strike in a New England manufacturing town, of a murder, of circumstantial evidence, of love and marriage. The reader knows it, and need not be reminded of the plot, which is unfolded from the end rather than the beginning,—a method which has its advantages and its disadvantages. Tourguénief has among recent writers used it with peculiar force in Spring-Floods, and Mr. Aldrich has managed it with such characteristic *finesse* that we venture to say no reader was in possession of any secret of it till the author chose to impart it. We confess to have been ourselves entirely surprised when it was Durgin, and not Torrini, who turned out to be the murderer; and we read the story from month to month with unflagging interest, and with a pleasure in certain passages which others must have shared with us. There are few finer effects of comedy than that scene in which Richard Shackford, going magnanimously to reconcile himself to his cousin Lemuel, comes away smacking his fists in the ecstasy of his unfulfilled desire to knock his kinsman down. In fact, the comedy is what strikes one most in this tragedy, which need not be the less a tragedy on that account. The whimsical discomfitures distributed with an impartial hand, to Richard when his eloquence has precipitated the dramatic opening of the strike, and to the detective when he fails to fix the murder upon Richard, and all the chorusing (if we may so call it) of the action by the village magnates in one room and the operatives in another, at Snelling's tavern, are very amusingly and freshly conceived. The description of the strike is a contribution to our knowledge of such matters: it is a vivid spectacle left to its own forcibleness for its impression. But in his presentation of the village life Mr. Aldrich does not escape the conventionality which we have before noted in similar work of his. Outside of Slocum's Yard—where all is new and real—it is the New England village and its interests and its characters which we know from literature. Like that other delightful writer whom we have named, Mr. Curtis, Mr. Aldrich seems to have a preference for looking at life through literature, and for giving not so much the likeness of what he might see if he rejected this medium as the likeness of something that has pleased him in books. He cannot deny himself the suggestion of traits endeared by literary association, as he cannot deny himself the pleasure of making witty and humorous remarks upon his action and people. This is English usage, sanctioned by all the great novelists, and yet we cannot help thinking it a vice. We are not sure that a novelist does not weaken his work by every good thing that he says in his own person; and Mr. Aldrich, unhappily, has his head full of good things! He must say them; we are charmed, instructed, amused, but the illusion suffers. In a romance, the author's position is different. There the illusion exists by the explicit and continual assent of the reader, who says, "All this could never have happened; but let us say that it did." So long as the author is true to the motive and the characters, nothing can be amiss; he may be as directly witty and wise as he likes, and as literary as he will.

We find ourselves making much the same strictures upon The Stillwater Tragedy that we made upon Prudence Palfrey, to which it is allied in method and material. It is a more interesting story, and the plot is less vulnerable; it is in fact a very good plot, of strong and close texture, through which the author's intention does not escape till he chooses. But both books are in the field of the novel, while Mr. Aldrich's other work is rather in the region of romance. They have in common a certain consciousness in the development of character, and that vice, if it is a vice, of confidential comment. The persons are characterized by the author rather than by themselves; but in compensation we have innumerable flashes of humorous description, of droll observation, which break irrepressibly from him, and which we should be stupid if we refused to enjoy. When Mr. Aldrich tells us that his Chinese laundry-man had no more facial expression than an orange, the stroke is as deliciously true as if some person of the story had said it; only, it would have been better for some person of the story to say it.

Mr. Aldrich, in fine, works in the novel with the instinct of the romancer. He is essentially a poet, of that order of imagination, gay and bright, which is even rarer than the gloomier cast, and we can fancy him occupied with some theme of pure romance, in which his poetic art would have free play, and which would remain a perfect delight. The novelist's trade,—that any one may learn, more or less well; but romance requires gift, and he is of the few who have gift. In Père Antoine's Date Palm, Marjorie Daw, and The Queen of Sheba, he has developed a species of romance in which we shall hope to see his hand again,—that kind which bases fanciful superstructure upon a solid foundation of realism. Poe does this in some of his dismal tales; but it remained for Mr. Aldrich to show us that the same principle could lend itself even more effectively to a cheerful purpose and a more delicate intention. He has accomplished this so lightly, so easily, that he has made the kind his own, and has become our debtor in a more considerable experiment than he has yet made,—an experiment which we would prefer in thoroughly modern material; but if not, then in something out of our American past. There is the life of the old Creole New Orleans, of his feeling for which he has given us hints; or there are matters in New England annals not wholly sombre. In the Scarlet Letter, the fearfulness of the Puritan conscience is embodied, once for all; but the later life which sprang up from the very heart of Puritanism, and rebelled against it, still waits to be portrayed in romance. We think it waits for Mr. Aldrich.

[*Atlantic Monthly*, November 1880]

Mark Twain.

In one form or other, Mr. Samuel L. Clemens has told the story of his life in his books, and in sketching his career I shall have to recur to the leading facts rather than to offer fresh information. He was remotely of Virginian origin and more remotely of good English stock; the name was well-known before his time in the South, where a Senator, a Congressman and other dignitaries had worn it; but his branch of the family fled from the destitution of those vast landed possessions in Tennessee, celebrated in The Gilded Age, and went very poor to Missouri. Mr. Clemens was born on the 30th of November, 1835, at Florida in the latter State; but his father removed shortly afterwards to Hannibal, a small town on the Mississippi, where most of the humorist's boyhood was spent. Hannibal, as a name is hopelessly confused and ineffective; but if we can know nothing of Mr. Clemens from Hannibal, we can know much of Hannibal from Mr. Clemens, who in fact has studied a loafing, out-at-elbows, down-at-the-heels, slaveholding, Mississippi river-town of thirty years ago, with such strong reality in his boys' romance of Tom Sawyer, that we need inquire nothing further concerning the type. The original perhaps no longer exists anywhere; certainly not in Hannibal which has grown into a flourishing little city since Mr. Clemens sketched it. In his time, the two embattled forces of civilization and barbarism were encamped at Hannibal as they are at all times and everywhere; the morality of the place was the morality of a slaveholding community, fierce, arrogant, one-sided— this virtue for white, and that for black folks—and the religion was Calvinism in various phases with its predestinate aristocracy of saints, and its rabble of hopeless sinners. Doubtless young Clemens escaped neither of the opposing influences wholly; his people, like the rest were slaveholders, but his father like so many other slaveholders abhorred slavery—silently, as he must in such a time and place. If the boy's sense of justice suffered anything of that perversion which so curiously and pitiably maimed the reason of the whole South, it does not appear in his books, where there is not an ungenerous line, but always on the contrary a burning resentment of all manner of cruelty and wrong.

The father, an austere and singularly upright man, died bankrupt when Clemens was twelve years old, and the boy had thereafter to make what scramble he could for an education. He got very little learning in school, and like so many other Americans in whom the literary impulse is native, he turned to the local printing-office for some of the advantages from which he was otherwise cut off. Certain records of the three years spent in the Hannibal Courier office are to be found in Mark Twain's book of Sketches; but I believe there is yet no history anywhere of the *wanderjahre*, in which he followed the life of a jour printer, from town to town, and from city to city, penetrating even so far into the vague and fabled East as Philadelphia and New York.

He returned to his own country—his *patria*—sated, if not satisfied, with travel, and at seventeen, he resolved to "learn the river" from St. Louis to New Orleans as a steamboat pilot. Of this period of his life he has given a full account in the delightful series of papers, Piloting on the Mississippi, which he printed seven years ago in The Atlantic Monthly. The growth of the railroads, and the outbreak of the civil war put an end to profitable piloting, and at twenty-four he was again open to a vocation. He listened for a moment to the loudly-calling drum of that time, and he was actually in camp for three weeks on the rebel side; but the unorganized force to which he belonged, was disbanded, and he finally did not "go with his section" either in sentiment or in fact. His brother having been appointed Lieutenant Governor of Nevada territory, Mr. Clemens went out with him as his private secretary; but he soon resigned his office and withdrew to the mines. He failed as a miner, in the ordinary sense; but the life of the mining-camps yielded him the wealth that the pockets of the mountain denied; he had the Midas-touch, without knowing it, and all these grotesque experiences have since turned into gold under his hand. After his failure as a miner had become evident even to himself he was glad to take the place of local editor on the Virginia City Enterprise, a newspaper for which he had amused himself in writing from time to time. He had written for the newspapers before this; few Americans escape that fate; and as an apprentice in the Hannibal Courier office his humor had embroiled some of the leading citizens and impaired the fortunes of that journal by the alienation of several delinquent subscribers.

But it was in the Enterprise that he first used his pseudonym of Mark Twain, which he borrowed from the vernacular of the river, where the man heaving the lead calls out "Mark *twain!*" instead of "Mark *two!*" In 1864, he accepted on the San Francisco Morning Call, the same sort of place which he had held on the Enterprise, and he soon made his *nom de guerre* familiar "on that coast"; he not only wrote "local items" in the Call, but he printed humorous sketches in various periodicals; and two years later he was sent to the Sandwich Islands as correspondent of a Sacramento paper.

When he came back he "entered the lecture-field," as it used to be phrased. Of these facts, there is, as all English-speaking readers know, full record in Roughing It; though I think Mr. Clemens has not mentioned there his association with that extraordinary group of wits and poets, of whom Mr. Bret Harte, Mr. Charles Warren Stoddard, Mr. Charles H. Webb, Mr. Prentice Mulford, were with himself, the most conspicuous: these ingenious

young men, with the fatuity of gifted people, had established a literary newspaper in San Francisco, and they brilliantly co-operated to its early
extinction.

In 1867 Mr. Clemens made in the *Quaker City* the excursion to Europe
and the East which he has commemorated in The Innocents Abroad. Shortly
after his return he married, and placed himself at Buffalo, where he bought
an interest in one of the city newspapers; later he came to Hartford, where
he has since remained, except for the two years spent in a second visit to
Europe. The incidents of this visit he has characteristically used in A Tramp
Abroad; and in fact, I believe the only book of Mr. Clemens's which is not
largely autobiographical is The Prince and the Pauper: the scene being laid
in England, in the early part of the sixteenth century, the difficulties presented to a nineteenth century autobiographer were insurmountable.

The habit of putting his own life, not merely in its results, but in its
processes, into his books, is only one phase of the frankness of Mr. Clemens's
humorous attitude. The transparent disguise of the pseudonym once granted
him, he asks the reader to grant him nothing else. In this he differs wholly
from most other American humorists, who have all found some sort of dramatization of their personality desirable if not necessary. Charles F. Browne,
"delicious" as he was when he dealt with us directly, preferred the disguise of
Artemus Ward the showman; Mr. Locke likes to figure as Petroleum V. Nasby
the cross-roads politician; Mr. Shaw chooses to masquerade as the saturnine
philosopher Josh Billings; and each of these humorists appeals to the grotesqueness of misspelling to help out his fun. It was for Mr. Clemens to
reconcile the public to humor which contented itself with the established
absurdities of English orthography; and I am inclined to attribute to the
example of his immense success, the humaner spirit which characterizes our
recent popular humor. There is still sufficient flippancy and brutality in it,
but there is no longer the stupid and monkeyish cruelty of motive and intention which once disgraced and insulted us. Except the political humorists,
like Mr. Lowell—if there were any like him—the American humorists for-
merly chose the wrong in public matters; they were on the side of slavery, of
drunkenness and of irreligion; the friends of civilization were their prey;
their spirit was thoroughly vulgar and base. Before John Phoenix there was
scarcely any American humorist,—not of the distinctly literary sort,—with
whom one could smile and keep one's self-respect. The great Artemus himself was not guiltless; but the most *popular* humorist who ever lived has not to
accuse himself, so far as I can remember, of having written anything to make
one morally ashamed of liking him. One can readily make one's strictures:
there is often more than a suggestion of forcing in his humor; sometimes it
tends to horse-play; sometimes the extravagance overleaps itself, and falls flat
on the other side; but I cannot remember that in Mr. Clemens's books I have
ever been asked to join him in laughing at any good or really fine thing. But I
do not mean to leave him with this negative praise; I mean to say of him that
as Shakespeare, according to Mr. Lowell's saying, was the first to make po-

etry all poetical, Mark Twain was the first to make humor all humorous. He has not only added more in bulk to the stock of harmless pleasures than any other humorist; but more in the spirit that is easily and wholly enjoyable. There is nothing lost in literary attitude, in labored dictionary funning, in affected quaintness, in dreary dramatization, in artificial "dialect"; Mark Twain's humor is as simple in form and as direct as the statesmanship of Lincoln, or the generalship of Grant.

When I think how purely and wholly American it is I am a little puzzled at its universal acceptance. We are doubtless the most thoroughly homogeneous people that ever existed as a great nation. There is such a parity in the experiences of Americans that Mark Twain or Artemus Ward appeals as unerringly to the consciousness of our fifty millions as Goldoni appealed to that of his hundred thousand Venetians. In our phrase, we have somehow all been there; in fact, generally, and in sympathy almost certainly, we have been there. In another generation or two perhaps it will be wholly different; but as yet the average American is the man who has risen; he has known poverty, and privation and low conditions; he has very often known squalor; and now in his prosperity he regards the past with a sort of large, pitying amusement; he is not the least ashamed of it; he does not feel that it characterizes him any more than the future does. Our humor springs from this multiform American experience of life and securely addresses itself in reminiscence, in phrase, in its whole material to the intelligence bred of like experience. It is not of a class for a class; it does not employ itself with the absurdities of a tailor as a tailor; its conventions, if it has any, are all new, and of American make. When it mentions hash, we smile because we have each somehow known the cheap boarding-house or restaurant; when it alludes to putting up stoves in the fall, each of us feels the grime and rust of the pipes on his hands; the introduction of the lightning-rod man or the book-agent, establishes our brotherhood with the humorist at once. But how is it with the vast English-speaking world outside of these States to which hash, and stove-pipes, and lightning-rod men and book-agents are as strange as lords and ladies, as donjon-keeps and battlements are to us? Why in fine should an English chief justice keep Mark Twain's books always at hand? Why should Darwin have gone to them for rest and refreshment at midnight, when spent with scientific research?

I suppose that Mark Twain transcends all other American humorists in the universal qualities. He deals very little with the pathetic,—which he nevertheless knows very well how to manage, as he has shown, notably, in the True Story of the old slave-mother—but there is a poetic lift in his work, even when he permits you to recognize it only as something satirized. There is always the touch of nature, the presence of a sincere and frank manliness in what he says, the companionship of a spirit which is at once delightfully open and deliciously shrewd. Elsewhere I have tried to persuade the reader that his humor is at its best the foamy break of the strong tide of earnestness in him. But it would be limiting him unjustly to describe him as a satirist; and it is hardly practicable to establish him in people's minds as a moralist: he has made them laugh too long; they will not believe him serious; they think some joke is always intended. This is the penalty, as Dr. Holmes has pointed out, of making one's first success as a humorist. There was a paper of Mark Twain's, printed in the Atlantic Monthly some years ago and called The Facts concerning the late Carnival of Crime in Connecticut, which ought to have won popular recognition of the ethical intelligence which underlies his humor. It was of course funny; but under the fun, it was an impassioned study of the human conscience; Hawthorne or Bunyan might have been proud to imagine that powerful allegory, which had a grotesque force far beyond either of them. It had been read before a literary Club in Hartford; a reverend gentleman had offered the author his pulpit for the next Sunday, if he would give it as a homily there. Yet it quite failed of the response I had hoped for it, and I shall not insist here upon Mark Twain as a moralist; though I warn the reader that if he leaves out of the account an indignant sense of right and wrong, a scorn of all affectation and pretence, an ardent hate of meanness and injustice, he will come indefinitely short of knowing Mark Twain.

His powers as a story-teller were evident in hundreds of brief sketches before he proved them in Tom Sawyer and The Prince and the Pauper. Both of these books, aside from the strength of characterization are fascinating as mere narratives, and I can think of no writer living who has in higher degree the art of interesting his reader from the first word. This is a far rarer gift than we imagine, and I shall not call it a subordinate charm in Mark Twain's books, rich as they otherwise are. I have already had my say about Tom Sawyer, whose only fault is an excess of reality in portraying the character and conditions of Southwestern boyhood as it was forty years ago, and which is full of that poetic sympathy with nature and human nature which I always find in Mark Twain. The Prince and the Pauper has particularly interested me for the same qualities, which in a study of the past we call romantic, but which alone can realize the past for us. Occasionally the archaic diction gives way, and lets us down hard upon the American parlance of the nineteenth century; but mainly the illusion is admirably sustained; and the tale is to be valued not only in itself, but as an earnest of what Mr. Clemens might do in fiction when he has fairly done with autobiography in its various forms. His invention is of the good old sort, like De Foe's more than that of any other English writer, and like that of the Spanish picaresque novelists, Mendoza and the rest; it flows easily from incident to incident, and does not deepen into situation; in the romance it operates as lightly and unfatiguingly as his memory in the realistic story.

His books abound in passages of dramatic characterization, and he is, as the reader knows, the author of the most successful American play. I believe Mr. Clemens has never claimed the reconstruction of Colonel Sellers, for the stage; but he nevertheless made the play, for whatever is good in it, came bodily from his share of the novel of The Gilded Age. It is a play which succeeds by virtue of the main personage, and this personage from first to last is quite outside of the dramatic action, which sometimes serves and sometimes does not serve the purpose of presenting Colonel Sellers. Where the drama fails, Sellers rises superior, and takes the floor, and we forget the rest. Mr. Raymond conceived the character wonderfully well, and he plays it with an art that ranks him to that extent with the great actors; but he has in nowise "created" it. If any one "created" Colonel Sellers, it was Mark Twain, as the curious reader may see on turning again to the novel; but I suspect that Colonel Sellers was never created, except as other men are; he was found somewhere, and transferred living to the book.

I prefer to speak of Mr. Clemens's artistic qualities because it is to these that his humor will owe its perpetuity. All fashions change, and nothing more wholly and quickly than the fashion of fun; as any one may see by turning back to what amused people in the last generation: that stuff is terrible. As Europe becomes more and more the playground of Americans, and every scene and association becomes insipidly familiar, the jokes about the old masters and the legends will no longer be droll to us. Neither shall we care for the huge Californian mirth, when the surprise of the picturesquely mixed civilization and barbarism of the Pacific coast has quite died away; and Mark Twain would pass with the conditions that have made him intelligible, if he were not an artist of uncommon power as well as a humorist. He portrays and interprets real types not only with exquisite appreciation and sympathy, but with a force and truth of drawing that makes them permanent. Artemus Ward was very funny, that can never be denied; but it must be owned that the figure of the literary showman is as wholly factitious as his spelling; the conception is one that has to be constantly humored by the reader. But the innumerable characters sketched by Mark Twain are actualities, however caricatured,—and usually, they are not so very much caricatured. He has brought back the expression of Western humor to sympathy with the same orthography of John Phoenix; but Mark Twain is vastly more original in form. Derby was weighed upon by literary tradition; he was "academic," at times, but Mr. Clemens is never "academic." There is no drawing from casts, in his work evidently the life has everywhere been studied; and it is his apparent unconsciousness of any other way of saying a thing except the natural way that makes his books so restful and refreshing. Our little nervous literary sensibilities may suffer from his extravagance, or from other traits of his manner, but we have not to beat our breasts at the dread apparition of Dickens's or Thackeray's hand in his page. He is far too honest and sincere a soul for that; and where he is obliged to force a piece of humor to its climax—as sometimes happens—he does not call in his neighbors to help; he does it himself, and is probably sorry that he had to do it.

I suppose that even in so slight and informal a study as this, something like an "analysis" of our author's humor is expected. But I much prefer not to make it. I have observed that analyses of humor are apt to leave one rather serious, and to result in an entire volitilization of the humor. If the prevailing spirit of Mark Twain's humor is not a sort of good-natured self-satire, in which the reader may see his own absurdities reflected, I scarcely should be able to determine it.

[*Century*, September 1882]

71

Henry James, Jr.

THE events of Mr. James's life—as we agree to understand events—may be told in a very few words. His race is Irish on his father's side and Scotch on his mother's, to which mingled strains the generalizer may attribute, if he likes, that union of vivid expression and dispassionate analysis which has characterized his work from the first. There are none of those early struggles with poverty, which render the lives of so many distinguished Americans monotonous reading, to record in his case: the cabin hearth-fire did not light him to the youthful pursuit of literature; he had from the start all those advantages which, when they go too far, become limitations.

He was born in New York city in the year 1843, and his first lessons in life and letters were the best which the metropolis—so small in the perspective diminishing to that date—could afford. In his twelfth year his family went abroad, and after some stay in England made a long sojourn in France and Switzerland. They returned to America in 1860, placing themselves at Newport, and for a year or two Mr. James was at the Harvard Law School, where, perhaps, he did not study a great deal of law. His father removed from Newport to Cambridge in 1866, and there Mr. James remained until he went abroad, three years later, for the residence in England and Italy which, with infrequent visits home, has continued ever since.

It was during these three years of his Cambridge life that I became acquainted with his work. He had already printed a tale—"The Story of a Year"—in the "Atlantic Monthly," when I was asked to be Mr. Fields's assistant in the management, and it was my fortune to read Mr. James's second contribution in manuscript. "Would you take it?" asked my chief. "Yes, and all the stories you can get from the writer." One is much securer of one's judgment at twenty-nine than, say, at forty-five; but if this was a mistake of mine I am not yet old enough to regret it. The story was called "Poor Richard," and it dealt with the conscience of a man very much in love with a woman who loved his rival. He told this rival a lie, which sent him away to his death on the field,—in that day nearly every fictitious personage had something to do with the war,—but Poor Richard's lie did not win him his love. It still seems to me that the situation was strongly and finely felt. One's pity went, as it should, with the liar; but the whole story had a pathos which lingers in my mind equally with a sense of the new literary qualities which gave me such delight in it. I admired, as we must in all that Mr. James has written, the finished workmanship in which there is no loss of vigor; the luminous and uncommon use of words, the originality of phrase, the whole clear and beautiful style, which I confess I weakly liked the better for the occasional gallicisms remaining from an inveterate habit of French. Those who know the writings of Mr. Henry James will recognize the inherited felicity of diction which is so striking in the writings of Mr. Henry James, Jr. The son's diction is not so racy as the father's; it lacks its daring, but it is as fortunate and graphic; and I cannot give it greater praise than this, though it has, when he will, a splendor and state which is wholly its own.

Mr. James is now so universally recognized that I shall seem to be making an unwarrantable claim when I express my belief that the popularity of his stories was once largely confined to Mr. Fields's assistant. They had characteristics which forbade any editor to refuse them; and there are no anecdotes of thrice-rejected manuscripts finally printed to tell of him; his work was at once successful with all the magazines. But with the readers of "The Atlantic," of "Harper's," of "Lippincott's," of "The Galaxy," of "The Century," it was another affair. The flavor was so strange, that, with rare exceptions, they had to "learn to like" it. Probably few writers have in the same degree compelled the liking of their readers. He was reluctantly accepted, partly through a mistake as to his attitude—through the confusion of his point of view with his private opinion—in the reader's mind. This confusion caused the tears of rage which bedewed our continent in behalf of the "average American girl" supposed to be satirized in Daisy Miller, and prevented the perception of the fact that, so far as the average American girl was studied at all in Daisy Miller, her indestructible innocence, her invulnerable new-worldliness, had never been so delicately appreciated. It was so plain that Mr. James disliked her vulgar conditions, that the very people to whom he revealed her essential sweetness and light were furious that he should have seemed not to see what existed through him. In other words, they would have liked him better if he had been a worse artist—if he had been a little more confidential.

But that artistic impartiality which puzzled so many in the treatment of Daisy Miller is one of the qualities most valuable in the eyes of those who care how things are done, and I am not sure that it is not Mr. James's most characteristic quality. As "frost performs the effect of fire," this impartiality comes at last to the same result as sympathy. We may be quite sure that Mr. James does not like the peculiar phase of our civilization typified in Henrietta Stackpole; but he treats her with such exquisite justice that he lets *us* like her. It is an extreme case, but I confidently allege it in proof.

His impartiality is part of the reserve with which he works in most respects, and which at first glance makes us say that he is wanting in humor. But I feel pretty certain that Mr. James has not been able to disinherit himself to this degree. We Americans are terribly in earnest about making ourselves, individually and collectively; but I fancy that our prevailing mood in the face of all problems is that of an abiding faith which can afford to be funny. He has himself indicated that we have, as a nation, as a people, our joke, and every one of us is in the joke more or less. We may, some of us, dislike it extremely, disapprove it wholly, and even abhor it, but we are in the joke all the same, and no one of us is safe from becoming the great American humorist at any given moment. The danger is not apparent in Mr. James's case, and I confess that I read him with a relief in the comparative immunity that he affords from the national facetiousness. Many of his people are humorously imagined, or rather humorously *seen*, like Daisy Miller's mother, but these do not give a dominant color; the business in hand is commonly serious, and the droll people are subordinated. They abound, nevertheless, and many of them are perfectly new finds, like Mr. Tristram in "The American," the bill-paying father in the "Pension Beaurepas," the anxiously Europeanizing mother in the same story, the amusing little Madame de Belgarde, Henrietta Stackpole, and even Newman himself. But though Mr. James portrays the humorous in character, he is decidedly not on humorous terms with his reader; he ignores rather than recognizes the fact that they are both in the joke.

If we take him at all we must take him on his own ground, for clearly he will not come to ours. We must make concessions to him, not in this respect only, but in several others, chief among which is the motive for reading fiction. By example, at least, he teaches that it is the pursuit and not the end which should give us pleasure; for he often prefers to leave us to our own conjectures in regard to the fate of the people in whom he has interested us. There is no question, of course, but he could tell the story of Isabel in "The Portrait of a Lady" to the end, yet he does not tell it. We must agree, then, to take what seems a fragment instead of a whole, and to find, when we can, a name for this new kind of fiction. Evidently it is the character, not the fate, of his people which occupies him; when he has fully developed their character he leaves them to what destiny the reader pleases.

The analytic tendency seems to have increased with him as his work has gone on. Some of the earlier tales were very dramatic: "A Passionate Pilgrim," which I should rank above all his other short stories, and for certain rich poetical qualities, above everything else that he has done, is eminently dramatic. But I do not find much that I should call dramatic in "The Portrait of a Lady," while I do find in it an amount of analysis which I should call superabundance if it were not all such good literature. The novelist's main business is to possess his reader with a due conception of his characters and the situations in which they find themselves. If he does more or less than this he equally fails. I have sometimes thought that Mr. James's danger was to do more, but when I have been ready to declare this excess an error of his method I have hesitated. Could anything be superfluous that had given me so much pleasure as I read? Certainly from only one point of view, and this a rather narrow, technical one. It seems to me that an enlightened criticism will recognize in Mr. James's fiction a metaphysical genius working to æsthetic results, and will not be disposed to deny it any method it chooses to employ. No other novelist, except George Eliot, has dealt so largely in analysis of motive, has so fully explained and commented upon the springs of action in the persons of the drama, both before and after the facts. These novelists are more alike than any others in their processes, but with George Eliot an ethical purpose is dominant, and with Mr. James an artistic purpose. I do not know just how it should be stated of two such noble and generous types of character as Dorothea and Isabel Archer, but I think that we sympathize with the former in grand aims that chiefly concern others, and with the latter in beautiful dreams that primarily concern herself. Both are unselfish and devoted women, sublimely true to a mistaken ideal in their marriages; but, though they come to this common martyrdom, the original difference in them remains. Isabel has her great weaknesses, as Dorothea had, but these seem to me, on the whole, the most nobly imagined and the most nobly intentioned women in modern fiction; and I think Isabel is the more subtly divined of the two. If we speak of mere characterization, we must not fail to acknowledge the perfection of Gilbert Osmond. It was a profound stroke to make him an American by birth. No European could realize so fully in his own life the ideal of a European *dilettante* in all the meaning of that cheapened word; as no European could so deeply and tenderly feel the sweetness and loveliness of the English past as the sick American, Searle, in "The Passionate Pilgrim."

What is called the international novel is popularly dated from the publication of "Daisy Miller," though "Roderick Hudson" and "The American" had gone before; but it really began in the beautiful story which I have just named. Mr. James, who invented this species in fiction, first contrasted in the "Passionate Pilgrim" the New World and Old World moods, ideals, and prejudices, and he did it there with a richness of poetic effect which he has since never equalled. I own that I regret the loss of the poetry, but you cannot ask a man to keep on being a poet for you; it is hardly for him to choose; yet I compare rather discontentedly in my own mind such impassioned creations as Searle and the painter in "The Madonna of the Future" with "Daisy Miller," of whose slight, thin personality I also feel the indefinable charm, and of the tragedy of whose innocence I recognize the delicate pathos. Looking back to those early stories, where Mr. James stood at the dividing ways of the novel and the romance, I am sometimes sorry that he declared even superficially for the former. His best efforts seem to me those of romance; his best types have an ideal development, like Isabel and Claire Belgarde and Bessy Alden and poor Daisy and even Newman. But, doubtless, he has chosen wisely; perhaps the romance is an outworn form, and would not lend itself to the reproduction of even the ideality of modern life. I myself waver somewhat in my preference—if it is a preference—when I think of such people as Lord Warburton and the Touchetts, whom I take to be all decidedly of this world. The first of these especially interested me as a probable type of the English nobleman, who amiably accepts the existing situation with all its possibilities of political and social change, and insists not at all upon the surviving feudalities, but means to be a manly and simple gentleman in any event. An American is not able to pronounce as to the verity of the type; I only know that it seems probable and that it is charming. It makes one wish that it were in Mr. James's way to paint in some story the present phase of change in England. A titled personage is still mainly an inconceivable being to us; he is like a goblin or a fairy in a story-book. How does he comport himself in the face of all the changes and modifications that have taken place and that still impend? We can hardly imagine a lord taking his nobility seriously; it is some hint of the conditional frame of Lord Warburton's mind that makes him imaginable and delightful to us.

It is not my purpose here to review any of Mr. James's books; I like better to speak of his people than of the conduct of his novels, and I wish to recognize the fineness with which he has touched-in the pretty primness of Osmond's daughter and the mild devotedness of Mr. Rosier. A masterly hand is as often manifest in the treatment of such subordinate figures as in that of the principal persons, and Mr. James does them unerringly. This is felt in the more important character of Valentin Belgarde, a fascinating character in spite of its defects,—perhaps on account of them—and a sort of French Lord Warburton, but wittier, and not so good. "These are my ideas," says his sister-in-law, at the end of a number of inanities. "Ah, you call them ideas!" he returns, which is delicious and makes you love him. He, too, has his moments of misgiving, apparently in regard to his nobility, and his acceptance of Newman on the basis of something like "manhood suffrage" is very charming. It is of course difficult for a remote plebeian to verify the pictures of legitimist society in "The American," but there is the probable suggestion in them of conditions and principles, and want of principles, of which we get glimpses in our travels abroad; at any rate, they reveal another and not impossible world, and it is fine to have Newman discover that the opinions and criticisms of our world are so absolutely valueless in that sphere that his knowledge of the infamous crime of the mother and brother of his betrothed will have no effect whatever upon them in their own circle if he explodes it there. This seems like aristocracy indeed! and one admires, almost respects, its survival in our day. But I always regretted that Newman's discovery seemed the precursor of his magnanimous resolution not to avenge himself; it weakened the effect of this, with which it had really nothing to do. Upon the whole, however, Newman is an adequate and satisfying representative of Americanism, with his generous matrimonial ambition, his vast good-nature, and his thorough good sense and right feeling. We must be very hard to please if we are not pleased with him. He is not the "cultivated American" who redeems us from time to time in the eyes of Europe; but he is unquestionably more national, and it is observable that his unaffected fellow-countrymen and women fare very well at Mr. James's hands always; it is the Europeanizing sort like the critical little Bostonian in the "Bundle of Letters," the ladies shocked at Daisy Miller, the mother in the "Pension

Beaurepas" who goes about trying to be of the "native" world everywhere, Madame Merle and Gilbert Osmond, Miss Light and her mother, who have reason to complain, if any one has. Doubtless Mr. James does not mean to satirize such Americans, but it is interesting to note how they strike such a keen observer. We are certainly not allowed to like them, and the other sort find somehow a place in our affections along with his good Europeans. It is a little odd, by the way, that in all the printed talk about Mr. James—and there has been no end of it—his power of engaging your preference for certain of his people has been so little commented on. Perhaps it is because he makes no obvious appeal for them; but one likes such men as Lord Warburton, Newman, Valentin, the artistic brother in "The Europeans," and Ralph Touchett, and such women as Isabel, Claire Belgarde, Mrs. Tristram, and certain others, with a thoroughness that is one of the best testimonies to their vitality. This comes about through their own qualities, and is not affected by insinuation or by downright *petting*, such as we find in Dickens nearly always and in Thackeray too often.

The art of fiction has, in fact, become a finer art in our day than it was with Dickens and Thackeray. We could not suffer the confidential attitude of the latter now, nor the mannerism of the former, any more than we could endure the prolixity of Richardson or the coarseness of Fielding. These great men are of the past—they and their methods and interests; even Trollope and Reade are not of the present. The new school derives from Hawthorne and George Eliot rather than any others; but it studies human nature much more in its wonted aspects, and finds its ethical and dramatic examples in the operation of lighter but not really less vital motives. The moving accident is certainly not its trade; and it prefers to avoid all manner of dire catastrophes. It is largely influenced by French fiction in form; but it is the realism of Daudet rather than the realism of Zola that prevails with it, and it has a soul of its own which is above the business of recording the rather brutish pursuit of a woman by a man, which seems to be the chief end of the French novelist. This school, which is so largely of the future as well as the present, finds its chief exemplar in Mr. James; it is he who is shaping and directing American fiction, at least. It is the ambition of the younger contributors to write like him; he has his following more distinctly recognizable than that of any other English-writing novelist. Whether he will so far control this following as to decide the nature of the novel with us remains to be seen. Will the reader be content to accept a novel which is an analytic study rather than a story, which is apt to leave him arbiter of the destiny of the author's creations? Will he find his account in the unflagging interest of their development? Mr. James's growing popularity seems to suggest that this may be the case; but the work of Mr. James's imitators will have much to do with the final result.

In the meantime it is not surprising that he has his imitators. Whatever exceptions we take to his methods or his results, we cannot deny him a very great literary genius. To me there is a perpetual delight in his way of saying things, and I cannot wonder that younger men try to catch the trick of it. The disappointing thing for them is that it is not a trick, but an inherent virtue. His style is, upon the whole, better than that of any other novelist I know; it is always easy, without being trivial, and it is often stately, without being stiff; it gives a charm to everything he writes; and he has written so much and in such various directions, that we should be judging him very incompletely if we considered him only as a novelist. His book of European sketches must rank him with the most enlightened and agreeable travelers; and it might be fitly supplemented from his uncollected papers with a volume of American sketches. In his essays on modern French writers he indicates his critical range and grasp; but he scarcely does more, as his criticisms in "The Atlantic" and "The Nation" and elsewhere could abundantly testify.

There are indeed those who insist that criticism is his true vocation, and are impatient of his devotion to fiction; but I suspect that these admirers are mistaken. A novelist he is not, after the old fashion, or after any fashion but his own; yet since he has finally made his public in his own way of story-telling—or call it character-painting if you prefer,—it must be conceded that he has chosen best for himself and his readers in choosing the form of fiction for what he has to say. It is, after all, what a writer has to say rather than what he has to tell that we care for nowadays. In one manner or other the stories were all told long ago; and now we want merely to know what the novelist thinks about persons and situations. Mr. James gratifies this philosophic desire. If he sometimes forbears to tell us what he thinks of the last state of his people, it is perhaps because that does not interest him, and a large-minded criticism might well insist that it was childish to demand that it must interest him.

I am not sure that my criticism is sufficiently large-minded for this. I own that I like a finished story; but then also I like those which Mr. James seems not to finish. This is probably the position of most of his readers, who cannot very logically account for either preference. We can only make sure that we have here an annalist, or analyst, as we choose, who fascinates us from his first page to his last, whose narrative or whose comment may enter into any minuteness of detail without fatiguing us, and can only truly grieve us when it ceases.

[*Century*, November 1882]

72

Maurice Thompson and His Poems.

THE question whether some life which makes poetry a rare and precious privilege to the poet does not afford better conditions for it than a purely literary calling is one that must present itself to the reader of "Songs of Fair Weather," if he knows anything of the author's history. Mr. Thompson is a very prosperous lawyer, in full practice in a little Western city, remote from literary associations and what are supposed to be literary incentives. If he were a young man, beginning the world, he would probably say to himself that Crawfordsville, Indiana, had no opportunities for a poet, and would make what haste he could to get into an environment of publication and criticism. But, as it is, he seems content to remain where he is, and apparently finds there all that is necessary to keep the will and the power of poetry alive in him. Literature must be a fresher and sweeter thing to such a man than it is to some of us who have been able to make it our shop; it must have still its primal zest; and I think that the peculiar qualities of "Songs of Fair Weather" are proof of this. Hereafter, perhaps, fiction, which is striving more and more to be truth, will study all the facts of a life like this poet's, and will inquire more closely than criticism can into the life around him: and then we may realize that the deepest sympathy with literature is not in Boston or New York; but in Crawfordsville, wherever Crawfordsville happens to be, east or west, north or south. It is in such small cities that a certain number of people read in a clear and unexcited atmosphere unknown to the so-called literary centers; they get the good of books which we, whom they come to as events, almost as mere matters of news, fail to get in equal measure. This is not saying that literature meets with the same technical appreciation in such places; that is impossible in the nature of things; but it does meet with profound sympathy, and not alone from women, who do the most of our reading, but from men also—at least in the West, where I have sometimes known them to keep, in the midst of affairs and public life, a romantic fondness for poetry and ideal fiction. They are a little old-fashioned in their tastes; that cannot be helped; and they come rather later to current literature than people in the great towns do; but they bring an unjaded sense to it, and more of it stays with them. In such a place, among such friends and neighbors, some of whom one need not idealize to find them what I have suggested, a poet, a literary man, has as favorable an environment as he need have anywhere; and he may devote himself as successfully to his art as in a nominal literary metropolis. For there are, happily, no schools of literature, as there are of other arts, to make him tame and academical; and he can command as much of real instruction from criticism and example there as he could find in London or Paris. The value of literary association, of the companionship of his kind, that is an unknown quantity, which we can only guess at from the quality of his performance. If he adds to his remoteness from this the practice of an alien profession, we are certainly brought to some such question as that I have felt in looking over Mr. Thompson's work. It will not do to say that, if you wish to write poems so delicately graceful, so full of a fresh, new speech for Nature as Mr. Thompson has written, you had better go practice law in an interior city of the second or third class; but the fact that he wrote them under these conditions remains, and suggests a revision of some of our preconceptions. It may only bring us in the end to saying that where the poet is there will be the poetry; but at least the poetry of Mr. Thompson is a most interesting study from the character of his circumstances.

Nothing more Western than this sensitively refined and lovely verse has yet come from the West. As we have understood from many supposed authorities the West ought to speak a dialect; it ought to be humorous in a huge, reckless, truculent sort, with moments of ungrammatical and hiccoughing pathos; it should be grotesque; it should be aggressively free. But here is something as fine as it is free, as gentle as it is native, as elect as it is wild in flavor, as lawful as it is sylvan in spirit; and yet it is all thoroughly and genuinely Western. The odor of the woods, pure and keen and clean, seems to strike up from this verse as directly as from the mold in the heart of the primeval forest; but it is as exquisite as if thrice distilled in some chemist's alembic, the last effect of his cunning in perfumes. Here, in a word, are conscious and instinctive art allied to a love of Nature, the most simple and joyous and unaffected that has for many a year found voice in rhyme.

I was going to say the most impassioned love for Nature; but then it occurred to me that no word could be more unfit for the dominant feeling in Mr. Thompson's poetry, which is cool and sweet, and as far from the heated and unwholesome mood of passion as a breath from the meadows or a fall of September sunshine; and it is this passionless, true feeling which makes it so rare in kind and so charming. His verse talks all the time in the poet's person, but it is singularly impersonal; it always puts the things he loves before his love of them. He exists merely to realize their loveliness to us. Here and there he strikes a thin, soft note of melancholy; but beyond this the suggestion of a presence gentle and shy, but very alert and manful, guiding our pleasure, is all that we have of the poet personally, to whom it may well seem a wrong that any one should try to detach him from the sylvan shadows with which he likes to mix. But a poet's work is of a sort that is always best appreciable through some knowledge of his life; and this poet's life has been picturesque and dramatic in full American variety.

He was born in Indiana; but his father an itinerant Baptist preacher, went early to Florida, and the poet grew up there amidst influences that deeply influenced his character and career. The nature, rich and wild, of the swamps and everglades, paints itself continually in his verse; and it was in their haunts that what comes nearest being a passion in him, his love of archery, grew. This world-old chase of wild things with bow and arrow, which, to our race, has been for five hundred years only a romantic dream of the poets, was an actuality with this poet and his brother, who ranged the Florida savannas with him, and who jointly with him has helped to revive a sport throughout the country among thousands, who, I am afraid, do not know how much more beautifully it lives in his poems than in their clubs, with all their meetings of pretty young girls and lithe and strong young fellows; though I am far from willing to disparage the charm of these. It trained the poet's eye to that minute acquaintance with every feature and expression of Nature's face which the hunter must have; but he was yet a boy when he must lay down the weapons of his mimic warfare for something that was altogether more serious in the business of killing. His family were in Florida when the War broke out, and the poet, like our great Southern romancer, Cable, fought through it on the losing side, with the same growing misgiving that it was the wrong side. He was still very young when, after the War, he drifted back to his native state, and began to study law at Crawfordsville. He had such culture as some Southern academy could give him; and he had as little means as possible short of having none. But this is the old American story which I need not dwell upon. We have nearly outlived it, especially we of the West. In due time Mr. Thompson was admitted to the bar, and his gifts and energies did the rest. His brother, whose name became even more famous in the revival of archery, was associated with him in the law, and the two married sisters and founded such houses, simple, quiet, refined, as make us willing to believe almost any good we hear of American life.

But at the threshold of these, if the reader pleases, we will pause, and not advance the foot, which any one may place on the table at Mr. Thompson's office, among the sociable boots of his clients. Here his prose life is passed; and in the modest home, on the border of the pleasant town, his poet life begins when he has trimmed his evening lamp and turned the key upon the world. He keeps his two lives quite distinct; one is not suffered to hurt the other. He is an able and business-like lawyer, as well as the author of these delicate poems and that charming romance which I do not know that I have the right to connect his name with. But he is even more strictly a poet than a romancer, with a love for fineness in his work which best satisfies itself in verse.

The first of his poems that I knew is one of the best in this collection. It came to me as editor of *The Atlantic Monthly*, ten or twelve years ago, and I remember sharing my pleasure in its freshness with that generous and gracious poet, who is in all our hearts, but shall cross our thresholds no more. We had a little question about a bird that was named in it—the sap sucker, as it is called in the West, but which Mr. Longfellow had never heard of, at least by that name; and I asked him if I had not better turn it into a blue-bird. He thought that I might harmlessly make this change; but now I desire to restore the sap-sucker to his place in literature, with the humble acknowledgement, long delayed, that the poet was right and the editor was wrong.

"AT THE WINDOW.

"I heard the woodpecker pecking,
　　The sap-sucker sing;
I turned and looked out of my window,
　　And lo, it was Spring!

"A breath from tropical borders,
　　Just a ripple, flowed into my room,
And washed my face clean of its sadness,
　　Blew my heart into bloom.

"The loves I have kept for a lifetime,
　　Sweet buds I have shielded from snow,
Break forth into full leaf and tassel
　　When Spring winds do blow.

"For the sap of my life goes upward,
　　Obeying the same sweet law
That waters the heart of the maple
　　After a thaw.

"I forget my old age and grow youthful,
　　Bathing in wind-tides of Spring,
When I hear the woodpecker pecking,
　　The sap-sucker sing."

There is something curiously touching in this poem, which I have never been able to read without a responsive thrill, both for its unaffected gladness and the pang that is somehow hidden in the heart of all rapture. The words and the images are simple and homely, but how good the first are, and how bold and strong the last!

Here is another poem in a different key, which I have always liked very much:

"NOVEMBER.

"A hint of slumber in the wind,
　　A dreamful stir of blades and stalks,
As tenderly the twilight flows
　　Down all my garden walks.

"My robes of work are thrown aside,
    The odor of the grass is sweet;
The pleasure of a day well spent
    Bathes me from head to feet.

"Calmly I wait the dreary change—
    The season cutting sharp and sheer
Through the wan bowers of death that fringe
    The border of the year.

"And while I muse, the fated earth
    Into a colder current dips—
Feels Winter's scourge with Summer's kiss
    Still warm upon her lips."

Is not this very subtly felt? There is the true imaginative touch in it, and the courage that trusts to reach the same emotion in the reader which the poet feels, by figures that say nothing to an alien mood. This courage is even greater in the very impressionistic little bit called

"BEFORE DAWN.

"A keen, insistent hint of dawn
    Fell from the mountain hight;
A wan, uncertain gleam betrayed
    The faltering of the night.

"The emphasis of silence made
    The fog above the brook
Intensely pale; the trees took on
    A haunted, haggard look.

"Such quiet came, expectancy
    Filled all the earth and sky;
Time seemed to pause a little space;
    I heard a dream go by!"

This is perfect of its kind; and I trust the reader appreciates the wholly unconventional character of its descriptiveness.

The poems I have quoted belong to a kind which I am in greater sympathy with than others in the book, though I own to liking them all; and in all I find a peculiar desire to say things simply and frankly that delights me. This is a poet who certainly does not get his love of Nature from literature, and who does not have to borrow the turns and touches of any other poet in reporting what he sees in her. What a waft from the woods is here, for instance:

"The belted halcyon laughs, the wren
    Comes twittering from its brushy den;

"The turtle sprawls upon its log,
 I hear the booming of a frog.

"*Liquidamber's keen perfume,
 Sweet-punk, calamus, tulip bloom*;

"Dancing wasp and dragon-fly,
 Wood-thrush whistling tenderly;

"Damp, cool breath of moss and mold,
 Noontide's influence manifold;

"Glimpses of a cloudless sky
 Soothe me as I resting lie.

"Bubble, bubble, flows the stream,
 Like low music through a dream."

The lines which I have italicized show the same joy in things and the names of things which one is aware of in the best songs of "the spacious times of great Elizabeth," when English was yet new and the poets were trying all its stops.

"Liquidamber's sweet perfume,
 Sweet-punk, calamus, tulip bloom,"

surely were never in verse before; but how musical they are; and how glad one is of the woodsy odor that seems to steal from such lines as

"Where the green walnut's outer rind
 Gives precious bitterness to the wind,"

and of the novelty of such a picture as

"I stand in some dim place at dawn
 And see across a forest lawn,

"The tall, wild turkeys swiftly pass,
 Light-footed through the dewy grass."

The verses that follow are scarcely more than a catalogue of the things named, yet their mere music and color are full of satisfying significance:

"Coolness all about me creeping,
 Fragrance all my senses steeping—

"Spicewood, sweet-gum, sassafras,
 Calamus and water-grass,

"Giving up their pungent smells,
Drawn from Nature's secret wells;

"On the cool breath of the morn,
Perfume of the cock-spur thorn,

"Green spathes of the dragon-root,
Indian turnip's tender shoot,

"Dogwood, red-bud, elder, ash,
Snowy gleam and purple flash,

"Hillside thickets, densely green,
That the partridge revels in."

Mr. Thompson is the first to say

"The busy nut-hatch climbs his tree,
Around the great bole spirally,"

as we have all seen him do; and in the "Death of the White Heron" and "The Fawn" he paints the whole unknown world of the Floridian glades and brakes. These are two sylvan tragedies, and it needs all their beauty to reconcile us to a catastrophe so realistically yet delicately limned as this:

"The wind drew faintly from the south,
Like breath blown from a sleeper's mouth,

"And down its current, sailing low,
Came a lone heron, white as snow.

"Then from my fingers leapt the string
With sharp recoil and deadly ring,

"Closed by a sibilant sound so shrill,
It made the very water thrill;

"Like twenty serpents bound together,
Hissed the flying arrow's feather!

"A thud, a puff, a feathery ring,
A quick collapse, a quivering—

"A whirl, a headlong downward dash,
A heavy fall, a sullen plash,

"And like white foam, or giant flake
Of snow, he lay upon the lake!

"And of his death the rail was glad,
  Strutting upon a lily-pad;

"The jaunty wood-duck smiled and bowed;
  The belted kingfisher laughed aloud,

"Making the solemn bittern stir
  Like a half-wakened slumberer;

"And rasping notes of joy were heard
  From gallinule and crying bird,

"The while with trebled noise did ring
  The hammer of the golden-wing!"

I should be sorry not to note how perfectly the sense of the waft and lull of a Summer wind is suggested in the line italicized; and as I read the close of the poem it is almost as if I heard that din of the golden-wing's bill and all the exultant clamor of the other forest denizens.

The reader may come to the other tragedy unprepared by quotation; but before leaving the book to him I must speak of a group of poems on classic subjects, poor old allegories, worn so smooth and flat by the touch of rhymers in all ages that one would say there could be no more form or motion in them. This group includes "Garden Statues," "Atalanta," "Ceres," "Avede," and "Diana," the last of which I will quote, to show how these conceptions spring to life, eternally beautiful, and walk the earth again whenever a true poet invokes them:

"She had a bow of yellow horn,
  Like the old moon at early morn.

"She had three arrows strong and good,
  Steel set in feathered cornel wood.

"Like purest pearl her left breast shone,
  Above her kirtle's emerald zone;

"Her right was bound in silk well-knit,
  Lest her bow-string should sever it.

"Ripe lips she had, and clear gray eyes,
  And hair pure gold blown hoiden-wise

"Across her face like shining mist
  That with dawn's flush is faintly kissed.

"Her limbs! how matched and round and fine!
  How free like song! how strong like wine!

"And, timed to music wild and sweet,
How swift her silver-sandaled feet!

"Single of heart and strong of hand,
Wind-like she wandered through the land.

"No man (or king or lord or churl)
Dared whisper love to that fair girl.

"And woe to him who came upon
Her nude at bath, like Acteon!

"So dire his fate that one who heard
The flutter of a bathing bird,

"What time he crossed a breezy wood,
Felt sudden quickening of his blood;

"Cast one swift look, then ran away
Far through the green, thick groves of May,

"Afeard, lest down the wind of Spring
He'd hear an arrow whispering!"

How plastic and how graphic all this is! And yet I feel sure that this poet never saw a master-piece of sculpture or painting: it is divined, as the Greek feeling of Keats's poetry was divined, by one who knew it only from the English translations; and it is purely delightful in spite of Mr. Thompson's Western insensibility to the claims of the subjunctive!

[New York, *The Independent*, 4 October 1883]

73

The Bread-Winners.[1]

THIS story did not lack comment, more or less impassioned, during the course of its publication in *The Century*, and its characteristics will probably have been canvassed still more thoroughly before these pages meet the eye of the reader. From the first it was noticeable that the criticism it received concerned the morality of the story, and even the morality of the writer, rather than the art of either; and, on the whole, we do not see why this was not well enough. It was, we think, a wholesome way of regarding the performance, and, even in those who most disliked it, implied a sense of conscience and of thinking in the book, however warped, however mistaken. It was a better way of looking at it than a mere survey of its literary qualities would have been, and it marked an advance in popular criticism. The newspapers did not inquire so much whether this or that character was well drawn, this or that incident or situation vividly reported, as whether the writer, dealing forcibly with some living interests of our civilization, meant one thing or another by what he was doing; though they did not fail to touch upon its literature at the same time. The discussion evolved an interesting fact, which we recommend to all intending novelists, that among us at least the novelist is hereafter to be held to account as a public teacher; that he must expect to be taken seriously, and must do his work with the fear of a community before his eyes which will be jealous of his ethical soundness, if nothing else. What did the author of "The Bread-winners" mean by making his rich and well-to-do people happy, and leaving all the suffering to the poor? Does he believe that it is wrong for the starving laborer and operative to strike? Are his sympathies with the rich against the poor? Does he think workingmen are all vicious? Does he mean that it was right for Captain Farnham to kiss Maud Matchin when she had offered herself to him in marriage and dropped herself into his arms, unless he meant to marry her? Was he at all better than she if he could do such a thing? Was it nice of Mrs. Belding to tell her daughter of this incident? Ought Alice Belding to have accepted him after such a thing as that?

Some of these voices—which still agitate the air—are unmistakably soprano and contralto; some, for which we have less respect, are falsetto. We

[1] The Bread-Winners. A Social Study. New York: Harper & Bros.

do not know whether it would be possible, or whether it would be profitable, to answer them conclusively. At any rate, we shall not attempt it; but we would like to call attention to the very important fact that the author of "The Bread-winners" shows no strong antipathy to strikers till they begin to burn and rob and propose to kill; and we will ask the abstract sympathizer to recall his own sensations in regard to the great railroad strike in 1877, after the riots began. In our own mind there is no question that any laborer, or any multiple of him, not being content with his hire, has the right to leave his work; and we should have been well content to see the strike of the telegraphers succeed, and not ill pleased to see those who thought them paid enough put to live awhile on their wages. But if the striking telegraphers, like the striking railroad men, had begun to threaten life and destroy property, we should have wanted the troops called out against them. We cannot see that the author of "The Bread-winners" has gone beyond this point in his treatment of the question of strikes.

We cannot see, either, that he has in any sort a prejudice against the workingman as a workingman. We are all workingmen in America, or the sons of workingmen, and few of us are willing to hear them traduced; but, for our own part, they do not seem to us preëminent for wisdom or goodness, and we cannot perceive that they derive any virtue whatever from being workingmen. If they were lawyers, doctors, or clergymen, they would be equally respectable, and not more so. They are certainly better than the idle rich, as they are better than the idle poor—the two classes which we have chiefly, if not solely, to dread; and it is the idle poor whom our author does not like, whom he finds mischievous, as other writers of romance have long found the idle rich. It is the Offitts and the Botts and the Bowersoxes whom he detests, not the Matchins, nor even the Sleenys. These are treated with respect, and Sleeny, at least in the end, is rather more lavishly rewarded than any of the millionaires, if his luck in escaping the gallows is not more than neutralized by the gift of Miss Maud Matchin as a wife. But there is no doubt the author meant well by him; and we think there is no doubt that he means well by all honest, hard-working people. He has not made them very brilliant, for still "the hand of little employment hath the nicer sense"; he has not heaped them with worldly prosperity, and it must be owned that Divine Providence has done no better by them. Let us be just before we are generous, even to the workingman. Let us recognize his admirable qualities in full measure; but let us not make a fetich of him, impeccable, immaculate, infallible. We suspect that in portraying a certain group of people as he has done, the author of "The Bread-winners" meant no more nor less than to tell the truth about them; and if he has not flattered the likeness of his workingmen, he has done the cause of labor and the cause of art both a service. Workingmen are in no bad way among us. They have to practice self-denial and to work hard, but both of these things used to be thought good for human nature. When they will not work, they are as bad as club men and ladies of fashion, and perhaps more dangerous. It is quite time we were invited to consider some of them in fiction as we saw some of them in fact during the great railroad strike.

When we come to the question whether Captain Farnham ought to have kissed Maud Matchin, or turned from her with loathing, we confess that we feel the delicacy of the point. Being civilians, we will venture to say that we fear it was quite in character for an ex-army man to kiss her, and so far the author was right. Whether it was in character for a perfect gentleman to do so, we cannot decide; something must be conceded to human nature and a sense of the girl's impudence, even in a perfect gentleman. But, having dodged this point, we feel all the more courage to deal with another, namely, whether he was not quite as bad as she. We think not, for reasons which his accusers seem to forget. Miss Matchin did not offer herself to him because she loved him, but because she loved his wealth and splendor, and wished to enjoy them; and, though she was careful to tell him that she would only be his wife, it is not clear to our minds that if she could have been equally secure of his wealth and splendor in another way, there was anything in her character to make her refuse. He did behave with forbearance and real kindness to that foolish and sordid spirit; he did use her with magnanimity and do what he could to help her, though she had forfeited all claim upon his respect. He may not have been a perfect gentleman, but he was certainly a very good sort of man, in spite of that questionable kiss.

We might wish to have Miss Matchin other than she was for her own sake; but if she were different, she would not be so useful nor so interesting. She is the great invention, the great discovery, of the book; and she is another vivid and successful study of American girlhood, such as it seems to be largely the ambition of our novelists to make. She is thoroughly alive, caught by an instantaneous process, in which she almost visibly breathes and pulsates. One has a sense of her personal presence throughout, though it is in the introductory passages that we realize most distinctly her mental and spiritual qualities, and the wonderful degree in which she is characterized by American conditions—by the novels of the public library, by the ambitious and inadequate training of the high school, by the unbounded freedom of our social life. These conditions did not produce her; with other girls they are the agencies of inestimable good. But, given the nature of Miss Maud Matchin, we see the effect upon her at every point. We can see the effect, also, of the daily newspaper and of the display of Algonquin Avenue, with its histories in brick and stone of swift, and recent, and immeasurable riches. The girl's poetry is money, her romantic dream is to marry a millionaire. She has as solid and sheer a contempt for the girl who dreams of an old-fashioned hero and love in a cottage as she has for her hard-working father and mother. There are no influences in her home to counteract the influences from without. She grows up a beautiful, egotistic, rapacious, unscrupulous fool. But take the novels and the high school away, and she would still have been some kind of fool. The art of the author consists in having painted her as she exists through them. The novelist can do no more. He shows us this creature, who is both type and character, and fitly leaves the moralist to say what shall be done about her. Probably nothing can be done about her at once; but if she is definitely ascertained as a fact of our civilization, it is a desirable step in self-knowledge for us.

At the end the author's strong hand seems to falter a little in the treatment of Miss Matchin. We read of her "rosy and happy face" when the man she has driven to murder is acquitted, and the chief weakness of the book here betrays itself. Something should have been done to show that those people had entered hand in hand into their hell, and that thenceforth there could be no hope for them.

There are some admirable passages of casual or subordinate interest in the book, and a great many figures drawn with a force that leaves a permanent impression. The episode of Maud's canvass for the place in the public library, and her triumph through the "freeze-out" that leaves Pennybaker "kickin' like a Texas steer"; the behavior of the rascal mayor during the strike; all the politicians' parlance; the struggle of Alice Belding with herself after her good-natured but not very wise mother has told her of Maud's offer to Farnham; her feeling that this has somehow stained or "spoiled" him;— these are traits vigorously or delicately treated, that may be set against an account of less interesting handling of some society pictures. The scenes of the riot and the attack on Farnham's house are stirringly done; that of the murderous attack on Farnham by Offitt less so; and it appears to us rather precipitate in Alice to fall asleep as soon as she hears that her lover is not fatally hurt. But these are very minor points. Generally speaking, we think the author has done what he meant to do. We believe that he has been faithful to his observation of facts. If the result is not flattering, or even pleasing, that is not his fault, and neither his art nor his morality is to blame for it.

[*Century*, May 1884]

74

Two Notable Novels.[1]

I have lately read two novels—or rather two fictions, for one of them, strictly speaking, is a romance rather than a novel—which struck me as being, in several ways, uncommonly interesting. Not the least interesting thing about them was the witness they bore of the prevalence of realism in the artistic atmosphere to such degree that two very differently gifted writers, having really something to say in the way of fiction, could not help giving it the realistic character. This was true no less of the romance than of the novel; and I fancied that neither the romancer nor the novelist had theorized much, if at all, in regard to the matter. Realism—the name is not particularly good—being almost the only literary movement of our time that has vitality in it, these two authors, who felt the new life in them, and were not mere literary survivals, became naturally part of it.

The novel was "The Story of a Country Town," and unless it shall have reached your readers in an Eastern republication, I imagine that I shall be giving most of them the first news of it. The author is Mr. E. W. Howe, who is also the editor of an evening paper in Atchison, Kansas, and who printed and published the first edition of his novel himself. In his preface he tells, with a frankness that is at once manly and appealing, how he wrote the book at night, after his day's work on the newspaper was done; but it is with the novel, and not with the novelist, that we have to do at present. It is simply what it calls itself, the story of a country town in the West, which has so many features in common with country towns everywhere, that whoever has lived in one must recognize the grim truth of the picture. It does not lack its reliefs,—which are of a humorous rather than a joyous sort,—but is very grim nevertheless, and at times intolerably sad. Its earlier chapters represent the hard-worked, almost hopeless life of the women in a country neighborhood, and the plodding disappointment of the men, in whom toil and privation have quenched the light of dreams in which they came out to possess the new land. Out of this general sentiment are materialized certain types, certain characters. They are commonly good, and nearly always religious people, with a passion for religious observances and for Scriptural discussions; and

---

[1] The Story of a Country Town. By E. W. Howe. Boston: J. R. Osgood & Co.
Miss Ludington's Sister. By E. W. Bellamy. Boston: J. R. Osgood & Co.

their gloom, one feels, is a temporary but necessary condition, out of which the next generation is sure to emerge. The author has instinctively chosen the form which, next to the dramatic, is the most perfect, and supposes himself the narrator of the story. His mother is one of those worn, weary women; his father is the sternest of the religionists, who, after leading a life of merciless industry and perfect morality, breaks under the strain of the monotony and solitude at last, and abandons his wife for a woman whom he does not love. This tragedy does not develop till the scene of the story has changed from the country neighborhood to the country town,—Twin Mounds it is called; and here the narrator's father buys the local newspaper and sets about making it prosperous with tremendous energy, which finally achieves success. But his curse is on him, and he goes away to ruin and disgrace, while his wife and son remain to a sorrow and shame that are depicted with unsparing and heart-breaking fullness. The wretched man returns the night following the death of his wife, and, after looking on her dead face with his pitying and forgiving son, goes out into the snow-storm from which he has come, and is heard of no more. This Rev. John Westlock is the great figure of the book, and not Jo Erring, of whom the author is fond, and who finally comes near spoiling the strong, hard-headed, clear-conscienced story. Yet Jo Erring is admirably imagined,—or discovered,—and even in his sentimental excess and unbalance is true to the West, and to a new country. His timorous, bewildered wife, who has yet a strange, womanly dignity, is very courageously and powerfully drawn; there are many such women in the world, but they are new to fiction. She is scientifically derived from her father, too, and the misery into which they both fall is the result of a weakness to which one cannot help being tender. Jo Erring becomes insanely jealous of a reprobate with whom Mateel had a boy-and-girl engagement; he kills the man, and commits suicide in prison. All that is treated deplorably enough as regards the narrator's blindness to the fact that Jo is really a culpable homicide; but on the artistic side, as regards the portrayal of character and conditions, there is no fault. The art is feeblest in the direction of Agnes, who is probably true to life, but seems rather more than the rest to have come out of books. Her termagant mother, on the other hand,—of whom we have scarcely more than a glimpse as she cuffs her way through a roomful of children,—and her uncle, the delicious cynic Lytle Biggs, with his frank philosophy and swindling life, are unmistakably out of the soil. It is not in the presentation of individuals, however, but rather in the realization of a whole order of things, that the strength of the book lies; and what I most admire in it is the apparently unconscious fearlessness with which all the facts of the case, good, bad, and indifferent, are recognized. Neither this thing nor that is exploited, but all things are simply and clearly portrayed. It is needless to note that, having something to say, the author has said it well; that follows. I do not care to praise his style, though, as far as that increasingly unimportant matter goes, it is well enough; but what I like in him is the sort of mere open humanness of his book. It has defects enough, which no one can read far without discovering; but, except in the case of Jo Erring, they are not important—certainly not such as to spoil any one's pleasure in a fiction which is of the kind most characteristic of our time, and which no student of our time hereafter can safely ignore. The book is full of simple homeliness, but is never vulgar. It does not flatter the West, nor paint its rough and rude traits as heroic; it perceives and states, and the results are perfectly imaginable American conditions, in which no trait of beauty or pathos is lost. There are charming things in it. Youth, with its ignorance, its ardor, its hopefulness and fearlessness, is more than once finely studied; and amidst the prevailing harshness and aridity there are episodes of tenderness and self-devotion that are like springs of water out of the ground. It is a fact so creditable to the community in which this remarkable novel was produced, without any aids of advertising or "favorable noticing," that I cannot forbear stating, at the risk of impertinence, that its uncommon quality was at once recognized, and the whole of the first edition sold there.

Mr. Bellamy works to an end very different in his romance, "Miss Ludington's Sister"; but he deals quite as frankly with his material, and has quite as little of that *mauvaise honte* which long prevented us from recognizing American conditions in the genteel presence of our English reviewers, as Mr. Howe. I observed that one of these critics lately arched a troubled eyebrow at a state of things presented in Mr. Bellamy's first story, "Dr. Heidenhoff's Process," where apparently the drug-clerk and the gunsmith's apprentice are members of village society. A little while ago, and we would not have dared to betray this low fact. But Mr. Bellamy had touched upon it in the most matter-of-fact, casual way, and as something that needed neither defense nor explanation; and his transatlantic reviewer, by a heroic effort, succeeded in praising his book in spite of it, though his noble reluctance was plain. In fact, Mr. Bellamy has done in both of his romances about the only thing left for the romancer to do in our times, if he will be part of its tendency: he has taken some of the crudest and most sordid traits of our life, and has produced from them an effect of the most delicate and airy romance. It always seemed to me that Hawthorne had some ironical or whimsical intention in his complaints of the unfriendliness of the American atmosphere and circumstance to his art; and the success of Mr. Bellamy, who is the first writer of romance in our environment worthy to be compared with Hawthorne, goes far to confirm me in this notion. By the boldness with which he treats our reality he wins a subtler effect for the fantastic and ideal when he introduces them. I think there can be in all fiction few stories more pathetic than "Dr. Heidenhoff's Process," in which the poor lost girl seems to find, in the physician's invention for the extirpation of any given memory, release from the shame of her fall. It would be a pity to dull the interest of any reader who has not happened to meet with the book, and I will tell its story no further. Of course I shall not reveal the secret of "Miss Ludington's Sister," but it can do no harm to ask the reader to note with what skill the clew is kept from him, with what cunning the irrefragable chain of logic is forged, and with what consummate craft the possible and the impossible are joined. All is told with the greatest quiet and plainness of manner, but there are moments when one's breath scarcely comes in the intense excitement of the situation: for example, where the medium suddenly dies in her trance, and the spirit which she has materialized remains in our world, bewildered, terrified, helpless. It is the earthly career of this strange being which fascinates the reader until the *éclaircissement* becomes almost intolerable; but, from first to last, nothing seems forced in character or situation. In this perhaps more daring flight of his imagination, Mr. Bellamy apparently finds himself no more embarrassed by fidelity to the every-day details of American life than he did in "Dr. Heidenhoff's Process." In both books these are treated with absolute unconsciousness of their difference from those of any other life. Up to a certain point it cannot be said that even Mr. Howe's novel is more realistic than Mr. Bellamy's romance, which, beyond that point, has earned the right to be as romantic as the author chooses. It indicates a direction in which a species of fiction, for which Hawthorne did so much that he may be almost said to have created it, can be continued and developed indefinitely. There is nothing antagonistic in realism to poetry or romance; perhaps the best and highest realism will be that which shall show us both of these where the feeble-thoughted and feeble-hearted imagine that they cannot exist. Mr. Howe's "Story of a Country Town" makes every stupid little American village poetic to the sympathetic witness, as geology renders every patch of earth historic; we grow indefinitely richer by such close and kindly study of human life, for if the study is close enough it is sure to be kindly; and realism is only a phase of humanity. Mr. Bellamy shows us that the fancy does not play less freely over our democratic levels than the picturesque inequalities of other civilizations, and both books enforce once more the fact that, whatever their comparative value may be, our own things are the best things for us to write of.

The new strength and the new freshness shown by these authors are not rare among our younger writers. Mr. Lathrop shows both, for example, in that beautiful book of his, "An Echo of Passion"; and I have just been reading Miss Jewett's last volume of sketches with exactly the keen delight with which one would meet her farmer and sailor folk in the flesh and hear them talk. Indeed, one does meet them really in her book; and it would be easy to multiply instances on every hand of the recognition of the principle of realism in our fiction. The books of Mr. Howe and of Mr. Bellamy happen to be the latest evidences, as well as very striking performances apart from this.

[*Century*, August 1884]

Notes to the Texts

THE following entries are keyed by page and line number to the contents of this volume. The count of lines begins at the top of each page (excluding running heads, page numbers, item numbers, and hairlines) and includes essay titles, bracketed editorial additions, section numbers or headings, bibliographical citations, and footnotes.

3.10   "Life . . . Sidney,": Sarah Matilda Henry Davis, *The Life and Times of Sir Philip Sidney* (Boston, 1859). Howells wrote to J. J. Piatt on 4 March 1859: "I have just been reading a foolish life of Sir Philip Sidney by a silly woman. If you want to laugh, read it—."

3.13   "A Bachelor's Story,": published 1859; by American novelist Oliver Bell Bunce (1828–1890).

3.14   "The Reveries" and "Dream Life,": *Reveries of a Bachelor* (1850) and *Dream-Life* (1851) by American novelist Donald Grant Mitchell (1822–1908), alias Ik Marvel.

3.35   Boston . . . *Patchquilt*: fictional titles suggesting mediocre literary magazines.

4.1–3   If . . . company: Dogberry's charge to the night watch in *Much Ado About Nothing*, III, iii, 25–51.

4.18   "rogues . . . serenades,": Tennyson, "The Princess: A Medley": "She wept her true eyes blind for such a one, / A rogue of canzonets and serenades" (IV, 116–117).

5.3–4   "*flammae inter nubes.*": *Latin*—a blaze in the gloom.

5.8–11   "Mein Herz . . . Bastei.": this and the allusions at 5.14, 5.17, and 5.18 are drawn from Heinrich Heine, *Buch der Lieder*, "Die Heimkehr," 3. The first four lines are translated—

> My heart, my heart is sad,
> Though May shines forth joyfully,
> I stand leaning against the linden tree,
> High atop the old bastion.

5.14   "fernes Gesunen,": Heine's line is "Ich höre sein fernes Gesumm"—I hear its distant hum.

5.17   *haupt-figur*: German—protagonist.

5.18   "Ich . . . todt!": Heine's line is "Ich wollte, er schösse mich tot."—
         I wished he would shoot me dead.

6.8   "Lotus Eater": Tennyson's "The Lotos-Eaters" (1833).

6.29–30 "suffer . . . strange?": *The Tempest*, I, ii, 400–402.

8.1   Clifton Pyncheon: error—authorial or otherwise—for Clifford
         Pyncheon.

9.2   poem: "Bardic Symbols," *Atlantic*, V (April 1860), 445–447.

9.8   scoop: used perhaps in the sense of a winnowing basket.

9.11–12 "Leaves of Grass,": the first edition was published in 1855, the
         second in 1856. The third, enlarged edition (1860) was in press
         when this article was written; for Howells' review of it, see item 4.

9.12–13 Ralph Waldo Emerson . . . age: on 21 July 1855 Emerson wrote
         Whitman the famous letter which Whitman published in the New
         York *Tribune*, 10 October 1855, and in the second edition of *Leaves
         of Grass*.

9.18   Some months ago: "A Child's Reminiscence," New York *Saturday
         Press*, 24 December 1859, p. 1, is the earliest printed version of
         "Out of the Cradle Endlessly Rocking."

9.19   dissension among the "crickets.": for the "crickets' " (critics') dis-
         sension, see "Walt Whitman's New Poem," New York *Saturday
         Press*, 7 January 1860, p. 1, and the parody "Yourn and Mine, and
         Any-Day," *Saturday Press*, 21 January 1860, p. 1.

10.11–14 "Break, break, . . . me!": the opening stanza of a poem without title
         (1842).

10.16   "divine despair.": Tennyson, "The Princess: A Medley": "Tears
         from the depths of some divine despair" (IV, 19).

11.2–3   Thayer and Eldrige: error, authorial or otherwise, for Thayer and
         Eldridge.

11.21–22 dead *Putnam*: Charles Eliot Norton, "Whitman's Leaves of Grass,"
         Putnam's, VI (September 1855), 321–323. *Putnam's* "died" in De-
         cember 1855 and was later revived.

11.24   Bardell and Pickwick: in Dickens' *The Pickwick Papers* (1837), vol. 2,
         ch. 6, Mr. Justice Stareleigh's instructions to the jury consist of
         useless truisms.

11.24–25 Emmerson: error, authorial or otherwise, for Emerson; see note
         9.12–13.

11.33   Nearly a year ago: see note 9.18.

12.1–5   The Misses . . . bulls: see note 3.19.

12.28   *Sie . . . lesen*: *German*—They are unreadable.

12.35   "the distinctive poet of America,": see note 9.12–13.

12.42   Heine: *Die romantische Schule*, III.

14.3   Caggeshall: error, authorial or otherwise, for William Turner Cog-
                geshall (1824–1867), state librarian at Columbus and literary editor
                of the *Ohio State Journal* when Howells joined the staff in 1858.

14.10   intention of the editor: Howells wrote four of the "Biographical
                Notices" (H. L. Bostwick, J. H. A. Bone, G. A. Stewart, M. A. Whit-
                tlesey) in *The Poets and Poetry of the West* and was himself represented
                in the volume by six poems.

14.18   we said: "Poets and Poetry of the West," *Ohio State Journal*, 5 May
                1860, p. 2.

14.27–28   "airy . . . habitation.": *A Midsummer Night's Dream*, V, i, 16–17.

14.37   "They love . . . songs,": source not identified.

15.14   Thomas Moore: according to the biographical notice in *The Poets
                and Poetry of the West*, "Bachelor's Hall," by John Finley (1797–
                1866), had been "very widely circulated in England, as well as in
                America, with Thomas Moore's name to it" (p. 83).

15.15   John L. Harney's: actually John M. Harney (1789–1825).

15.16   Perkins': James H. Perkins (1810–1849).

15.25–28   Gallagher's verse . . . "Mary Robbins,": William Davis Gallagher
                (1808–1894), Alice Cary (1820–1871), Phoebe Cary (1825–1871),
                Rebecca S. Nichols (1819–1903), Amelia B. Welby (1819–1852),
                William W. Fosdick (1825–1862), William Ross Wallace (1819–
                1881), Coates Kinney (1826–1904), William Wallace Harney
                (1831–1912; son of John M. Harney; for Howells' essay on his
                poems, see item 6), John J. Piatt (1835–1917; co-author with How-
                ells of *Poems of Two Friends* [1860]; for Howells' review of his later
                volumes, see item 60), Louisa Amelia M'Gaffey-Pratt (1833–?; alias
                "Ruth Crayne"), and Mary Robbins Whittlesey (1832–?).

17.3   Mr. Coggeshall's book: William Turner Coggeshall, ed., *The Poets
                and Poetry of the West* (1860); see item 5.

17.5   a series: the "series" consisted of this and one other article, "Some
                Western Poets of To-Day: Helen H. Bostwick," *Ohio State Journal*,
                1 October 1860, p. 2.

17.19   William Wallace Harney: (1831–1912) teacher, attorney, author,
                and associate editor of the Louisville *Daily Democrat*. Born at

Bloomington, Indiana, Harney moved to Kentucky at the age of five. His later works include "Who Won the Pretty Widow," published under Howells' editorship in the *Atlantic*, XXIX (May 1872), and *The Spirit of the South* (1909).

20.7   Drayton's "Dawsabel,": Michael Drayton, *Pastorals*. Fourth Eclogue:

> Quoth he, So Had I done full well,
> Had I not seene faire Dowsabell
>   Come forth to gather May.

20.21–24   "absorbed . . . politics.": despite the quotation marks, Howells is paraphrasing rather than quoting the biographical sketch of Harney in *The Poets and Poetry of the West*, p. 634.

20.32   "Ah! . . . days!": source not identified.

21.16   Manzoni . . . Grossi: Alessandro Manzoni (1785–1873), Silvio Pellico (1789–1854), Francesco Domenico Guerazzi (1804–1873), Massimo d'Azeglio (1798–1866), and Tommaso Grossi (1791–1853) were all patriots whose writings reflect their romantic nationalism.

21.42   Ruffini: Giovanni Ruffini (1807–1881).

22.42   1859: the year of the Italian war against Austria, which finally led to the unification of Italy.

22.44   *hunkers*: entrenched reactionaries in the New York Democratic Party.

23.19   Goldoni: Carlo Goldoni (1707–1793).

23.23   Giacometti: Paolo Giacometti (1816–1882).

24.12   *facchini*: *Italian*—porters.

25.2   *capa y espada*: *Spanish*—cloak and dagger.

25.4   *righe di biglietto*: *Italian*—intimate note, *billet doux*.

26.2   *è fatto così*: *Italian*—he is made so; it is his nature.

26.29   Gigli . . . Faggiuoli: Girolamo Gigli (1660–1722), Jacopo Martelli (1665–1727), Niccolo Amenta (1659–1717), Francesco Scipione Maffei (1675–1755), and Giovanni Battista Fagiuoli (1660–1742).

26.35   autobiography: Goldoni's *Memoirs*, first published in French in 1787; Howells edited an 1877 English translation and wrote an introduction which first appeared in the *Atlantic*, XL (November 1877), 601–613.

26.42   Dall' Ongaro: Francesco Dall'Ongaro (1808–1873).

27.2   *imbroglione*: *Italian*—swindler, intriguer.

28.5   Ridotto: *Italian*—literally a foyer or retreat, but used also to refer to a public entertainment.

28.13   *scaldini*: *Italian*—braziers for warming the hands.

28.27   Alfieri: Vittorio Conte Alfieri (1749–1803); Howells' edition of his autobiography was published in 1877.

28.31   Alberto Nota: 1775–1847.

28.38   Augusto Bon: Francesco Augusto Bon (1778–1858). The plays mentioned were published between 1832 and 1837.

29.29   *civetta*: *Italian*—flirt.

29.37   *cavalieri serventi*: *Italian*—ladies' men.

30.31   battle . . . won: the unification of Italy in 1861 under King Victor Emmanuel II did not include Venetia, Rome, or the Papal States.

30.37–38   "New men . . . past,": Tennyson, "Godiva," lines 6–7.

31.40   Ciconi: Teobaldo Ciconi (1824–1863).

31.41   *White Flies*: *Le mosche bianche* (1863).

32.1   *birbante matricolato*: *Italian*—consummate rascal.

33.9   Paolo Ferrari: 1822–1889.

33.11   Castelvecchio . . . Botto: Riccardo Castelvecchio, pseudonym of Count Giulio Ceasare Baldassare Leopoldo Pullè (1814–1894); Luigi Gualtieri (1826–1901); Leone Fortis (1824–l898); Domenico Francesco Botto (? – ?) also published *Ingegno e speculazione: Commedia in quarto atti* (186?).

34.6   "*Ricordatevi . . . Fornaretto!*": *Italian*—Remember poor Fornaretto!

35.4   Veneto: from the province of Venetia.

35.20   "*pittoraccio di scenarii*,": *Italian*—an inferior landscape painter.

35.20–21   "*sovvertitore . . . scuola.*": *Italian*—a would–be rebel against any rule and an enemy to any school.

37.9   *extra domum, extra civitatem*: *Latin*—outside the home, outside the protection of the law.

39.39   "E perchè . . . originali.": *Italian*—And why not? The English are all eccentrics.

40.16   *La Scuola delle Vedove*: (1748) written and staged anonymously by Pietro Chiari (1711?–1785?).

41.32   *condottieri*: Italian—soldiers of fortune.

43.7–8   Lucretia Maria Davidson: 1808–1825; posthumous collections of her poetry were published in 1829 (*Amir-Khan, and Other Poems*) and 1841 (*Poetical Remains*).

43.45   Theodore Winthrop: 1828–1861; this writer's heroic death during the Civil War gave particular pathos to the praise accorded his posthumously published novels, *Cecil Dreeme* (1861), *John Brent* (1862), and *Edwin Brothertoft* (1862).

44.3   Aleardo Aleardi: 1812–1878.

44.20   *buon genere*: Italian—of the better sort.

44.28–29 "Can . . . . weep!": source not identified.

45.18   eloquent critic: Dall'Ongaro; see Howells' note, p. 26 in this text. Dall'Ongaro read and admired "Recent Italian Comedy" and later corresponded with Howells.

48.4   first book: *Leaves of Grass* (1855); for Howells' review, see item 4.

48.6   great sage: the basis of Howells' allusion has not been identified.

48.20   French critic: on 12 November 1860, in his "Literary Gossip" department for the *Ohio State Journal*, Howells translated the following paragraph from *Bibliographie Impériale*: "One reading him [Whitman] comprehends nothing; and the more one reads him, the less one comprehends. Nevertheless, something is believed to be acquired. You feel your soul launched upon a new orbit: *it is not the power which you understand*, it is the inspiration of *the poet which you partake*. You are not simply a reader—*you become associated in the great poetic enterprise.*"

52.2   Since . . . Tupper: *Littell's Living Age* for 13 April 1861 compared the Scotsman Andrew K. H. Boyd (1825–1879), author of the widely read *Recreations of a Country Parson* (1860) and its sequels, to Martin F. Tupper (1810–1889), author of *Proverbial Philosophy* (1838–1842), a didactic work of great popularity.

52.4   "Timothy Titcomb.": J. G. Holland's pseudonym.

53.43   Ruskin . . . slavery: probably a reference to Ruskin's "Essays on Political Economy" in the April 1863 number of *Fraser's Magazine*, later published as chapters V and VI ("Government" and "Mastership") of *Munera Pulveris* (1872).

59.16   "inarticulate natures;": in "No. II. Model Prisons," *Latter-Day Pamphlets* (1850), p. 46, Carlyle describes an elderly prison official who made a spirited formal defense of prison policy but whose "nature and all his inarticulate persuasion (however much forbidden to articulate itself) taught him the futility and unfeasability of the system followed here."

60.9   Mahomet's coffin: John Milton, *Eikonoklastes* (1649): "Legend has it that Mahomet's coffin is suspended in mid-air at Medina without any support, but kept in position by lodestones."

61.12   Byron's advice: Byron, *English Bards and Scotch Reviewers*, lines 75–77:

> . . . Believe a woman or an epitaph
> Or any other thing that's false, before
> You trust in critics who themselves are sore.

61.33   "nothing if not critical.": *Othello*, II, i, 120.

63.5   The author: Edward Colvil was the pseudonym of Mary Lowell Putnam (1810–1898); Howells wrote a second review of the book for the *North American Review*, CIII (October 1866), 620–621.

64.10   Mandingo's observations: the Mandingos included several black nations of West Africa, an area heavily preyed upon by slave traders.

65.9   moralities and proprieties: the serialization of *Griffith Gaunt* in the *Atlantic* (December 1865–November 1866) was widely criticized as "morally unfit for introduction to families" (*Round Table*, III [28 July 1866], 472) and affected the magazine's sales. The central problem addressed in this review—the relationship between good morals and true art—Howells treats again in a later review of Reade's *A Terrible Temptation*, in the *Atlantic*, XXVIII (September 1871), 383–384; see also *My Literary Passions* (1895), pp. 191–197.

65.21–22   "C'est . . . guerre.": *French*—it is magnificent, but it isn't war. Attributed to Pierre Bosquet (1810–1861), on the charge of the Light Brigade.

65.25   "Golden Dustman,": an allusion to Nicodemus Boffin, servant to the old dust contractor John Harmon in *Our Mutual Friend*; Boffin inherits Harmon's fortune.

66.35   "Romola,": George Eliot's novel, published 1862–1863.

67.22   Henry Esmond: Thackeray's novel, *The History of Henry Esmond, Esquire* (1852).

69.4   Atlantic: *The Biglow Papers, Second Series* appeared in six monthly parts in the *Atlantic* (January–June 1862) prior to collection in English editions (1862, 1864, and 1865) and an American publication in a single volume (1867). The original series of *Biglow Papers* was published as a book in 1848 after appearance in the Boston *Courier* in 1846.

73.22   "The living . . . pictures.": *Macbeth*, II, ii, 54–56:

> The sleeping and the dead
> Are but as pictures, 'tis the eye of childhood
> That fears a painted devil.

76.19   "As pure . . . bread,": source not identified.

76.38   "moralized his song,": Pope, *Epistle to Dr. Arbuthnot*, line 340.

77.19–22   "All can raise . . . weed,": Tennyson, "The Flower," lines 19–20, 23–24.

81.8   this *goldene . . . Jugend: German*—this golden time which does not rust is not an eternal youth.

84.2   first article: Howells' earlier essay was apparently "The Coming Translation of Dante," *Round Table*, III (19 May 1866), 305–306.

85.3–14   " 'Io son . . . . him.' ": *Purgatorio*, XIX, 19–24.

85.16   Cary's translation: *The Vision; or, Hell, Purgatory, and Paradise of Dante Alighieri*, translated by Henry Francis Cary (1814).

85.30–86.22   "Cruel . . . . not do.": *Inferno*, XXXIII, 40–75.

86.26–31   "Quivi . . . . digiuno,": *Inferno*, XXXIII, 70–75; line 74 reads "E che [not *tre*] dì gli chiamai, poich' e' fur morti."

86.40   Mr. Ford: *The Inferno of Dante*, translated by James Ford (1865).

87.8   Mr. Brooksbank: *Dante's Divine Comedy. The First Part. Hell.* "Translated in the metre of the original with notes" by Thomas Brooksbank (1854).

87.10   Mr. Cayley: *Dante's Divine Comedy*, "Translated in the original ternary rhyme" by Charles Bagot Cayley, 4 vols. (1851–1855).

87.15   Mrs. Ramsay: *Dante's Divina Commedia*, "Translated into English, in the metre and triple rhyme of the original. With notes," by Mrs. Claudia Hamilton Ramsay, 3 vols. (1866).

87.17–18   "Tu ne . . . . spoglia,": *Inferno*, XXXIII, 63–64.

87.24   Mr. Wright's: *Dante*, translated by Ichabod Charles Wright, 3 vols. (1845).

87.33   Mr. Rossetti: *The Comedy of Dante Alighieri*, "Translated into blank verse" by William Michael Rossetti, Part I, "The Hell" (1865).

88.4–5   episode of Francesca: *Inferno*, V, 98–143.

90.25   these lines: *Inferno*, III, 1–9.

91.35   Thomas: *The Trilogy; or, Dante's Three Visions*, "Translated into English, in the metre and triple rhyme of the original; with notes and illustrations" by the Rev. John Wesley Thomas, 3 vols. (1859–1866).

92.10   "If were . . . . friend,": *Inferno*, V, 91.

92.28–93.16   "And lo . . . . within.": *Purgatorio*, II, 13–45.

93.21–94.18   "And lo . . . . hands.": *Purgatorio*, XXVIII, 15–58.

94.28–31   "I suppose . . . English.": evidently a paraphrase from memory; no such quotation has been identified.

98.2   Thomas Purnell: English author (1834–1889) whose works also include *Dramatists of the Present Day* (1871).

110.12   "Evening—by a Tailor": in Holmes's *Poems* (1836), lines 1–4.

112.36–37   Schiller . . . Frederick: Thomas Carlyle, *Life of Friedrich Schiller* (1825) and *History of Friedrich II of Prussia* (1858–1865).

114.15   "Easy Chair": Curtis wrote "Editor's Easy Chair" for *Harper's Monthly* from 1853 until his death in 1892. The column was revived by Howells when he joined *Harper's* in 1900, and he remained its author until his death in 1920.

114.27   the Cable: the first permanent transatlantic telegraph cable had been laid in 1866 by Cyrus West Field.

115.39–40   Uhland's overpaid boatman: probably a reference to Ludwig Uhland's poem "Auf der Überfahrt," in which a man crossing a river (not necessarily the Rhine) is reminded of two friends, who had been in this same boat with him before they died years ago, and pays the boatman triple fare.

115.41   Drake's Culprit Fay: "Culprit Fay" (written in 1816, published posthumously in 1835), by Joseph Rodman Drake (1795–1820), takes the highlands of the Hudson River for its setting.

115.43   "Princess": Tennyson, "The Princess: A Medley," VII, lines 175–176: "she found a small / Sweet Idyl . . . ."

116.1   "Gipsey's Malison": "The Gipsy's Malison," a poem by Charles Lamb, first printed in *Blackwood's* in 1829.

117.28   that address: Curtis's oration, "The Duty of the American Scholar to Politics and the Times," delivered on 5 August 1856, at Wesleyan College, and printed in the New York *Tribune*, 7 August 1856. Pointing to the struggle between slaveholders and abolitionists in Kansas, Curtis concluded: "Brothers! the call has come to us . . . . I summon you to the great fight of freedom."

117.37   authentic vocation to politics: Curtis was a delegate to the Republican national conventions in 1860 and 1864, an unsuccessful candidate for Congress in 1864, and a Presidential elector in 1868. He served as president of the National Civil Service Reform League from its founding in 1881 until his death in 1892.

118.1   Hughes: Thomas Hughes (1822–1896), M. P. (1865–1874) and principal of the Working Men's College in London, was the author of *Tom Brown's School-Days* (1857).

118.2   D' Azeglio: Massimo d'Azeglio (1798–1866), Italian statesman and author.

118.30   his "Lounger's" attitude: from 1857 to 1863 Curtis contributed a column, "The Lounger," to *Harper's Weekly*.

118.38–39   political writing: before 1868, these included *The President: Why He Should Be Re-Elected* (1864) and *Equal Rights for Women* (1867).

121.8   season just ending: for Howells' earlier criticism of English extravaganzas on the New York stage, see "The New Play at Wallack's," *Nation*, I (2 November 1865), 570–571.

121.20   Tostée: Lucille Tostée (?–1874), singer and actress in opera bouffe.

121.27   Edmund Kirke: pseudonym of James Roberts Gilmore (1822–1903), businessman and author. His early books, *My Southern Friends* (1862) and *Down in Tennessee* (1863), presented realistic scenes of Southern life.

121.32   "Vous voyez bien le tableau!": *French*—you get the picture!

122.10   *La Belle Hélène*: comic opera (1864) by J. Offenbach.

122.15   Booth, Hackett, and Forrest: Edwin Booth (1833–1893), James Henry Hackett (1800–1871), and Edwin Forrest (1806–1872) were famous American actors.

122.25   Irma, and Aujac: Mlle. Irma, known as "the statuesque lady" for her performance in *tableaux vivants*, and Aujac, an actor and singer, appeared in the opera bouffe company headed by Lucille Tostée.

122.33   Ristori: Adelaide Ristori (1821–1905), Italian actress, had earlier appeared on the American stage and was to become famous for her performance as Lady Macbeth.

123.3   *La Grande Duchesse*: comic opera (1867) by Offenbach.

123.12–13   "'aime . . . . favorable!": *French*—I delight in collecting my thoughts in front of this family picture! My father, my mother, they are both here! O my father, turn upon your child an approving beak!

123.15–17   "Soit! . . . théâtre.": *French*—so be it! but without telling her who I am—I want to maintain the strictest anonymity until the moment when the situation will be favorable for a dramatic revelation.

123.19   *Un Mari sage*: "A Wise Husband," song in Act II of Offenbach's *La belle Hélène*.

123.42–43   "pas . . . épique": *French*—not an ordinary husband, an epic one.

124.5–6   "The Black . . . Auction.": *The Black Crook* (1866) by Charles M. Barres and Giuseppe Operti, often cited as the first American musical comedy; *The White Fawn* (1868), an English extravaganza by Francis Cowley Burnand (1836–1917); *The Devil's Auction* (1867), a singing and dancing extravaganza probably created by John de Pol.

124.18   "The Three Fast Men,": probably an English theatrical piece subtitled *The Female Robinson Crusoes*, by W. B. English (first produced as early as 1858).

124.36–37   *soirée . . . chantante*: *French*—an evening of singing and dancing.

124.45   "Ixion" or "Orpheus" or "Lucrezia Borgia?": *Ixion* (1863), an English burlesque by Burnand; "Orpheus" is probably *Orphée aux Enfers* (1858), a comic opera by Offenbach; *Lucrezia Borgia, M. D.* (1868), an English extravaganza by Henry James Byron (1835–1884).

127.26   Lemprière's Dictionary: John Lemprière, *Bibliotheca Classica: or, A Classical Dictionary* (1788).

127.42   "Ivanhoe,": melodrama (1822) by Alexandre Dumas, père.

128.8–9   Mr. Reverdy . . . spoons: Reverdy Johnson (1796–1876), noted American lawyer, was U. S. ambassador to the Court of St. James during negotiations to settle the Alabama claims (1868–1869); Benjamin Franklin Butler (1818–1893), lawyer, soldier, and politician, pursued the impeachment of President Andrew Johnson.

128.19   Mr. Fiske: James Fisk (1834–1872), one of the agents in the complex conspiracy to control the Erie Railroad in 1866–1868; he and his partners employed such illegal means as the issuance of unauthorized stock ("Erie shares"). Their practices were publicly attacked by Samuel Bowles (1826–1878), editor of the Springfield *Republican*, who was sued for libel by Fisk.

129.2–3   Vision of Sin: by Tennyson (1842), lines 33–41.

129.20   Signorina Morlacchi: Giuseppina Morlacchi (?–1886), Italian dancer who starred in *The Devil's Auction*.

129.27   Jardin Mabille: Le bal Mabille, established in 1840, was one of the many public dance halls of Paris frequented by students, artists, and bohemians.

131.3   "Dora.": 1867; by Charles Reade.

131.11   "School,": 1869; by English actor and dramatist Thomas William Robertson (1829–1871).

131.15   "My Lady Clara": Robertson's play opened in 1869 and was subsequently retitled *Dreams*. When published in 1875, the title was further changed to *Dreams, or My Lady Clara*.

131.20   "Foul Play,": 1868; English comedy by Dion Boucicault and Charles Reade, adapted from their novel. Howells reviewed it in *Atlantic*, XXII (August 1868), 254–255.

131.23   "After Dark," and the "Lancashire Lass,": *After Dark, a Tale of London Life* (1868) by Dion Boucicault; *Lancashire Lass, or Tempted, Tried and True* (1867) by Henry James Byron.

133.42   artist: True W. Williams.

137.8   to be given: the review for the New York *Tribune* was volunteered by Howells to be used a few days in advance of the poem's publication in the *Atlantic* (XXV [January 1870], 1–15). On 11 December 1869 Howells wrote to Whitelaw Reid: "Fields and Osgood have allowed me to notice Lowell's new poem for you . . . it is to my thinking by far the greatest poem yet written in America. . . . I don't wish to be known as having written the review, especially where the fact would come back to Lowell."

138.18   "Vision of Sir Launfal.": Lowell's poem (1848), which begins with a lengthy "Prelude to Part First."

150.40   a tale for older heads: Aldrich's first novel "for older heads," *Prudence Palfrey*, appeared in 1874 and was reviewed by Howells; see item 48. See also Howells' later essay, "Mr. Aldrich's Fiction," item 69. *The Story of a Bad Boy* appeared serially in *Our Young Folks* (January–December 1869).

151.13   "Philip": for Howells' review of *The Adventures of Philip* (1861–62), see "Literary," *Ohio State Journal*, 20 February 1861, p. 1.

151.25   here produced anew: the *Miscellanies* had first been published in 1854–1857 (4 vols., London).

154.13   that unique essay: John Richard Dennett (1838–1874), "The Glut in the Fiction Market," *Nation*, III (6 December 1866), 453–455.

154.24–25   Miss Mühlbach: Louise Mühlbach, pseudonym of Klara Müller Mundt (1814–1873), writer of popular historical fiction.

154.36–37   the three books: a fourth English translation, a collection under the title *Ovind*, had appeared in London in 1869.

159.17   Auerbach: Berthold Auerbach (1812–1882), German novelist.

166.4–5	"The Overland Monthly,": during its first two-and-a-half years, the San Francisco magazine (1868–1875, 1883–1935) was edited by Bret Harte, who contributed "The Luck of Roaring Camp" (1868) and other works.
172.14	later yearnings: in a review in the *Atlantic*, XXV (February 1870), 249–250, Howells compared Tennyson's "The Holy Grail" unfavorably with his earlier "Morte d'Arthur" (1842).
173.4	*Festa Campestre*: a painting by the Venetian painter Giorgione (ca. 1418–1510).
175.16	living with the cattle: the allusion is to the line, "Of men that live among cattle or taste the ocean or the woods"—"Song of Myself," line 256.
178.28	Constance: mother of Arthur in Shakespeare's *King John*.
178.32	saint: St. Francis of Assisi (1181?–1226).
179.2	hero's character: Keeler was perhaps the most bohemian of Howells' Cambridge friends and served as a model for Fulkerson in *A Hazard of New Fortunes*; see *Literary Friends and Acquaintance* (Bloomington and London, 1968), pp. 231–234.
179.4	Atlantic papers: "Three Years as a Negro Minstrel," *Atlantic*, XXIV (July 1869), 71–85; and "The Tour of Europe . . . ," *Atlantic*, XXVI (July 1870), 92–105.
179.25	Gil Blas: Alain René Le Sage (1668–1747), *L'Histoire de Gil Blas de Santillane* (1715–1735).
179.31	first book: *Gloverson and His Silent Partner* (1869).
180.4	old romance: Sylvester Judd (1813–1853) first published *Margaret* in 1845.
180.14	"Wilhelm Meister": Goethe's *Wilhelm Meisters Lehrjahre* (1796).
183.5–6	"An illiterate . . . . writings.": quoted from Henry Crabb Robinson's *Diary, Reminiscences, and Correspondence*, ed. Thomas Sadler (1869), 2:266.
183.24–25	"Get . . . heart,": Charles Lamb, "A Quaker's Meeting," *London Magazine*, April 1821; later collected in *Elia* (1823).
183.29	Whittier: Woolman's *Journal* was first published in 1774; the 1871 edition reviewed by Howells was edited by John Greenleaf Whittier, himself a prominent Quaker.
184.4	a new creation: *Songs of the Sierras* appeared in 1871 and was a revised and enlarged edition of the collection which had been privately printed in England as *Pacific Poems* the year before. English

critics hailed Miller as "the Byron of the Oregon"; the reception by American critics (with the exception of Whitman) was considerably cooler.

184.9   "The consecration . . . dream.": Wordsworth, "Elegiac Stanzas, Suggested by a Picture of Peele Castle in a Storm," lines 15–16.

189.3   no sense of it: in his *American Notes* (1842), Dickens complained that the Americans "certainly are not a humorous people, . . . their temperament always impressed me as being of a dull and gloomy character" (Chapter XVIII, "Concluding Remarks").

189.6   Taine's History: *Histoire de la Littérature Anglaise* first appeared in 1863, *Philosophie de l'Art en Grèce* in 1869.

189.15   full amends hereafter: Howells "made amends" for the brevity but not for the negative tenor of his review: he printed Henry James's long review of Taine's *History of English Literature* (*Atlantic*, XXIX [April 1872], 469–472) and discussed Taine's premises and their consequences at greater length in his own review of Taine's *Notes on England* (*Atlantic*, XXX [August 1872], 240–242).

189.22   Lowell's essay: "Dryden," *Among My Books* (1870), pp. 1–80. Howells reviewed the collection of essays in *Atlantic*, XXV (June 1870), 757–758.

192.44   appeared serially: *Hearth and Home*, III (30 September–30 December 1870).

193.22   these pages: *Atlantic*, XXVII–XXVIII (January–December 1871).

194.24   As we said: see Howells' review of De Forest's novel *Overland* (1871), *Atlantic*, XXIX (January 1872), 111.

195.13   "Miss Ravenel's Conversion": for Howells' review of this novel, see item 18.

195.42   "breathes full East.": source not identified.

197.4   American Note-Books: *Passages from the American Note-Books of Nathaniel Hawthorne* (1868).

197.7   English journals: *Passages from the English Note-Books of Nathaniel Hawthorne* (1870).

197.31   Mr. Brown . . . Claude: most likely references to Ford Madox Brown (1821–1893), English historical painter, and Claude Lorrain (1600–1682), French landscape painter.

198.31   Miss Bremer: Frederika Bremer (1801–1865), Swedish writer and feminist.

198.43   Mrs. Jameson: Anna Brownell Jameson (1794–1860), English essayist.

198.44–45   Story . . . Powers: William Wetmore Story (1819–1895), American painter; Robert (1812–1889) and Elizabeth Barrett (1806–1861) Browning; and Hiram Powers (1805–1873), American sculptor.

199.43   criticism of "The Marble Faun,": for Howells' review, see item 2.

203.3   the first: the first volume of Forster's biography appeared in 1872 and was reviewed by Howells in the *Atlantic*, XXIX (February 1872), 239–241; for Howells' review of the third volume (1874), see *Atlantic*, XXXIII (May 1874), 621–622.

204.22   Pictures from Italy: in 1844 Dickens undertook a long visit to Italy and produced a series of sketches for the *Daily News* (January–March 1846); they were published in book form as *Pictures from Italy* (1846).

204.29   President Felton: James T. Fields's memoir, *Yesterdays with Authors* (1872; for Howells' review, see *Atlantic*, XXIX [April 1872], 498–499), contains several letters from Dickens to Cornelius Conway Felton (1807–1862), president of Harvard College (1860–1862).

205.16   Jerrold: Douglas William Jerrold (1803–1857), English humorist and playwright.

205.31   Our Mutual Friend: for Howells' review, see item 10.

205.42   Dr. Mackenzie's statement: Robert Shelton Mackenzie (1809–1880) recounts the story involving Cruikshank in his *Life of Charles Dickens* (1870), pp. 164–165.

207.4   Revenge: W. F. West's translation of *La Revanche de Joseph Noirel* (1872), by French novelist Victor Cherbuliez (1829–1899), had been reviewed by Howells in the *Atlantic*, XXXI (January 1873), 105–106.

213.13   Harris of Hanover: Johann Georg Karl Harrys (1780–1838), an English attaché to the court of Hannover, served briefly as secretary and interpreter for Paganini.

215.13–14   Matthew Arnold: "Heinrich Heine," *Essays in Criticism, First Series* (1865).

215.17   Lord Houghton's Monographs: *Monographs* (1873) by Richard Monckton Milnes, first Baron Houghton (1809–1885).

216.8   *Erinnerungen*: *Heinrich Heine: Erinnerungen* (1856) by Alfred Meissner (1822–1885).

217.3   excellent version: *Every Saturday*, III (25 January–26 April 1873); the translator may have been Eugene Schuyler (1840–1890).

220.8   Halleck, and Verplanck: Fitz–Greene Halleck (1790–1867), American poet, and Gulian Crommelin Verplanck (1796–1870), New York lawyer, journalist, politician, and satirist.

221.3   journalist: Bryant was co-editor of the *New York Review and Athenaeum Magazine* and later editor-in-chief of the New York *Evening Post*.

223.12   New England Tragedies and Divine Tragedy: *New England Tragedies* (1868), *Divine Tragedy* (1871), and *The Golden Legend* (1851) form a trilogy first brought together in *Christus: A Mystery* (1872). For Howells' review of *The Divine Tragedy*, see *Atlantic*, XXIX (February 1872), 237–239.

223.23   Dante: for Howells' review of Longfellow's translation of the *Divine Comedy* (1869), see item 17.

223.25   Tales of the Wayside Inn: published in three separate parts in 1863, 1872, and 1873.

223.28   Idyls of the King: Tennyson published "Morte d'Arthur" in 1842; his treatment of Arthurian legend continued to grow and change through 1885, when he published "Balin and Balan." For Howells' review of *The Holy Grail, and Other Poems*, see *Atlantic*, XXV (February 1870), 249–250; for his review of *The Last Tournament*, see *Atlantic*, XXIX (February 1872), 236–237.

225.25   Scanderbeg: *Atlantic*, XXXI (May 1873), 618–621.

225.27–28   "liked . . . sound,": "The Musician's Tale: The Mother's Ghost," *Tales of the Wayside Inn* (1863), lines 18–19.

225.31   The Rhyme of Sir Christopher: *Atlantic*, XXXII (September 1873), 332–335.

229.15–16   The Mother's Ghost: a Danish ballad to be found in Svend Herselb Grundtvig's *Danmark's Gamle Folkeviser* (1856), 2:478.

230.8   extravagant admiration: in an undated letter (early in 1833), Charles Lamb wrote to Landor: " 'tis for Rose Aylmer, which has a charm I cannot explain. I lived upon it for weeks." *The Letters of Charles Lamb*, ed. E. V. Lucan (1935), 3:361.

230.25   American essayist: the words of this person (who has not been identified) are quoted in the "Introduction" to the volume being reviewed (p. 16).

231.2   Percival . . . Morris: James Gates Percival (1795–1856) wrote poetry noted for its romantic excesses; George Pope Morris (1802–1864) was best known for the poem "Woodman, Spare that Tree!"

231.10–11   Aftermath, and Changed: for Howells' comments on Longfellow, see item 45.

235.8   *Revue de Deux Mondes*: *La Révue des Deux Mondes* printed a translation of *The Hoosier Schoolmaster* (Series 2, CII [1872], 125–176) under the title *Le Maître d'École du Flat Creek*. *The Hoosier Schoolmaster* (1871), *The End of the World* (1872), and *The Mystery of Metropolisville* (1873) were republished in England in 1872, 1872, and 1873, respectively. *Le Prédicateur Ambulant* (*The Circuit Rider*) was also published in that journal (Series 3, CV [1874], 678–707, 789–835).

235.13   went West: Horace Greeley (1811–1872) used the "famous" phrase "Go West, Young Man!" in an editorial in the New York *Tribune*, but did not coin it; it first appeared in an article by John Babsone Lane Soule (1815–1891) in the Terre Haute (Indiana) *Express* (1851).

236.5   *Arne*; and Turgénieff: for Howells' reviews, see items 28, 40, and 43.

236.13   The Hoosier Schoolmaster: for Howells' review, see item 36.

239.7   Marjorie Daw and Mademoiselle Zabriski: stories in Aldrich's collection *Marjorie Daw and Other People* (1873), which Howells reviewed in *Atlantic*, XXXII (November 1873), 625–626.

241.12   Hawthorne: "Preface," *The Marble Faun* (1860).

241.13   Mr. Hale: Edward Everett Hale (1822–1909). Howells reviewed *If, Yes, and Perhaps* in *Atlantic*, XXII (November 1868), 634–635; and *The Ingham Papers* in *Atlantic*, XXIV (July 1869), 128.

241.38   three books of Dr. Holmes's: presumably *The Autocrat of the Breakfast-Table* (1858), *The Professor at the Breakfast-Table* (1860), and *The Poet at the Breakfast-Table* (1872); Howells reviewed the last in *Atlantic*, XXX (December 1872), 745–746.

242.2   Aldrich: the paragraphs preceding this section of "Recent Literature" are a review of T. B. Aldrich's *Prudence Palfrey* (see item 48).

242.7   discussed his merits: see Howells' reviews of *Miss Ravenel* (item 18), of *Kate Beaumont* (item 36), and of *Overland*, in *Atlantic*, XXIX (January 1872), 111.

245.21   will recall: *Concepcion de Arguello* was printed in *Atlantic*, XXIX (May 1872), 603–605.

248.4–5   his earliest appearance in The Atlantic: James's first story in the *Atlantic* was "The Story of a Year," XV (March 1865), 257–281.

249.34   will remember: "A Passionate Pilgrim" had first appeared in *Atlantic*, XXVII (March–April 1871), 352–371, 478–499.

253.41   Donatello: for Howells' review of *The Marble Faun*, see item 2.

256.7   already know: "Solomon," *Atlantic*, XXXII (October 1873), 413–
             424; "The Lady of Little Fishing," *Atlantic*, XXXIV (September
             1874), 293–305; "Wilhelmina," *Atlantic*, XXXV (January 1875),
             44–55.

261.11   Mark Twain's petition: when this facetious petition was favorably
             received, Mark Twain addressed a serious one to Congress on inter-
             national copyright law in 1875.

261.43   Jumping Frog: Mark Twain's "Celebrated Jumping Frog of
             Calaveras County," first printed in the New York *Saturday Press* of
             18 November 1865, was published in French translation in *La Ré-
             vue des Deux Mondes*, Series 2, C (1872), 314–319 ("La Grenouille
             Sauteuse du Comte Calaveras").

262.5   in these pages: "A True Story, repeated Word for Word as I heard
             it," Mark Twain's first contribution to the *Atlantic* (XXXIV [Novem-
             ber 1874], 591–594), appeared under Howells' editorship.

263.25   The Hanging of the Crane: for Howells' review, see *Atlantic*,
             XXXIV (December 1874), 745.

263.30   friends of his: Cornelius Conway Felton (1807–1862), Louis Agassiz
             (1807–1873), and Charles Sumner (1811–1874).

265.40–41   "We . . . best.": Howells' paraphrase of the central idea in "Mori-
             turi Salutamus," in the volume reviewed.

267.6–8   the Ring . . . Country: *The Ring and the Book* (1868–1869), *Fifine at
             the Fair* (1872), and *Red Cotton Night-Cap Country* (1873); for How-
             ells' review of the last, see item 41.

271.2   A Bad Boy: Thomas B. Aldrich, *The Story of a Bad Boy* (1870); for
             Howells' review, see item 26.

272.5   the boy's point of view: after reading the book in manuscript, How-
             ells advised Clemens to "treat it explicitly *as* a boy's story," and
             jotted suggestions in the manuscript to further unify the point of
             view. See *Selected Letters*, 2:109.

272.33   Mr. William M. Baker: 1825–1883; best known for his autobio-
             graphical account of the Civil War, *Inside: A Chronicle of Secession*
             (1866), published under the pseudonym of George F. Harrington.
             Howells reviewed two of Baker's novels in the *Atlantic*: *The New
             Timothy* (XXVI [October 1870], 504–506) and *Moses Evans* (XXXIV
             [August 1874], 230).

272.36   Tom Brown and Tom Bailey: see Howells' introduction to the 1911
             edition of Thomas Hughes's *Tom Brown's School Days*; Tom Bailey is
             the hero of Aldrich's *The Story of a Bad Boy*.

274.18–19   Biglow Papers . . . Cathedral: for Howells' reviews, see items 14 and 25.

275.3   certain sketches: the following stories were published in the *Atlantic*: "Shore House" (XXXII [September 1873], 358–368); "Deephaven Cronies" (XXXVI [September 1875], 316–329); and "Deephaven Excursions" (XXXVIII [September 1876], 277–290).

277.6   in these pages: unsigned and unindexed reviews of Piatt's *Poems in Sunshine and Firelight* (1866) and *Landmarks and Other Poems* (1872) appeared in *Atlantic*, XVII (May 1866), 653–655, and XXIX (March 1872), 367, respectively—both attributable to Howells. Howells first met Piatt in 1851 in Columbus, where both worked on the *Ohio State Journal*, and the two collaborated on *Poems of Two Friends* (1859).

280.14   *causeur*: *French*—talker.

280.14   famous Causeries: Charles Auguste Sainte-Beuve (1804–1869) published several series of critical articles, including his "Causeries du Lundi," beginning in 1850.

281.27   Sainte-Beuve treats him: Sainte-Beuve's writings referred to are presumably "M. de Balzac" (1834) in *Portraits Contemporains* (1855), 1:432–454; and "M. de Balzac" (Lundi, 2 Septembre 1850) in *Causeries du Lundi* (1882), 2:443–463.

283.2   Mr. Bishop: William Henry Bishop (1847–1928), American author, college instructor, and U. S. consul (Genoa, 1903–1904; Palermo, 1905–1910).

283.9   remember it: *Detmold* was serialized in *Atlantic*, XL–XLI (December 1877–June 1878).

286.3   Morley's: John Morley (1838–1923), English statesman and man of letters, was general editor of the "English Men of Letters" series of biographies, which had begun publication in 1878. Other monographs in this series reviewed by Howells are Henry James's *Hawthorne* (see item 64) and Goldwin Smith's *Cowper* (see item 67).

289.2   Miss Hogarth and Miss Mary Dickens: Georgina ("Georgie") Hogarth (1827–1917), sister of Dickens's wife and mentioned in his will as "the best and truest friend man ever had"; Mary Dickens (1838–1896), the author's daughter.

289.4   his biography: John Forster, *The Life of Charles Dickens*, 3 vols. (1872–1874); for Howells' reviews of the individual volumes, see *Atlantic*, XXIX (February 1872), 239–241; XXXI (February 1873), 237–239 (see item 39); and XXXIII (May 1874), 621–622.

289.14–15   domestic happiness: Dickens's marriage to Catherine Hogarth (1836) ended in separation in 1858.

289.25   letters from America: the letters written during Dickens's second visit to America (1867–1868); a first visit had taken place in 1842.

290.1   Mr. Dolby: manager of Dickens's second American lecture tour; author of *Charles Dickens As I Knew Him* (1887).

290.23   Staunton: Henry M. Stanton (1814–1869) was appointed secretary of war by Lincoln in 1862.

290.35   copyright: international copyright legislation by the U. S. Congress, petitioned for by Mark Twain in 1875 (see note 261.11, above) and repeatedly and publicly demanded by Howells, was not passed until 1909.

290.43   Eyre massacre: Edward John Eyre (1815–1901), British governor of Jamaica (1864–1866), was accused of brutally suppressing an uprising of blacks in Jamaica in 1865.

291.1   Canon Kingsley: Charles Kingsley (1819–1875), English author, had been appointed canon of Westminster in 1873.

292.9–10   Forty-six, fifty, sixty-four: dates of the publication of *Mosses from an Old Manse* (1846) and *The Scarlet Letter* (1850), and of Hawthorne's death (1864).

293.18   "little hymn.": "Concord Hymn. Sung at the Completion of the Battle Monument, July 4, 1837."

294.12   the note-books: Hawthorne's posthumously published *Passages from the American Note-Books* (1868), *Passages from the English Note-Books* (1870), and *Passages from the French and Italian Note-Books* (1872); for Howells' review of the last, see item 37.

294.22   The Marble Faun: for Howells' review, see item 2.

296.4–9   "Most . . . weed.": Tennyson, "The Flower," lines 19–24.

296.14–15   "Thieves . . . wall": Tennyson, "The Flower," line 11.

297.25   Innocents Abroad: for Howells' review, see item 24.

299.3   American life: eight papers by Jonathan Baxter Harrison (1835–1907), listed in the next sentence, were first published in *Atlantic*, XLII (October 1878), 385–402; (November), 521–530; (December), 717–727; XLIII (January 1879), 59–71; (February), 129–134; (June), 689–705; and XLIV (August 1879), 129–137; (October), 488–500.

299.28   Thackeray's "Spec.": Mr. Spec was Thackeray's pseudonym for the author and narrator of *Sketches and Travels in London* (1853).

302.4   Irish History: Smith's *Irish History and Irish Character* (1862).

302.14   printed here: "Pessimism," *Atlantic*, XLV (February 1880), 199–201.

304.26   Southey: "Life of Cowper," in *The Works of William Cowper*, ed. Robert Southey (1835), 1:1.

306.5   these pages: "Père Antoine's Date Palm," *Atlantic*, IX (June 1862), 778–781.

306.8   its charm: the letter is not from Nathaniel Hawthorne but from Mrs. Sophia Hawthorne (28 October 1866).

306.9   Curtis . . . sketches: see Howells' essay, "George William Curtis," item 22.

306.13   reputation of a poet: for Howells' reviews of Aldrich's poetry, see *Atlantic*, XVIII (August 1866), 250–252, and XXXIX (January 1877), 90–91.

306.24   The Story of a Bad Boy: for Howells' review, see item 26.

306.32   Marjorie Daw: published in *Atlantic*, XXXI (April 1873), 407–417, and in *Marjorie Daw and Other People* (1873); for Howells' review of the book, see *Atlantic*, XXXII (November 1873), 625–626.

307.10–11 Miss Mehetabel's . . . Zabriskie: first published in *Atlantic*, XXXI (June 1873), 719–730, and XXXII (October 1873), 385–392; reprinted in *Marjorie Daw and Other People*.

307.12   Prudence Palfrey: serialized in *Atlantic*, XXXIII (January–June 1874), and published in book form the same year; for Howells' review, see item 48.

307.20–21 The Queen of Sheba: serialized in *Atlantic*, XL (July–November 1877), and published in book form the same year; for Howells' review, see *Atlantic*, XLI (January 1878), 141–142.

307.36   The Stillwater Tragedy: serialized in *Atlantic*, XLV–XLVI (April–September 1880), and published in book form the same year.

310.8   The Gilded Age: (1873); for Howells' review of the dramatized version, see *Atlantic*, XXXV (June 1875), 749–751.

310.16–17 Tom Sawyer: (1876); for Howells' review, see item 57.

311.4   book of Sketches: *Mark Twain's Sketches* (1875); for Howells' review, see item 54.

311.5   *wanderjahre*: German—years of travel.

311.12   Piloting on the Mississippi: *Old Times on the Mississippi*, serialized in *Atlantic*, XXXV–XXXVI (January–August 1875).

311.42   Roughing It: (1872); for Howells' review, see item 38.

312.1–2   a literary newspaper: *The Californian* (1864–1868).

312.5   Innocents Abroad: (1869); for Howells' review, see item 24.

312.9–10   A Tramp Abroad: (1880); for Howells' review, see item 66.

312.11   The Prince and the Pauper: (1881); for Howells' review, see New
            York *Tribune*, 25 October 1881, p. 6.

313.33   chief justice: probably Sir John Duke Coleridge (1820–1894), lord
            chief justice of England (1880–1894), noted for his enthusiastic and
            entertaining telling of stories.

313.39   True Story: "A True Story, repeated Word for Word as I heard it,"
            Atlantic, XXXIV (November 1874), 591–594.

313.43   Elsewhere: see, for example, item 54.

314.6   Carnival of Crime in Connecticut: *Atlantic*, XXXVII (June 1876),
            641–650.

314.11   literary Club: in 1875 Mark Twain read his "Carnival of Crime"
            story for the Monday Evening Club, organized in the 1860s and
            counting among its members several ministers, including Joseph
            Twichell.

315.4   Raymond: John T. Raymond (1836–1887), the American actor and
            producer, claimed to have created the character of Colonel Sellers;
            in reporting this claim to Howells, Clemens commented: "The truth
            is that the finer points in Sellers's character are a trifle above Ray-
            mond's level."

317.22–23   "The Story of a Year": *Atlantic*, XV (March 1865), 257–281.

317.28–29   "Poor Richard": *Atlantic*, XIX–XX (June–August 1867).

318.24   Daisy Miller: it appears that Howells did not review *Daisy Miller*
            when it was first published in 1878; his only known discussions of
            the novel are "Mr. James's Daisy Miller" in the second volume of
            Heroines of Fiction (1901) and his "Introduction" for the Modern
            Library Edition of *Daisy Miller* (1919). The earlier items attributed
            to Howells in Albert Mordell's *Discovery of a Genius: William Dean
            Howells and Henry James* (1961) are not by Howells.

318.36   "frost . . . fire,": Milton, *Paradise Lost*, II, line 595: "and cold per-
            forms th' effect of Fire."

319.13   "Pension Beaurepas,": *Atlantic*, XLIII (April 1879), 460–488.

319.32–33   "A Passionate Pilgrim,": *Atlantic*, XXVII (March–April 1871); reprinted in *The Passionate Pilgrim and Other Tales* (1875); for Howells' review, see item 51.

320.13   Dorothea: Dorothea Brooke in George Eliot's *Middlemarch* (1871–1872).

320.32   "The Madonna of the Future": *Atlantic*, XXXI (March 1873), 276–297.

323.6   European sketches: *Transatlantic Sketches* (1875); an unsigned review in *Atlantic*, XXXVI (July 1875), 113–115, attributed to Howells in Albert Mordell's *Discovery of a Genius* (1961), contradicts major arguments consistently presented in Howells' other reviews of James and does not appear under Howells' name in the *Atlantic Index*.

323.9   essays on modern French writers: *French Poets and Novelists* (1878); for Howells' review, see item 61.

326.2   Florida: in a letter of 8 October 1883 (MS at Harvard), Thompson corrected Howells' "geographical lapse," explaining that "in fact my father took me to Georgia instead of Florida and I was reared in a North Georgia mountain-vale"; he added that he knew Florida from boyhood expeditions and adult business trips.

326.5   archery: Howells reviewed Thompson's *The Witchery of Archery* (1878) in *Atlantic*, XLIV (August 1879), 269.

326.26   His brother: there is no evidence that Will Henry Thompson (1848–1918) was more significantly associated with archery than his brother Maurice.

326.37   charming romance: *A Tallahassee Girl* (1881); Howells' statement that "I do not know that I have the right to connect his name" with the book refers to its anonymous publication.

327.6   AT THE WINDOW: *Atlantic*, XXXI (April 1873), 461; in that printing the bluebird replaced the sap-sucker in the second and twentieth lines.

329.14–15   "the spacious times of great Elizabeth,": Tennyson, "A Dream of Fair Women," line 7.

333.2   comment, more or less impassioned: the novel appeared in serial form in *Century*, n.s., IV–V (August 1883–January 1884). John Hay was not at the time publicly identified as the author of the anonymous work, but he was certainly known to Howells, who had been instrumental in arranging for *Century* publication. Some of the "comment" on *The Bread-Winners* was so vituperative about the novel's content and authorship that Hay was compelled to respond in two—also anonymous—letters in the same "Open Letters" column of the *Century* (November 1883 and March 1884) in which Howells' review appeared. Howells' review is signed only "*W.*"; his authorship is known from references in his correspondence.

334.33   "the hand . . . sense": *Hamlet*, V, i, 75: "The hand of little employ-
              ment hath the daintier sense."

339.18   *mauvaise honte*: *French*—bashfulness, reticence.

339.20   these critics: this reference remains unidentified.

339.33   American atmosphere: "Preface" to *The Marble Faun* (1860).

340.8   *éclaircissement*: *French*—explanation.

340.34   Miss Jewett's last volume: presumably *The Mate of the Daylight and
              Friends Ashore* (1884).

TEXTUAL APPARATUS

Textual Commentary

THIS volume of Howells' criticism consists of seventy-four items selected from the years 1859 through 1884. Of these, fifty-nine exist in only one form and are reprinted here with either minimal or no editorial changes. In addition, fifteen essays exist in more than one form. Two of these (items 22 and 70) exist as full manuscripts, and for one essay (item 72) there is a single page of manuscript. Three others (items 2, 3, and 6) were printed both in the *Ohio State Journal* and the *Ohio State Weekly Journal*, the same setting of type apparently having been used for both newspapers. Six essays were reprinted in *My Mark Twain* after initial appearance in the *Atlantic Monthly* (items 24, 38, 54, 57, and 66) or the *Century* (item 70; as mentioned above, this is one of the full-manuscript texts). The four remaining essays extant in more than one form appeared, complete or in part, as follows: item 1 in the New York *Saturday Press* and Ferris Greenslet's *The Life of Thomas Bailey Aldrich* (1908); item 4 in the *Ashtabula Sentinel* and the New York *Saturday Press*; item 23 in the *Atlantic Monthly* and *Suburban Sketches*; and item 74 in the *Century* and the 1917 edition of E. W. Howe's *The Story of a Country Town*.

Given the variety of textual situations represented in these three volumes of selected criticism, the usually conservative editorial policy of "A Selected Edition of W. D. Howells" is particularly necessary. Each of the texts presented here is based on a copy-text chosen from the pertinent extant materials on the basis of careful examination of available internal and external evidence. Into that text are introduced authorial revisions made in other forms, culminating in the first published appearance. These volumes emphasize the immediacy of newspaper or periodical publication and thus present the form of the material as Howells' audience would first have seen it in print. For that reason, the copy-text is emended to incorporate authorial revisions made to the point of first publication, but not to include revisions made later in preparation for inclusion in collected volumes—as is the case, for example, with "The New Taste in Theatricals," which first appeared in the *Atlantic Monthly* (1869) and then was extensively revised for inclusion in the second edition of *Suburban Sketches* (1872). In addition, the copy-text is corrected to remove nonsense readings. In all other details the texts printed here reproduce the copy-texts, even to the point of printing without correction Howells' misquotations of the items he is discussing. Significant misquotations are pointed out, however, in the Notes to the Texts. No attempt has been made to regularize either spelling (including the wide variation among essays in the Anglicization of foreign proper names) or punctuation.

The general typography and other non-essential, visual appurtenances of the texts have been disregarded. The variant typography of the bodies of the texts and of any inset material, the spacing and relative indentation of paragraphs, and the styling of initial paragraphs and of section numbers are made to conform to the style of the present edition. Extended quotations from the texts reviewed by Howells are inset in smaller type regardless of the style used in the copy-text.[1] Regardless of the treatment of punctuation marks after italic letters in the copy-text, this edition consistently italicizes only exclamation points and question marks when they follow a word or letter in italics. The essays are reprinted without their original by-lines or authorial attributions and without the copyright notices, credits, or reprint information which may have accompanied them in their printed versions. All footnotes are part of the copy-text; however, varying symbols (asterisks, daggers, superscript numbers) and placements of footnotes have been regularized and appear as sequentially numbered footnotes at the bottom of the page. Explanatory notes added by the editors of these volumes appear in the Notes to the Texts. The only non-authorial information provided is the citation of the place and date of first publication at the end of each item, and—for items which lack distinctive descriptive titles—either newly created titles or brief catalogs of the general content. Any such editorially supplied information appears in square brackets, except for sequential item numbers, which have been added for convenient reference. Generic titles of newspaper columns or magazine "departments" (for example, "Reviews and Literary Notices" or "Editor's Study") are not used as titles or parts of titles; that information is given in the textual commentary for each item. Similarly, when the text printed here represents only a portion of the original item (typically a review column dealing with several books), the relationship of the printed section to the whole is described in the textual commentary.

For the convenience of the reader in dealing with a large number of short texts, all information pertinent to the history of a text—the textual commentaries, Textual Notes, Emendations and Rejected Substantives lists, and part A of the two-part Word-Division list that deals with the resolution of compounds hyphenated at the end of a line in the copy-text—is assembled in one place. These individual sections of textual apparatus follow the order of the texts themselves, and are cross-referenced to them by item number and title. Only part B of the Word-Division list, which provides a guide for transcription of end-line hyphenations in the present edition, appears as a separate unit applicable to all of the texts, since it contains information necessary not only for the reader interested in the history and record of each text but for anyone who wishes to cite portions of it.

The specific textual commentary for each item begins with its identification as an essay appropriately attributed to Howells. If it is recorded in William M. Gibson and George Arms, *A Bibliography of William Dean Howells* (New York, 1948; rpt. 1971), the identification appears parenthetically, immediately following the title, listing the entry number in the bibliography. If it is not recorded in Gibson and Arms, another basis of attribution is provided. Next, the textual commentary provides a record of the symbols assigned to the pertinent forms of the text and used for citation within the Emendations and Rejected Substantives lists.[2] This record is followed by a description of the choice of copy-text and other significant textual details. This information in-

---

[1] This policy affects blocks of text printed inset on the following pages in the present edition (the framing quotation marks and paragraph indentations of the originals have been retained): 155, 156–157, 158, 160–161, 161–162, 169, 192, 208–209, 209–210, 213–214, 218, 218–219, 221–222, 237, 250, 250–251, 251–252, 252, 287–288, and 295.

[2] The symbols are assigned by general physical category and, within categories, by numbers consistent with the chronology of texts. Thus, MS is used for autograph manuscript; TS for authorial typescript; RG for galley material authorially revised; N1, N2, N3, and so on for newspaper publications in sequence; P1, P2, P3, and so on for periodical appearances in sequence; and A1, A2, A3, and so on for book publications in sequence.

cludes, where necessary, a discussion of the relationship of the copy-text to other extant texts, a description of the relationship of excerpted materials to the full essays and reviews of which they are a part, a description of extant manuscripts, and a discussion of specific textual cruces. If these last are especially complicated or a number of them occur within a single text, the general textual commentary is followed by a section headed "Textual Notes," which is keyed to the page and line numbers of entries in the Emendations and Rejected Substantives lists; in the lists themselves these entries are in turn cross-referenced to the Textual Notes by asterisks.

The list of Emendations records all changes in substantives and accidentals introduced into the copy-text, with the exception of the typographical regularizations described above or mentioned in the textual commentary. Within an Emendations entry, the reading of the present edition appears to the left of the bracket, and immediately to its right the symbol for the text which is the historical source of the reading, followed by a semicolon; this in turn is followed by the reading of the copy-text and the copy-text symbol. Emendations which simply correct copy-text errors in spelling or punctuation cite the first extant form which makes the correction (if any extant text does so), not because that text has any authority, but because the information may be of historical interest; responsibility for such corrections lies with the present editors. When a correction has not been made in any of the extant texts but originates entirely with the present edition, the symbol HE is used. Readings which fall, according to the chronological sequence described, between the copy-text and the text whose reading is accepted in the present edition should be assumed to agree with the copy-text unless they are recorded following the copy-text reading in the entry. The Emendations list records neither non-authorial revisions of accidentals in texts between copy-text and the text whose reading is accepted nor apparently non-authorial accidentals at points where substantive readings are accepted. Readings of texts subsequent to the source of the adopted reading in the chronology should be assumed to agree with the adopted reading unless they are recorded in Rejected Substantives. Whenever a text is reprinted in this edition without emendations, the textual apparatus omits the "Emendations" heading altogether. The only exception to this practice occurs when any part of the text requires the clarification "[*sic*]," which is used to identify the copy-text as the source of certain errors; for the sake of convenience, these entries are included under Emendations.

The Rejected Substantives list appears only for those items for which more than one form of text is extant. It records all substantive variants occurring in texts subsequent to the reading accepted at each point in the present edition. The accepted reading appears to the left of the bracket and immediately to its right the source of that reading, followed by a semicolon; this in turn is followed by the variant reading or readings and their sources. The reading of any unlisted text other than the copy-text should be assumed to agree with the reading to the left of the bracket unless it is recorded in Emendations; if the source of a reading at any point is other than copy-text, the copy-text reading is recorded in Emendations.

In both the Emendations and Rejected Substantives lists other special conventions are employed. The curved dash (~) represents the same word that appears before the bracket and is used in recording punctuation and paragraphing variants. The use of "*omitted*" means that the reading to the left of the bracket does not appear in the text or texts cited to the right of the semicolon.

Word-Division List A records the resolution of compounds or possible compounds hyphenated at the end of the line in the copy-text (or in other texts at points where readings have been adopted from them). Editorial judgment informed by familiarity with Howells' normal usage at the time of composition has been exercised in resolving these as either hyphenated or one-word forms. If the words occur in consistent form elsewhere in the copy-text, resolution was made on that basis; if these other occurrences are inconsistent, resolution was based on the treatment of a similar form in closest proximity to the possible compound in the copy-text. If neither of these recourses was available, then the problem was resolved first on the basis of Howells' usage in other manuscripts of the same period and then, if necessary, on the evidence of his other published works.

All entries in the Textual Apparatus are identified by page and line numbers in the present volume: the page number precedes the period, and the line number or numbers follow it. The count of lines begins at the top of each page (excluding running heads, page numbers, item numbers, and hairlines) and includes essay titles, bracketed editorial additions, section numbers or headings, bibliographical citations, and footnotes.

Commentaries and Lists

1. A Book Read Yesterday.

(G&A 59–30; misdated)

No manuscript or other pre-publication form of this review is known to exist. It appeared in print only once in its entirety during Howells' lifetime: in the New York *Saturday Press*, 30 July 1859, p. 2, which serves as copy-text for this edition. "Chispa," one of Howells' pseudonyms of the period, is given as the author's name. An excerpt was reprinted in Ferris Greenslet, *The Life of Thomas Bailey Aldrich* (New York, 1908), pp. 47–48, but since it contains no variants that suggest Howells' attention to the text, it is not cited in the apparatus. It does, however, correct various misquotations, which have been identified in the Notes to the Texts.

Word-Division List A
4.38   inkhorn-

2. Hawthorne's "Marble Faun."

(G&A 60–14)

No manuscript or other pre-publication form of this review is known to exist. It appeared in print twice without authorial attribution: first in the *Ohio State Journal*, 24 March 1860, p. 2 (N1), which serves as copy-text for this edition, and in the *Ohio State Weekly Journal*, 3 April 1860, p. 1 (N2). The two forms are identical both textually and physically, apparently having been printed from the same type.

Emendations
7.28   delighte [*sic*]
7.31   art.]HE; art N1–N2
7.34   Faun]HE; Fame N1–N2
8.1   Clifton [*sic*]

3. Bardic Symbols.

(G&A 60–16)

No manuscript or other pre-publication form of this review is known to exist. It appeared twice in print without authorial attribution: in the *Ohio State Journal*, 28 March 1860, p. 2 (N1), which serves as copy-text for this edition, and in the *Ohio State Weekly Journal*, 3 April 1860, p. 1 (N2). The two forms are identical, both textually and physically, apparently having been printed from the same type.

Emendations
9.1   Bardic Symbols.]HE; "~ ~." N1–N2
9.25   the true]HE; the the true N1–N2

4. [Whitman's Leaves of Grass]
(G&A 60–25)

No manuscript or other pre-publication form of this review is known to exist. It first appeared without authorial attribution in the *Ashtabula Sentinel*, 18 July 1860, p. 4 (N1), and without title other than the bibliographical information identifying the work under review. That printing serves as copy-text for this edition. The text was reprinted, again without authorial attribution, under the title "A Hoosier's Opinion of Walt Whitman" in the New York *Saturday Press*, 11 August 1860, p. 1 (N2), under the note "From the Ashtabula (Ohio) 'Sentinel,' July 18."

Emendations

11.3	Eldrige [*sic*]	12.11	it?"]HE; ~.?" N1; ~?' N2
11.24–25	Emmerson [*sic*]	12.14	together]N2; to/gether N1
11.29	infurried [*sic*]	12.30	altogether,]N2; altogher, N1

Rejected Substantives
11.28   as that]N1; as N2
11.29   infurried]N1; infurried (*sic*) N2

Word-Division List A
11.31   new-fashioned
12.13   clover-heads
12.21   fifty-sixth

5. [Poets and Poetry of the West]
(G&A 60–41)

No manuscript or other pre-publication form of this review is known to exist. It appeared without authorial attribution in the *Ohio State Journal*, 1 September 1860, p. 2 (N1), and without title other than the bibliographical information identifying the book under review.

Emendations
14.3   Caggeshall [*sic*]
14.25   substantialy [*sic*]
15.1   pride."]HE; ~. N1
15.23   away" / but]HE; away." ¶ But N1
15.26   Amelia Welby,]HE; ~ , ~ N1

Word-Division List A
14.31   go-ahead

6. Some Western Poets of To-Day
(G&A 60–42)

No manuscript or other pre-publication form of this essay is known to exist. It appeared twice in print without authorial attribution: first in the *Ohio State Journal*, 25 September 1860, p. 1 (N1), which serves as copy-text for this edition, and then again in the *Ohio State Weekly Journal*, 2 October 1860, p. 1 (N2). The two forms are identical both textually and physically, apparently having been printed from the same type.

Emendations

17.5	animadversive]HE; admadversive N1–N2
17.34	in]HE; in in N1–N2
18.31	doubtless]HE; doubless N1–N2
19.25	inadequency [*sic*]
19.40	rats slinks [*sic*]
20.2	cooling-floor]HE; cooling-flour N1–N2
20.12	observation [*sic*]

Word-Division List A

17.9	songbirds
19.15–16	after-glance
19.20	-into-nine-
19.21	-but-he-
19.29	coffin-poetesses

7. [Recent Italian Comedy]

(G&A 64–19)

No manuscript or other pre-publication form of this essay is known to exist. It appeared without authorial attribution in the *North American Review*, XCIX (October 1864), 364–401 (P1). In accordance with the policy of that journal, the text is identified in its heading only as "ART. II" in the sequence of contents; the full title, however, appears both in the index and in the running-title, and is supplied as the formal title in the present edition.

Emendations

21.2	1. *Opere*]HE; ART. II.—1. *Opere* P1
25.2	accessaries [*sic*]
39.26	Johnson [*sic*]
39.27	Suthampton [*sic*]

Word-Division List A

25.3–4	serving-maids	29.28	old-maiden
26.36	play-wright	35.23	scene-painter
27.2	fellow-servant	36.15	assurance-companies
27.10	sweet-blooded	42.20	well-contrived
28.8	lace-makers	42.35	sharply-cut
28.10	old-fogy	43.25	deep-seated
29.5–6	money-lender	45.31	father-in-
29.24	scandal-monger	46.26	play-goers

8. Drum-Taps

(G&A 65–16)

No manuscript or other pre-publication form of this review is known to exist. It appeared in the *Round Table*, 11 November 1865, 147–148, over the author's initials, "W. D. H." (P1).

Emendations

48.34	"Drum-Taps."]HE; ~–~." P1
49.16	out the [*sic*]

9. Concerning Timothy Titcomb.

(G&A 65–18)

No manuscript or other pre-publication form of this review is known to exist. It appeared, without authorial attribution, in the *Nation*, I (23 November 1865), 659.

Word-Division List A
53.4   schoolroom
54.1   anticlimax

10. Our Mutual Friend.

(G&A 65–24)

No manuscript or other pre-publication form of this review is known to exist. It appeared in the *Round Table*, 2 December 1865, pp. 200–201 (P1), over the author's initials, "W. D. H."

Emendations
55.11   Sharpe [*sic*]
55.25   Sharpe [*sic*]
55.26   resemblances.]HE; ~ P1
57.4   idiotcy [*sic*]

Word-Division List A
59.12   warm-blooded

11. Literary Criticism.

(G&A 66–13)

No manuscript or other pre-publication form of this essay is known to exist. It appeared, without authorial attribution, in the *Round Table*, 27 January 1866, p. 49.

12. [Slavery in M. L. Putnam's Novel]

(G&A 66–39)

No manuscript or other pre-publication form of this review is known to exist. It appeared, without title or authorial attribution, in "Reviews and Literary Notices," *Atlantic Monthly*, XVIII (July 1866), 128.

13. [Charles Reade's Remarkable Novel]

(G&A 66–48)

No manuscript or other pre-publication form of this review is known to exist. It appeared, without title or authorial attribution, in "Reviews and Literary Notices," *Atlantic Monthly*, XVIII (December 1866), 767–769.

Emendations
65.23   *elan* [*sic*]

Word-Division List A
65.26   spellbound
66.40   stumbling-block
67.14   gold-lace

14. [Lowell's Biglow Papers]
(G&A 67–1)

No manuscript or other pre-publication form of this review is known to exist. It appeared, without title or authorial attribution, in "Reviews and Literary Notices," *Atlantic Monthly*, XIX (January 1867), 123–125.

Word-Division List A
70.16   Heaven-given
71.24   high-toned

15. [Melville's Battle-Pieces]
(G&A 67–3)

No manuscript or other pre-publication form of this review is known to exist. It appeared, without title or authorial attribution, in "Reviews and Literary Notices," *Atlantic Monthly*, XIX (February 1867), 252–253.

Word-Division List A
73.16   greenwood

16. [Henry Wadsworth Longfellow]
(G&A 67–8)

No manuscript or other pre-publication form of this review is known to exist. It appeared, without authorial attribution, in the *North American Review*, CIV (April 1867), 531–540 (P1). In accordance with the policy of that journal, the text is identified in its heading only as "ART. VII" in the sequence of contents; the full title, however, appears both in the index and in the running title, and is supplied as the formal title in the present edition.

Emendations
76.2   1. *The*]HE; ART. VII.—1. *The* P1
81.21   bass-relief [*sic*]
82.8   poet's [*sic*]

Word-Division List A
77.1   travel-sketches
78.1   Redman

17. Mr. Longfellow's Translation of the Divine Comedy.
(G&A 67–10)

No manuscript or other pre-publication form of this review is known to exist. It appeared, without authorial attribution, in the *Nation*, IV (20 June 1867), 492–494 (P1).

Emendations
88.43   much-longed for [*sic*]
91.25   CAYLEY.]HE; ~ P1
92.32   coming]HE; co ing P1
93.6   pinions]HE; p nions P1
94.1   Spring]HE; S ring P1

18. [De Forest's Miss Ravenel]
(G&A 67–12)

No manuscript or other pre-publication form of this review is known to exist. It appeared, without title or authorial attribution, in "Reviews and Literary Notices," *Atlantic Monthly*, XX (July 1867), 120–122. The text is reprinted here without alteration even though De Forest's name is misspelled ("De Forrest") in the bibliographic heading and throughout the review itself.

Word-Division List A
95.11–12   stage-coach
95.18   fence-rails
97.4   warm-hearted
97.23   strongly-flavored

19. [Literature and Its Professors]
(G&A 67–13)

No manuscript or other pre-publication form of this review is known to exist. It appeared, without title or authorial attribution, in "Reviews and Literary Notices," *Atlantic Monthly*, XX (August 1867), 254–255.

Word-Division List A
98.5   self-satisfied
99.23   Hero-Worship

20. [Emerson's Poetry]
(G&A 67–15)

No manuscript or other pre-publication form of this review is known to exist. It appeared, without title or authorial attribution, in "Reviews and Literary Notices," *Atlantic Monthly*, XX (September 1867), 376–378.

Word-Division List A
102.2   harebells

21. [J. G. Holland's Feeble Poetic Fancy]
(G&A 67–17)

No manuscript or other pre-publication form of this review is known to exist. It appeared, without title or authorial attribution, in "Reviews and Literary Notices," *Atlantic Monthly*, XX (December 1867), 762–764 (P1).

Emendations
109.33   forever?"]HE; ~?' P1
109.36   accept our]HE; ~. ~ P1

Word-Division List A
106.3   Bitter-Sweet
110.6   dry-goods

22. [George William Curtis]
(G&A 68–12)

In addition to its publication as Article V in the *North American Review*, CVII (July 1868), 104–117 (P1), this essay is represented by a complete holograph manuscript (MS), in Howells' hand in black ink and bearing his signature. Now located in the Princeton University Library, the manuscript consists of seventy-nine leaves, numbered 1–2, 2A, 3, [4], 5–21, A=1–A=4, 22–25, 26=27=28, 29–31, 31[bis]–33, 35–70, 71–72, 7[3?]–78.[1] Leaves 41–45, 57–59, 64–65, and 70 were originally numbered 23–27, 33–35, 37–38, and 47, respectively, suggesting that the final form of the manuscript was the result of the revision and expansion of an earlier draft. Only leaf 70 in the final numbering bears any text on the verso, but the three lines there, originally intended for incorporation into the recto, are cancelled.

The only details on the leaves not in Howells' hand are the penciled heading on leaf 1, "Art. V—George William Curtis," the numbers 1–6 before the book titles that preface the essay, and the names Wyle [?] (twice), West, and Powers (twice) which occur at different points in the text. The presence of these names, which can be explained only as defining compositorial assignments, indicates the use of the manuscript directly as printer's copy for the *North American Review*. Though internal revisions of the text appear throughout the manuscript, Howells' hand is especially legible and the order of the material is sufficiently clear to allow typesetting without difficulty.

The finished manuscript, as revised by Howells (but excluding the few editorial revisions on leaf 1), constitutes copy-text for the present edition; however, the internal revisions made by Howells are not recorded. The material was elaborately revised between this stage and the form finally published in the *Review*, and no evidence exists to suggest that this revision was not undertaken by Howells himself, presumably working on galleys or proofs. The alterations range from substitution of one word for another (e.g., "poor" for "wretched" at 111.18, "expression" for "tone" at 120.16), to the rewriting and relocation of lengthy sections (e.g., the passage finally located at 116.22–23 originally appeared at a point corresponding to 115.19 in the present text, and that at 116.25–117.8 at a point corresponding to 111.35–112.2).

The editors of the present edition, therefore, have accepted into the manuscript copy-text all the substantive revisions that appeared in the *North American Review* printing except for those made in the opening list of Curtis' books. Except in cases of clear manuscript error or where the revision of specific passages requires alteration of punctuation, however, the accidentals of the manuscript have been retained; thus, the italicization of "littérateur" (117.38) and "dilletante" [*sic*] (118.22) and alterations of Howells' punctuation have been rejected.

Howells did not supply a title to the essay, and it is headed, in accordance with *Review* policy, only "ART. V." The present edition uses the more formal title given in the table of contents of the journal and repeated in its running heads.

---

[1] In this list, hyphens indicate conventional inclusive numberings of leaves in series; square brackets signify numbers supplied by the editors; capital letters are Howells' own; and equal signs represent single- and double-line hyphens used by Howells to mark leaves inserted into the normal sequence (e.g., four leaves—A=1, A=2, A=3, and A=4—were inserted between leaves 21 and 22).

Textual Notes

111.23–25   Deterioration of the upper right edge of the manuscript leaf prevents
              the reconstruction of the material signalled by the bracketed
              question marks in this Emendations entry and that at 111.25.
120.22–24   Deterioration of the lower right corner of the manuscript leaf
              containing this portion of the text prevents the reconstruction of
              the material signalled by the bracketed question marks in this
              Emendations entry.

Emendations

111.17	have to]P1; have MS	111.28	accomplished . . .
111.18	poor]P1; wretched MS		from]P1;
111.21	wanting.]P1; The		accomplished, and
	reader must share		at least separated it
	in this		from MS
	dissatisfaction with	111.29	future, and . . .
	the numerical		completeness.]P1;
	estimate, and the		future. MS
	critic's result will	111.30	years, now]P1; years
	be received as it		now, MS
	offered, with	111.31	past,]P1; ~,, MS
	misgiving and	111.31	absolute]P1; tangible
	exception.		and absolute MS
	Conceive the	111.35–112.2	¶ The cordial . . . .
	lamentable attitude		work; but]P1; ¶
	of a critic who had		Many who were in
	told us exactly what		their earlier loves
	Dr. Holmes was		and later teens
	just before Dr.		when the book
	Holmes published		named "Prue and
	the Autocrat of the		I" appeared, could
	Breakfast Table! MS		hardly have been
111.23	regret]P1; grieve MS		easily persuaded
111.23	infallible.]P1; ~.. MS		that it was not the
*111.23–25	Yet . . . than]P1; Yet		most charming
	there is a certain		book ever written,
	degree of		and we have heard
	completion in the		of true lovers, now
	period described by		growing a little bald
	the above-cited		but still in their first
	books of Mr.		passion, who
	George[?] Curtis		continue to think
	which makes it safer		"Prue and I"
	grou[?] than MS		exquisitely fine,
111.25	afford, for Mr.]P1;		tender, delightful,
	affor[?] or which at		and who give it
	the worst gives us		away to friends
	an excuse for		upon all occasions
	attempting some		of making a
	study of them. Mr.		present. We do not
	MS		despise their taste,
111.27	lecturing]P1; the		nor yet that of
	letters of lecturing		many thousands of
	MS		fresh-hearted and

bright-minded young girls (now mostly mothers or old maids) east and west, who, educated beyond their opportunities to enjoy and appreciate beautiful and splendid things, adored "Lotus-Eating," and caught their first vivid glimpse in its pages of the great world of American fashion,—saw there its dazzling and delightful watering-places in the light of European refinement and elegance, and learned to appreciate its gay life while they envied it. We have not yet forgotten the sensation, the satisfaction with which we all hailed "Our Best Society and the social studies that came afterward to be "The Potiphar Papers," and we cannot refuse to see now how far they

would have buoyed up any machinery less ponderous and intricate than that put into the work, and which would have made triumph for a meaner attempt; while each of the author's two first books has a charm as characteristic as the others, and valuing perhaps even more to give the author his distinct and separate place in our literature. ¶ To be sure, in the diction of the "Nile Notes of a Howadji," the maturer reader feels a want of simplicity which did not trouble him at eighteen; but then such a one can now discover some things there not so conspicuous to him before; while it is certain that in all his succeeding books the author's style has steadily grown simpler and stronger. But MS

succeeded with	112.2	well]P1; *omitted* MS
types and	112.4	those melting
conditions difficult		hues,]P1; *omitted*
from their inherent		MS
extravagance to	112.5	the earlier]P1; that
handle. In		other MS
"Trumps" itself	112.9	more and]P1; *omitted*
which even the		MS
warm admirers of	112.11	It]P1; That MS
Mr. Curtis make a	112.11	pleasing]P1; beautiful
kind of scapegoat		MS
for his sins, we find	112.11	is]P1; was MS
characters and	112.11	best]P1; first MS
situations which	112.12	truth]P1; fidelity MS

112.12	for]P1; that MS	Howadji as she
112.13	always]P1; forever MS	stalks large from the
112.14	and]P1; that MS	English steamer to
112.17	neither . . . than]P1;	the temples of Aboo
	at least as	Simbel across the
	ignorantly as MS	Sahara and a track
112.18	twenty-seven]P1;	of many thousand
	twenty-six MS	years? ¶ When the
112.24	that]P1; it MS	worst is said, any
112.28	expression]P1; the	sayer must own in
	sensibilities MS	his heart that he
112.29	gifted]P1; *omitted* MS	would be glad to
112.37	*versa!*]P1; *versa!* How	have written a book
	melancholy for	one tenth as good,
	Goethe if he had	and to have never
	ended with the	worse books to
	Sorrows of the	read. MS
	Young Werther! MS	113.11 alliterations]P1;
112.38	do]P1; Do MS	alliterations is there
112.40	What]P1; What ever	are many things in
	MS	it which MS
112.40–41	imagination, lively	113.13 like]P1; good MS
	humor,]P1; lively	113.14 scarcely]P1; not MS
	imagination MS	113.14 impulse]P1; motive
112.42	veritable]P1; tangible	MS
	MS	113.15 doubting]P1;
112.44	angular]P1; jagged	unfriendly MS
	MS	113.17 "Ultima]P1; "Ultimate
112.44	graceful]P1; stately	T "Ultima MS
	MS	113.19 some of]P1; *omitted*
112.45–113.1	thought . . .	MS
	dreams]P1; the	113.20 touch]P1; hand MS
	loom into mind-	113.37–114.3 This . . . . poetry is]P1;
	woven fabrics of	Is not this
	mist MS	surpassingly tender
113.1–3	times; in . . . those]P1;	and beautiful? Is it
	times. Moreover, to a	not true and subtle
	greater degree, we	feeling, delightful
	think, than the	even in its dulcet
	author intends there	excess? From it,
	is, a want of	learn the mood if
	chronological	not the quality of the
	perspective. Those	whole book from
	MS	which it is taken. It is
113.8–10	time. ¶ Grant . . .	poetry of a very
	effect.]P1; time; and	sweet and delicate
	who is that poet	kind, and MS
	Harriet, with the	114.3 corrupts]P1; can
	horns of Isis upon	corrupt MS
	her brow, and Mrs.	114.3 it; not even the]P1; it.
	Gamp's umbrella in	Even those MS
	her hand, so daintily	114.4 and who]P1; *omitted*
	mocked by the	MS

114.4	only]P1; *omitted* MS	114.22	civilization or civility in its wide significance]P1; civilization, MS
114.5–6	passion, ... the song]P1; tenderness, in which there is more pity than passion, though there is no warmth of color or significant expression in their life unrendered. The song MS	114.23	he . . . fatigues]P1; how well he does it the failure of most essayists in the same direction can best testify MS
114.6–7	it is not didactic]P1; not MS	114.26	barbarities . . . sensations]P1; ill-breeding and accidents MS
114.7	a nature]P1; an individuality MS	114.31	Curtis, however unconsciously,]P1; Curtis MS
114.8–10	sound, . . . individual]P1; serene. Thus early shows the natural bent of one who is a moralist more than anything else—but a moralist of so winning and new MS	114.33	literary art]P1; literature MS
		114.33	likely to be]P1; commonly MS
		114.34	singular]P1; *omitted* MS
		114.37–38	before, . . . photography.]P1; before. MS
114.11	describe him]P1; fit him well MS	114.39	he]P1; that he MS
114.12–13	The reader . . . charming]P1; The tendency of Mr Curtis's mind in this direction has been more and more decided in each successive book, and in those frequent MS	114.40	scenes]P1; pictures MS
		114.40	evidence]P1; evidences MS
		114.41	to give]P1; giving MS
		114.41	names]P1; ~, MS
		114.42	characteristics . . . classes]P1; classes, is a result quite the reverse of failure MS
114.14	years,— . . . homilies]P1; years. We can speak in this place as well as in any of those graceful homilies, MS	114.44	effectively.]P1; effectively; and with all their faults "The Potiphar Papers" remain the first of our social satires, unless we except Mr. De Forrest's picture of New Haven life in "Miss Ravenel's Conversion." MS
114.16	admirable]P1; perfect MS		
114.18	hearty sense]P1; cordial pleasantness MS		
114.20	papers are]P1; papers MS	115.2	though]P1; but MS
		115.2	not]P1; *omitted* MS
114.21	essentially]P1; inwardly MS	115.8	insist, at times,]P1; insist MS

115.10	Sharpe [*sic*]
115.10	Pendennises]P1; Pendennsis MS
115.13	it]P1; this MS
115.14	not only]P1; *omitted* MS
115.15–17	but . . . . so]P1; and they pay him a homage not given to writers of less manly qualities of mind. To tell the truth, he deserves well at their hands. He seems MS
115.18	affection]P1; affection, so MS
115.18	never]P1; hardly MS
115.19	unlovely.]P1; unlovely, and in this he is wiser than the master whom he has so long studied with so little effect. Mrs. Potiphar, though silly, is far from bad-hearted; Aurelia is a fine conception of a high-souled woman of society; Prue has a most original sweetness and tenderness, though outwardly but a conventional type of housewifehood; that poor lost thing who clings to the wreck of Abel Newt is kept from despite and antipathy by her truth to him. MS
115.21	books,]P1; authors MS
115.23	whole]P1; beautiful MS
115.24	he]P1; Mr. Curtis MS
115.28	people]P1; the people MS
115.29–36	It . . . . plain. ¶ Mr.]P1; Fold on fold the influences of the

time are gathered about Mr. Curtis until it appears impossible for him to touch man or nature save through some charming quotation or felicitous allusion; nay things seem so interwoven with his own entity, that one might say with pardonable Irish excess that he is never quite so much himself as when he is somebody else. He enjoys the beautiful with a double sense, once for its own sake, and again for the sake of those whom it has delighted. Shakespeare and this world, Dante and the other world are reciprocally infinite and sublime. And who, after all cares so much for the roses that were born to blush unseen? For our own part we would not give one that suggested the blush on Chloe's cheek to a poet for a whole wilderness of them. In reading Mr. Curtis one must often question himself: Have we then no fine instincts, and are all intellectual perceptions and delights traditional, the mere work of association and suggestion? These things that have

been authentic once,
are they now only
authorial? Have all
facts and feelings
been again and again
celebrated and
expressed in
literature, and is it
but the reproduction
of them that
surprises and charms
each of the
somewhat
monotonously
repeated generations
of men? MS

115.36	respect]P1; direction MS
115.37	"Prue]P1; ~ MS
115.38	it . . . sympathy.]P1; much of it comes out of Mr. Curtis's memory and how little out of Mr. Curtis; how much it is the fruit of association, how little of inspiration. MS
116.3	traveller]P1; to traveller MS
116.6–14	rescue?—with . . . . intelligence.]P1; rescue? MS
116.15	In "Prue]HE; "~ ~ MS, P1
116.17	all]P1; *omitted* MS
116.18	work]P1; book MS
116.19	actuated]P1; motivated MS
116.21	sometimes]P1; *omitted* MS
116.22–23	Aurelia . . . sketch.]P1; *omitted* MS
116.23	chief]P1; *omitted* MS
116.25–117.8	volume, for . . . . present.]P1; volume. Where was ever a sweeter and fairer revery than "My Chateaux in Spain"? It is the

very breath of
longing and regret,
the sad grave of the
hopes that must
perish to make even
happiness, the
sweetness of the
blossom that had to
fall before there
could be fruit. The
allegory of
"Titbottom's
Spectacles" is of
exquisite fineness
and point; in "Sea
from Shore" and
the "Cruise of the
Flying Dutchman,"
the unattained and
the unattainable are
alike enjoyed. It is
one of the truest
books of travel ever
written—a book of
universal travel
giving the sentiment
of all lands and
climes through the
fantasy of the
home-keeping
voyager. MS

117.9	as original . . . beautiful]P1; is very original in kind MS
117.14	book]P1; book's sentiment MS
117.16	uncertain]P1; vague MS
117.16–19	suspense . . . . already in]P1; suspense in which letters, like politics, religion, and commerce, were not yet emancipated from the influence deforming the national life—in which literature must become an indignant outcry against slavery, a

satire or a sermon,		and lies, as highly
or beguile itself in		Genteel!—when
revery or romance.		Mr. Curtis, in MS
It is difficult not to	117.19	made a jest of]P1;
leave the fact still		from the very heart
		of society sneered
"unsaid in part,		at MS
Or say it in too	117.20	in finding]P1; found
great excess,"		MS
but we think most	117.21	negros' [*sic*]
readers recalling	117.21–23	had . . . that]P1; he
the conditions of		discovered a high
that time will feel		degree of courage,
the truth we		and he was in
indicate. We were		advance of his time
once, and but a		¶ He was afterwards
little while since, a		truer to the
nation of three		contemporary spirit
hundred thousand		of literature in the
slaveholders and		pensiveness and the
thirty million snobs,		regrets of "Prue
and though the		and I," but MS
snob still survives	117.24	sadly]P1; languidly
among us, and will		MS
probably live to	117.26	politician]P1;
hear the last		politician, well
trump, the		understood, MS
slaveholder is	117.26	liberal]P1; *omitted* MS
extinct, and we	117.26	generous]P1; *omitted*
cannot well		MS
remember how we	117.28	his]P1; Mr. Curtis's MS
could ever have	117.29	celebrated . . .
feared him. Yet we		Kansas]P1;
did use to pay him		declared that
homage explicit or		Kansas was the
tacit, in arts and		Thermopylae of
letters; the books		their day, and
from which we		celebrated the
learned to read		irrepressible
confessed his		conflict MS
power; the pulpit	117.31	yet]P1; then MS
shielded him; the	117.34	right]P1; truth MS
press defended	117.34	of]P1; young men on
him; the legislature		MS
made him a law;	117.35–36	and bolder . . .
society looked		accession.]P1; in the
upon the savage		company of this
thing, with his lust		*preux chevalier.* His
of dominion and		accession had much
his manifold		of that heroic grace
cruelties and		which clings to the
licences, his		thought of Wendall
murders, adulteries		Phillips's turning his

back upon all the traditions of political respectability, and ranging himself by the side of the despised abolitionists. His act ought perhaps to have even a greater value since it was done from New York. MS

117.44   with]P1; with with MS

118.1   they:]P1; ~. MS

118.1–2   Hughes . . . Lamartine]P1; Mill and Hughes, with Thiers and Guizot MS

118.5   office.]P1; office. The men who are still young enough to be moved by generous example think all the better of him that he does not think himself too good for the primary meetings, the conventions and the mass-meetings, while they take heart to believe that self-respect and political influence are not incompatible. MS

118.5   he]P1; Mr. Curtis MS

118.15–16   must sympathize]P1; sympathizes MS

118.22   dilletante [sic]

118.26   is doing]P1; has done MS

118.27   his]P1; omitted MS

118.28   ablest]P1; aptest MS

118.36   his party]P1; the party MS

118.38   caprices,]P1; superfluous envelopes; MS

118.39–119.2   note . . . . poet.]P1; see how the

sentimentality is wrung out of his style. The alliterations are gone, so are the quotations, so are the allusions. In his strong grasp upon us we feel more sensibly than ever before the pulsation of a true courageous heart, and know that the hand is not the hand of that most despicable of fine gentlemen, a fine literary gen=/ gentleman. MS

119.4   honor]P1; are old-fashioned enough to honor MS

119.5   think]P1; to think MS

119.10   him]P1; him for good MS

119.13–14   precarious honors]P1; easy triumphs MS

119.14   prophesy [sic]

119.14   he]P1; Mr. Curtis MS

119.18   have written]P1; write MS

119.20   stumps and]P1; stumps=and MS

119.22   unique]P1; exquisite MS

119.25   actual]P1; substantial MS

119.25   world]P1; world of fashion and affairs MS

119.26   rank]P1; place MS

119.28–29   refinement . . . execution.]P1; refinement, and in a certain immediate affect upon contemporaries. MS

119.30   he has]P1; but with MS

119.31   Providence. He has]P1; Providence. He has more

poetical feeling than Irving, while he lives more than Longfellow in an atmosphere of literary association, as distinguished from literary knowledge. He has MS

119.33   found]P1; *omitted* MS

119.34–35   has not . . . much]P1; is a less archaic spirit than Irving, but because his writings have always dealt more or less MS

119.36   have . . . with]P1; they seem less modern than MS

119.36–120.3   In most . . . . in]P1; ¶ What is Mr. Curtis, then, in our literature? One feels that he is a positive element in it, of the same kind with some of our best writers, and that with occasional palpable failure, he has contributed much to refine and universalize it. He has traits of a cosmopolitan which have appeared to our advantage in his writings. If he is nowhere intense, he is seldom over-intense; he is

sentimental, but with a manly, impersonal sentimentality, so frank that at the worst we only wish it were something else. In some of his shorter works he has given us what seems almost a new species in fiction, and in his criticisms his exquisitely intelligent and subtile praise has sometimes made praise appear the only virtue of MS

120.10   too]P1; too direct and MS

120.11–12   doing it is openly declared]P1; doing, as much is assumed MS

120.12   partly]P1; *omitted* MS

120.15   Lotus-Eating]P1; Lotus Eating MS

120.16   expression]P1; tone MS

120.19   to]P1; *omitted* MS

120.19–21   but . . . poet.]P1; he is a moralist, and not a romancer. MS

*120.22–24   which . . . beginning.]P1; which [?] arrive is this: How can a morali[?] be so wholly charming? But this perpl[?] in the beginning. MS

Rejected Substantives

111.2   Nile]MS; ART. V.—1. *Nile* P1

111.4   The]MS; 2. *The* P1

111.7   Lotus-]MS; 3. *Lotus-* P1

111.10   The]MS; 4. *The* P1

111.12   Prue]MS; 5. *Prue* P1

111.14   Trumps . . . Curtis]MS; 6. *Trumps: A Novel.* By George William Curtis P1

113.8   chaunt]MS; chant P1

113.23   hareem]MS; harem P1

116.1   "Gipsey's Malison"]MS; Gypsy's Malison, P1

120.14   novels]MS; travels P1

Word-Division List A
114.37   all-but
115.5   book-backs
115.36–37   "Lotus-Eating"
116.36   dream-people

23. The New Taste in Theatricals.

(G&A 69–8)

No manuscript or other pre-publication form of this essay is known to exist. It was first printed, without authorial attribution, in the *Atlantic Monthly*, XXIII (May 1869), 635–644 (P1), and then extensively revised—and retitled "Some Lessons from the School of Morals"—for inclusion in the enlarged second edition of *Suburban Sketches* (Boston: James R. Osgood, 1872), pp. 220–240 (A). The alterations for book publication are of five kinds: (1) addition of an initial passage intended to establish for the essay the authorial tone of the Cambridge suburbanite that informs the other chapters of the book; (2) the deletion of the final three paragraphs, which turn from drollery about burlesque theatricals to more serious consideration of imported European drama; (3) alterations of tense and references to time so as to create a sense of historical retrospect rather than of reviewing the theatrical season just past—e.g., "in those far-off winters" was substituted for "last winter" at 124.2; (4) a few changes intended to emphasize the suburban perspective—e.g., "two suburban friends" substituted for "two friends" at 126.3; (5) alterations which may be regarded as the author's second thoughts on matters of style. In keeping with the policy of presenting the development of Howells' criticism, it is the original essay, not the chapter from *Suburban Sketches*, that is reprinted here; hence, the alterations have not been accepted as emendations but are listed in the Rejected Substantives list.

Emendations
121.28   Artemas [*sic*]
126.19   ruthlessly]A; ruthlesssly P1
127.5   dulness [*sic*]
128.19   Fiske [*sic*]
130.34   traversties [*sic*]

Rejected Substantives
121.2   There is]P1; Any study of suburban life would be very imperfect without some glance at that larger part of it which is spent in the painful pursuit of pleasures such as are offered at the ordinary places of public amusement; and for this reason I excuse myself for rehearsing certain impressions here which are not more directly suburban, to say the least, than those recounted in the foregoing chapter. ¶ It became, shortly after life in Charlesbridge began, a question whether any entertainment that Boston could offer were worth the trouble of going to it, or, still worse, coming from it; for if it was misery

to hurry from tea
to catch the
inward horse-car
at the head of the
street, what sullen
lexicon will afford
a name for the
experience of
getting home again
by the last car out
from the city? You
have watched the
clock much more
closely than the
stage during the
last act, and have
left your play
incomplete by its
final marriage or
death, and have
rushed up to
Bowdoin Square,
where you achieve
a standing place in
the car, and,
utterly spent as
you are with the
enjoyment of the
evening, you
endure for the
next hour all that
is horrible in
riding or walking.
At the end of this
time you declare
that you will never
go to the theatre
again; and after
years of suffering
you come at last to
keep your word. ¶
While yet,
however, in the
state of formation
as regards this
resolution, I went
frequently to the
theatre—or school
of morals, as its
friends have
humorously called
it. I will not say
whether any

desired
amelioration took
place or not in my
own morals
through the
agency of the
stage; but if not
enlightened and
refined by
everything I saw
there, I sometimes
was certainly very
much surprised.
Now that I go no
more, or very, very
rarely, I avail
myself of the
resulting leisure to
set down, for the
instruction of
posterity, some
account of
performances I
witnessed in the
years 1868–69,
which I am
persuaded will
grow all the more
curious, if not
incredible, with
the lapse of time.
¶ There is A

121.8	season just ending]P1; years mentioned A
121.34	are]P1; were A
122.1	letters]P1; in letters A
122.3	we]P1; I A
122.7	the present]P1; a now waning A
122.13	that]P1; that have A
122.13	the past winter]P1; recent years A
122.13–28	The season . . . . mistaken.]P1; *omitted* A
122.30	appeared]P1; appeared in Boston A
122.32	enjoys]P1; enjoyed A
122.38	is now scarcely]P1; was no A

122.41	is]P1; was A	127.7	in]P1; *omitted* A
122.44	ought to]P1; should A	127.7	winter]P1; ensuing winter A
122.44	is]P1; was A	127.31	charms]P1; personal charms A
122.45	can]P1; could A		
122.45	is to]P1; was to A	128.1	are]P1; were A
123.1	music is]P1; music was A	128.8	all]P1; *omitted* A
		128.9	Johnson's]P1; Johnson's now historical A
123.3	is]P1; was A		
123.12	'aime]P1; J'aime A		
123.23	understanding and]P1; *omitted* A	128.12	our]P1; the A
		128.19	to Mr.]P1; to the late Mr. A
123.24	new]P1; *omitted* A		
123.24	is]P1; was A	128.19	Fiske, and to Mr. Samuel Bowles.]P1; Fiske. A
123.25	does]P1; did A		
123.41	alone]P1; only A		
123.44–45	be. ¶ It]P1; ~. ~ A	128.34–36	It . . . confidence.]P1; *omitted* A
123.45	can]P1; could A		
124.1	can]P1; could A		
124.2	last winter]P1; in those far-off winters A	129.22–23	faces, evidently of but]P1; faces of A
		129.26	have]P1; had A
124.5	we]P1; I A	129.27	have]P1; had A
124.12	the past winter]P1; at the time of which I write A	129.28	has]P1; had A
		129.29	the new]P1; this new A
124.15	last]P1; the previous A	130.28–29	of the new taste in theatricals]P1; *omitted* A
124.43–45	I . . . it.]P1; *omitted* A		
126.3	two]P1; two suburban A	130.30–132.15	The new . . . . statute.]P1; *omitted* A
126.9	is]P1; was A		

Word-Division List A

122.25–26	overflowing	129.20	*cancan*
123.36	over-delicacy	130.25	hard-working
124.40	morning-coats	130.44	playgoers
126.36	full-blown	131.23	steam-power
128.9	speech-making		

24. [Mark Twain's Innocents Abroad]

(G&A 69–19)

No manuscript or other pre-publication form of this review is known to exist. It was first printed, without title or authorial attribution, in "Reviews and Literary Notices," *Atlantic Monthly*, XXIV (December 1869), 764–766 (P1), and later collected in the "Criticisms" section of *My Mark Twain* (New York and London: Harper and Brothers, 1910), pp. 107–112 (A). The later reprint was not revised by Howells and varies from the *Atlantic* text—which is the copy-text for the present edition—only in punctuation and spelling.

Textual Notes
133.8 Here and at 133.14, 133.24, 133.37, 134.6, 134.28, 134.30, 135.7, 135.11, 135.18, 135.26, and 136.4 the misspelling "Clements" (sometimes as the possessive "Clements's") of the *Atlantic* text is retained. In the text as reprinted in *My Mark Twain* the spelling was corrected throughout to "Clemens" (and "Clemens's"). The middle initial of Clemens' name ("S.") at 133.8 is given here as it appears in the *Atlantic* review.

Emendations
133.33   pseudonyme [*sic*]

Rejected Substantives
*133.8   Clements]P1; Clemens A

Word-Division List A
133.4   Pleasure-Excursion

25. Mr. Lowell's New Poem.

No manuscript or other pre-publication form of this review is known to exist. It appeared, with the title as given here, under the general heading "New Publications," in the New York *Tribune*, 16 December 1869, p. 6 (N1). Although the review appeared without authorial attribution, Howells can be identified as the author on the basis of his letter of 11 December 1869 to Whitelaw Reid (MS at Harvard); see the entry at 137.8 in Notes to the Text. Error or styling of the text by the newspaper may have occasioned the nonsense reading "worder" for "wonder" at 141.20 and the spelling "hight(s)" for "height(s)" at 143.8, 143.22, and 145.7. Possibly these differences were occasioned by Howells' quotation from proof-sheets or some other preliminary form of the *Atlantic* text of "The Cathedral," since the poem as published there differs in a significant number of substantive details from Howells' quotation of it.

Emendations

140.5	nabitang?']HE; ~?" N1	143.22	hight [*sic*]
140.13	fly."]HE; ~.' N1	144.29	that poet [*sic*]
141.21	worder [*sic*]	145.7	hight [*sic*]
143.8	hights [*sic*]	147.27	us.]HE; ~ N1

Word-Division List A
144.23   many-sided

26. [T. B. Aldrich's Bad Boy]
(G&A 70–2)

No manuscript or other pre-publication form of this review is known to exist. It appeared, without title or authorial attribution, in "Reviews and Literary Notices," *Atlantic Monthly*, XXV (January 1870), 124–125.

Word-Division List A
149.4   boy-theatricals
149.13   whirlpool

27. [William Makepeace Thackeray]
(G&A 70–3)

No manuscript or other pre-publication form of this review is known to exist. It appeared, without title or authorial attribution, in "Reviews and Literary Notices," *Atlantic Monthly*, XXV (February 1870), 247–248.

28. [Björnson's Fiction]
(G&A 70–5)

No manuscript or other pre-publication form of this review is known to exist. It appeared, without title or authorial attribution, in "Reviews and Literary Notices," *Atlantic Monthly*, XXV (April 1870), 504–512.

Emendations
155.27   fidler [*sic*]

Word-Division List A
156.11   drinking-bouts
159.12   wedding-gear
162.15   lifelong
162.25   Anglo-Saxon

29. [Bret Harte's Fiction]
(G&A 70–6)

No manuscript or other pre-publication form of this review is known to exist. It appeared, without title or authorial attribution, in "Reviews and Literary Notices," *Atlantic Monthly*, XXV (May 1870), 633–635.

Word-Division List A
167.25   Hair's-breadth
170.9   roadside

30. [Rossetti's Poetry]
(G&A 70–9)

No manuscript or other pre-publication form of this review is known to exist. It appeared, without title or authorial attribution, in "Reviews and Literary Notices," *Atlantic Monthly*, XXVI (July 1870), 115–118 (P1).

Emendations
171.23   seven.]HE; ~ P1
173.10   Giorgiona [*sic*]

Word-Division List A
177.18   -means-blessed

31. [Ralph Keeler's Adventures]
(G&A 70–15)

No manuscript or other pre-publication form of this review is known to exist. It appeared, without title or authorial attribution, in "Reviews and Literary Notices," *Atlantic Monthly*, XXVI (December 1870), 759–760.

Emendations
178.19   happen him [*sic*]

32. [Sylvester Judd's New England Romance]
(G&A 71–2)

No manuscript or other pre-publication form of this review is known to exist. It appeared, without title or authorial attribution, in "Recent Literature," *Atlantic Monthly*, XXVII (January 1871), 144.

33. [John Woolman's Journal]
(G&A 71–13)

No manuscript or other pre-publication form of this review is known to exist. It appeared, without title or authorial attribution, in "Recent Literature," *Atlantic Monthly*, XXVIII (August 1871), 251–252.

Word-Division List A
182.20   overworking

34. [Joaquin Miller's Verses]
(G&A 71–17)

No manuscript or other pre-publication form of this essay is known to exist. It appeared, without title or authorial attribution, in "Recent Literature," *Atlantic Monthly*, XXVIII (December 1871), 770–772 (P1).

Emendations
187.28   still."]HE; ~. P1

35. [Taine and the Science of Art-History]
(G&A 72–2)

No manuscript or other pre-publication form of this review is known to exist. It appeared, without title or authorial attribution, as part of "Recent Literature," *Atlantic Monthly*, XXIX (February 1872), 241. In a change from its previous format—a separate bibliographic heading introducing each review—"Recent Literature" now took the form of a continuous, undivided essay without authorial attribution and all the titles under consideration identified in a footnote on the opening page; hence the change to the footnote format in the present edition. The material on Taine printed here begins with the second sentence of a paragraph and ends with a paragraph break.

Word-Division List A
189.9   -a-lantern

36. [Three Recent American Works of Fiction]
(G&A 72–3)

No manuscript or other pre-publication form of these reviews is known to exist. They appeared, without title or authorial attribution, as part of "Recent Literature," *Atlantic Monthly*, XXIX (March 1872), 362–366. The format is similar to that described in the commentary on item 35, above. The material printed here begins with the beginning of the whole review section and ends with a paragraph break.

Emendations
194.22   one of most [*sic*]

Word-Division List A

192.12	cob-pipe	193.15	Saxonburgers
193.4	slaveholding	193.17	twenty-five
193.10	Flat-Creekers	195.17	Oldtown
193.14	spelling-school	195.31	backwoods

37. [Hawthorne's French and Italian Notebooks]
(G&A 72–6)

No manuscript or other pre-publication form of this review is known to exist. It appeared, without title or authorial attribution, as part of "Recent Literature," *Atlantic Monthly*, XXIX (May 1872), 624–626. Its format is similar to that described in the commentary on item 35, above. The material printed here begins and ends with paragraph breaks.

Word-Division List A
197.15–16   New-Englandish
198.30   self-examination
198.41   tea-drinking
199.4   many-mindedness

38. [Mark Twain's Roughing It]
(G&A 72–7)

No manuscript or other pre-publication form of this review is known to exist. It first appeared, without title or authorial attribution, as part of "Recent Literature," *Atlantic Monthly*, XXIX (June 1872), 754–755—in a format similar to that described in the commentary on item 35, above. The material printed here begins and ends with paragraph breaks and was later collected in the "Criticisms" section of *My Mark Twain* (New York and London: Harper and Brothers, 1910), pp. 113–114. This reprint was not revised by Howells and varies from the *Atlantic* text—which serves as copy-text for the present edition—only in punctuation.

Emendations
201.33   Samuel T. Clemens [*sic*]

39. [Forster's Biography of Dickens]
(G&A 73–4)

No manuscript or other pre-publication form of this review is known to exist. It appeared, without title or authorial attribution, as part of "Recent Literature," *Atlantic Monthly*, XXXI (February 1873), 237–239. Its format is similar to that described in the commentary on item 35, above. The material printed here begins at the beginning of the whole review section and ends with a paragraph break.

Word-Division List A
204.13   -countrymen

40. [Turgenev's Novel of Russian Life]
(G&A 73–4)

No manuscript or other pre-publication form of this review is known to exist. It appeared, without title or authorial attribution, as part of "Recent Literature," *Atlantic Monthly*, XXXI (February 1873), 239–241 (P1). Its format is similar to that described in the commentary on item 35, above. The material printed here begins and ends with paragraph breaks.

Emendations
207.2   The reader]HE; —~ ~ P1

Word-Division List A
208.40   street-lamps
209.21   underwood
209.36   drawing-room
209.43   half-hidden

41. [Robert Browning's Antic Night-Cap Poem]
(G&A 73–9)

No manuscript or other pre-publication form of this review is known to exist. It appeared, without title or authorial attribution, as part of "Recent Literature," *Atlantic Monthly*, XXXII (July 1873), 114–115 (P1). Its format is similar to that described in the commentary on item 35, above. The material printed here begins and ends with paragraph breaks.

Emendations
211.2   The Red]HE; —~ ~ P1

Word-Division List A
211.14   love-letters
211.29   life-use

42. [Heine's Fantastic Attitudes]
(G&A 73–10)

No manuscript or other pre-publication form of this review is known to exist. It appeared, without title or authorial attribution, as part of "Recent Literature," *Atlantic Monthly*, XXXII (August 1873), 237–239. Its format is similar to that described in the commentary on item 35, above. The material printed here begins at the beginning of the whole review section and ends with a paragraph break.

Word-Division List A
215.12   self-criticism
215.23   fellow-revolutionists

43. [Turgenev's Study of Character]
(G&A 73–11)

No manuscript or other pre-publication form of this review is known to exist. It appeared, without title or authorial attribution, as part of "Recent Literature," *Atlantic Monthly*, XXXII (September 1873), 369–370. Its format is similar to that described in the commentary on item 35, above. The material printed here begins at the beginning of the whole review section and ends with a paragraph break.

44. [Bryant's Orations and Addresses]
(G&A 73–12)

No manuscript or other pre-publication form of this review is known to exist. It appeared, without title or authorial attribution, as part of "Recent Literature," *Atlantic Monthly*, XXXII (October 1873), 498–500 (P1). Its format is similar to that described in the commentary on item 35, above. The material printed here begins and ends with paragraph breaks.

Emendations
220.2   Mr.]HE; —Mr. P1
220.16   subtilety [*sic*]
222.16   absolete [*sic*]

45. [The Perfection of Longfellow's Poetry]
(G&A 73–13)

No manuscript or other pre-publication form of this review is known to exist. It appeared, without title or authorial attribution, as part of "Recent Literature," *Atlantic Monthly*, XXXII (November 1873), 622–625 (P1). Its format is similar to that described in the commentary on item 35, above. The material printed here begins at the beginning of the whole review section and ends with a paragraph break.

Emendations
228.31   'You]HE; "~ P1
228.33   more.']HE; ~." P1
229.18   reveal]HE; reveals P1

Word-Division List A
223.4   self-rivalry
226.2   footsteps
226.33   to-morrow

46. [Landor's Poetic Conceits]
(G&A 74–4)

No manuscript or other pre-publication form of this review is known to exist. It appeared, without title or authorial attribution, as part of "Recent Literature," *Atlantic Monthly*, XXXIII (March 1874), 368–370. Its format is similar to that described in the commentary on item 35, above. The material printed here begins at the beginning of the whole review section and ends with a paragraph break.

Word-Division List A
231.8   tuberose

47. [Eggleston's Story of Backwoods Ohio]
(G&A 74–7)

No manuscript or other pre-publication form of this review is known to exist. It appeared, without title or authorial attribution, as part of "Recent Literature," *Atlan-

tic Monthly, XXXIII (June 1874), 745–747. Its format is similar to that described in the commentary on item 35, above. The material printed here begins at the beginning of the whole review section and ends with a paragraph break.

Emendations
235.8   *Revue de* [*sic*]

Word-Division List A
236.20   Southwest
236.22   horseback
236.36–37   horse-stealing

48. [Aldrich's New England Romance]
(G&A 74–11)

No manuscript or other pre-publication form of this review is known to exist. It appeared, without title or authorial attribution, as part of "Recent Literature," *Atlantic Monthly*, XXXIV (August 1874), 227–229. Its format is similar to that described in the commentary on item 35, above. The material printed here begins at the beginning of the whole review section and ends with a paragraph break.

Word-Division List A
240.12   brother-in-
241.31   high-spirited

49. [J. W. De Forest: The Only American Novelist]
(G&A 74–11)

No manuscript or other pre-publication form of this review is known to exist. It appeared, without title or authorial attribution, as part of "Recent Literature," *Atlantic Monthly*, XXXIV (August 1874), 229–230 (P1). Its format is similar to that described in the commentary on item 35, above. The material printed here begins and ends with paragraph breaks.

Emendations
242.2   Mr.]HE; —Mr. P1
242.5   DeForest [*sic*]
242.15   DeForest [*sic*]
242.34   DeForest [*sic*]

50. [The Abounding Charm of Bret Harte's Poetry]
(G&A 75–2)

No manuscript or other pre-publication form of this review is known to exist. It appeared, without title or authorial attribution, as part of "Recent Literature," *Atlantic Monthly*, XXXV (February 1875), 234–236 (P1). Its format is similar to that described in the commentary on item 35, above. The material printed here begins at the beginning of the whole review section and ends with a paragraph break.

Emendations
247.3   "Vainly]HE; '~ P1

51. [Henry James's Marvelous First Book]

(G&A 75–3)

No manuscript or other pre-publication form of this review is known to exist. It appeared, without title or authorial attribution, as part of "Recent Literature," *Atlantic Monthly*, XXXV (April 1875), 490–495. Its format is similar to that described in the commentary on item 35, above. The material printed here begins at the beginning of the whole review section and ends with a paragraph break.

Word-Division List A

251.4	ear-locks	253.38–39	self-contradictory
251.16	fern-collector	254.9	eighteenth-century
252.25	drawing-room	255.2	well-considered
253.26–27	old-fashioned	255.13	poverty-stricken

52. [Miss Woolson's Lake-Country Sketches]

(G&A 75–6)

No manuscript or other pre-publication form of this review is known to exist. It appeared, without title or authorial attribution, as part of "Recent Literature," *Atlantic Monthly*, XXXV (June 1875), 736–737. Its format is similar to that described in the commentary on item 35, above. The material printed here begins at the beginning of the whole review section and ends with a paragraph break.

Word-Division List A
257.29   fur-hunters

53. [The Quaintness of William Morris's Poems]

(G&A 75–10)

No manuscript or other pre-publication form of this review is known to exist. It appeared, without title or authorial attribution, as part of "Recent Literature," *Atlantic Monthly*, XXXVI (August 1875), 243–244 (P1). In the newly adopted format of the review section, the bibliographical identifications of the texts under review are given in separate footnotes keyed to appropriate sentences in each subsection; the present text reflects this new format. The material printed here begins and ends with paragraph breaks.

Emendations
258.2   Mr.]HE; —Mr. P1

Word-Division List A
258.29   Haystack

54. [Mark Twain's Sketches, Old and New]

(G&A 75–12)

No manuscript or other pre-publication form of this review is known to exist. It first appeared, without title or authorial attribution, as part of "Recent Literature," *Atlantic Monthly*, XXXVI (December 1875), 749–751 (P1)—in a format similar to that described in the commentary on item 53, above—and was later collected in the "Criticisms" section of *My Mark Twain* (New York and London: Harper and Brothers,

1910), pp. 120–124, under the title "Mark Twain's 'Sketches, Old and New' " (A). The later reprint was not revised by Howells and varies from the *Atlantic* text—which serves as copy-text for the present edition—in punctuation and in three words, apparently all non-authorial in origin.

Emendations
260.2   It]A; —It P1
260.34   Company.]HE; ~ P1

Rejected Substantives
261.7   amongst]P1; among A
261.36   amongst]P1; among A
262.9   we]P1; one A

55. [The Genius of Longfellow's Art]
(G&A 76–1)

No manuscript or other pre-publication form of this review is known to exist. It appeared as part of a comprehensive essay, "Four New Books of Poetry," *Atlantic Monthly*, XXXVII (January 1876), 109–111, over the initials "W. D. H." The material printed here follows the original in the format of presenting the bibliographical identification of the work under review; it begins with a paragraph break and ends at the conclusion of the whole review essay.

56. [Browning's Formless Melodrama]
(G&A 76–2)

No manuscript or other pre-publication form of this review is known to exist. It appeared, without title or authorial attribution, as part of "Recent Literature," *Atlantic Monthly*, XXXVII (March 1876), 372–374. Its format is similar to that described in the commentary on item 53, above. The material printed here begins at the beginning of the whole review section and ends with a paragraph break.

Word-Division List A
267.23   high-souled

57. [Mark Twain's Boys' Book]
(G&A 76–4)

No manuscript or other pre-publication form of this review is known to exist. It first appeared, without title or authorial attribution, as part of "Recent Literature," *Atlantic Monthly*, XXXVII (May 1876), 621–622 (P1)—in a format similar to that described in the commentary on item 53, above—and was later collected in the "Criticisms" section of *My Mark Twain* (New York and London: Harper and Brothers, 1910), pp. 125–128 (A). The later reprint was not revised by Howells and varies from the *Atlantic* text—which serves as copy-text for the present edition—only in punctuation.

Emendations
271.2   Mr.]A; —Mr. P1

Word-Division List A
272.17   human-nature

58. [Lowell's Complete Poetical Works]
(G&A 77–1)

No manuscript or other pre-publication form of this review is known to exist. It appeared as part of a special review, "Some New Books of Poetry," *Atlantic Monthly*, XXXIX (January 1877), 93–94, over the initials "W. D. H." The material printed here follows the original in the format of presenting the bibliographical identification of the book under review; it begins with a paragraph break and ends at the conclusion of the whole review essay.

Word-Division List A
273.14   self-righting
273.27   war-poems
274.16   sounding-board

59. [Sarah Orne Jewett's Sketches of Local Life]
(G&A 77–6)

No manuscript or other pre-publication form of this review is known to exist. It appeared, without title or authorial attribution, as part of "Recent Literature," *Atlantic Monthly*, XXXIX (June 1877), 759 (P1). Its format is similar to that described in the commentary on item 53, above. The material printed here begins and ends with paragraph breaks.

Emendations
275.2   The]HE; —The P1

60. [J. J. Piatt: A Poet of Genuine Promise]
(G&A 78–2)

No manuscript or other pre-publication form of this review is known to exist. It appeared, without title or authorial attribution, as part of "Recent Literature," *Atlantic Monthly*, XLI (January 1878), 139–141 (P1). Its format is similar to that described in the commentary on item 53, above. The material printed here begins and ends with paragraph breaks.

Emendations
277.2   In]HE; —In P1
277.33   *Poems.*]HE; ~ P1

Word-Division List A
277.18   highways

61. [Henry James's Essays on French Authors]
(G&A 78–8)

No manuscript or other pre-publication form of this review is known to exist. It appeared, without title or authorial attribution, as part of "Recent Literature," *Atlantic Monthly*, XLII (July 1878), 118–119 (P1). Its format is similar to that described in the commentary on item 53, above. The material printed here begins at the beginning of the whole review section and ends with a paragraph break.

Emendations
280.34   1878.]HE; ~ P1

Word-Division List A
280.29   overshadowed

62. [W. H. Bishop's Blending of Romance and Novel]
(G&A 79–4)

No manuscript or other pre-publication form of this review is known to exist. It appeared, without title or authorial attribution, as part of "Recent Literature," *Atlantic Monthly*, XLIV (August 1879), 264–265 (P1). Its format is similar to that described in the commentary on item 53, above. The material printed here begins and ends with paragraph breaks.

Emendations
283.2   Mr.]HE; —Mr. P1

63. [Trollope's Lucubrations on Thackeray]
(G&A 79–4)

No manuscript or other pre-publication form of this review is known to exist. It appeared, without title or authorial attribution, as part of "Recent Literature," *Atlantic Monthly*, XLIV (August 1879), 267–268 (P1). Its format is similar to that described in the commentary on item 53, above. The material printed here begins and ends with paragraph breaks.

Emendations
286.2   Reading]HE; —Reading P1
287.26   prevades [*sic*]

Word-Division List A
287.44   schoolmaster

64. Dickens's Letters.
(G&A 80–3)

No manuscript or other pre-publication form of this review is known to exist. It appeared as a separately titled essay, without authorial attribution, in the *Atlantic Monthly*, XLV (February 1880), 280–282, which is here reprinted without change.

Word-Division List A
290.29   horseplay

65. James's Hawthorne.
(G&A 80–4)

No manuscript or other pre-publication form of this review is known to exist. It appeared as a separately titled essay, without authorial attribution, in the *Atlantic Monthly*, XLV (February 1880), 282–285, which is here reprinted without change.

66. Mark Twain's New Book.

(G&A 80–6)

No manuscript or other pre-publication form of this review is known to exist. It first appeared as a separately titled essay, without authorial attribution, in the *Atlantic Monthly*, XLV (May 1880), 686–688, and was later collected in the "Criticisms" section of *My Mark Twain* (New York and London: Harper and Brothers, 1910), pp. 129–133. The later reprint was not revised by Howells and varies from the *Atlantic* text—which serves as copy-text for the present edition—only in punctuation and spelling.

Word-Division List A
296.21   garden-plot
297.18   -times-repeated
298.13   undercurrent

67. A New Observer.

(G&A 80–7)

No manuscript or other pre-publication form of this review is known to exist. It appeared as a separately titled essay, without authorial attribution, in the *Atlantic Monthly*, XLV (June 1880), 848–849, which is here reprinted without change.

Word-Division List A
299.7   Workingmen
299.25   first-class

68. Goldwin Smith's Cowper.

(G&A 80–10)

No manuscript or other pre-publication form of this review is known to exist. It appeared as a separately titled essay, without authorial attribution, in the *Atlantic Monthly*, XLVI (September 1880), 425–427. That text is here reprinted with only one change: the superscript number for the bibliographical footnote, which was erroneously omitted from any part of the *Atlantic* text, is here inserted at the end of the title.

Word-Division List A
303.13   card-playing

69. Mr. Aldrich's Fiction.

(G&A 80–11)

No manuscript or other pre-publication form of this review is known to exist. It appeared as a separately titled essay, without authorial attribution, in the *Atlantic Monthly*, XLVI (November 1880), 695–698, which is here reprinted without change.

Word-Division List A
307.42   Spring-Floods
309.13   superstructure

70. Mark Twain.

(G&A 82–3)

The essay was printed twice during Howells' lifetime: as a separate and titled essay over the author's name in the *Century*, XXIV (September 1882), 780–783 (P1), and after Clemens' death as part of the "Criticisms" section of *My Mark Twain* (New York and London: Harper and Brothers, 1910), pp. 134–144 (A). It is also represented by a complete holograph manuscript, now in the Beinecke Library at Yale University (MS), consisting of fifty leaves numbered in the final sequence [1], 1=1, 2–10, 2=10, 11–20, 22&23, 24–32, 2=32, 35–51.[1] The text, in black ink throughout, appears mostly on the rectos of the sheets, but with some verso material on leaves [1], 2, 29, and 32. The only details on the leaves not in Howells' hand are the penciled headings on leaf [1], "O S LP Sept. Century" [Old Style Long Primer September Century], designating the typeface to be used and the issue of the magazine in which the material was to appear; the names "Miss Levasseur" (four times), "Clara" (twice), "Emily" (twice), and "Silloway" (once) at various points, indicating the assignment of compositors to portions of the text; and an asterisk between "Hartford" and "gentleman" on leaf 34 (314.11–12 in the present edition), accompanied below Howells' text on the leaf by "*; a reverend" in Samuel L. Clemens' hand and signed "SLC." It is well known that Howells read Clemens' manuscripts. This is one of the few evidences that Clemens read Howells', though it was not unusual for Howells to invite his literary friends to review his major commentaries about them. In this instance, the revision is corrective rather than interpretive, the interpolation completing the sense of the manuscript. The revision has been adopted in the present text, and its physical difference from the rest of the manuscript is designated by the siglum *MS* in the list of Emendations.

The finished manuscript constitutes copy-text for the present edition. Howells' internal revision of the manuscript has not been recorded in the apparatus here. The presence of typographical instructions and compositorial marks indicates the use of the manuscript as setting copy for the *Century*. Differences between these two forms of the material suggest that Howells made substantive revisions in proof before magazine publication (for example, the change from "a thousand" to "hundreds of" at 314.18), but that at the same stage of preparation twelve other substantive changes were introduced which do not appear to be authorial in origin. The authorial changes are incorporated into the manuscript copy-text and recorded in the Emendations list below; the non-authorial variants have not been accepted and appear only in the Rejected Substantives list. The present edition also introduces into the copy-text changes in punctuation and other accidentals—also recorded in Emendations—to make it clear and accurate. All these corrections first appeared in the *Century*, but no claim is made for Howells as their source: the *Century* is cited in the Emendations list only for historical reasons, and the changes are made here on the authority of the present edition.

The reprinting of the essay in *My Mark Twain* appears to have been based on the *Century* text. The reprinting repeats the authorial and non-authorial variants from the manuscript which had first appeared in the magazine—with the exception of the apparently coincidental return to the manuscript readings "characterizes" rather than the *Century* "characterized" at 312.27, "our" rather than "one" at 313.13, and "picaresque" rather than "picturesque" at 314.36. It also introduces a number of new substantive variants, some of them of sufficient significance to raise the question

---

[1] In this list, hyphens indicate conventional inclusive numberings of leaves in series; square brackets signify numbers supplied by the editors; equal signs represent single- and double-line hyphens used by Howells to mark leaves inserted into the normal sequence (e.g., one leaf, marked 2=10, was inserted between leaves 10 and 11); the ampersand is Howells' own.

of Howells' attention to revision. But the absence of authorial revision in the other essays collected in that volume and the fact that the most striking of the variants appear to be responses to immediate context rather than larger changes of meaning suggest that these revisions were not Howells'. The change from the *Century* reading "style" to "sum" at 313.2, for example, corrects the magazine misreading, but without restoring "stock," Howells' original manuscript reading. Hence, the book variants are rejected as non-authorial and listed in the Rejected Substantives list. Even if they were authorial, the emphasis in this selection of critical essays on the chronological development of Howells' critical thought would have been sufficient reason for preferring the manuscript and/or periodical readings.

Emendations

310.9	went]P1; came MS		312.12	century,]P1; ~ MS
310.9–10	on the 30th of November, 1835,]P1; *omitted* MS		312.15	processes,]P1; ~ MS
			312.16	attitude.]P1; ~ MS
			312.19	Charles]P1; Chas. MS
310.23	Calvinism]P1; calvinism MS		312.22	Mr.]P1; Mr MS
			312.45	saying,]P1; ~ MS
310.31	always]P1; *omitted* MS		313.31	strange]P1; ~, MS
310.31	resentment]P1; resentment always MS		314.11–12	Hartford; a reverend gentleman]*MS*; Hartford gentleman MS
311.6	from city]P1; city MS			
311.10	St.]P1; ~ MS			
311.20	Mr.]P1; Mr MS		314.14	moralist;]P1; ~.; MS
311.36	had]P1; *omitted* MS		314.18	hundreds of]P1; a thousand MS
311.44	Charles H.]P1; Chas. H. MS			
			314.33	an]P1; a MS
312.4	in the *Quaker City*]P1; *omitted* MS		315.5	to that extent]P1; *omitted* MS
312.5	East]P1; East in the Quaker City MS			

Rejected Substantives

310.9	the 30th of November]P1; November 30 A		313.2	stock]MS; style Pl; sum A
			313.13	our]MS; one P1
310.16	boys']MS; boy's P1, A		313.32	as donjon-]MS; dungeon-P1, A
311.9	country]MS; town A			
311.34	*twain*]MS; twain P1, A		314.7	which underlies]MS; underlying A
311.34	*two*]MS; two P1, A			
312.27	humaner]MS; humane P1, A		314.36	picaresque]MS; picturesque P1
312.27	characterizes]MS; characterized P1			
			315.8	are;]MS; are; that P1, A
312.37	*popular*]MS; popular P1, A		316.2	determine]MS; define A

Word-Division List A

310.5	well-known		313.30	English-speaking
310.15	slaveholding		313.31	book-agents
311.5	*wanderjahre*		315.24	showman
313.26	boarding-house			

71. Henry James, Jr.

(G&A 82–4)

No manuscript or other pre-publication form of this essay is known to exist. It appeared, with the title as given here, in the *Century*, XXV (November 1882), 25–29, over the author's name. The text in the present edition introduces no changes and even retains Howells' consistent misspelling of "Belgarde" for "Bellegarde" at 319.14, 320.39, 321.18, and 322.12.

Word-Division List A
319.13   bill-paying
321.7   story-book
323.15–16   story-telling

72. Maurice Thompson and His Poems.
(G&A 83–4)

The review was printed only once during Howells' lifetime, in the New York *Independent*, 4 October 1883, pp. 1249–1250 (P1); immediately below the title is the by-line "By W. D. Howells" and at the end of the essay, in a separate line, "Boston, Mass." Both of these have been omitted in the present edition. There also exists in the University of Southern California Library a single leaf of holograph manuscript (MS) containing the text of the last paragraph of the essay, signed "W. D. Howells." The leaf is a 5 3/16 in. x 8 5/8 in. sheet, with Howells' handwriting in black ink and the number "29" in the upper right corner. The presence of this number and of internal deletions and insertions into the text (which are not recorded below) suggest that the leaf is a portion of an original draft of the essay and not a later fair or presentation copy, though there are no editorial or compositorial marks verifying its use as setting copy for the *Independent*. The journal text is substantially identical to the final form of the manuscript: it varies from the latter only in printing "painting. It" for "painting: it" at 332.18. The manuscript constitutes copy-text for the last paragraph, and the *Independent* printing for the rest.

Emendations
325.9   looking]HE; loooking P1
326.45   sap sucker [*sic*]
328.19   hight [*sic*]
329.26   "The]HE; ~ P1
331.17   subjects,]HE; ~ P1

Word-Division List A
324.22   so-called

73. The Bread-Winners.
(G&A 84–1)

No manuscript or other pre-publication form of this review is known to exist. It appeared under the subheading "Recent American Novels" in the "Open Letters" column of the *Century*, XXVIII (May 1884), 153–154 (P1). The essay itself bears the title "The Bread-Winners" and the authorial attribution "*W.*"

Emendations
333.1   The Bread-Winners.]HE; "~ ~–~." P1

Word-Division List A
334.12   railroad
334.18   workingmen
335.40   hard-working

74. Two Notable Novels.

(G&A 84–2)

No manuscript or other pre-publication form of this review is known to exist. It appeared, with the title as given here, in the "Open Letters" column of the *Century*, XXVIII (August 1884), 632–634 (P1), over the authorial attribution "*W. D. Howells.*" Portions of the section dealing with Howe were excerpted under the title "An Appreciation" in the 1917 Harper and Brothers edition of *The Story of a Country Town* (A). Those portions—corresponding to 337.16–26, 338.36–45, and 339.4–15 in the present edition—vary from the *Century* text only in punctuation and in the one substantive variant listed below. The magazine text constitutes copy-text for the present edition.

Rejected Substantives
338.45   humanness]P1; humaneness A

Word-Division List A
337.27   hard-worked
339.26   transatlantic

Word-Division

LIST B

THE following list is a guide to transcription of compounds or possible compounds hyphenated at the end of the line in the present text. Compounds recorded in this list should be transcribed as given; words divided at the end of the line and not listed should be transcribed as one word.

5.13	mill-wheel	155.10	back-alleys
11.25	china-shop	158.33	nutting-party
18.23	well-flavored	162.18	Fisher-Maiden
19.15	after-glance	162.41	Fisher-Maiden
19.20	-nine-go-	163.26	novel-reading
19.21	-we-wont-	169.9	bowie-knife
22.29	office-holders	185.23	long-spurred
23.13	society-romance	194.37	low-downers
25.3	serving-maids	197.15	New-Englandish
29.5	money-lender	199.43	Note-Books
32.13	old-womanish	201.27	stage-drivers
32.16	print-shops	205.35	letter-press
36.10	fire-assurance	206.3	high-pressure
36.18	good-hearted	229.2	brute-character
38.34	heart-break	236.36	horse-stealing
39.9	scene-shifter	237.3	camp-meeting
45.28	self-assertion	240.8	good-naturedly
46.40	self-respect	249.9	fellow-countrymen
53.41	second-rate	250.41	fellow-man
56.40	dress-maker	251.14	weather-beaten
57.18	well-educated	253.14	figure-maker's
60.5	fault-finding	253.26	old-fashioned
61.29	title-page	262.13	non-committally
63.20	New-Englander	268.43	soon-spreading
70.3	merry-andrew	269.7	Night-Cap
73.10	bulletin-boards	271.13	Sunday-school
95.11	stage-coach	272.9	love-affair
105.5	out-of-	272.26	well-conceived
114.27	forty-nine	274.21	many-sidedness
115.36	Lotus-Eating	282.19	well-seated
116.2	farewell-song	283.18	fellow-townsmen
116.7	bounty-jumpers	292.6	fellow-countrymen
117.44	politico-literary	292.9	sixty-four
120.14	watering-places	297.4	Alp-climbing
122.17	poverty-stricken	300.42	thrice-exploded
123.38	love-making	302.24	old-fashioned
127.17	Anglo-Saxon	305.1	singing-robe
132.11	theatre-going	313.30	stove-pipes
133.26	good-humored	318.26	new-worldliness
137.9	book-form	321.42	fellow-countrymen
149.28	sea-faring	323.15	story-telling
152.2	first-rate	339.24	matter-of-

List of Authors and Titles Reviewed

THE following list refers the reader to the consecutively numbered essays in this volume which either review a particular work by the cited author or present a general discussion of that author's works. The beginning page number for each numbered essay can be most conveniently located by referring to the Table of Contents. Title entries under each author's name in the following list are arranged in chronological rather than alphabetical order. The list does not include authors who are only briefly mentioned in the discussion of another writer's works.